D0899061

Modern Peoplehood

Modern Peoplehood

John Lie

HARVARD UNIVERSITY PRESS

Cambridge, Massachusetts

London, England

WITHDRAWN

Copyright © 2004 by the President and Fellows of Harvard College
All rights reserved
Printed in the United States of America

Library of Congress Cataloging-in-Publication Data

Lie, John.
    Modern peoplehood / John Lie.
        p. cm.
    Includes bibliographical references and index.
    ISBN 0-674-01327-1 (alk. paper)
    1. Group identity. 2. Identity (Psychology) 3. Race awareness.
    4. Ethnicity. 5. Nationalism. I. Title.

HM753.L54 2004
305—dc22   2004040585

for Charlotte

Contents

Preface

"When the soul of a man is born in this country there are nets flung at it to hold it back from flight. You talk to me of nationality, language, religion. I shall try to fly by those nets." Unlike Stephen Dedalus, I shan't fly by those nets that I call modern peoplehood. Instead, I strive to disentangle and displace them. I hope at once to illuminate and to sublate the major categories of modern peoplehood—race, ethnicity, and nation—and the cognate phenomena of racism and genocide—the nightmares from which we are still trying to awake.

Caveat lector: I have excised expressions of my scholarly limitations and doubts, as well as warnings about the tentative nature of all propositions. Cowardly creatures we scholars are; I ask of you not so much the suspension of disbelief as of distrust. I also want you to read the whole book. In order to entice you to do so, I have sought to smooth the textual flow. Alas, its texture is encrusted by the canard of scholarship. Quite obviously, a habit of an academic lifetime is hard to halt. The gravitas of citations drags the narrative thrust—not to mention the aesthetic blight—but the academic apparatus also expresses scholarly exactitude and gratitude. The Reverend Stephen Dedalus, S.J., would have approved. There is, in any case, curious comfort in citing authorities, especially in languages with which one must struggle. I spent an inordinate amount of time eliminating citations during the final stage of revision. As long as the list of references remains, it is humbling to ponder that many other uncited but excellent essays and books exist and disturbing to realize that I have undoubtedly failed to learn from many of them.

The solitary pleasure and pain of reading and writing—that voluntary servitude we call research—depended on all sorts of peoples and institutions. I am afraid that I was an agent for entropy at the libraries of the University of Oregon, University of Illinois at Urbana-Champaign, Harvard University, and the University of Michigan. I wish to thank my colleagues and students at Oregon, Illinois, Michigan, and elsewhere. In particular, I am grateful to Aya Ezawa, Bob Lee, Libby Schweber, Charis Thompson, Thembisa Waetjen, Maxim Waldstein, and Brennon Wood for reading a preliminary draft. Serife Genis, Nao Terai, and Leslie Wang helped me with the references and the index. Most importantly, Charis read and discussed this book, even as she carried, gave birth to, and nurtured Charlotte, to whom it is dedicated.

Ann Arbor, Michigan
May 2003

Prelude

By modern peoplehood I mean an inclusionary and involuntary group identity with a putatively shared history and distinct way of life. It is inclusionary because everyone in the group, regardless of status, gender, or moral worth, belongs. It is involuntary because one is born into an ascriptive category of peoplehood. In addition to common descent—a shared sense of genealogy and geography—contemporary commonality, such as language, religion, culture, or consciousness, characterizes the group. It gropes toward a grouping larger than kinship but smaller than humanity. It is not merely a population—an aggregate, an external attribution, an analytical category—but, rather, a people—a group, an internal conviction, a self-reflexive identity.

The discourse of modern peoplehood is rich and resonant, providing a comprehensive and comprehensible vocabulary to make sense of the world. It is a commonplace belief that the major categories of modern peoplehood—race, ethnicity, and nation—reveal something profound about the human condition. As a repository of deep truths about our subjectivity and individuality, peoplehood identity is primal, experienced as somehow ineffable and infallible, authentic and cathartic. Whether grounded in the memes of cultural tradition or the genes of racial belonging, individuals are described and explained in terms of their peoplehood. The metaphysic of modernity turned out to be closer to the irrational Being of Heidegger than to the rational Reason of Kant.

Why is peoplehood identity so important? What is identity?

1

2

Identity is one of those topics that, like time for Saint Augustine (1991: 230), is at once obvious and obscure: "We surely know what we mean when we speak of it. We also know what is meant when we hear someone else talking about it. . . . Provided that no one asks me, I know." Posing the question seems to expunge the answer; the mind hankers for the certainty that seemed to be. I am I, but who is this I, me, myself?

John Locke's classic discussion in *An Essay Concerning Human Understanding* (1689) equates personal identity with the psychic unity and temporal continuity of individual consciousness. According to Locke (1975: 342, 344): "*Personal Identity* consists, not in the Identity of Substance, but . . . in the Identity of *consciousness*. . . . Nothing but consciousness can unite remote Existences into the same Person." In his view, the faculty of memory underpins the unity and continuity of the self. The Lockean idea informs Erik Erikson's (1985:142) influential formulation of identity as something that "provides the ability to experience one's self as something that has continuity and sameness." Occasional oscillations are categorized as identity crises and mark important but infrequent biographical stages (cf. Erikson 1958:14).

Countering Locke's confident and commonsensical account in *A Treatise on Human Nature* (1777); David Hume (1978:259) stresses the indefinable and impermanent nature of personal identity: "The identity, which we ascribe to the mind of man, is only a fictitious one." Rather than a unitary entity, he (1978:253) envisions it as "a kind of theatre, where several perceptions successively make their appearance; pass, re-pass, glide away, and mingle in an infinite variety of postures and situations. There is properly no *simplicity* in it at one time, nor *identity* in different." Rather than Locke's continuity and homogeneity, Hume suggests discontinuity and heterogeneity.

Hume's pronouncement resonates with self-conscious and self-reflexive people. John Keats's (1990:418) letter of 27 October 1818 to Richard Woodhouse reads: "As to the poetical Character itself . . . it has no self. . . . A Poet . . . has no Identity." This is because the poet is constantly "filling some other Body." Consciousness is fleeting and flowing, eluding easy identification. Indeed, a hallmark of the modern self, whether for J. W. G. von Goethe's Faust or W. E. B. Du Bois's black folk, is divided or double (cf. Miller 1985:viif,49). The intimation of a fluctuating and multiple self becomes the commonsense of literary modernism, whether in Virginia Woolf's *Orlando* (1928) or Robert Musil's *Der Mann ohne Eigenschaft* [The Man without Qualities] (1930–43). As Franz Kafka's (1994:225) diary entry of 8 January 1914 records: "What do I have in common with Jews? I have hardly anything in common with myself." The indeterminacy of identity, dislodged from the unity of memory and the entelechy of life, shapes the source of the ludic, and at times ludicrous, self. Extending Keats's theme, Jorge Luis Borges (1995:4) observes: "It is to my other self, to Borges, that things happen. . . . But I recognize myself much less in the books he writes than in many others or in the clumsy plucking of a guitar. . . . I cannot tell which one of us is writing this page."

Diversity and discontinuity in self-identity, we should recall, manifest themselves as mental illnesses: multiple-personality disorder and amnesia. The stability of the self is the condition of possibility of mental sanity and social life. As Thomas Reid (1846:344) noted in 1785: "The conviction which every man has of his Identity . . . needs no aid of philosophy to strengthen it; and no philosophy can weaken it, without first producing some degree of insanity." The Lockean criteria of continuity and unity are in fact necessary for self and identity, even if the Humean recognition of discontinuity and diversity captures the reality of consciousness.

3

The very question of identity, despite its philosophical provenance, tends to be shunned by contemporary philosophers—ever in search of conceptual clarity and logical rigor—who frequently vaporize its substantive motivation (Kripke 1980:97–101; Wiggins 1980:179–182). As Ludwig Wittgenstein (2001:61) put it: "To say of *two* things that they are identical is nonsense, and to say of *one* thing that it is identical with itself is to say nothing." Rather than scrutinizing affiliation or belonging that gives sustenance to personal identity—analyzing the sense of self one has or the kind of person one is—Peter Strawson (1959:113) resolves the contradiction between personal identity and group membership by noting that the former often dissolves into the latter. The question of personal identity is largely a nonissue—a muddle that should be skipped in favor of more clear terrains (cf. Strawson 1959:133). Although people may be interested in the very contradiction, or the confusing dialectic, between the individual and the social, philosophers wonder, "Am I essentially my brain?" (Parfit 1984:

273) or probe the psychological continuity between "people who are just like us, except that they are reproduced by natural division" (Parfit 1984: 302). The modal operation is to flee the realm of social life in favor of science fiction. Yet most contemporary discussions of identity are about people's social belonging and the meaning attached to it. Rather than the disembodied mind or genetic engineering, the animating concern is decidedly less abstract and lower tech. Put simply, it is about what it means to say that one is French or Flemish or Fulani, or woman or gay or disabled. It queries one's sense of self and probes the significance of one's social identification.

Most people, therefore, turn to fiction to read and reflect on identity. In John Updike's novel *Rabbit, Run* (1960), the protagonist Harry "Rabbit" Angstrom lives out his life in the refracted memory of his high school basketball heroics. Basketball shapes his way of thinking, his way of living. In common parlance, his personality and worldview cannot be separated from the formative experience of high school basketball. As Updike traces his peregrinations in the Rabbit tetralogy, our understanding of Rabbit cannot be torn apart from the changing context of the late twentieth-century United States. Rabbit's identity comes close to being coterminous with narratives about his life and times. In locating the intersection of biography with history and society, many *Bildungsroman* realize what the sociological imagination aspires to achieve. Identity is, thus, not a matter of analytic speculations but a stuff of personal narratives.

Beyond novels, autobiographies and biographies seek to unravel the puzzle of identity. Consider two contrasting masterpieces from the late eighteenth century. The opening passage of Jean-Jacques Rousseau's (1995: 5) *Les Confessions* (1764–70) underscores its reputation as the first modern autobiography: "I am forming an undertaking which has no precedent, and the execution of which will have no imitator whatsoever. I wish to show my fellows a man in all the truth of nature; and this man will be myself. . . . If I am worth no more, at least I am different." Indeed, for well over five hundred pages Rousseau delineates his differences. In contrast, Hume's (1987:xxxi) "My Own Life" (1777) says: "It is difficult for a man to speak long of himself without vanity; therefore, I shall be short." Between them, there is no doubt who proved to be prophetic. Not only are the genres of autobiography and biography notorious for their prolixity, but they are also, above all, exercises in vanity triumphant.

In contrast to premodern biographies, which were hagiographies, exemplary lives, or moral fables, whether Suetonius on the Caesars, Einhard on Charlemagne, or the lives of the saints, modern written lives eschew ordinary virtues. Unlike Plutarch's lives—devoured by both Rousseau and Hume—modern biography presents not so much a model, or someone to emulate, but an anti-model. We take interest in people who are, like Rousseau, different. Hence, the historian Alain Corbin's (1998:10) biography of an unknown nineteenth-century clog maker—Louis-François Pinagot, being neither the fantastic Menocchio nor the madman Pierre Rivière—seems so exotic.

Being different loses its pejorative connotations and becomes a point of pride, a virtue rather than a sin, in modern life. People have personality and are fascinating to the extent that they are colorful, or deviant, from the colorness norm. Indeed, ordinariness and sameness suggest inauthenticity. In his rant against mass society, Heidegger (1962:164) excoriates the mass man, or *they* [*das Man*]: "We take pleasure and enjoy ourselves as *they* [*Man*] take pleasure; we read, see, and judge about literature and art as *they* see and judge; likewise we shrink back from the 'great mass' as *they* shrink back." The average, faceless man is the inauthentic Other, the bugbear of all critics of mass society. Profundity, however, comes at the expense of clarity; a few moments of clarity plumb the meaningless depth of profundity. Who exactly are *they?* "In utilizing public means of transport and in making use of information services such as the newspaper, every Other is like the next" (Heidegger 1962:164). Other philosophers may celebrate ecologically correct or politically concerned citizens, but Heidegger exaggerates our tendency to celebrate authenticity and individuality, which points to people's distinct passions, experiences, and aspirations.

How does one distill authenticity and individuality into manageable essences, or principal predicates? How does one capture a life, to satisfy the insistent demand for principle, harmony, and meaning instead of randomness, chaos, and meaninglessness? Where is the will or the soul that threads life's fabric? How can one come to know—intuitively, as it were, but intimately—oneself or another? Epitaphs may be lapidary, but eulogies are known for their longueurs. Encyclopedic coverage, in any case, does not guarantee the veracity of facts or the accuracy of interpretation. Perhaps God can help us, but our closest equivalent—the omniscient narrator—tends to be all too human. Even the most realist of Victorian novelists, Charles Dickens (1948:169), has David Copperfield say: "When my thoughts go back now, to that slow agony of my youth, I wonder how much of the histories I invented for such people hangs like a mist of fancy over well-remembered facts." In "making his imaginative world out of such strange experiences and sordid things" (Dickens 1948:169)—in recalling sounds and smells, chatters and characters—Dickens aspires to no less than what Marcel Proust attempts in *À la recherche du temps perdu* [In Search of Lost Time] (1913–27). Though both proffer the remembered past in all its expansiveness, neither grants us certitude.

If fictive characters are shrouded in mists of fancy, then what hope do we have for real-life human beings? We need at least to dampen the dynamism of lived life. As D. H. Lawrence (1971:75) put it: "To *know* a living thing is to kill it. You have to kill a thing to know it satisfactorily. For this reason, the desirous conscience, the SPIRIT, is a vampire." Biographers may be vampires, as Henry James might have said, but the dead, in a Jamesian fashion, do not rest in peace. Not surprisingly, biographers are perforce in perpetual search.

"What, at this point in time, can we know about a man?" begins Jean-Paul Sartre's (1981:ix) study of Gustave Flaubert. Although Sartre (1981: ix) endeavors "to *summing up* all the data on him at our disposal," *L'idiot de la famille* [The Family Idiot] (1971–72), for the few who have finished it, is hardly satisfactory. Rather, we would probably come to the same conclusion as that poignant passage in *Madame Bovary* (1857): "Whereas the truth is that fullness of soul can sometimes overflow in utter vapidity of language, for none of us can ever express the exact measure of his needs or his thoughts or his sorrows; and human speech is like a cracked kettle on which we tap crude rhythms for bears to dance to, while we long to make music that will melt the stars" (Flaubert 1993:180). Ironically, Antoine Roquentin—the protagonist of Sartre's literary breakthrough *La nausée* [Nausea] (1939) who endeavors to write a biography of an obscure eighteenth-century figure—does not begin to live, to act as it were, until he jettisons biography in favor of art.

If literary immortals have trouble comprehending fictional characters or dead authors, then what of mere mortals who must struggle with the vagaries of life, with limited information and insight? Reflective beings though we all may be, the more we ponder and the more we know, the less we seem to understand—this is the fundamental paradox of identity. Certitude appears to be the luxury of the less reflective; as Oscar Wilde (1982:434) declaimed: "Only the shallow know themselves." The quest for identity opens the proverbial Pandora's box, unleashing intractable questions about the meaning of life—not only as a semantic query—and the human condition. Although every individual may be a world authority on oneself, that does not ensure illumination or insight. Surely, Samuel Beckett was one of the more self-reflective writers of the reflexive twentieth century. Yet, his *L'innommable* [The Unnameable] (1953), that lengthy meditation and interrogation of the narrating subject, demonstrates the inscrutability of the writing self.

Even if we bypass the confusion and complexity of personal identity by embracing the identity of modern peoplehood, we are unlikely to achieve self-satisfaction and reflective reconciliation. Flaubert or Sartre may be French, but what can the simple predicate sentence tell us? It takes a heroic leap into the mindset of modern peoplehood to believe that Flaubert's Frenchness somehow meaningfully describes or explains him. Could such a crystalline formulation illuminate the opacity of a life that humbled Sartre?

To put it prosaically, why should the inscrutable self be adequately captured by any identity? Even in the least differentiated societies, people are inescapably enmeshed in kinship and neighborhood relations, and their roles and identities are far from singular or stable. Slash-and-burn agriculturalists of Guiana Highlands recognize individuality, gender, the nuclear family, the extended family, and villages, as well as the political-religious roles of the headman or the shaman (Rivière 1984:10–13). Social organization is coterminous with role and categorical differentiation. Complex societies, needless to say, offer numerous roles and categories.

Important institutions mandate a sense of belonging and identification. Why shouldn't what one does for a great part of one's waking life generate meaning and commitment? Occupational groups, in fact, constitute distinct subcultures, such that the anthropologist Abner Cohen (1974:xxi) famously characterized the City of London men "as 'ethnic' as any ethnic group can be." Consumption—music, dress, cuisine—produces individuals with a common mode of self-fashioning. Subcultures and social divisions generate salient categories, revealing remarkable instances of auto-essentialism, whether in schismatic political and religious groups or even fan clubs and recovery movements.

In the era of reflexive modernization, reflexivity penetrates every sphere of social life (Giddens 1991:27–34). When people are constantly asked to ponder on identity, the fundamental paradox of identity deepens. Posing the very question is corrosive, forcing us to reconfigure settled identities.

Even Robinson Crusoe—the modern solitary par excellence—has retrospectively become replete with identities, whether as *Homo oeconomicus* or European imperialist. From psychoanalysis to psychobabble, from Freud to Foucault, psychological discourses at once colonize and construct interiority.

Intellectual ferments meet their match in technological innovations. Massive transformations in transportation and communication systems corrode the stability of the here and now (Gergen 1991:53–61). Centripetal spatial forces and disaggregated temporal schemes shatter any notion of unitary social consciousness. Our experiential space expands and becomes more mobile; diurnal life makes a long journey into night to a cathemeral society. Reproductive technologies and other advances in bioengineering, as well as electronization and digitation, transform science-fiction speculations into quotidian topics of commercial and policy discussions.

The multiple and social sources of identity present each individual with manifold circles of belonging from the human race to the self. The sociological cliché that we moderns are ensembles of relations and roles has become ever more fully appreciated by many individuals. Although our repertoire of identities is not infinitely malleable, everyone experiences opportunities to choose, reflexively and strategically, affiliation, belonging, and community. Technologies of self enable individuals to transcend, whether in spirit or in body, their ascribed attributes. Parameters of self-presentation expand. People shift, negotiate, and present a myriad of identities.

Finally, in spite of the thoroughgoing social character of identity, most people cultivate their inner psychic life and preserve their ineffable interiority. The triumph of the therapeutic does not ensure the victory of the superego, whether in the form of a Panopticon or the psychiatric gaze. Individuals may call on experts to point out and prescribe cures for their inadequacies, but the culture of narcissism rests on, however illusory it may be at times, the belief in the self-legislating subject. The emphasis on authenticity is in part an injunction that a modern individual should not unreflexively embrace ascribed identities. We distinguish between a true, private self and a false, public self (Winnicott 1971:65–71). In common understanding, we do not conflate the social sources of identity and the relatively autonomous realm of self—the inviolable, deep, and true core. The construction of the essential self does not make us a product of a stereotype but rather a performer in an open-ended drama. Socialization is, after all, not destiny, and we do not need to be a Sartre to believe in the existential possibility of self-determinacy or the autonomy of actions, beliefs, and commitments. The authorship of modern life stubbornly resides in the "I." We are, at least potentially, autotelic and autonomous. Does anyone genuinely believe in determinism?

We cannot but fail to acknowledge the complexity of individual lives once we take an interest in them. Who would be content with three adjectives or a single group membership to describe, much less to explain, oneself? We dismiss undesirable plants as weeds and unpalatable insects as bugs, but we need not be a horticulturist or an entomologist to acknowledge and appreciate the diversity or individuality of plant or insect species. Frans de Waal (1982:83) writes: "The chimpanzees themselves discriminate between individuals . . . both with their own circle and outside it. They notice practically every familiar human face, even if it appears amongst an immense crowd of visitors." If chimpanzees can recognize and distinguish human individuals, then we can surely do the same for our fellow human beings. In our Blakean moments we know that no two snowflakes or human lives are identical.

Modern life is too complex and the modern self is too inscrutable to provide credible but concise narratives of self. One is—one has been and may well become—hundreds and thousands of predicates, with innumerable belongings and longings. It is puzzling, then, that the question of identity should highlight the categories of modern peoplehood, that modern peoplehood should become a master identity. If we question the continuity and sameness of personal identity, then we should be all the more skeptical about individual identification with a static group membership. The paradox of modern identity is that in spite of the complexity of modern social life—and coexistent with the difficulty of discussing personal identity—we frequently find simplified articulations of belonging and identification. Needless to say, one should not be surprised that it should be part of one's identity kit. However, unlike kinship and local identities that are concrete and thick, modern peoplehood—usually aggregates of millions—seems rather thin: abstract and amorphous. Thick identity allows for a concrete and cogent narrative of people who trace their lineage or allegiance to a particular place or people, a mere extension of the extended family. Categorical belonging, in contrast, constitutes thin identity, with tangential claims to common descent and belonging. Why should thin identity triumph over the thick? Why should modern peoplehood be more significant than kinship roles or occupations, political ideologies or world-views, passions or experiences? How do we reconcile the complexity of the modern self with the simplicity of racial, ethnic, or national identity? Why do so many people regard modern peoplehood as a primary identity?

4

Consider two leading intellectuals in the contemporary Anglophone aca-deme: Stuart Hall and Yi-fu Tuan. In the conceptual universe of modern peoplehood, we would say that one is black and the other Chinese. But even cursory queries reveal the implausibility of the conventional racial, ethnic, or national identification.

Celebrated as the leading postcolonial theorist, Hall is routinely char-acterized as black. But he (1990:231) says of growing up in Jamaica in the 1940s and 1950s: "Although almost everyone around me was some shade of brown or black . . . I never once heard a single person refer to themselves or to others as, in some way, or as having been at some time in the past, 'African.' " It is only in the 1970s that "Jamaicans discovered themselves to be 'black' " (Hall 1990:231). According to Hall (1996:484), his "family was ethnically very mixed—African, East Indian, Portuguese, Jewish." In fact, his mother thought of herself as English and regarded England as "the mother country" (Hall 1996:485). Learning "Latin, English history, English colonial history, European history, English literature, etc." in Jamaica, he recalls the first time he drove through English West Country landscape: "I've never seen it, but I know it. I read Shakespeare, Hardy, the Romantic poets. Though I didn't occupy the space, it was like finding again, in one's dream, an already familiar idealized landscape" (Hall 1996:486,491). He attended Oxford—"the pinnacle of Englishness, it's the hub, the motor, that creates Englishness" (Hall 1996:492)—and spent virtually all of his adult life in England. In spite of being the product of Oxford and knowing "England from the inside," he says that he "never will be 'English' " (Hall 1996:490).

Tuan is an influential geographer, known for his humanistic reflections on place and culture. Being born and reared in China, one may expect him to identify himself as Chinese. Yet he (1999:88) declares outright that: "I am less a Chinese than a Greek." This is because he defines himself as a scholar, and he measures his life by the books he has written. "No matter how far they fall short of my original intention or some abstract ideal, they undeniably exist. . . . I feel content, fulfilled" (Tuan 1999:118). Having been educated at Oxford and Berkeley, he has taught at several universities in North America, but he does not feel particularly at home anywhere. Rather than lamenting his rootlessness, he ascribes his sense of homelessness to "immaturity." In fact, he (1999:129) defines "immaturity" as "the feeling of never being quite in place, truly at home." Writing obliquely about his romantic and sexual longings, he is hesitant to encapsulate himself in one or another form of social identity. When Tuan (1999:119) poses the question, Who am I? he answers that he has "been afraid of life."

The sense of homelessness unites Hall and Tuan, but they share a great deal more, including Oxford education: are they therefore English? Would it be so ridiculous to observe the similarities between Hall and Tuan and to belittle their peoplehood identities? As Hall states, few in his native Jamaica considered themselves to be black, as did he until he was ensconced in England. Is he Jamaican, Black Briton, East Indian, or perhaps Asian—like Tuan? What would it mean to ascribe Chineseness to Tuan, who says he is more Greek? What does it mean to be a member of a group that is estimated to number 1.5 billion? Even if one were to spend only a second to count each Chinese person, it would still take nearly a half-century to complete the chore.

Polemically put, isn't the very idea of modern peoplehood absurd? By contemporary racial, ethnic, or national categorization, we might call Moses black or Egyptian and Abraham Arab or Syrian. What do we gain by identifying Apuleius or Saint Augustine as Algerian except perhaps as a fodder for the contemporary nationalist pride of Algerians? Should we regard Santa Claus as Turkish? Was Saladin a Muslim or Arab hero, or an Iraqi, a Syrian, an Egyptian, or a Kurd? What do we learn of Hume and Rousseau by observing that they are Scotch and Swiss? Should we consider Kant—born in present-day Kaliningrad and who came to his professorship during the Russian occupation of Königsberg (Kuehn 2001:112)—as Russian? Many Russians commemorate Pushkin as "Russia's greatest poet and the founder of her literature" (Pipes 1974:279), but he would be a black writer in the dominant American ethnoracial classificatory scheme (cf. Binyon 2002:4). If we follow the halakhic definition, then V. I. Lenin would be Jewish, but a compelling case can be made for him being Muslim or Buddhist, Chuvash or Mordvinian, or Kirgiz or Kalmyk, but not Russian except as a political or cultural identity (cf. Service 2000:16,21). What would it mean to classify the Riga-born Isaiah Berlin as Russian, Latvian, or Jewish, rather than as a

representative British intellectual? Is the father of nationalism Johann Gottfried von Herder, also born in Riga, Latvian? What if he had become an
Oxford don? Have we said something of significance by observing Hall's
blackness or Tuan's Chineseness? Why do we simplify and reify people
into essentialized categories of modern peoplehood? Even more bizarre,
why do people identify principally with one or another category of modern
peoplehood?

These observations and intimations, doubts and queries motivate *Modern
Peoplehood*.

In Search of Foundations

Social classification is a cultural universal, and categorical differences are coeval with human history. The impulse to classify and categorize people appears in the founding work of Western history, Herodotus's *History,* which is replete with reports of foreign peoples. Yet these proto-ethnographies—certainly ethnocentric and frequently xenophobic—do not imply that Herodotus held the same conceptualization of peoplehood that we do. The modern sense of peoplehood is an involuntary and inclusionary identity based on descent and commonality that is larger than lineage or village, clan or city. In classical Greece, being an Athenian meant being a citizen. Citizens and slaves constituted qualitatively different kinds of people. Mandarin disdain mandated disidentification. In contrast, today even the richest citizens of rich countries do not begrudge an identity of peoplehood to their poorest counterparts. Whereas a wealthy American and indigent American are equally American, the same cannot be said for Athenian citizens and Athenian slaves. In any case, Athens is a city, which does not intuitively meet the minimum threshold of peoplehood. We may speak of New Yorkers as a distinct group, but no one would seriously suggest that they are a racial, ethnic, or national group.

The naturalness and necessity of modern peoplehood is difficult to desist. Equipped with contemporary categories, we are wont to use them to make sense of the past. Given that everyone is from somewhere and lives in some sort of a community, toponyms and political nomenclatures seem to signal the existence of peoplehood. Certainly, analytical categories—as transhistorical and transcultural constructs—can be applied to all times and places. Hence, one may very well identify the efflorescence of modern peoplehood in the distant past, revealing race relations in ancient Egypt or medieval Europe (Redford 1992:229; Bartlett 1993:197). Yet these modern retrojections are anachronistic, akin to the way in which vulgar Marxists found class consciousness and class struggle everywhere. Premodern instances of an inclusionary and involuntary peoplehood are almost always external attributions that essentialize the putative others. Whether the classic Roman *stirpa,* the medieval European *natio,* or the classic Arabic *waṭan,* categories that refer to one's place of birth lack the modern connotation of identity. Otherwise, we would call Aristotle a Macedonian and Herodotus a Turk. The category of Greeks denoted a civilizational affiliation: a matter of achievement not ascription.

Before modernity, civilization (center v. periphery or urban v. rural), religion (faithful v. infidel), status (aristocrat or citizen v. peasant or slave), and locality (village or town) provided the major bases of classifying people. In contrast, the modern sense of peoplehood largely eschews exclusions based on civilization, religion, or status, although they often legitimate the idea of peoplehood. Communities based on civilization or religion hold the possibility of acculturation or conversion. That is, civilizational or religious identity may be inclusionary, but it is not involuntary. Whether expressed as orders or estates, status belonging is descent-based and is therefore involuntary. But it is precisely such division that modern peoplehood denies.

The conditions of possibility of modern peoplehood are the infrastructural development of identity transmission (cultural or horizontal integration) and the decline of status hierarchy or qualitative inequality (status or vertical integration). As I elaborate in Chapter 3, they began in early modern Europe, accelerated there after the French Revolution, consolidated in the late nineteenth century, and then spread around the world. Beyond repetitive face-to-face interactions that is possible in a very small collectivity, any large group depends on institutions and technologies to sustain a common language and law or culture and custom. In their absence, people in a neighboring village or region may very well be aliens or foreigners. The narcissistic inflation of minor differences would ensure the assertion and acceptance of social distinction. Furthermore, whereas we may think of lords and peasants in medieval France as French, they almost certainly did not. Modernity, whether defined as the transition from status to contract or aristocracy to democracy connotes the decline of status hierarchy. Quantitative inequality may persist, but qualitative inequality disappears. Today, rich or poor French are equally French: an inclusionary, involuntary, and indivisible identity.

Let me consider three common claims to premodern peoplehood: language, religion, and culture. These are all cultural universals; human collectivities all have language, faith or value, and tradition or culture. However, given dynamism and hybridity, as well as geographical diversity and social heterogeneity, none of them offers a solid basis for modern peoplehood. The most potent ground is common consciousness, which remained weak until modernity when identity transmission expanded and status distinction diminished.

2

There are some compelling reasons to privilege language as a, if not *the,* fundamental basis of peoplehood. As *homo loquens,* any social solidarity would be difficult to imagine or sustain without linguistic communication. If people in the same category could not converse with each other, then it would be denuded of meaning for most people. It was not only disciplinary chauvinism that led Ferdinand de Saussure (1983:306) to declare that "the only essential unity is that which is constituted by social bonds," which in turn is characterized by "a community of language." Hence, the classic Greek etymology of barbarians—those who don't speak Greek—or the Shakespearean riposte to the hubris—"It's all Greek to me"—points to the linguistic gulf as an indisputable basis of distinction. These observations give credence to the Romantic celebration of language as the soul of peoplehood. As Herder (1991:65) trenchantly expressed it in the late eighteenth century: "In [language] lives all of people's wealth of ideas on tradition, history, religion, and principles of life—all its heart and soul." The Romantic idea that language suffuses culture has become something of a cliché, whether articulated by Benjamin Whorf (1956:152–156) or Ludwig Wittgenstein (1958:8). Certainly, language conflict can be highly volatile. As Gwyn Williams (1985:294) quipped: "Whom the Gods wish to destroy they first afflict with a language problem."

Does the existence of 5,000–7,000 languages or 250 large language families suggest that there are 5,000–7,000 or 250 ethnic groups? Does it mean that there are 750 ethnic groups in Papua New Guinea alone, or that the expansion of Tok Pisin there suggests the emergence of a panethnic Papua New Guinean identity (Romaine 1992:341)? Are there four groups in Switzerland because of four official languages there and 70 in Burkina Faso? Do (native) English speakers constitute a people (including English speakers in Papua New Guinea)? Should we consider the estimated half of humanity that is bilingual (Crystal 2000:45) as biracial or binational? Does the possible extinction of three thousand languages in the next century (Crystal 2000:19) portend a massive wave of genocide? Alternatively, was there only one people at the time of the Tower of Babel (Borst 1957:18–31)? If Gypsies define themselves as Romany speakers, then are Romany speakers—including an alien anthropologist—Gypsies (Stewart 1997:44,58)? Do sign language users constitute an ethnic group (Neisser 1983:281)? A synchronic correspondence between language and peoplehood is not a universal law.

A commonsense idea is, however, that there is in principle one language for one people. In this line of thinking, Italian people have always spoken Italian. This is false. Bereft of integrative forces—extensive trading networks or educational institutions—fourteenth-century Italians spoke dialects that were often mutually unintelligible. As Dante (1996:21) queried: "why people who live close together still differ in their speech (such as the Milanese and the Veronese, or the Romans and the Florentines) . . . and, what is more remarkable, why it is true of people living in the same city (such as the Bolognese)." Dante (1996:3) may have been a champion of the vernacular, but he bemoaned its diversity: fourteen major variations that were not so much dialects as distinct languages (Alinei 1984:196–199).

Contemporary standard Italian is based on Tuscan, or more exactly Florentine, which owes in no small part to Alessandro Manzoni, whose definitive 1840 edition of *I promessi sposi* [The Betrothed] provided a touchstone for the convergence of the written and the spoken word (Migliori and Griffith 1984:362–366). In the celebrated novel, characters from "all social classes . . . speak the same Italian language of Florentine extraction. . . . [In fact] the two protagonists Renzo and Lucia, who do not know how to read or write, would have spoken in a horrible brand of Lombard dialect, structurally entirely different from Tuscan" (Devoto 1978:275).

At the time of political unification, less than 3 percent of the population spoke standard Italian (De Mauro 1972:43; cf. Migliorini 1990:109–118). Italian linguistic integration occurred in the twentieth century, resulting from national systems of education, transportation, and communication (especially radio and television), universal male conscription, and other integrative forces (De Mauro 1972:334–354; Mengaldo 1994:16–24).

Christ may have stopped at Eboli, but the Italian state penetrated the far-thest reaches of the peninsula. Even so, only a third of Italians exclusively used standard Italian at home in the 1980s (Maiden 1995:9).

The Italian case is not the exception but the norm; linguistic diversity is an indisputable fact of human life. Lingua franca may facilitate governance, economic transactions, and cultural interactions within a nation-state or the world at large. But that does not mean that language correlates with race, ethnicity, or nation (Sapir 1921:215). We cannot even claim a natural correspondence between language and tribe; neighboring villagers may very well speak different dialects. For example, the three thousand Yolngu of northern Australia speak nine different languages (I. Keen 1994:4).

Against the reality of polyglottism, nationalists have aspired to imbricate language and nation. Perhaps the most notable is the case of France. The history of the French language reveals the overlapping influences and in-flections of Anglo-Norman, German, and Gothic tongues and other Euro-pean and Mediterranean languages from its Latin and Indo-European ori-gins. Yet the ancestor of contemporary French (Francien, or Parisian French) was far from being a national language until recently (Brunot 1905–72:i,ix,525–599).

Status and geographical differentiation made communication elusive. In feudal France, "the language of the educated . . . was almost uniformly Latin [and that of the non-educated was] the variety of tongues in everyday use" (Bloch 1961:75). As late as the sixteenth century, the literature in France was cosmopolitan (Brunot 1905–72:ii,3). The learned language was Latin, polite society conversed in Francien, and the rest spoke their local dialect (Padley 1988:322; Brun 1927:12). Jean Racine's 1661 visit to Lyon provoked him to write to Jean La Fontaine: "I could no longer understand the language of the country [*pays*], and could not make myself understood" (Walter 1988:105). Although he thought he'd asked for a chamber pot, the maid provided a heater. A Parisian in Lyon, wrote Racine, was like a Mus-covite in Paris. More systematically, Abbé Grégoire's 1794 survey showed that the number of fluent French speakers did not exceed three million in a population of twenty-six million (de Certeau, Julia, and Revel 1975:302). For many people in France, the French Revolution "was conducted in a foreign language" (Jones 1988:208). More tellingly, as late as 1863, one-fourth of French people were ignorant of *langue nationale* (Weber 1976: 498–501).

The linguistic unification of France was a protracted process. First, national language had to be established. The 1539 Ordonnance de Villers-Cotterets legislated *langage maternel françois* as the language of the law courts. François I's edict asserted his political supremacy over the church and its language, Latin, and in so doing dislodged Latin as the language of the elite. Simultaneously, it secured the supremacy of Francien over other dialects and languages (Brunot 1905–72:i,364;ii,27–32). The crystallization of seventeenth-century French, modeled after classical Latin (Fumaroli 1980:87), propagated the belief in the clarity and logic of the French language. In so doing, language engineers, such as Claude Favre de Vaugelas and François de Malherbe, sought "to immobilize that which by nature is mobile" (Brunot 1905–72:i,iv,60). Ferdinand Brunot (1905–72:iii,4) excoriates in particular Malherbe, who inflicted "the reign of grammar which was more tyrannical and lasted longer [in France] than in any other country" and "killed lyricism in France for 200 years" (Brunot 1891:590). Be that as it may, the standardization of written French provided a sense of continuity, such that contemporary readers have little trouble deciphering Racine's letter, even though the master of the French language was unable to order a chamber pot. The temporal continuity of the scriptural does not guarantee the spatial communality of the oral.

Secondly, mass education and mass communication spread French throughout France. Even after establishing it as the official language, the state did not impose it on the subjects (Peyre 1933:217–221). Linguistic integration was part and parcel of the egalitarian and secular impetus of the Revolution, which sought to squelch status and regional distinctions (Balibar and Laporte 1974:116). As Abbé Grégoire intoned: "The unity of language (*l'idiome*) is an integral part of the Revolution" (de Certeau, Julia, and Revel 1975:309). The rapid expansion and intensification of the nationwide systems of production and distribution facilitated the spread of standard French (cf. Balibar and Laporte 1974:80). As we have seen, however, the linguistic unification of France was completed only in the twentieth century and contemporary France remains a multilingual society (Walter 1982).

As the French case suggests, the presupposition of one people, one language is made plausible in part by the stability of the scriptural. Scholars have often neglected language diversity in light of textual unity and continuity (Steinberg 1987:199). The relative immobility of the written—the language of administration and civilization—provides nominal continuity and homogeneity, thereby effacing the ephemerality and heterogeneity of the oral. A central language provides the patina of imperial unity. As the pioneering grammarian Antonio de Nebrija (1946:5) wrote in 1492: "Language is always the companion of empire." Thus, Chinese may have been the lingua franca of the Chinese empire, but the unity was largely scriptural and restricted to the elite. In the late twentieth century, dialects "are as different from each other as French from Italian and, when taken together, are probably more complex than the whole Romance family" (Ramsey 1987:16). The ideal of chirographic unity faces everywhere the reality of oral diversity.

Language integration entails overcoming status and geographical differentiation. If aristocrats claim to be a different kind of people from their subjects, then they may very well buttress the distinction by linguistic means. Russian aristocrats spoke French or German, while the Mughal elite spoke Persian. English aristocrats spoke French until the fifteenth century, and some English kings spoke German better than English as late as the eighteenth century. Colonialism provides another source of linguistic stratification. Political or military superiority frequently spawns a belief in linguistic superiority—based on aesthetic or scientific criteria—whether in French, British, or Japanese colonialism (Calvet 1974:chap. 11; Phillipson 1992:chap. 6; Shi 1993:chap. 2).

Beyond status integration, linguistic unification requires the development of mass education and mass communication. The task is especially intractable in large countries. The Soviet Union in the 1970s had 130 major languages despite the effort to create a single "speech community" (M. Smith 1998:168–176). But it is no different in relatively small countries. In the early nineteenth century, there were five major languages in Norway: Danish (the language of the colonizer), literary standard ("a Norweigian reading pronunciation of Danish used on solemn occasions"), colloquial standard ("the daily speech of the educated classes"), urban substandard (spoken by artisans and workers), and rural dialects ("varying from parish to parish") (Haugen 1966:31). Even today, the language of the official elite (Bokmål) remains distinct from that of the folk elite (Landmål) (Kerswill 1994:36–45). Postcolonial societies often face the challenge of linguistic unification that generates language conflicts (cf. Laitin 1992:chap. 5).

Inter-regional economic and cultural interactions generate and sustain a lingua franca, but the fundamental force of linguistic unification has been the modern state. Its importance can be illustrated by comparing the fates of Hebrew and Esperanto. By the mid-nineteenth century, Hebrew, if not quite dead, was in a category of languages that had to be painfully acquired, like Latin for their Gentile counterparts in central and eastern Europe. The language of the Diaspora was not Hebrew; Sephardic Jews spoke Ladino and other Jewish-Spanish languages, and Ashkenazic Jews primarily used Yiddish. The language of instruction in *yeshivah* was Yiddish (Alter 1988: 6), which—if we follow the logic of racial philology—made Yiddish-speaking Jews Aryans (Hobsbawm 1992:98). Furthermore, post-Emancipation European Jewry generally adopted the dominant language of their resident country. To be sure, Haskalah (Hebrew Enlightenment led by Moses Mendelssohn in the eighteenth century) sought to revive Hebrew, but the first novel in Hebrew—Avraham Mapu's *'Ahavat Tsiyon* [The Love of Zion]—appeared only in 1853, when no one spoke the language (Alter 1988:17,24). Symptomatically, German was the language of instruction at Mendelssohn's first modern Jewish school, *Freischule* (Epstein 1959:290).

Eliezar Ben Yehuda sedulously resuscitated spoken Hebrew after moving to Palestine in 1881 (Avineri 1981:83–87; cf. Harshav 1993:84), though as late as 1901 only ten families regularly used Hebrew (Cooper 1989:13). Against Jewish religious opposition, Zionists sought to unite language and territory (Avineri 1981:85). The establishment of the Israeli state in 1948 and its adoption of Hebrew as the official language ensured its efflorescence (Spolsky and Cooper 1991:59–73). Ironically, some of the founding Israeli leaders had limited fluency in the country's official language (Segev 2000: 98), and linguistic diversity persists in contemporary Israel (Ben-Rafael 1994:pt.3).

No one would deny the place of Modern Hebrew among the world's major languages, but many people would begrudge a place to Esperanto. However, the estimated number of Esperanto speakers was fifteen million in the early 1970s (Janton 1973:112), much larger than the three million Hebrew speakers today (Dalby 1998:245). Furthermore, Ludwig Zamenhof invented Esperanto in 1887, roughly coeval with Ben Yehuda's effort to revive Hebrew. Esperanto itself was not created de novo, just as Modern Hebrew had to be adapted for modern parlance (cf. Ornan 1985:22). Indeed, Esperanto was intended explicitly to be cosmopolitan. As Zamenhof poignantly wrote: "No one more than a Jew can feel the tragedy of human division. No one more than a Jew, who must pray to God in a dead language, can feel the need for a neutral and non-national language" (Janton 1973:30).

What differentiated their fate was the power of the modern state. The

Israeli state designated Hebrew as its official language, thereby terminating the long tradition of Jewish diglottism (Ornan 1985:23). Had the state of Israel adopted one or more of the Diasporic languages, or even Esperanto, Hebrew would have remained in the category of classical languages spoken only by a few cognoscenti. Esperanto, in contrast, lacked the support of modern states. Although it expressed the utopian desire for human unity, international organizations, such as the League of Nations, avoided adopting Esperanto as one of its official languages. Stalin went so far as to suppress its use in the Soviet Union (Forster 1982:185,202).

Many nationalists seek the essence of peoplehood in language because it appears primordial, articulating something deep and authentic (Fishman 1972:40–55). The idea of mother tongue expresses the intimate and natural social bond that anchors collective identity. Yet the fatal flaw of language as a nationalist icon is that outsiders can learn it. Though capable of eliciting deep emotional attachment, language is ultimately an instrument of communication. A child capable of learning a language is able to learn any language. Many people, after all, grow up bilingual. Given the plasticity of language acquisition, as well as the undeniable dynamism and hybridity of actually existing languages, language is not as robust an anchor for modern peoplehood as it seemed to the Romantics and their followers. Thus, we should reformulate Saussure's proposed relationship between ethnicity and language. Modern peoplehood neither emerged from nor is congruent with premodern linguistic community. Syllogistically, if politics defines language and language defines peoplehood, then politics defines peoplehood (cf. Meillet 1918:331).

3

Religion provides a potent underpinning of peoplehood, expressing its deepest values and longings. To be sure, religious unity is often nominal. Whether for medieval Christians (Delumeau 1992:333–336) or contemporary Javanese religious adherents (Geertz 1960:6), heterogeneity and heterodoxy, as well as dynamism and diversity, are rife. Furthermore, articulated in the language of belief, the idea of religion is ethnocentric (Smith 1977:v). The epistemological conception of religion dates from the Enlightenment, forged in the crucible of Christian theological and anti-Christian philosophical writings (Harrison 1990; cf. Greisch 2002:44–50). Nonetheless, religious peoplehood asserts a common identity among the faithful, or an inclusionary identity based on spiritual descent (tradition) and commonality (culture) (Smith 1979:12; cf. Hanson 1978:76–90). Although a harbinger of modern peoplehood, religious peoplehood is not circumscribed by geography or by physiological descent. Major world religions hanker toward the universal (Smith 1981:3), including individuals regardless of their territorial origins or ethnoracial background. Many people follow the faith of their parents, but they may very well convert to Jainism or Judaism. Modern peoplehood is not voluntary; one cannot, in principle, convert to Flemish or Fulani race or ethnicity.

Ecumenical impulse is clear in Christianity. Against the claim of particular descent, John the Baptist exhorts: "Do not presume to say to yourselves, 'We have Abraham as our ancestor'; for I tell you, God is able from these stones to raise up children to Abraham" (Mt 3.9). Not physiological lineage but spiritual descent is what matters (Rom 9.6). A Christian may renounce parents and families (Mt 10.34–37), and instead embrace strangers who are fellow Christians (Mk 3.31–35). The Pharisaic Jew Paul's (Phil 3.5) interpretation of the Gospel is "the power of God for salvation to everyone who has faith" (Rom 1.16; cf. 1 Tim 4.10), which means that: "There is no distinction between Jew and Greek; the same Lord is Lord of all" (Rom 10.12; cf. Gal 3.28). Egalitarianism is a critical element of Christian fellowship (Mk 10.25; Lk 6.20–25, Jn 5.1–7; cf. Kautsky 1925:323–336). The fundamental distinction is, then, between Christians and non-Christians (Rom 9), which is a matter neither of descent nor of status but of faith (Kee 1995:199–207). That is, this-worldly criteria of birth, wealth, and, indeed, the modern notion of peoplehood should be immaterial to Christian fellowship.

The concrete manifestation of Jesus in a particular place and time does not limit the potential community of Christians to a particular people, but, rather, extends it to all of humanity (Rahner 1978:234,430; Pannenberg 1983:13). The question of who Jesus was or who he thought he was is not a query about his racial, ethnic, or national origin (O'Neill 1995:188; cf. Sanders 1985:116–119). Christian philosophical anthropology asserts that human beings, who are made in God's image, are essentially one. Thus, Saint Augustine (1998:581) wrote: "God chose to create the human race from one single man. His purpose in doing this was not only that the human race should be united in fellowship by a natural likeness, but also that men should be bound together by kinship in the unity of concord, linked by the bond of peace." The idea of "one, holy, catholic and apostolic" church is a constant theme from the Gospels (Jn 17.20–23; 1 Cor 1.13; Eph 4.4), the early formulations of Tertullian (Rankin 1995:111–116) and Cyprian (1840:134) to modern theologians from Schleiermacher to Barth (Sykes 1984:239–261). The Christian community is transnational and transhistorical: "Our citizenship is in heaven" (Phil 3.20; cf. Bultmann 1957:34–37). In rejecting particularistic claims for Christians (Niebuhr 1941–43:ii,41), there is a strong impulse to universalize "the unity between love of God and love of neighbor" to include non-Christians as well (Rahner 1978:456). Needless to say, Christian love has been vitiated by a wide array of hatreds. However, the dark side of Christian history does not deny that Christian identity and hatred were based on faith, not modern peoplehood.

H. Richard Niebuhr (1957:6) states the sociological truism that: "The division of the churches closely follows the division of men into the castes of national, racial, and economic groups." Although Christianity's entanglement with power and wealth is undeniable, its alignment with race, ethnicity, or nation is a modern phenomenon. Niebuhr (1957:122) himself dates it from the Reformation. Only after the 1648 Treaty of Westphalia— though the 1555 Treaty of Augsberg is a significant precedent—did the state decisively supersede the church (cf. Ward 1999:1). The Wesphalian Peace, furthermore, stunted efforts to achieve the isomorphism of polity and religion. The diffusion of the vernacular, the entwinement of absolutist states and national churches, and the transformation of religion into mass politics facilitated the alignment of Christianity with modern peoplehood. But the equation remained restricted to the elite, whether in the form of ecclesiastical patriotism or the unholy alliance between absolutist states and national churches, until the nineteenth century (Bossy 1982:289; Cameron 1991:52–55).

Universalism is equally explicit in Islam. The self-surrender to Allah is a route to salvation open to everyone, underscored by the Qur'an's emphasis on "essential human egalitarianism" (Rahman 1982:19). The community of Muslims, *umma,* is transtribal; the sphere of Islam, *dar al-Islam,* is not a territorially based or bound but denotes the extension of the faith (Hodgson 1974:i,252). The Qur'an is critical of particularistic claims: "When it is said to them: 'Follow what God has revealed,' they reply: 'No, we shall follow only what our fathers had practiced,'—even though their fathers had no wisdom or guidance" (2:170; cf. 5:104; 31:21). Tribal solidarities and genealogical claims pale in comparison to the light of Islamic faith: "If you do not know their fathers, they are then your brothers in religion and your friends. . . . The Prophet is closer to the faithful than they are themselves" (33:5). The very existence of human diversity is taken to be a divine sign: "Among other signs of His is . . . the variety of your tongues and complexions" (30:22), but it does not deny the unity of humanity, which stems from a single origin (4:1; cf. Lewis 1990:21). The fundamental distinction is between Muslims and *kafīr* (unbelievers), but, unlike gender or status, it is a matter of choice not birth (Lewis 1984:9).

In spite of considerable doctrinal schisms—Islamic history is coterminous with them—Islamic unity is no less valorized than Christian unity. The sense of Muslim peoplehood has frequently superseded other claims of allegiance, whether territorial or tribal (Goldziher 1966:73; Hitti 1970: 753). As Ibn Khaldun pointed out, Muslim unity supersedes all forms of *'aṣabīyah,* or group cohesiveness, including family and tribal ties (cf. Kāmil 1970:26–45). Like Christianity, Islam came to justify empires, but premodern empires did not promote modern peoplehood. Rather, the universalistic elements made them amenable as an imperialist ideology (cf. Fowden 1993:170), which in turn constituted a common inheritance of Islamic civilization (cf. Hourani 1983:341).

Islam did not expunge particularistic ties or avoid expressions of ethnocentrism (von Grunebaum 1953:35–40), but the alignment of Islam and modern peoplehood occurred in the early twentieth century as a reaction to Western impact (Porath 1986:284–290; Roy 1994:110). Because of the universalistic impulse of Islam, as well as its penchant for political theocracy (Hitti 1970:753), however, the dominant expression of nationalism has been secular in the Muslim world (Smith 1957:73–85). Atatürk was vehemently antireligious; Reza Khan named his dynasty after a pre-Islamic Iranian language; and Gamal Abdel Nasser in Egypt or the Ba'th party in Iraq and Syria claimed to be socialist.

The most influential articulation of modern peoplehood in the modern Middle East has been pan-Arab nationalism, which is based principally on shared language and history, not religion (Hourani 1983:260; Porath 1986: 314). Two of the most influential Arab nationalist intellectuals, Sati' al-Husri and Michel 'Aflaq, were influenced by German Romanticism (Tibi 1990:pt.3). Symptomatically, Christians, not Muslims, initially promoted Arab nationalism (Antonius 1938:45–60). Christians traditionally belonged to a protected community (*dhimma*) in *dar al-Islam,* and began to claim the rights of citizenship or homeland (*waṭan*) after the late nineteenth century (Samir 1998:75). However, *waṭan* had no connotation of being the basis of modern peoplehood, and the very term to describe nations referred to religious groups in classical usage (Lewis 1988:38–42,131, 1998:83).

Universalism is also evident in Asian religions. Buddha opened the possibility of nobility (*ārya*) to the ignoble (*anārya*), and in so doing envisioned a community of faith regardless of status hierarchy or geographical origins (Takakusu 1956:18; Nakamura 1985:227–287). In *Suttanipāta* (136–142), Buddha taught that nobility or nirvana is not a product of birthright but of rightful conduct. The egalitarian impulse of Buddhism challenged existing social stratification, whether in Buddha's India or Shinran's Japan (Chakravarti 1987:108–111; Yoshimoto 1984:14–18). Needless to say, Buddhism has been mobilized to justify autocratic rule (Wright 1959:57), but few have claimed to locate the source of modern peoplehood in Buddhism. The same can be said of Taoism, which is "a two-thousand-year tradition of individualism and of revolt against tyranny" (Welch 1965:157). The teachings of Laozi or Zhuangzi frequently appealed to the peasantry (Wright 1959:25), but no one has yet claimed either as the basis of racial, ethnic, or national identity.

Not all religions are inclusionary or universalist. Hieratic and hierarchical religions, such as Hinduism, or explicitly nationalist religions such as State Shintō, exist. Hinduism denotes a congeries of South Asian religions that are not Muslim, Sikh, Jain, Christian, or Buddhist, but what unites the mixture is the traditional exclusion of Untouchables, or Dalits, from society (Flood 1996:59). Privileged Hindus, especially high-caste Brahmans, regarded Untouchables as a distinct and despised group of people. Facing British colonialism, Christian missions, and the Muslim Khilafat movement, the Hindu Sangathan movement began to integrate Untouchables in Hindu peoplehood in the 1920s (Jaffrelot 1996:11). By the late twentieth century, Hindu nationalism—a predominantly middle-class movement that was at once conservative and populist—sought to expunge non-Hindu religions (Veer 1994:196; Hansen 1995:5–9). Religion and nationality were to be isomorphic: India for Hindus, Pakistan for Muslims (Ahmad 1964: 271–276; Pandey 1993:12). However, this is a modern state of affairs. Similarly, Shintō emerged as a state religion in Japan after the late nineteenth century. The strength of local faiths and rival religions, however, prevented it from achieving national religious integration (Hardacre 1988:131).

How about primitive religions? Thorkild Jacobsen (1976:147) describes the religion of Mesopotamia in the second millennium BCE as "personal religion": "The individual matters to God, God cares about him personally and deeply." Tribal religions are more promising: in a social organization based on descent and kinship, religious practice often focuses on ancestor and lineage (Fortes 1983:11). However, once ethnographers jettison the myth of tribal isolation from history and the world, they shatter the simple equation of religion and peoplehood. For example, Uduk-speaking people on the border of Sudan and Ethiopia include many refugees and migrants and there is nothing "corresponding to the older anthropological image of a coherent tribal cosmos, an integrated system of discourse, an orthodoxy" (James 1988:3). Uduk religion, which itself is diverse, exists alongside Nilotic, Christian, and Islamic faiths (James 1988:pt.2). Even in Australia, where Émile Durkheim (1995:90–93) located the most primitive religion, the claim of religious and social solidarity is spurious. Each patrifocal group in the aforementioned Yolngu practices a relatively autonomous form of religious ritual and knowledge, and they too have not been spared the Christian missionary effort (I. Keen 1994:1,22–35).

Thus, religious peoplehood should not be equated with modern peoplehood. Although modern racial, ethnic, or nationalist movements and identities may align religion and modern peoplehood, such a conceptualization is inevitably modern. One case, however, requires an extended commentary.

The controversy over Jewish identity is a longstanding one, beginning with Moses—an Egyptian (Assmann 1997:21) married to a Cushite (Num 12)—but the primary basis of premodern Jewish identity was religious. Like all religions, Judaism began among a particular people, place, and time, but the fate of the faith is not congruent with the descendants of the original tribes (cf. Gottwald 1979:688–693). It is not by dint of birth but faith that one is chosen; Amos (1.2–2.16; 9.7–10), for instance, offers little solace for the faithless. Although some of Abraham's descendants, such as Isaac and Jacob, inherited Israel's covenant with Yahweh, others were disinherited, such as Esau and Ishmael. Quite clearly, not all descendants are equally chosen, and, as Spinoza (1951:247) famously argued, the covenant was annulled by the Babylonian exile. The Tanakh does not promote ethnoracial purity or the bond between Israel and land (Lev 25.23). The very term Israel connotes a mixed community of faith rather than an ethnonational group (Harvey 1996:271).

Given its universalist impetus (Ps 102.22; cf. Segal 1986:165–171; Levine 1998:96–104), the ambit of Judaism has included Gentiles (Kee 1995:50; cf. Feldman 1993:293). As Isaiah (56.7) notes: "For my house shall be called a / house of prayer / for all peoples." Most compellingly, Gentiles could convert: "The convert (*ger* or *ger tzedek*) becomes a new creature, 'similar to a new born infant'; his previous, non-Jewish kinship ties are completely severed. He is now included in the category of 'Israel,' and is therefore 'an Israel in all respects' " (Stern 1994:90; cf. Cohen 1987: 50–58).

The halakhic definition of Jewish identity—Jews as children of Jewish mothers—seems to suggest that premodern Jews held an ethnoracial conception of peoplehood. Were that the case, however, one would expect Jews to valorize patrilineal as well as matrilineal descent. When the Torah gives an injunction against intermarriage, the reason is religious: "for that would turn away your children from following me, to serve other gods" (Deut 7.4; cf. Ezra 9.1–4; Neh 13.27). Although the Midrash, Zohar, Judah Halevi, and other authorities appear to provide a proto-ethnoracial definition of premodern Jewish identity, discounting in places the possibility of conversion or even of apostasy, no less an authority than Moses Maimonides argued that converts were Jews whereas apostates were not (Kellner 1991:101–104; Novak 1995:235–239). Joseph, we should recall, did not subscribe to the halakhic definition (Gen 41.45).

The modern conception of Jewish peoplehood can only be applied anachronistically, and hence misleadingly, to first-century Palestine (cf. Noethlichs 1996:125–131), which was a differentiated community of various tongues, widespread intermarriage, and a mixture of customs and mores (Hengel 1980:60–77, 1989:53; Horsley 1995:104–107). Physical appearance, clothing, language, names, occupations, or penile circumcision (androcentric a mark though it may be) did not distinguish Jews from Gentiles (Cohen 1999:27–49). Some Jews became Hellenized to the extent that they claimed common ancestry and cultural origins with Greeks (Gruen 1998:261–267; cf. Bartlett 1985:184). To be a Jew meant to belong to one of the Judaic sects, but schisms, frequently following status distinctions, divided them. Thus Sadducees and Samaritans or Scribes and Pharisees appear as separate peoples (Saldarini 1988:pt.3). The ruling strata and the indigenous peasantry constituted distinct groups of people (Horsley 1995:7; cf. Kreissig 1970:80–87).

The destruction of the Temple in Jerusalem in 70 CE, the Bar Kochba Revolt of 132–135 CE, and the ensuing Pharisaic Rabbis' emigration to Galilee accelerated the fission of Judaism from the Roman Empire and Christianity (Goodman 1987:239–251). Christian identity became manifest after 200 CE (Markus 1980:4–7; cf. Acts 11.26), when Christians began to define non-Christians as *ethne* (nations), a term similar to the Jewish goyim (Goodman 1994:14). *Ethne* and goyim are religious, not ethnic, terms, though boundaries were fuzzy and permeable (Wilken 1984:24). In turn, Rabbinic Judaism became normative Judaism after the Rabbis' emigration to Galilee (Schäfer 1983:150–155; Cohen 1987:215–224). The Rabbis transformed their view of Christians from being Judaic to heretics (*minim*) and even non-Jewish (Kimelman 1981:243; Schiffman 1985:75–78). Although tolerant of Gentiles and pagans before, the early Rabbinic literature came to characterize non-Jews as polluted and wicked, as animal-like beings who are prone to theft, rape, and murder, in contradistinction to holy, righteous, and angel-like Jews (Stern 1994:22–42). Aspersion was cast on deviants from the new orthodoxy. Ethnic Jews—not only Christians, but also Sadducees, Samaritans (*Kutim*), and slaves—were cast outside the boundaries of Jews (Schiffman 1985:36; Stern 1994:99–113). In other words, in the disinherited tradition of Esau and Ishmael, the heterodox, whether Sadducees or Christians and their descendants, ceased to be Jewish. Needless to say, they would comfortably pass the ethnoracial or ethnonational test of Jewish peoplehood. The integral definition of Jewry was, however, fidelity to normative Judaism. Even 'am ha-'arets (people of the land) were suspect because the Rabbis regarded them as lax in faith (Stern 1994:156–170).

To put the matter more polemically, consider Galileans, most of whom were what we would today call Jewish farmers. Galilee then exhibited, as it does today, considerable regional, status, religious, and linguistic variety (Goodman 1983:31–40; Cohen 1992:185–189). Despite being the home of the Jesus movement, many Galileans resisted Christianity until the missionary efforts under Constantine I (Horsley 1996:184–189). Contemporary descendants of first-century Galileans, having largely converted to Christianity or Islam (Gil 1992:9,140,836), have transmogrified into another racial (Arab) or ethnonational (Palestinian) group (cf. Landau 1993:8; Laurens 1999:200–206). However, a strict application of an ethnoracial or halakhic definition would classify many of them as Jews. In this spirit, David Ben-Gurion exhorted in 1924: "The fate of the Jewish worker is linked to the fate of the Arab worker. We will rise together or sink together. . . . We Jewish and Arab workers are the sons of the same country, and our paths are united for ever" (Shapira 1984:85). The identification of Israel as the Jewish state, however, rendered long-term residents as racial, religious, and national others (Rabinovitz 1997:187; cf. Rouhana 1997:146–150). Palestinians thereby faced a situation not unlike that of their second-century ancestors confronting the Rabbinic immigration to Galilee.

Between ancient Galilee and eighteenth-century European emancipation lies a long history of the Jewish Diaspora. Here, again, the basis of Jewish communities, whether in the twelfth-century Latin Kingdom of Jerusalem (Prawer 1988:94–98) or eighteenth-century Egypt (Beinin 1998:7), was faith. Conversions to and out of Judaism occurred throughout medieval Europe (Cohen 1984:73–76; Goitein 1999:303), including the intermittently successful Christian missionizing in medieval Europe (Chazan 1989: 169) and the Islamic conversion of Sabbatai Sēvi's followers (Scholem 1973:823). Did Christian and Muslim converts remain Jews? The primacy of religion accounts for the exclusion of Karaites (who rejected Talmudic authority) from the ambit of Jewry (Beinin 1998:2).

Enlightenment and Emancipation at once liberated the Jewish religious minority and posed the question of identity. Many Jewish Germans in the early twentieth century, for example, advocated Enlightenment values and identified themselves as Germans (Mosse 1985:42–46; cf. Deutscher 1982: 51). Emil Ludwig (1931:573) exemplified the Enlightenment universalism of educated Jewish Germans, writing in his autobiography that Goethe stood for his faith.

The quest for the modern Jewish identity was ironically the search for the Jewish identity *tout court*. As Ahad Ha-Am put it in 1892: "We are not yet a people; we are only [individual] Jews" (Meyer 1990:69). Although Mendelssohn regarded Jews as a religious group, later thinkers considered them as a matter of modern peoplehood (cf. Meyer 1990:16–19). Moses Hess at first sought a synthesis between Germans and Jews and Judaism and Christianity in his 1837 *Die heilige Geschichte der Menschheit* [The Holy History of Humanity] (Avineri 1985:21) and found Jewish national consciousness lacking (Lundgren 1992:75), but he advocated a Jewish community in Palestine in his 1862 treatise *Rom und Jerusalem* [Rome and Jerusalem] (Hertzberg 1969:138). By the mid-nineteenth century Heinrich Graetz (1891:vf) delineated the history of Jewish "race" and "nation," which systematically excluded dissident currents (Shmueli 1990:194). More dramatically, Franz Rosenzweig (1972:298) wrote in the early twentieth century: "There is only one community in which such a linked sequence of everlasting life goes from grandfather to grandson, only one which cannot utter the 'we' of its unity without hearing deep within a voice that adds:

'are eternal.' It must be a blood-community, because only blood gives present warrant to the hope for a future."

The transformation from religious to racial identity can be seen in the German debate on the Jewish Question. Karl Marx's concern in his celebrated 1843 essay, "On the Jewish Question," was fundamentally religious. By the time of German unification, it denoted concerns over civil or political emancipation (cf. Sorkin 1987:21–43). By the turn of the twentieth century, the Jewish Question queried whether Jews were a religious-cultural or racial group (Abraham 1992:90). Max Weber, for example, considered Jewish Germans as a status group, much like Catholics (Abraham 1992:289).

The idea of the blood community fused with a territorial-based ideology in Zionism, easily the most influential formulation of Jewish peoplehood, which is, according to Avishai Margalit (1998:167), "a junkyard for almost every European ideology" (cf. Talmon 1970:88,101). Assimilated Jews, such as Leon Pinsker and Theodor Herzl, embraced the European idea of Romantic nationalism (Avineri 1981:12; cf. Aschheim 1982:100). Zionism marked the abdication of apocalyptic eschatology in favor of modern nationhood, as Pinsker's 1882 manifesto, *Auto-Emancipation,* makes clear (Hertzberg 1969:198).

Zionism arose in part because of anti-Semitism. The very term anti-Semitism was coined in 1879 (Rürup 1975:101). The "motto of modern anti-Semitism" was: "On the Jew's *faith* I do not look, his *race* is what I cannot brook" (Kautsky 1926:11). That is, the basis of anti-Semitism shifted from Christian hostility to ethnoracial denigration (cf. Arendt 1968: vii). While Abbé Grégoire equated Jewish assimilation with Christian conversion in the late eighteenth century, Edouart Drumont and other anti-Semites did not a century later (Birnbaum 2000:16–19).

In contradistinction to religious-based argument, anti- or non-Christian anti-Semitism celebrated the Romantic and biological idea of the *Volk.* As the self-proclaimed patriarch of anti-Semitism, Wilhelm Marr—who married thrice, all to Jewish women and later castigated as a Jew (Zimmermann 1986:vii,13,114)—wrote in 1880: "There must be no question here of parading religious prejudices when it is a question of race and when the difference lies in the 'blood' " (Pulzer 1988:48). In a similar vein, Eugen Dühring argued in 1881: "Jewish influence can be removed . . . only with the removal of the Jews themselves" (Graml 1992:65).

The shift from religious to racial anti-Semitism can also be seen in the development of Nazi racial ideology. Dieter Eckart—the " 'spiritual' god-father of National Socialism" (Wistrich 1995:45) and the man to whom *Mein Kampf* is dedicated—stressed the spiritual aspect of Jewish identity (Lane and Rupp 1978:xiii). The religious definition was supplanted by the biological by Alfred Rosenberg and Adolf Hitler, who (1943:56) argued that Jews were "not Germans of a special religion, but a people in them-selves." In fact, the "first and greatest lie" is the idea "that the Jews are not a race but a religion" (Hitler 1943:307). After realizing the racial ontology that separated Jews from Germans, he "had at last come to the conclusion that the Jew was no German" (Hitler 1943:61). Rather than the German Romantic definition that stressed language and culture, he (1943:336) ar-gued that "nationality or rather race does not happen to lie in language but in the blood." After Hitler and the Holocaust, that Jews constituted a racial, ethnic, or national group became an article of faith.

Nazism completed the transition from religious to racial identity. As Peter Gay (1998:47) observes: "By 1933 . . . we had suddenly become Jews." The 1935 Nuremberg Laws emphasized both maternal and paternal ancestry, in contrast to the 1913 Reich law in which citizenship passed through men (Wildenthal 1997:265). Though Jewish Germans may have regarded the racial definition of Jewry as "just another lie that we repudi-ated as unhistorical and unscientific" (Gay 1998:110), the Nazi regime transformed all of them into racial Jews (cf. Herzl 1946:92). Once estab-lished, historical anti-Judaism was transformed into anti-Semitism, delin-eating two millennia of continuous Judeophobia (cf. Poliakov 1955–77).

The transition from religion to race did not completely expunge the past. Racial anti-Semites, such as Houston Stewart Chamberlain (1968:334), stressed the primacy of peoplehood over religion: "There would be no Jewish religion if there were no Jewish nation." Ironically, for Chamberlain (1968:336), a telltale proof of Jewish distinctiveness was religious: "One single trait is all that is necessary to reveal in an almost alarming manner to our consciousness the yawning gulf which here separates soul from soul: the revelation of Christ has no significance for the Jew." Even the Nazi racial law could not but be based ultimately on the religious definition of Jewry (Hilberg 1985:i,68). Herzl's (1946:72) *Der Juden Staat* [The Jewish State] (1896) had proclaimed that: "We are a people—one people," but, after discussing the diversity of Jews, he (1946:146) noted: "Our com-munity of race is peculiar and unique, for we are bound only by the faith of our fathers."

Traditionalists, such as Yeshayahu Leibowitz (1992:83), bemoan the disjuncture between Judaic faith and Jewish identity: "The national identity of the historic Jewish people is *Judaism,* the actuality of which is life according to the Torah" (also 206–212; cf. Levinas 1990:247–258). Consider in this regard Yehuda Bauer's (2001:vii) belief that it is "best to look at the Holocaust from a Jewish perspective," because "the theology of the Holocaust is . . . a dead end." This should not be surprising given that Rabbi Yoel Taitelbaum notoriously argued that the Holocaust was an expression of God's vengeance on the Jews (Funkenstein 1993:307).

The contemporary wisdom is that Judaism is a civilization and Jewish identity is ethnonational (de Lange 1986:81). Rather than faith alone, as Rosenzweig (1955:30) wrote to Hermann Cohen in 1917, "what is necessary for the continuation of Judaism [is] a Jewish world." The ethnonational definition can be seen in a 1930s Jewish German (Altmann 1991:44) or a 1990s Jewish American (Eisen 1998:262). Symptomatically, Leo Baeck's major work before the Nazis was entitled *Das Wesen des Judentums* [The Essence of Jewishness] (1905), which stressed religion, while that after the Nazis was entitled *Dieses Volk* [This People] (1955–57), which emphasized peoplehood. Many European immigrants to Palestine embraced the idea of blood and land, thereby ultimately betraying the founding ideal of labor Zionists (Almog 2000:96–103; cf. Sternhell 1998:324–327). In 1848, no one thought of Jews as a nation (Vital 1999:253–257); a century later, very few did not.

In modern societies, religious-based groups frequently function as quasi-ethnic communities, such as the Jains in India or Britain (Banks 1992:221); the Mennonites in Germany, Russia, and Canada (Ens 1994:4–8); the Catholics in the United States (McGreevy 1996:83); or the Church of the East in Kurdistan, better known as Nestorians in the borderlands of Iran and Turkey (Coakley 1992:11–18). The Sikhs, though religious in origin, are frequently regarded as an ethnonational group (McLeod 1989:104–108). Similarly, Muslim immigrants are racialized as Muslims (cf. Metcalf 1996). Roughly 40,000 Hutterites in North America claim descent from 425 settlers in the 1870s, exercise endogamy, and continue a distinct way of life. Would their categorization as an ethnonational group distort their fundamental identity as a religious community? Polemically put, shouldn't Christians in first-century Anatolia be characterized as racial or ethnic Jews (cf. Mitchell 1993:11–43)? If not, why not as Christians? Was Paul Jewish or Christian (Boyarin 1994:2)? Why shouldn't we consider Christians, like

Jews, as a racial or ethnic group? In fact, in contemporary Muslim societies, religious minorities, such as Christians, function as quasi-ethnic groups (Samir 1998:70).

In this regard, Mormons view themselves as a schismatic community from Christianity, just as Christianity emerged out of Judaism (Shipps 1985:148). The Saints, as Mormons call themselves, share "a common culture, social institutions, traditions, and of course religion—adding up to a sense of group identity" (Arrington and Bitton 1992:216). Since its beginning with the family of Joseph Smith, Jr., (Bushman 1984:3), Mormon history cannot be considered apart from the Saints' awareness of their distinctiveness from and persecutions by Gentiles (Anderson 1942:420; Leone 1979:223–226). As the Book of Mormon teaches, the religion is universalist (2 Ne. 27:1) but descends from Israelites (1 Ne.:17; 2 Mosiah 3:19; Moro. 8:26). Indeed, the rhetoric of Mormonism is saturated with the language of Judaic apocalypticism, and the similarities between Mormons and Jews are manifold (Mauss 1994:64). Not only did Mormons seek Zion, but they also believed themselves to be the chosen people and unique to boot (Shipps 1985:122). Descent was not merely spiritual but also assumed the character of kinship and blood (Shipps 1994:71). The primary purpose of "the blessing was to identify the tribe of Israel to which the Saint belonged" (Hansen 1981:193). Spiritually and physiologically, then, the Saints can be said to be Jewish, and Joseph Smith, Jr., claimed to belong to Aaronic Priesthood (Bushman 1984:100). To be sure, converts, as in Judaism, were allowed to become part of the extended kinship group via adoption (Hansen 1981:193). However, intermarriage, especially with African Americans, was discouraged (Hansen 1981:184–195), and relatively few converted to Mormonism between 1880 and 1960 (Shipps 1994:65). Given their identity as Saints (as opposed to Gentiles), a distinct way of life, presumed kinship, and group closure, Mormons are regarded as a quasi-nationality (O'Dea 1957:16) or as an ethnicity (May 1980:726).

Nonetheless, many dispute the classification of Mormons as an ethnonational group. If they are not, however, why are Jews one? Mormons, like Jews in the past, have attracted converts and excluded apostates. They also face anti-Mormonism, which remains something of an anti-Semitism for intellectuals. Furthermore, contemporary Mormons have abdicated any desire for peoplehood identity. Mormon history is also short and hence not shrouded in mystery as is Jewish history. All that live long become saturated with naturalness and necessity.

In premodern societies, faith constituted a major mode of identity, especially as a nominal and expansionary identity of the supreme institution of the early modern world (cf. Wallerstein 1974–89:i,209). Although some religious groups have transmogrified themselves into categories of modern peoplehood, religious peoplehood should be distinguished from modern peoplehood if only by the dynamic of apostasy and conversion.

4

If language and religion cannot define peoplehood in and of itself, then what about a congeries of folkways, customs, tradition—what we call culture? Does it provide a basis for modern peoplehood?

The concept of culture crystallized as something that everyone has or shares in a delimited area in the late nineteenth century (cf. Boon 1973:2). E. B. Tylor (1970:1) defined it in *Primitive Culture* (1871) as "that complex whole which includes knowledge, belief, art, morals, law, custom, and any other capabilities and habits acquired by man as a member of society." In spite of the siren calls of cultural relativism, most nineteenth-century scholars shared the Enlightenment belief in the unity of human nature. Tylor (1970:7) himself noted that humanity is "homogeneous in nature." Even Herder had used the term culture only in the singular (Frisch 1992: 711). The master explanation for human diversity was the idea of evolution—"the main tendency of human society has been to pass from a savage to a civilized state" (Tylor 1970:32; cf. Burrow 1966:98). Whereas primitive people were believed to share folkways and customs because they were homogeneous and timeless, the predominant characterization of modern societies stressed refinement and cultivation in the manner of Matthew Arnold's *Culture and Anarchy* (1869). Culture in the Arnoldian sense is precisely what is not widely disseminated. That is, culture is something that distinguishes the haves from the have-nots. Imperial Roman or Chinese civilization may have been encompassing, but most people were not part of it. The democratic revolution leveled the field of culture as a shared terrain. Rather than the best that has been thought and said, it came to denote demotic thought and lifestyle, though the glorious achievements of the past became part and parcel of people's inheritance. Indeed, the culture concept became entrenched in the West only in the mid-twentieth century (cf. Kuper 1999:15).

Culture is a concatenation of creative and productive processes, and is neither autochthonous nor autotelic. That is, it does not flow majestically and uninterruptedly from past to present. Inevitably, there are external influences and influxes, as well as internal conflicts and contradictions. Only a selective narrative allows one to delineate a singular descent, masking manifold ancestral influences. Furthermore, many beliefs and practices that are believed to be from the misty past turn out to be relatively recent constructs. Tradition, as Eric Hobsbawm (1983a:4) notes, is "essentially a process of formalization and ritualization." Though nothing is invented out of nothing—recall that the Latin *invenire* means both to make and to discover—creativity is a crucial constituent of cultural reproduction. Even if tradition seems merely received and repeated, the past must be constantly reconstructed in order to provide a lineage. In other words, the present seeks a past that grants a sense of continuity.

Let us consider components of culture associated with peoplehood: folklore and literature, clothing and cuisine, and memory and history. The Romantics believed that folklore and mythology, like language, expressed the spirit of the people *(Volkgeist)* (Grimm and Grimm 1997:21). In this line of thinking, the more primitive the tale is the more authentic it is (Zink 1998:73–76). Folklore may express a variety of identities, but the Romantic equation between a specific set of tales and a particular people is untenable. As a literary genre, it is no older than Charles Perrault. Folklore and mythology became associated with peoplehood in the eighteenth century (Lincoln 1999:49–54).

The idea of a pure and pristine people's tale is chimerical. Many that supposedly express the spirit of the people, such as James Macpherson's *Ossian* or Elias Lönnrot's *Kalevala,* more properly belong to the genre of fakelore (Dundes 1989:42–47). They are modern compositions that depended on creative imagination (cf. Dégh 1969:59). In keeping with Perrault's literary ambitions, the Grimm Brothers' celebrated folktales are not direct dictation or reflection of the folk but constitute a particular genre, replete with non-German sources, and express a middle-class morality (Ellis 1983:9–12; Tatar 1987:32). The nineteenth-century bourgeois version expressed an orderly and genteel universe, in stark contrast to the eighteenth-century, unpolished peasant version. For example, Little Red Riding Hood is rescued in the former, but devoured in the latter (Darnton 1984:9).

More generally, the Linnaeus of folklore studies, Antti Aarne (1981), showed in 1910 that folktales have generic or universal features. As Italo

Calvino (1980:xx) curtly summarized: "Folktales are the same the world over." The tale that resolved Leo Tolstoy's personal religious crisis in *Confession* (1884) direly depicts the human condition; a man flees a beast, only to face falling into a well with a dragon (Tolstoy 1983:30). Although he manages to hang onto a bush, he is surely to die imminently as mice are gnawing at its roots. Tolstoy regarded the fable as Russian in origin. Wilfred Cantwell Smith's (1983:6–11) search for the fable's ancestry, however, takes him around the world. The Russian version is taken from a Greek story, which was adopted from an Islamic tale, which in turn hailed from the Manichees in Central Asia. The Central Asian version derived from a Buddhist legend, which may have a pre-Buddhist ancestry. Moving forward, Tolstoy had an impact on Gandhi, who in turn influenced Martin Luther King, Jr.

In general, the lability of literature is irrepressible. The extension of a literary language marks the rough boundaries of world literatures—Latin in medieval Christendom or Chinese in early modern East Asia—that extends well beyond any modern notion of peoplehood (Curtius 1953:viii). As T. S. Eliot (1968:190) observed: "No one nation, no one language, would have achieved what it has, if the same art had not been cultivated in neighboring countries and in different languages. We cannot understand any one European literature without knowing a good deal about the others." Would it make more sense to regard Virgil and Dante as formative influences on world literature or Italian literature? In fact, *Cambridge History of Italian Literature* begins with Saint Francis, "whose very name indicates how fashionable French culture was, and who sang in French when jolly, who liked to name his companions after the characters in the Round Table" (Usher 1996:5). A history of English literature can be written as a trajectory from Beowulf to Virginia Woolf, but only at the cost of eliding extra-English influences and ruptures. The final volume of the *Oxford History of English Literature* (Stewart 1963) features eight writers whom we would call Irish, American, and Polish. The lone *English* writer is the India-born Hardy.

National literature emerged in modern Europe (Curtius 1953:13; Casanova 1999:148–154). The eighteenth-century European novel often assumed a nationalist cast (Moretti 1998:38). It presupposed the emergence of mass literacy and readership, which in turn shaped aesthetic and cultural nationalism. If Ireland were invented by its literature, then it occurred in the early nineteenth century when the common consciousness of peoplehood was forged in the smithy of its writers' brains (Deane 1997:18–21).

Non-Europeans often emulated European literature, including their nationalist impulse, but they are indisputably of more recent vintage. Latin American national romances flourished between 1850 and 1880 (Sommer 1991:15–19), while East Asian nationalist writings blossomed in the very late nineteenth and early twentieth centuries (Liu 1995:47).

Literature, along with other arts, neither expresses nor embodies modern peoplehood. Romanticism contributed to nationalism, but the two should not be conflated (Riasanovsky 1992:96). Goethe (1986:190) wrote in 1795 that Germany will not produce classical works until national unification, but his work came to be considered the high point of German culture, and he (1986:224) himself pioneered the very idea of world literature. The realm of literature has consistently squelched racial or somatic genealogy in favor of an imagined and idiosyncratic lineage. Percy Bysshe Shelley (1974:319) exclaimed in *Hellas* (1822): "We are all Greeks. Our laws, our literature, our religion, our arts, have their roots in Greece." This should not be surprising as Erasmus declared in 1517: "Anyone is a Greek who has worked hard and successfully at Greek literature" (Goldhill 2002:14).

Historical ruptures, internal heterogeneity, and cultural hybridity are not restricted to the imaginative realm of literature and the arts. Clothing is often taken as a mark of ethnonational identity (Eichner 1995:1), but gender, status, urban-rural, regional, and other differences characterized premodern societies (Roach and Eicher 1965:pt.4). In fact, national differences in clothes have never been well established (Roche 1994:254). Haute couture has always been cosmopolitan (Lipovetsky 1994:57–60). Fashion has been the true vanguard of globalization.

The trend toward convergence has harbored the countertrend that insists on an endless play of distinction (König 1973:62–65; Perrot 1994:80–86). Fashion, by definition, depends on emulation and differentiation. In particular, distinction is at the heart of sartorial ethos; the very workings of differentiation limit the national convergence in clothing. Because the upper strata in most premodern societies followed the fashion of cultural metropolis, elite clothing provided a poor basis for a nationally distinct costume. Yet, except for a few romantics, they resisted the garb of lower status people, who would have provided a more robust foundation for a folk costume (Bell 1976:116). Thus, national or ethnic identity expression via clothing has remained a marginal phenomenon (cf. Davis 1992:26–29), cultivated largely for national holidays and tourist posters (Bell 1976:102).

The seeming exceptions prove the modernity of tradition. Although the sight of kilt and the sound of bagpipes evoke Scottish Highland today, Scotland was long a colony of Ireland and possessed no distinctive, independent cultural tradition until the Union. According to Hugh Trevor-Roper (1983), the cultural revolt against Ireland in the early nineteenth century severed Scotland's dependence on Ireland. The vacant tradition was clothed by tartan philibeg, or the modern kilt. Tartan hailed from Flanders in the sixteenth century, and philibeg was invented by an Englishman in the early eighteenth century. Seeing a lucrative market, William Wilson & Son devised distinctive patterns to symbolize lineage, which was being assembled by antiquarians. In other words, romantic nationalists and commercial interests concocted the Scottish ethnonational costume in the eighteenth century. Go to Glasgow today, however, and one finds there roughly the same clothing as in Göttingen or Guangdong.

"Tell me what you eat: I shall tell you what you are" (Brillat-Savarin 1995:16). Food and cuisine, as much as they are human universals, express social and cultural particulars. Taste buds vividly and viscerally distinguish people, being notoriously redolent of nostalgia (Mennell 1985:17; Gelder 2000:27). Both *The Epic of Gilgamesh* and *The Iliad* define human beings as bread eaters and claim food as a basis of social distinction (Garnsey 1999: 62). Certainly, the modern world is replete with alimentary metaphors from cognition to copulation as it is with national and ethnic stereotypes about food. Common epithets—Froggy or Kraut—use food in the work of national and ethnic distinction. But does the kind of food people eat tell us to which peoplehood they belong? In spite of being something of a patriot befitting a provincial, Jean Anthelme Brillat-Savarin (1995:139) is more eager to tell his readers that "gourmands live much longer than other folk," rather than to discourse on distinct ethnonational cuisine.

A particular food item usually cannot be traced to a particular group. Few would doubt the Jewish provenance of bagels, but Jewish Israelis regard bagels as American, and the Israeli *bagele* are largely Arab made and sold (Gabaccia 1998:2). Brought over to the United States by Eastern European Jews, bagels first gained prominence in the 1920s in New Haven, Connecticut (Gabaccia 1998:3). Soon, it became an iconic urban, northeastern food, usually eaten with cream cheese, which was developed by eighteenth-century English Quakers in Pennsylvania (Gabaccia 1998:4). The folklorist Yanagita Kunio (1978:50–55) identified rice as the basis of Japanese culture, but it came proximately from the Korean peninsula and became the chief staple only in the nineteenth century (Ohnuki-Tierney 1993:39). Medieval peasants ate millet and wild grass (Nagahara 1990: 325), and taro was the chief staple in some areas (Tsuboi 1979:274–285).

No distinct ethnic or national cuisine emerged until modernity. "The basic unit in gastronomy is the region, not the nation" (Revel 1982:215). Yet Provençal cuisine in the fifteenth century was generic to the Mediterranean, and it did not develop into a distinct regional cuisine until much later (Stouff 1970:261). Furthermore, status distinctions, albeit not universal (Goody 1982:95–98), are frequently profound (Mennell 1985:40–47). What aristocrats ate in medieval France had little in common with what peasants ate (Bloch 1970:231). Among the European court and church elite, Gothic international style predominated from the twelfth to the fifteenth century (Bober 1999:230–237), which is not surprising in an age when the aristocratic and ecclesiastical networks were transnational (Flandrin 1984:75). Religious differences were significant, such as the exercise of faith-based food proscriptions. One of the manifold consequences of the Protestant Reformation was the division of Europe into two major culinary zones (Montanari 1994:113–116).

National differences emerged in Europe during the seventeenth century (Mennell 1985:133). In particular, François Pierre de La Varenne's treatise, *Le cuisinier François* (1651), was a landmark for French cuisine, which henceforth held pride of place as the premier Europe cuisine. The eighteenth-century *Encyclopédie* article articulates the triumph of French cuisine from its ancient Greek and Roman origins via Italian cookery, but Arabic influences suffused high-European cooking of the Renaissance (Peterson 1994:21). La Varenne's treatise, far from marking continuity, signaled a rupture, which invented French cuisine by expunging the Arabic impact (Peterson 1994:203). By the nineteenth century, with the emergence of charismatic chefs, such as Antonin Carême and Georges Auguste Escoffier, French national cuisine reigned triumphant (Mennell 1985:134), but as Jean-François Revel (1982:214) observes: "The French cuisine is . . . *international* cuisine." Other European national cuisine, however, came to be defined against the French.

Reified notions of national cuisine mislead by neglecting internal differences and historical changes. Consider class distinction. George Orwell (1986:92) wrote of the early twentieth-century British working class: "But the English palate, especially the working-class palate, now rejects good food almost automatically. The number of people who *prefer* tinned peas and tinned fish to real peas and real fish must be increasing every year, and plenty of people who could afford real milk in their tea would much sooner have tinned milk—even that dreadful tinned milk which is made of sugar and cornflour and has UNFIT FOR BABIES on the tin in huge letters." Although he is right to highlight class difference in English cuisine, the negative evaluation of English cuisine *tout court* has become a historical relic in turn-of-the-millennium London (James 1996:82). A British M.P. cites chicken tikka masala as the national dish, and Chinese food, along with McDonald's, exemplifies culinary globalization (Goody 1998:165–171).

Finally, national history is a compelling way to assert the priority and primacy of peoplehood. As Thomas Carlyle (n.d.:151) declared in his essay, "On History" (1830): "Of all mankind, there is no tribe so rude that it has not attempted History, though several have not arithmetic enough to count Five." Echoing Locke's philosophy of personal identity, John Stuart Mill (1977:546) highlighted the role of history in national identity: "But the strongest of all is identity of political antecedents; the possession of a national history, and consequent community of recollections; collective pride and humiliation, pleasure and regret, connected with the same incidents in the past."

Until the eighteenth century, the dominant modes of European historiography delineated and served churches and dynasties (Schorske 1995: 388). National history remained marginal until Montesquieu and Herder (Meinecke 1972:121,341–357), and its efflorescence occurred in the nineteenth century by the likes of Jacob Burckhardt, Jules Michelet, Thomas Macaulay, and George Bancroft (Breisach 1994:chap. 15). Only then did the nation become a privileged unit of analysis (Teggart 1977:40–43). In seeking a continuous and pure descent of people, nationalist narrative effaces past heterogeneity and exogenous influences, and singularly stresses national achievements. Not surprisingly, architects and chroniclers of the modern state were frequently the same people; many leading politicians of nineteenth-century Europe, such as François-Pierre-Guillaume Guizot and Theodor Mommsen were also noted historians (Gilbert 1990:9). The new politics of democratic nationalism projected an inclusionary vision of peoplehood, which mandated its own history. Although nineteenth-century historians may have rhetorically invoked the people, they in fact focused on the elite, producing heroic tales of captains and kings. The Annales school, the British Marxist historians, and others redressed the exclusion of workers, women, and others in the twentieth century, thereby completing the status integration in historiography (Burke 1990:110).

There are, then, fundamental flaws in attempting to ground peoplehood on culture or, for that matter, on language or religion. Modern peoplehood draws on the past but very selectively. Claims of continuity miss the ruptures and radically alien character of the past. In the imagination of modern peoplehood, people living in medieval France are recognizably French, but the presumption of pure descent erases the reality of dialectal diversity or the Arabic influence on French cuisine. The premodern world is also marked by local differences. The reality of heterogeneity contradicts the assumption of homogenous, essential peoplehood. In premodern societies, moreover, culture or civilization is precisely what the demos lacked. To refer to people living in medieval France as all French is anachronistic. They may have been people *an sich,* but they were far from being people *für sich.* This is the distinction I stress between population—an analytical category, an external attribution—and people(hood)—an experiential entity, an internal conviction.

Language, religion, and culture are not coterminous with peoplehood. On the one hand, they often expand well beyond the limited boundary of an actually existing group. The German language—once we ignore dialectal diversity—extends across much of continental Europe; Christianity is a worldwide religion; and Western culture or civilization can be found outside of the West. On the other hand, we witness the influx and outflow of people from one language, religion, or culture into another, as well as the inevitable process of hybridity that results from fluctuating allegiances and identities. In a matter of a generation, people learn a new language, become adherents of another faith, and even exemplify the heights of cultural or civilizational achievements. In short, assimilation and acculturation are powerful forces.

The anti-entropic force of the modern state linked the subject (peoplehood) and the predicates (language, religion, culture, and so on). As I elaborate in Chapter 3, the modern state was the principal institutional force that made modern peoplehood. Its bureaucratic development was critical in disseminating a common identity over a far-flung territory. In addition, the democratic revolution rendered the conceptualization of people living in the same territory as the same kind of people. The alignment of peoplehood and its predicates depended on cultural and status integration.

5

The indisputable source of peoplehood is common consciousness. The primordial sense of belonging captures not only the intuitively obvious but also the je ne sais quoi character of people's identity. Subjective though such definition may seem, it has been the most robust precisely because of its tautological character. Ernest Renan (1990:20) defined the nation in his celebrated 1882 lecture: "Man is a slave neither of his race nor his language, nor of his religion, nor of the course of rivers nor of the direction taken by mountain chains. A large aggregate of men, healthy in spirit and warm of heart, creates the kind of moral conscience which we call a nation." According to Renan, a shared memory and ideal—in the realm of the mind and the imagination—and not the shared geographical or biological endowment, or language or culture, brings people together as a nation. Social distinction owes not so much to predicates but rather to the very articulation of categorical differentiation. In short, thinking makes it so; peoplehood is collective consciousness.

As the preceding discussion on language, religion, and culture suggests, the very search for the basis of peoplehood is a modern enterprise. The Romantics on language and folktale or the early anthropologists on primitive culture articulate a vision of an inclusionary and involuntary identity based on descent and commonality. However, they are post-Enlightenment ideas. In classical civilizations, the modern conception of peoplehood was vaguely intuited and usually attributed to marginalized others. Self-definitions, in contrast, revolved around other axes of differentiation, such as civilization and religion or status and occupation. The reality of people-for-itself (peoplehood) must be made from the idea of people-in-itself (population). This accounts for the characteristic trope of nationalist historiography that trumpets the dawn or awakening of a people. The insistent vision of modern peoplehood retrospectively identifies a past aggregate as a meaningful, if latent, community.

The search for common consciousness vaporizes the seeming solidity of past peoples. One may very well begin at the point zero of recorded human history: ancient Mesopotamia, the cradle of civilization and the home of Abraham (Pollock 1999:1). Were we to visit a Mesopotamian city at the time of Hammurabi's reign and survey people's identity, we would be unlikely to generate responses such as Mesopotamian, Babylonian, Akkadian, or other terms that we use today to categorize them. It was not ethnic identity as we conceive of it that animated Mesopotamia, but rather the distinction between those within the city and those without (Snell 1997: 11). The Mesopotamian city was a political and religious center and the basis of culture and civilization (Van de Mieroop 1997:42–52). It was multiethnic in our sense—Sumerians, Akkadians, Amorites, Elamites, Kassites, Hurrians, Guti, and so on—but boundaries were permeable (Nissen 1988: 186–197). Moreover, social status divided the population. The Laws of Hammurabi strictly separated slaves (*wardum*), subjects (*muškēnum*), and people (*awīlum*) (Gadd 1973:196). Scribes, for example, did not share their language with others, though there was no necessary correlation between language and ethnoracial grouping (Oppenheim 1977:48). Perhaps ethnoracial origins mattered a great deal, but we possess no evidence that they did (Gadd 1971:625; Dandamaev 1982:173). Because few claim to be descendants of Amorites or Hurrians, the idea of ethnically distinguishing the ancient Mesopotamian population is mercifully moot.

In contrast, classical Athenian writers provide fertile grounds for discussions of peoplehood, ranging from the professed superiority of Athenians expressed by Aristotle (1327,23–29) to M. I. Finley's (1981:126) suggestion that there was "a deep-rooted consciousness of belonging to a single and unique culture" (cf. Gernet 1981:287). However, there is little evidence of a common Greek identity in the Archaic period (Malkin 1998:17–20). Homeric poems refer to Achaens, Argive, and Danaans, which are often translated as Greeks, but the first two are localities, whereas the third fell into desuetude (Finley 1981:83; cf. Hall 2002:53). The principal literary evidence remains Herodotus's (8:144) report of Athenians speaking to Spartans: "We are one in blood and one in language; those shrines of the gods belongs to us all in common, and the sacrifices in common, and there are our habits, bred of common upbringing." Spartans, however, called everyone else foreigners (*xenoi*) (Herodotus 9:11–55), which makes a mockery of the Athenian entreaty regarding Greek unity. Panhellenic, or Greek, identity existed in an inchoate form by the fifth century BCE, but Greece was not a society in any substantive sense (Walbank 1985:1; Cartledge 1993:3–10).

Language and culture distinguished Greeks from barbarians (Jaeger 1939:xvii; Hartog 1988:258). Articulated most clearly in Greek tragedies during the war against Persians (Hall 1989:1–14), polar contrasts were drawn between them in line with a favored way of argumentation (Lloyd 1966:pt.1). In fact, the rhetoric of pure descent and categorical distinction masked the reality of extensive cultural interactions between them (West 1997:606–624), as well as the actually existing diversity of languages, religions, and cultures in both (Walbank 1992:78). Furthermore, most Greek writers ascribed differences between civilized urbanites and uncivilized rustics to climate and custom. They may have been ethnocentric, but they were not racist in the modern sense (Snowden 1983:56–59; Gassi 2001: 24). As Herodotus (3:38) reported Darius as saying: "I think Pindar is right when he says, 'Custom is king of all.' " The pre-Socratic philosopher Antiphon expressed the dominant tenor of classical Greek thought: "We are, in our relations with one another, like barbarians, since we are all by nature born the same in every way, both barbarians and Hellenes" (Freeman 1948: 148). Non-Greeks could become Greeks by learning language and culture (cf. Swain 1996:10). People intermarried, runaway slaves passed as Athenians, and metics and foreigners assimilated (W. R. Connor 1994:36). Identities were achieved, rather than ascribed. That is, to be an Athenian meant to look and act like an Athenian. In this spirit, Plato (262CE) found the distinction between Greeks and barbarians specious.

The distinction between center and periphery was expressed as that between *polis* and *ethnos,* denoting the cosmopolitan city against the rural community (Larsen 1968:4; Ehrenberg 1969:22). Anthony Snodgrass (1980:42) characterizes *ethnos* as "a population scattered thinly over a territory without urban centres, united politically and in customs and religion, normally governed by means of some periodic assembly at a single centre, and worshipping a tribal deity at a common religious centre." This characterization is synonymous with the contemporary meaning of peoplehood, but a tribal state or *ethnos* was "an artificial creation of geography and politics" (Larsen 1968:6) and did not claim common descent (Snodgrass 1980:25).

Polis constituted the basic unit of political affairs (Aristotle 1252b19), practice (Parker 1996:3), and social identity (Meier 1990:141–146). In the classic ideal of the *polis,* citizens were alike *(homoioi),* equal *(isoi),* and bound by friendship *(philia),* constituting something of a Durkheimian mechanical solidarity (Vernant 1982:60,101). In addition, Pericles claimed both the indigeneity and pure descent of Athenians (Thucydides 1.2.5; 2.36.1; cf. Ober 1989:261–266). Thus, the putatively cosmopolitan *polis* claimed the garb of kinship and descent more than the supposedly traditional *ethnos* (Pomeroy 1997:167).

Polis identity seems to express the modern notion of peoplehood, but few moderns would consider a small city—with perhaps forty thousand citizens (Stockton 1990:16; cf. Gomme 1933:34)—an adequate basis of peoplehood (cf. Cohen 2000:10). Citizenship status was alienable and attainable (Osborne 1981–83:iv,139), and boundaries between insiders and outsiders were neither stable nor clear (Manville 1990:210–217). Far from the ideal of homogeneity, Athens was a diverse community, owing to its status as a colonial power and cultural metropolis (Gschnitzer 1981:113). Aristotle regarded *polis* as socially differentiated and bereft of collective identity (Yack 1993:29). For many Athenians, *deme* (territorial division) and occupation provided more salient sources of identity (Whitehead 1986:356; Garnsey 1999:65).

Furthermore, to be an Athenian meant to be a male citizen, denoting a status more than an ethnonational origin. Greek *poleis* were fraternities that excluded women, slaves, and others (Gschnitzer 1981:117–124; Bleicken 1985:281–288). The autochthonous myth of Athenians did not include women or slaves (Vidal-Naquet 1986:218; Garlan 1988:155–163), who numbered some one hundred thousand in fifth-century Athens (Gomme 1933:34). The Aristotelian (1253b32, 1254a20) argument about the inferiority of slaves remained powerfully persuasive (Strasburger 1976:49; Brunt 1993:343–388). Yet neither slave nor metic was an ethnic category (Garnsey 1996:77; Whitehead 1977:114). Status distinction manifested itself in the disjunction between Attic Greek and demotic Greek (Horrocks 1997:81–86; Swain 1996:33–35). Similarly, the fabled egalitarianism of Sparta was restricted to Spartacites, or *homoioi*, and did not extend to *perioikoi* (subjects) and helots (cf. Cartledge 2001:73). Qualitative inequality among status groups remained a fundamental ideology of classical Greek civilization. The concept of human unity (Baldry 1965:4) existed comfortably with that of status inequality.

In general, the salience of status distinction stunted the development of an inclusionary identity in premodern societies. That is, proto-peoplehood identity was restricted to the elite. This was true for medieval Europe as it was for classical Athens. According to Georges Duby (1980a), the dominant ideology in France from 1025 to 1225 projected a society comprised of people who pray, fight, and work. In spite of the complexity of social relations—merchants, for example, did not fit neatly into the tripartite schema—the ideology remained remarkably robust. The mode of social classification is frequently rigid and conservative, and outlives the social reality that it claims to represent. Adalbero, bishop of Laon, believed that:

"Nobles and serfs constituted two species, two 'races' " (Duby 1980a:51). Few today would regard rich and poor French people as distinct species or races, but Adalbero used the criterion of descent to distinguish them. "The entire nobility shared 'the blood of kings,' as Adalbero, who was a part of it and knew his genealogy by heart, was convinced" (Duby 1980a: 51). Ancestry in France around 1000 CE was traced along patrilineal "house," which was regarded as "race" (Duby 1980b:101).

Status was visible and racialized. Beyond the binary of nobles and serfs, each social type—the monk, the prince, the peasant, and so on—had its particular clothing, footwear, and haircut (Le Goff 1988:358), and a distinct code of behavior and way of life (Constable 1995:263). Speaking of a slightly earlier period, Marc Bloch (1961:255) distinguished between free men and slaves. The latter "appeared as an alien being, outside the ranks of the community" (Bloch 1961:225). In addition to their distinct social stations and appearances, the two groups often spoke different tongues (Bloch 1961:75). "That the *populus francorum* was composed only of free men, independently of any ethnic distinction, is proved by the fact that the national name and the legal status came in the end to be synonymous" (Bloch 1961:255). In other words, to be French meant to be a free man, and free men constituted an ethnic group in our sense of common descent and identity (cf. Benveniste 1973:263). All others were, to use an anachronism, racial or ethnic others.

Because of the poor level of inter-regional communication and transportation, education, and other means of cultural integration, most people in France—the territory of which fluctuated greatly over the centuries—were peasants whose social identity did not expand beyond their village or region (Bloch 1961:61–65; Goubert 1986:chap. 11). Emmanuel Le Roy Ladurie's (1979) study of fourteenth-century Montaillou offers a suggestive snapshot. In spite of considerable geographical mobility, "the basic perception was that of the locality or village—the *terra*" (Le Roy Ladurie 1979: 283). The village was bound by nature (e.g., mountains and rivers) and society (e.g., language and cuisine). A different dialect, food, and religion marked Sabathès, a village about twenty miles away (Le Roy Ladurie 1979: 284). That is, a village of roughly one thousand people constituted the basic unit of society, divided though it was by clan conflicts, gender distinctions, and so on (Le Roy Ladurie 1979:266–276).

The identification and imagination of French peoplehood are coeval with the birth of France (Beaune 1985:337–351), but it usually denoted the linguistically and religiously unified nobility (cf. Clark 1995:3774). France achieved a degree of political unity by the seventeenth century (Le Roy Ladurie 1981:9–19), but early modern France remained a society of orders or estates (Mousnier 1970:7–16). The idea of the French nation "was synonymous with the French nobility"; being endogamous, it had "a racial, caste quality" (Bakos 1997:61). Henri de Boulainvilliers notoriously argued that the distinction between the nobility and the masses was based on the Frank conquest of Gauls (Ellis 1988:26–83). French urbanites regarded peasants as savage and barbaric, constituting "another race" (Weber 1976:7; cf. Muchembled 1985:154). The ideas of homeland and patriotism referred to localities (Jones 1995:12). Villagers regarded all non-villagers as foreigners, whether French or English (Weber 1976:46; cf. Le Roy Ladurie 1987:188–193). Louis-François Pinagot—the nineteenth-century clog maker we encountered in the Prelude—almost certainly had little inkling of French national identity (Corbin 1998:33–41). This is not surprising when the French countryside was characterized by regional language, barter economy, localized gossip, and widespread illiteracy (Corbin 1998: 83–106). The construction of national culture depended on the fusion of high and low culture (cf. Muchembled 1990:178), which did not diffuse throughout France until the twentieth century (Weber 1976:486).

Against the stereotype of stasis, agrarian societies that encompassed much of Europe and elsewhere in the last two millennia exhibited considerable dynamism and diversity. However, status inequality and the peasantry—though itself a problematic category of analysis (Shanin 1990:6–16)—predominated. Peasants lived in villages and differentiated themselves from outsiders as well as their status superiors (cf. Ginzburg 1982:16). In spite of migration, trade, and other modes of contact with the outside world, most peasants were circumscribed in their experience and worldview (Blum 1978:29–34; Le Roy Ladurie 1987:361–364). Families and lineages, not ethnic or national groups, were important in their social identification (cf. Segalen 1986:61–71). There existed numerous networks and identities, whether based on language, religion, or culture, but they were far from permanent (cf. Reynolds 1984:335). Categories and memberships shifted, whether due to intermarriage or migration. Facing local variation, premodern societies lacked institutions and technology to crystallize and disseminate a common identity over a large territory. In any case, the conception of inclusionary peoplehood was absent. People, after all, cannot imagine or identify without appropriate categories (cf. Bloch

1963:355). Peasant nationalism may occur, but usually as a result of Western-educated intellectuals' organizational efforts (cf. Feierman 1990: 105–112) or later incorporation by the modern state (cf. Mallon 1995:317; Wolf 2001:298–303). It is not an accident that the disappearance of the peasantry coincides with the ascent of modern peoplehood.

Even if technology and institution were available to disseminate a common identity, in status-based societies, people we would regard as co-racials, co-ethnics, or co-nationals constituted different types of people (Zagorin 1982:i,62–65). Characterized by a sense of superiority and status endogamy, the European nobility demonstrated many elements of modern peoplehood (cf. Benveniste 1973:264), but they were at once supranational and infranational (Blum 1978:15; Dewald 1996:17–20). European aristocracy was transnational, marrying freely across present-day national boundaries. In contrast, the nobility and the peasantry constituted different stocks. They certainly looked different, whether in terms of clothing or stature (cf. Scott and Storrs 1995:12). As Stanislaus Leszcyski wrote in the eighteenth century: "We look upon the peasant as a creature of an entirely different sort, and deny him even the air which we breathe with him, and make hardly any distinction between him and the animals who plow our fields. Often we value them even lower than the animals" (Blum 1978:46). In this spirit, nineteenth-century Estonian peasants were Maarahvas (country people) in contradistinction to Saks (Germans, or lords) (Hobsbawm 1992:48), while Polish peasants were "Austrian" or "imperial" because Poles referred to landlords (Hagen 1980:27).

6

Ancient Mesopotamia, classical Greece, and medieval France do not exhaust the variety of premodern societies. The absence of peoplehood consciousness in premodern polities cannot be proved definitively. As long as names exist to represent a collectivity, proto-peoplehood sentiments remain possible, especially as an elite identity. The Whiggish temptation to impute modern peoplehood on geographical or administrative categories is irresistible, leading us to systematically misread past records. This is true especially in cases of nominal continuity, which offers a conceptual underpinning to generate discourses of continuous identity. Nations in the sense of polities—but not culturally and status-integrated society—existed before nationalism. Yet premodern polities were at once incapable of and indifferent to achieving cultural and status integration. That is, they failed to forge a common national culture or to establish the unity of the rulers and the ruled. Hence, attributions of premodern peoplehood are proleptic, projecting present understanding onto the past. Let me consider in turn imperial, caste, tribal, and island polities.

Empires by definition entail one polity's control over another (Doyle 1986:45), and are therefore inevitably multiethnic in our sense. The metrople does not usually attempt to integrate and assimilate the periphery. After all, it does not even integrate its own population. State bureaucracy was underdeveloped, and status inequality was ideologically critical. In other words, the universalistic claim of imperial rule does not depend on racial, ethnic, or national isomorphism.

Roman rule unified the political and cultural elite under the rubric of civilization but did not seek cultural uniformity or popular integration (Sherwin-White 1967:86). "Most Roman provinces comprised a hotchpotch of tribes and cities, mutually hostile, and not linked by any of the ties [of modern nationalism]" (Brunt 1990:126). The mark of civilization was city life, which defined Romanitas (Woolf 1998:106–112). Agricultural workers not only constituted distinct groups (Garnsey 1998:144–147), but they were lower status and uncivilized as well. Status hierarchy was significant, especially the distinction between *servus* and *liber* (Garnsey 1970: 260–263). Peasants and rulers frequently spoke different languages (Brunt 1990:273).

Roman rule was based on political citizenship, not peoplehood identity (Finley 1973:47). The expansion of Roman citizenship followed the extension of Roman imperial rule (Badian 1968:62–69). Roman citizenship was given to the provincial elite to acknowledge subjection and to participate in imperial rule (Balsdon 1979:82–96). Becoming Roman meant to become a Roman imperial citizen (Woolf 1998:246–249). "If by culture and sentiment men were Romans, Romans they were" (Brunt 1990:132). The contrast between civilized Romans and uncivilized barbarians was cultural (Sherwin-White 1939:282–289), as there was no clear-cut distinction between Romans and non-Romans (Elton 1996:20). Most classical authors attributed cultural difference to distinct material circumstances. Skin color was not equated with status nor did it divide people (Thompson 1989: 140–156). Neither racial nor religious origin posed an insurmountable barrier (Syme 1958:11). Status mobility was by no means impossible—as slaves could become citizens (Hopkins 1978:116)—and cultural assimilation occurred throughout the Roman world (MacMullen 2000:134–137). In this regard, the Roman word *tribus* did not have the connotation of an ethnoracial group that the modern term tribe does (Fried 1975:3). The term was a construct of imperial rule (Wells 1999:116–119). Regional and status distinctions marked "barbarian" tribes (cf. Amory 1997:26–33), though the category of Germans, for example, did not imply a common identity (Wells 1999:113). In short, as P. A. Brunt (1990:126) concludes: "In the ancient world there was hardly any nationalism in the modern sense."

Similarly, as diverse as different dynasties that claimed the mandate of heaven were, Chinese empires were culturally integrated only at the elite level, united by a vision of the Sinocentric world order (Fairbank 1968:5). Although the political and cultural elite of the tributary states may have become Sinified, the cultural category of Sinification bypasses the historically transient allegiance to different dynasties (Mote 1999:268–271). The Qing dynasty may appear retrospectively as a congeries of ethnic groups, but ethnic identities were historically constructed constituencies (Crossley 1999:3–7; cf. Elliott 2001:346–355). Immense regional diversity existed, and status hierarchy was well established (Gernet 1970:127–132). Crucially, the vast majority of the population—peasants or farmers—were excluded (Eberhard 1965:135). It is doubtful that they identified themselves as Chinese (Gernet 1970:106). Well into the twentieth century, most peasants' lives were demarcated by the narrow horizon of village life (Shue 1988:48–52). Chinese ethnic nationalism is a late nineteenth-century and early twentieth-century phenomenon (Fitzgerald 1996:346; Zheng 1999:26).

The Mughal Empire provides another example of a multiethnic polity. Its legendary rulers, Babur (whom we might today call Chaghatai Turkish), Akbar, or Shah Jahan, lorded over a geographically and religiously heterogeneous nobility and territory (Richards 1993:143–148). Islamic emperors nominally ruled a non-Muslim population; the Islamic conception of *dhimma* (protected religious minority community) turned out to incorporate virtually the whole realm (Richards 1993:36–40). As we have seen, Hindu or Indian nationalism has sought to obliterate the past of Muslim India, just as much as Sun Yat-sen denied the legitimacy of Qing China by advocating Han Chinese ethnonational identity (Zheng 1999:68).

Given the presumption of "common descent, as well as a claim of common geographical origin, and a particular occupational ideal" (Bayly

1999:10), caste appears to be functionally equivalent to modern peoplehood. However, it would be misleading to equate them. It is not caste as
varna (four- or fivefold divisions based on Vedic texts) but as *jati* (an endogamous, occupational group) that provides most South Asians with a
recognizable and basic identity (Mandelbaum 1970:i,13). India was and is
not neatly divided into four or five castes (cf. Milner 1994:63–79). "To the
average peasant . . . the names of castes in other linguistic areas are pure
abracadabra" (Srinivas 1966:3). *Jati* denotes a subjectively held social identity; it is not an instance of modern peoplehood. Caste organization is more
like a political rather than kinship unit (Quigley 1993:166). In spite of
beliefs in common descent and status, the Coorgs of southern India in the
1940s spoke different languages and exhibited significant divisions (Srinivas 1952:8,34–37). Furthermore, *jati* is not an immobile identity, as individual and communal mobility is possible (Srinivas 1966:29–45; Mandelbaum 1970:ii,421–436). Finally, village identity is fundamental
(Srinivas 1987:56–67). "When a man goes outside his village, he is apt to
be identified first of all by his village rather than by jati or other reference
category" (Mandelbaum 1970:ii,329).

Tribe is defined as "a descent group which constitutes a political community," which tends to be egalitarian and participatory (Crone 1986:51)
and mirrors the very idea of modern peoplehood. E. E. Evans-Pritchard
(1940:279) notes that "the whole Nuer people form a single community,
territorially unbroken, with common culture and feeling of exclusiveness."

Rather than being an elementary and isolated social organization, tribe
usually emerges in reaction to outsiders (Fried 1967:15; Colson 1967:201).
Tribal name is often "a designation applied to a population by outsiders,
or from a word equivalent to the concept 'person' or 'human being' " (Fried
1967:14). The Nuer, for example, was classified by outsiders and crystallized in response to external forces (Johnson 1994:244; Hutchinson 1996:
37). The Mahafaly, who reside in the southern part of Madagascar, claimed
neither Mahafaly identity nor membership, but: "Whenever they had to
interact with French officials, or individuals they identified with them, they
called themselves *Mahafaly* and behaved as they knew *Mahafaly* were supposed to behave" (Eggert 1986:334). Furthermore, tribe frequently includes different language speakers and religious adherents, and tribal
boundaries—overstepped by migration and intermarriage—are never as
rigid as many ethnographers and colonial administrators believed
(Moerman 1967:166; Wilson 1977:21–27). In this regard, Edmund Leach's

(1965:285) analysis of shifting tribal identity in highland Burma points to the centrality of political allegiance (cf. Gluckman 1940:28).

Durkheim (1995:93) regarded Australian tribes as "completely homogeneous" and "the most primitive," but the aforementioned Yolngu in the late 1970s and early 1980s showed regional variations and historical transformations, and "did not think of themselves as one ethnic entity," despite numbering only three thousand (I. Keen 1994:4). Jean Briggs (1970:1) lived among the Utkuhikhalingmiut in northern Canada, who were "the sole inhabitants of an area 35,000 or more miles square." However, the twenty to thirty individuals were divided into three kin groups, but two households were regarded as "not real Utku" (Briggs 1970:40). Hoping to find a shamanistic religion, Briggs (1970:2) found Anglicans. The !Kung in southern Africa in the 1960s lived in camps of ten to thirty individuals, "but the composition of these camps changes from month to month and from day to day" (Lee 1979:54).

Tribe is often a way of describing an extended kinship group. A. R. Radcliffe-Brown (1964:16), for example, identified ten tribes in the Great Andaman population of 625 (cf. Thomas 1990:19–26). Kinship ties may be robust in tribal life (Fortes and Evans-Pritchard 1940:6), but so they are also industrial societies. In this regard, clan is "usually a larger body" that cannot trace descent to "a known common ancestor" (Radcliffe-Brown 1950:39). Clan in this sense is a form of consortium; it is not blood that ties the group, but group identity expresses itself in kinship terms (cf. Gaunt 2001:261–271).

Similarly, nomadic groups may claim common descent and kinship, but the reality of geographical mobility and political-economic instability ensure the influx and integration of outsiders (Khazanov 1994:139–142). The unity of the Gypsies—including the very nomenclature—is likewise externally imposed (Fonseca 1995:276; Lemon 2000:179,234).

Continents provide ample opportunities for mixture and movement. How about isolated islands? The Siuai of the Solomon Islands numbered 4,700 in the 1930s (Oliver 1967:xvii). Although aware of neighboring islands and peoples, there was "a fuzziness about the boundaries of Siuai" (Oliver 1967:103). This is not surprising given that they had no tribal unity or organization. There was another group, Terei, about 1.5 miles west, and in border villages bilingualism and intermarriage were the norm (Oliver 1967:103). Plantation owners encouraged tribal identity by making fellow language users work and live together (Oliver 1967:104). The returnees, not surprisingly, came back to their villages with a heightened sense of Siuai identity.

Raymond Firth (1963:88) characterized Tikopia, an island in the South Pacific, in the 1920s as an extremely isolated group: "The use of a common language and sharing of a common culture, all that is implied by the natives when they speak of themselves as '*tatou ŋ Tikopia,*' 'We the Tikopia,' and distinguish themselves from the folk of Tonga, of Samoa, or of Santa Cruz, or from that still more alien creature, the *papalaŋgi,* the white man." His (1963:3) claim that they were "homogeneous in speech and culture" and "almost untouched by the outside world," evokes the essential tribe that is homogeneous, isolated, and without history. However, "for nearly a century and a half they have been subjected to various influences of the 'civilized' order" (Firth 1963:31). Tikopians themselves claimed to hail from various places, and nearly half of them were Christians (Firth 1963:32,43–50). Two major groups, Sa Faea and Sa Reveāga, were characterized by "mutual suspicion and distrust" (Firth 1963:72). Their religions and even cooking styles were different (Firth 1963:73). There were, then, effectively two ethnic groups on the island of Tikopia in the 1920s, when the population numbered 1,281 (Firth 1963:368). It is not clear whether Firth (1963:11), who has "been assured a number of times that I was 'just like a Tikopia,' " included himself in the census count.

Finally, contemporary Icelanders valorize Icelandicness that is at once homogeneous and egalitarian (Tomasson 1980:51–55). Certainly, its history of emigration from present-day Norway in the eighth and ninth centuries, its relative isolation, the heroic sagas, and the medieval freestate that was proto-democratic all provide potent bases of Icelandicness. However, the Icelandic Freestate was colonized by Norway in 1262 and by Denmark in 1380. Danes regarded Iceland as an exemplar of the common Norse experience until its independence in 1944 (Wylie 1987:177).

Medieval Iceland was rigidly divided between free farmers and slaves (Hastrup 1985:107). Although slavery was abolished around 1100, the category of Icelander did not encompass the population of Iceland. The twelfth century *Landnámabók* listed only important settlers, befitting a society marked by rigid status hierarchy (Hastrup 1985:169,176, 1998:30). Vagrants, beggars, and others were regarded as "inhuman men" (*ómenskumenn*) and, as late as the eighteenth century, some questioned whether they should be allowed to marry (Hastrup 1990b:194). As Kirsten Hastrup (1990b:289) argues: "Icelandicness was continually defined by the narrow circle of settled farmers in control of their lands and lives," which thereby excluded not only the poor, but also fishermen and workers (Hastrup 1990a:131). Ironically, if we apply the test of Icelandicness, which equates courage exemplified in the heroic sagas with humanity, then most Icelanders were "at risk of being classified as not human at all" (Hastrup 1990b:196). The European Enlightenment and the French Revolution gave rise to Icelandic Romantic nationalism in the early nineteenth century (Gjerset 1924:367–381), but the standardization of the Icelandic language did not occur until after independence (Pálsson 1989:134). As much as they may essentialize themselves against tourists and anthropologists, they think of themselves as "rampant individualists" (Lacy 1998:11).

In this chapter, I criticized the retrojection of contemporary categories into the past. Premodern societies lacked cultural and status integration—the institutional impetus to immobilize the mobile and to unify diversity—to make modern peoplehood possible. Language, religion, and culture did not lead inexorably to modern peoplehood, although peoplehood identity draws on them. Cultural and status integration reified the flux of population into the stasis of peoplehood. In this regard, correlative efforts sought to ground the categories of modern peoplehood in nature. In the following chapter, I argue that the pedestal of scientific foundation was in fact and remains dependent on the very conception of modern peoplehood. Neither history nor nature anchors modern peoplehood.

Naturalizing Differences

Who has trouble distinguishing a German shepherd from a golden retriever? Canine pedigree and psychology mark breeds, just as common descent and contemporary commonality characterize peoplehood (Goldsby 1977:17–21). Indeed, dog breeds often stand for human racial or national differences (Kete 1994:65). As the ur-Nazi racial theorist Houston Stewart Chamberlain (1968:261) wrote: "The human races are, in reality, as different from one another in character, qualities, and above all, in the degree of their individual capacities, as greyhound, bulldog, poodle and Newfoundland dog."

The very idea of breeds became popular in nineteenth-century England where the notion of dog-as-pet came to symbolize middle-class lifestyle. Currently popular breeds, such as collies, emerged in Victorian England as dog breeders and dog club activists focused on "arbitrary and conventional points" to differentiate and define them (Ritvo 1987:114). The American Kennel Club's (1985) official standards highlight their "arbitrary and conventional points." For example, the golden retriever's "General Appearance" is prescribed as: "A symmetrical, powerful, active dog, sound and well put together, not clumsy nor long in the leg, displaying a kindly expression and possessing a personality that is eager, alert and self-confident. Primarily a hunting dog, he should be shown in hard working condition. Over-all appearance, balance, gait and purpose to be given more emphasis than any of his component parts" (American Kennel Club 1985:106). Subjective characterizations are complemented by objective caninometric guides: "Male 23–24 inches in height at withers. . . . Deviation in height of more than one inch from the standard shall disqualify" (American Kennel Club

55

1985:106). In addition to stature deviation, "undershot or overshot bite is a disqualification" (American Kennel Club 1985:106). Physiological exactitude is accompanied by the popularity of dog psychology (the meanness of chows) and sociology (the Germanness of German shepherds). Phenotypical differences, however, correlate weakly with behavior (Scott and Fuller 1965:385).

Far from being natural kinds, human insistence is necessary to reproduce breeds against the entropic force of interbreeding. We can talk about breeds of dogs because they are artificially reproduced to exaggerate differences. Although hybridity appears to enhance physical and spiritual well-being (Derr 1997:207), a mongrel is often called a mutt, whose first definition in the *Oxford English Dictionary* is "stupid, ignorant, awkward, blundering, incompetent, or the like; a blockhead, dullard, or fool." While hybrids of a century ago are prized, hybrids of today experience canine racism, replete with efforts to eradicate them.

In this chapter, I argue that the racial classification of human difference is "arbitrary and conventional," eternalizing the ephemeral and marking qualitative ruptures where only quantitative gradations exist. Human history cannot be considered apart from migration and hybridity, which casts doubt on racial ontology. In the absence of social constraints, such as legal or customary proscription on interracial or mixed-race procreation and marriage, human beings interbreed. People often overcome enormous constraints, and may even find their passion burning brighter as a result. Beginning in the eighteenth century and intensifying in the twentieth century, racial scientists sought a solid ground for human classification. They provided scientific justifications for the modern notion of peoplehood, giving credence to the immutability of geographically and descent-based groups. The claim of racial ontology, however, falters against the recalcitrant reality that nature and culture are inextricably intertwined. Nature contributes to human differences, but all social classification correlates categories and bodies by naturalizing differences. Race and racism—far from being constitutive categories of nature—presuppose the modern categories of peoplehood.

2

Like well-known dog breeds, well-disseminated racial categories, such as blacks and whites in the United States, are intuitively obvious. Indisputable phenomenology seems grounded in intergenerational heredity. In the language of modern biology, the infrastructure of separate gene pools supports the superstructure of distinct appearance. In this line of thinking, races are natural kinds, the like reproducing the like (Mayr 1997:136). As Adolf Hitler (1943:284) put it: "The titmouse seeks the titmouse, the finch the finch, the stork the stork, the field mouse the field mouse, the dormouse the dormouse, the wolf the she-wolf, etc. . . . The consequence of this racial purity, universally valid in Nature, is not only the sharp outward delimitation of the various races, but their uniform character in themselves. A fox is always a fox, a goose a goose, a tiger a tiger, etc."

The concept of species corresponds to the notion of, natural kinds. Its primacy in biological taxonomy is well established. As Theodosius Dobzhansky (1982:306) observed, species is "a single systematic category which, in contrast to others, has withstood all the changes in the nomenclature with an amazing tenacity" (cf. Mayr 1991:31). However, determinants of species classification remain contested. The most frequently cited definition by Ernst Mayr (1982:120) identifies species as "groups of actually or potentially interbreeding natural populations, which are reproductively isolated from other such groups." Yet his biological species concept is problematic—what of asexual organisms?—and other proposals, ranging from the ecological species concept to the recognition concept, have not generated a consensus (Ereshefsky 1992; Wilson 1999). Hence, contemporary biologists are left with the triumph of tacit knowledge. As Charles Darwin (1993:71) memorably, if problematically, concluded: "The only guide" to species determination should be "the opinion of naturalists having sound judgment and wide experience" (cf. Dobzhansky 1982:310–314).

Since Linnaeus's 1735 *Systema naturae,* most biologists have regarded Homo sapiens as a single species. Different groups do not constitute distinct species; people do not mate exclusively among group members. Most compellingly, people of presumably different races have produced healthy offspring. To be sure, racial scientists prophesied that miscegenation would lead to degeneration. Attempting "to cast doubt on the viability of racial hybridity," F. G. Crookshank (1924:440) argued that "where there is parental *conflict* (as when a pure-bred Nordic crosses with a pure-bred Lapp) the 'mongoloid' offspring will be very likely degenerate, ill-developed, and imbecile." Even Hitler (1943:286), however, did not deny the existence of mixed-race offspring (cf. Broca 1864:60).

The more plausible approach regards race as subspecies, which has a venerable antecedent in biology. As Dobzhansky (1982:47) noted: "The term 'race' is used quite loosely to designate any subdivision of species which consists of individuals having common hereditary traits." What the concept captures is the undeniable existence of geographical variation. Humanity has been singularly successful in adapting to virtually every ecological niche on earth: "specializing in despecialization" (Mayr 1976:543). The fact of diversity underscores the claim that race is "a group related by common descent, blood or heredity . . . often used interchangeably with the term subspecies" (Rushton 1995:283).

George Gaylord Simpson (1990:172) proposed two criteria to justify the use of subspecies: "1. Is there any non-arbitrary element (or 'objective basis') in subspecies? 2. Is the recognition of a formal subspecific category (whether wholly arbitrary or not) useful to taxonomists?" For human beings, geographical variation is almost always gradual, constituting cline, rather than the qualitative distinction implied by the use of subspecies (cf. Mayr 1982:280–283). Although one may posit race as an analytic category, one should not mistake it as being rooted in nature.

Most racial scientists, however, assume the reality of their taxonomy and characterize race as a pure and static type, rather than as a hybrid and dynamic population. As an essentialist and typological category, members of a race are said to show limited variation, share essential attributes, and are qualitatively distinct from members of other races (cf. Mayr 1997:128). In fact, in-group variations are great and they are also qualitatively indistinct from between-group variations (Haldane 1990:3). Therefore, once a commitment is made to identify a static type or an essence among a population that demonstrates geographical and individual variation, the consequence is inevitably a mismatch between the category and the population. Few racial scientists would question Swedes as part of the Nordic race. Yet, in a major study of Swedish army recruits in the late nineteenth century, only 10 percent were identified as Nordic (Dahlberg 1942:202). If 90 percent of Swedes are not Nordic, then who are they? The early twentieth-century racial scientist Hans F. K. Günther encountered a similar problem with the German *Volk*. He identified 6–8 percent as "pure Nordic," 3 percent as "pure Alpine," 2–3 percent as "pure Mediterranean," and 2 percent as "pure Baltic." The rest were impure, hybrid, or mixed (Proctor 1998:151). The German Idealist quip that it is so much the worse for the facts provides a poor excuse for the disjuncture. It is symptomatic that the two greatest proponents of the Aryan myth—the Englishman Chamberlain and the Austrian Hitler—should have deviated from the idealized Aryan appearance. In general, as Mayr (1991:27) put it: "Types or essences do not exist in living nature."

The claim of racial ontology faces the problem of racial classification and the antipodal pulls of lumpers and splitters. Popular classificatory schemes propose a handful of races. From the second edition of *Systema naturae,* Linnaeus identified four races: white Europeans, red Americans, yellow Asians, and black Africans (Hannaford 1996:204). Carleton Coon (1963: 3) claimed that there are five major races: Caucasoid, Mongoloid, Australoid, Congoid, and Capoid (the latter two are usually lumped together as Negroid). According to Coon (1963:2), the Caucasoid race "includes Europeans and their overseas kinsmen, the Middle Eastern Whites from Morocco to West Pakistan, and most of the peoples of India, as well as the Ainu of Japan." The category of Caucasoid, Caucasian, or white remains widely used today, but few would follow Coon and include what many would call Arabs and Asians.

Because lumpers appear blunt and crude, the desire for scientific rigor seems to favor splitters. William Z. Ripley (1923) divided Caucasian into Teutonic, Alpine, Nordic, Mediterranean, and other distinct races. A 1971 textbook proposed thirty-two "large races" in the world (Garn 1971:169–178). Refined divisions rest on a slippery slope that descends toward ever finer distinctions. They risk the criticism of claiming qualitative differences between peoples who are not qualitatively distinct. What exactly makes Teutonic, Alpine, and Nordic races so different? Geography provides few obvious and natural breaks; continents correspond poorly to races (Lewis and Wigen 1997:120–123). "Classification is not an exact science," as Simpson (1963:18) declared.

Consider in this regard the fluctuating definitions of whiteness in the United States. Writing in 1751, Benjamin Franklin (1987:374) observed: "The Number of purely white People in the World is proportionably very small. . . . And in *Europe,* the *Spaniards, Italians, French, Russians* and *Swedes,* are generally of what we call a swarthy Complexion; as are the *Germans* also, the *Saxons* only excepted, who with the *English* make the principal Body of White People on the Face of the Earth." In the nineteenth century, Irish immigrants—black in the British colonial, religious, and racial imaginary (Lebow 1976)—frequently mixed with African Americans, generating the census category of mulattoes (Ignatiev 1995:40). Furthermore, "Irish were frequently referred to as 'niggers turned inside out'; the

Negroes, for their part, were sometimes called 'smoked Irish' " (Ignatiev 1995:41; cf. Williams 1990:136–144). In the early twentieth-century immigration debate, Slavic, Mediterranean, and other southern and eastern European races were excluded from the ambit of white Americans (Jacobson 1998:68–90). When Franz Boas (1969:15) was traveling in the Pacific Northwest in the early twentieth century, a fellow passenger insisted that: "There is not a single white man among the lumbermen" because "they are all Swedes and Norwegians." Similarly, poor whites were deemed not really white in the U.S. Southwest (Foley 1997:5–9). Only in the early twentieth century did the expansive notion of whiteness become dominant (Guterl 2001:6–13).

Racial classification is not an exact science because race is not a constitutive category of nature. Hence, it must justify its existence by its usefulness. But why is it useful to classify people into races? If convenience provides the impulse to classify, then the impulse becomes reified and fortifies racial classification as obvious, natural, and convenient.

3

In spite of its arbitrary and convenient origins, most racial scientists insist on the natural foundations of race. The lapidary assertion of racial ontology provides the basis for painstaking data collection; the pride of racial science is its dogged empiricism. Generations of scholars have collected data on "human characters of racial value" (Wilder 1926:284). And it would almost be a pity to condemn in toto a century's worth of sustained human inquiry—as motivated as they were by a category mistake. Racial scientists attempted to achieve rigor and exactitude in their measurement and analysis, and it is not an accident that major advances in biostatistics emerged from racial science. Yet, just as we may laud Tycho Brahe's empirical precision and methodological virtuosity, we would be remiss to believe in the phenomenologically persuasive Ptolemaic worldview.

Anthropometric data, whatever their quality, cannot justify racial classification. How does one identify and measure race? Roland B. Dixon (1923:4) observed that "the criteria of race may be divided into two groups: (1) external or superficial, and (2), internal, structural, or skeletal," but he also noted the limitations of the first type because they were "useless for the study of the skeletal remains of ancient peoples." More importantly, he also found the second type of data wanting: "In practice it has been found extremely different to determine with real accuracy the great number of intermediate shades or forms [of skin and hair color, etc.]." In spite of his own caveats, Dixon persisted in racial measurements.

Exact measurements or high correlations do not prove the existence of categories. The assertion of racial permanence—"the races of men have been absolutely the same" (Knox 1850:34)—is contradicted by the reality of historical change. As we have seen, the constituent groups of the Caucasian race have changed dramatically. Once the categories are accepted, however, they provide receptacles for evidence of racial difference. Good data can cast doubt on the suitability of classification and categorization, but the mountain of data collected by racial scientists merely reinforced their conviction about racial ontology.

Because past pronouncements deviate so greatly from contemporary certitudes, it is easy to puncture the scientific claims of racial science and to collect howlers from the past, for the long list is neither inspiring nor edifying (Tucker 1994; Gould 1996). For example, Arthur de Gobineau (1966:151) observed that: "The negroes . . . have less muscular power. . . . In strength of fist, the English are superior to all the other European races." Few today would accept his propositions given the presumption of black athletic superiority (Hoberman 1997:xxvf). Gobineau's commonsense has merely disappeared into the repository of the wrong opinions of dead men. To take another example, early twentieth-century serologists believed that blood group served as a race marker. Arguing that Group A denoted intelligence and industry and Group B imbecility and sloth, some German scientists asserted that pure Germans had Group A blood and eastern Europeans Group B blood (Starr 1998:74–77). Given the actual mixture of blood types in both groups, they then sought to prove that Slavs and Jews had infused tainted blood into Germans (Mazumdar 1995:294). In fact, blood types and racial categories offer poor correlation (Zack 2002:53). The belief in racially distinct blood, however, sustained the segregation of blood in the United States into the 1960s (Starr 1998:169).

The failures of racial science stem in part from its presumption of biological or genetic determinism, which ignores the plasticity of human biology (Lasker 1969; Mascie-Taylor and Bogin 1995). The fact of heritability does not prove the primacy of genetics or biology. Seemingly stable and heritable features are profoundly affected by environmental factors. For example, nutritional and environmental changes led the average male Norweigian height to increase from under 160 cm in 1761 to just under 180 cm by 1984 (Floud, Wachter, and Gregory 1990:6). More dramatically, the average Japanese male stature rose over 5 inches in the second half of the twentieth century (French 2001:A4). Migrant studies, pioneered by Franz Boas (1912), demonstrated that whether of Japanese, Mexican, or Swiss origins, immigrants to the United States were taller than their native counterparts (Roberts 1995:4). In contrast, famines have resulted in shorter stature and head length, even among adults (Roberts 1995:2). Contextually affected morphological changes include body composition and the distribution and structure of tissues (Roberts 1995:8–12).

Nonetheless, hope springs eternal that a better science will validate racial ontology and epistemology. Indeed, recent advances in genetics promise the possibility of correlating the recalcitrant reality of geographical variation with genetic distribution (Cavalli-Sforza, Menozzi, and Piazza 1994:18). Modern genetics appears to make true racial science possible.

When population geneticists and biological anthropologists examine the existing distribution of gene pools, they find considerable diversity in small areas and among seemingly similar people. This is true for Oxfordshire villagers (Harrison 1995), Bougainville islanders (Friedlaender 1975), Pacific islanders (Houghton 1996), and Australian aborigines (Birdsell 1993). There are no obvious qualitative divisions in genetic distribution. "No single gene is therefore sufficient for classifying human populations into systematic categories" (Cavalli-Sforza, Menozzi, and Piazza 1994:19). If there are innumerable genetically distinct populations, then should we exceed the wildest desire of splitters and suggest thousands, perhaps millions, of races?

Furthermore, variation within any population tends to be greater than that across populations (Lewontin 1974:152–156). This is not surprising given the Darwinian postulate regarding evolution as the outcome of individual, not geographical, variation. The Jewish Diaspora evinces a certain genetic similarity across dispersed Jewish communities around the world, but each community—whether the Yemeni Jews or the Karaites—shows similar genetic composition to the surrounding non-Jewish populations (Mourant, Kopec, and Domaniewska-Sobczak 1978:57; cf. Kautsky 1926: 118). As we will see for African Americans, the ideology of racial purity contradicts the reality of hybridity.

Finally, the pitfalls of genetic determinism remain. Along with the quixotic quest for crime or cancer genes, the search for a race gene merely demonstrates the dogged insistence of racial scientists. Genotype does not

ineluctably manifest itself as phenotype, as multiple genes account for morphological features (Haldane 1990:25). We do not inevitably inherit our
appearance, behavior, or character (King 1981:60). The double meaning
of breeding suggests that biological reproduction is inadequate to sustain
social or cultural reproduction. The triple helix of gene, organism, and
environment mutually interacts in contingent and complex manners (Lewontin 2000:16–38). Even the most sophisticated practitioners of human
population genetics incorporate social data, such as linguistic evidence
(Cavalli-Sforza, Menozzi, and Piazza 1994:22) and surname distribution
(Lasker 1985:73–80), to trace transformations in populations. Precisely
when a truly scientific foundation for racial classification seemed possible,
genetic data requires social categories and sociological information.

Human biology—and biology in general—cannot expunge the social. If
environmentalism that dominated the European human sciences in the
eighteenth century is untenable, so too is the overweening ambition of
sociobiology, evolutionary psychology, and other doctrines of biological
determinism. An organism and its environment are inextricably intertwined; we can neither reduce one to the other nor use one to make deterministic claims about the other (Levins and Lewontin 1985:51–58; Rose
1997:278–299). The natural and the social are mutually constituted.

Racial classification presumes the existence of qualitatively distinct and
homogeneous populations when they are only quantitatively different and
heterogeneous. The concept of race is not necessary to make sense of
human biological diversity (e.g. Brace 1964; Bogin 1993). Contemporary
genetics finds little justification for the continued use of race. Because of
"the complexity, one might also say the impossibility, of the task of framing
a consistent classification of mankind" (Haddon 1925:151), many biologists eschew the concept of race altogether, preferring to lump everyone
into the category of Homo sapiens (Medawar and Medawar 1983:254; Futuyma 1998:737). After reviewing different proposals of dividing human
beings from two to sixty-three races, Charles Darwin (1981:i,226) expressed his skepticism about the very effort because the purported races
"graduate into each other, and that it is hardly possible to discover clear
distinctive characteristics between them." He (1981:i,232) also observed
"the close similarity between the men of all races in tastes, dispositions and
habits." Not surprisingly, Darwin postulated "sexual selection," rather than
"natural selection," to make sense of human variety. Given the artificiality
of racial demarcations and the unity of human beings, he (1981:i,227)

suggested that the scientist has "no right to give names to objects which he cannot define." Privileging the biological racial science effaces the social, thereby transforming contingency into destiny. Race should be expunged from the vocabulary of the human sciences. The term is soiled not only by two centuries of racist science, but it is also a category mistake.

4

What animates racial science is folk biology or common sense. The link between the past of descent and the present of commonality is well-nigh irrefutable. The imagery of kinship underscores the naturalness and necessity of racial distinction, which is at once transhistorical and transcultural. Don't we inherit something eternal and essential from our ancestors?

Because prestigious pedigrees are sought for everything from horses to books, we should not be surprised that many people—following longstanding aristocratic practice—seek illustrious ancestors. Whereas the genealogy of book ownership may be delineated as a single line of provenance, the same cannot be said for human genealogy. In the conventional imagery, a kinship chart fans out from an original couple, leading to an exponential growth of descendants. However, if one were to trace one's ancestry, a similar fanning out would occur as one traces one's ancestors (two parents, four grandparents, eight great grandparents, and so on). Indeed, the exponential growth in the number of ancestors suggests that every contemporary European may descend from Charlemagne and every human being from Confucius (Chang 1999).

Contemporary concerns inevitably shape the family tree, whether in ignoring ignominious ancestors or in claiming glorious but dubiously ascertained forebears. Purity is preserved by pruning unwanted branches of ancestry. While some seek ancestors that they aspire to deserve—Hellenized Jews claimed Greek ancestry, Greeks sought Egyptian and Persian roots (Hadas 1972:34,84)—others attempt to save the souls of the deceased infidels by converting them posthumously, as contemporary Mormons have been doing (Wright 2002:49). Every culture is replete with rituals to naturalize kinship relations.

The desire for pure lineage faces the messy reality of biological reproduction. Kinship is underdetermined by biology (Thompson 2001:175). Parents often present adopted children as "real" progenies. The patriarchal basis of most family genealogies risks the unsavory fact of false paternity, a rate that is estimated at up to 5 percent for the contemporary United States (Seabrook 2001:58). *Mater certa pater incertus.* Incidences of adultery, fornication, and other forms of extramarital sexual reproduction are surely not negligible (Betzig 2002:37). As Posthumus proclaims in *Cymbeline:* "We are all bastards." Only Siamese twins can be certain of consanguineous kinship.

Most individuals today can hardly hope to produce accurate genealogies. Family trees were the preserve of the landed elite in agrarian societies, and record keeping was never the model of scholarly rectitude. As we saw in the previous chapter, Icelandic genealogy—the basis for the genetic mapping project DeCode—was far from comprehensive. Beyond a few generations, genealogical charts face the misty mess of past prevarication and present projections. Genealogy is a strategic construct, a convenient fiction. As Rousseau (1994:133) memorably mocked it: "I have said nothing about king Adam or emperor Noah. . . . I hope this moderation will be appreciated, for as I am a direct descendant of one of these Princes, and perhaps of the eldest branch, how am I to know whether, through the verification of titles, I would not discover that I am the legitimate king of the human race?"

As we saw in the previous chapter, European nobility and peasantry generally claimed distinct lineages. Karl Friedrich von Baden observed: "If there are races among animals, there are races among men; for that reason the most superior must put themselves ahead of others, marrying among themselves and reproduce a pure race: that is the nobility" (Epstein 1966: 184). The French nobility imagined their ancestors to have conquered their peasant counterparts (Ellis 1988:26). The Polish nobility claimed Sarmatian origin, thereby distinguishing themselves from their plebeian counterparts (Walicki 1989:6–9), who, as I noted in the previous chapter, did not identify themselves as Polish until the nineteenth century. Similarly, free men were Slavs whereas peasants were "black" in medieval Russia (Blum 1961: 27,93). Contemporary caste differences in India are often racialized and stress skin color difference (Béteille 1965:48), however much outsiders are wont to call them all Indians.

Consider in this regard African Americans. Although racialized as black, African Americans do not hail from pure and pristine African ancestry. To begin with, though the vast majority of Africans arrived as slaves, they did not assume racial identification. "In the Americas, men and women identified as Angolans, Igbos, or Males frequently gained such identities not from their actual birthplace or the place from which they disembarked but because they spoke, gestured, and behaved like—or associated with—Angolans, Igbos, or Males" (Berlin 1998:104). To be sure, they had become a "race" by the nineteenth century but they were neither pure nor homogeneous. Julian Herman Lewis (1942:1) begins *The Biology of the Negro* by noting that "Negroes in the United States form a sharply delineated but well-integrated racial element of the American population," but a few pages later he mentions the considerable "intermixing" and suggests that over a fifth of African Americans in 1910 are "mixed" (Lewis 1942:9). Similarly, R. Ruggles Gates (1949:4) seeks to identify racial inheritance, but remarks that "American Negroes of course possess much white ancestry," and his sample of "Negro families" include African American families with "American Indians, Chinese, Hawaiians, and other peoples" as ancestors. In other words, there is a long history of miscegenation. As Ishmael Reed (1989: 227) wryly remarked: "If Alex Haley had traced his father's bloodline, he would have traveled twelve generations back to, not Gambia, but Ireland." One-drop rule was rarely codified. In the state of Virginia, for example, the definition of blackness was one-fourth African ancestry in 1785, one-sixteenth in 1910, and "one drop" of African blood in 1930 (Nash 1999: 17). Melville Herskovits (1930:1), realizing the hybrid character of African Americans, argued that they offer "what practically amounts to a laboratory condition for the study of race crossing." Consequently: "the term 'Negro' . . . as applied in the United States is a sociological one, and indicates any person who has partial Negro ancestry" (Herskovits 1930:271).

Ancestral confusion also bedeviled British intellectuals in the early twentieth century. J. Reid Moir (1927:162) argued that: "What is now England was the home of the earliest men." In contrast, L. A. Waddell (1925) suggested the Phoenician origin of Britons, whereas Nottidge Charles Mac-Namara (1900:165) noted the Iberian root of English people. R. N. Bradley (1926:13) found "Mediterranean, Beaker, Alpine and Nordic origins and traditions." Others were convinced of the Germanic—the Angles, Saxons, and Jutes (Whitelock 1954:11)—origins of the British race. In response, C. L'Estrange Ewen (1945:15) exhorted British people to cease considering "themselves as Anglo-Saxons or to claim cousinship with bestial German gangsters." E. Odlum (1916:v) went so far as to suggest: "We, the Anglo-Saxon peoples, are the ancient Ten-tribed House of Israel, in *a national and official sense.*" Some saw the ancestral unity and others the historical diversity of British people. MacNamara (1900:179–191) claimed that Scottish

Highlanders were Scandinavian and that Welsh and Irish were Iberian and Mongolian in origin. Probably the most scientific theory of the time had colonial British and colonized Indians hailing from the same stock (Pagden 2001:144–147).

My point is not to adjudicate among these competing and contradictory claims or to demonstrate the mixture of idle speculation and circumstantial evidence that animated them. Rather, intra-racial variation provided prima facie plausibility to a rather wide range of theories. Like all works of genealogy, contemporary prejudices projected themselves into the past. In the early nineteenth century, Teutonic affiliation was favored in part because of Protestant affiliation, defined against the Catholics and the Celts (Levine 1986:79). World War I contributed, however, to define Britishness against the enemy Germans (Winter 1996:265). Ultimately, the decline of nationalism and colonialism dampened interest in ancestral speculations (MacDougall 1982:127–130).

We all hail from ancestors, but how we define them is far from obvious. William Blake wondered: "Am not I / A fly like thee?" This is not quite as absurd as it may seem because "of the 289 known human 'disease' genes, 177 have direct counterparts in the fruit fly" (Ackerman 2001:12). Few would wish to claim commonality with and trace ancestry to amoebas, flies, or even chimpanzees, but contemporary physical anthropology suggests that we are all Africans. When people took biblical monogeny seriously, they at times depicted Adam and Eve as what we would call an interracial couple (Sollors 1997:32). Racial theories—however grounded they may be in science—refract speculations that reflect contemporary common sense (cf. Stoczkowski 1994). However much ancestral and contemporary bodies were and are real, genealogy and identity are inevitably essentially contested constructs.

If the search for roots confuses human beings with plants and confounds the constant mobility and hybridity of our ancestors, then the same cautionary note applies to territorial claims. As preposterous as it may seem, after a few generations, some U.S. Midwesterners say they are "native" Americans. Yet, as Randolph Bourne (1964:109) observed in 1916: "We are all foreign-born or the descendants of foreign-born, and if distinctions are to be made between us they should rightly be on some other ground than indigenousness." Even Native Americans were new settlers in North America not so long ago (Cavalli-Sforza, Menozzi, and Piazza 1994:303–308). People do not spontaneously generate from the earth. Claims of aboriginality, indigeneity, and nativity mask movements and conquests in the past.

5

Even if descent, lineage, and genealogy are problematic, don't common-sense perceptions provide potent foundations for racial classification? Racial typology reflects contemporary convention. Like dog breeds, what ultimately matters is the convenience of the classifier and not the composition of the classified. Faced with the reality of past interbreeding, racial scientists can deny its salience. "From the standpoint of taxonomy . . . how a race was formed is irrelevant. A race is a race is a race whether it goes back unchanged for six millennia or whether it resulted from admixture after 1850" (Garn 1971:6). Who today would have trouble distinguishing an African from an Asian? The implacable logic of Hitler's racial commonsense reduces individuals to different breeds or animals, which suffuses even the anti-Nazi mindset. For example, Art Spiegelman's *Maus* (1986–91) depicts different peoples as different animals. In racial fundamentalism, race is race is race, as obvious as black and white. The problem with crackpot realism is the inability to distinguish categories and metaphors from individuals and realities. The naturalness of racial science depends on the historically specific presupposition of modern peoplehood.

Appearance is a cogent basis of everyday racial classification. To put it crudely, people who look different are assumed to be different. "It is strange that race differences should ever have been taboo, since human groups obviously do vary, for instance in skin color and facial figures" (Levin 1997: 1); "when a six-foot Swede and a five-foot Pygmy shake hands, they are not mistaken for brothers, no matter how amicable and warm" (Goldsby 1977:4). Language, clothing, religions, and other elements of social life can be acquired with more or less ease over a generation; the same cannot be said for heritable physiological characteristics, which appear immutable.

Somatic pigmentation is the most popular basis of racial taxonomy. Skin color in fact has limited biological significance (Robins 1991:211; cf. Smith 1993:12). Though a proxy for recent ancestry, as the racial scientist Dixon noted above, it is useless for discerning our ancestors' racial categorization. The primacy of color results from its visual immediacy and heritability, which presumably correlates it with geographical variety. Perhaps the most common scheme highlights the three major continents: "The three highly differentiated human races are in order the White, the Yellow, and the Black, or more technically, the Caucasian, the Mongolian, and the Ethiopian" (Wilder 1926:338; cf. Coon 1965:3; Rogers 1990:19).

In general, the paler the skin, the higher the status. White has been the color of power and prestige in the West as delineated in Herman Melville's tour de force, "The Whiteness of the Whale" in *Moby Dick* (1851). A proximate reason is the primacy of agricultural work in the preindustrial world. Because daylong field work darkens the skin, color provided a ready-made means of differentiating peasants from nobles. Lighter skin is therefore a common proxy for higher status. In the British West Indies, for example, lighter skin connoted higher income and educational attainment (Smith 1965:60–66). Modern colonialism predominantly enslaved people from tropical zones; colonial power relations correlated with and thereby strengthened the hierarchy of light over dark skin.

Status inequality and symbolic hierarchy go hand in hand and are at times convertible. That is, power, wealth, and prestige whiten. As Frantz Fanon (1967:18) observed: "The Negro of the Antilles will be proportionately white—that is, he will come closer to being a real human being—in direct ratio to his mastery of the French language." During the race-conscious nineteenth century in the United States, the Mediterranean Jew Jesus became a blond-haired and blue-eyed Christ, exemplified by Warner Sallman's best-selling portrait, "Head of Christ" (Dyer 1997:68; cf. Firth 1973:406–411). In contrast, lower status groups are often "black" (Gilman 1986:10). The pioneering race theorist Gobineau (1966:205) regarded Mediterraneans as "black," just as contemporary Russians call Romani (Gypsies) "black" (Lemon 2000:63).

The symbolic valence of color has been far from fixed, however. "Among the Arabs and Ottoman Turks white slaves were specially prized [while in] Imperial China and Islamic India, black slaves were valued for their exotic appearance" (Patterson 1982:178). Some cultures have favored darker skin pigmentation, and some seemed to have been relatively indifferent to color gradation (Robins 1991:166–170). "The relationship between the black and white Lolo [of southern China] is that between members of the upper and lower classes" (Lin 1961:102). Contemporary Hawaii, for instance, is characterized by significant prejudice and discrimination against *haole* (outsiders, usually white Americans) (Whittaker 1986:154–163). The mark of the leisure class in the contemporary United States is sporty tan, denoting the ability to sun and surf in the age of office work.

Skin color is not a black-and-white affair; the existence of gradients makes many people capable of passing as a member of another race. A person who may be "white" in Dominican Republic would be "colored" in Martinique and "black" in the United States (Mintz 1984:315). Native Australians, South Asians, and Central Africans tend to have darker skin, but they are usually classified as different races. Given that South Asians are said to be the original Aryan and are frequently classified as Caucasian, the mismatch between color and race becomes all the more poignant. Even when slave status entailed presumed racial differences, such as in much of the Americas, "it was not so much color differences as differences in hair type that become critical as a mark of servility" (Patterson 1982:61). Skin color was a useful status marker, but others, such as clothing, body markings, and hairstyle, were just as common (Patterson 1982:58–62). Early British colonizers in North America did not use skin color to demarcate themselves from Native Americans (Seed 2001:131).

Color is reified as both a cause and effect of racial differentiation, but it is also important in nonracial forms of social distinction. As I noted in the previous chapter, the claim of hereditary superiority sustained status hierarchy. Quite literally, nobles and peasants were regarded as different races. In medieval Europe, both sacred and secular history legitimated the subordination and status distinction of the peasantry, whether as a result of Noah's curse or aristocratic conquest (Freedman 1999:107–110). Medieval French intellectuals depicted peasants (pagani) as "medieval Caliban" (Le Goff 1980:92–97). "One strategy in such mythologizing was to type the original conquered population and their descendants as servile by emphasizing right of conquest or by arbitrarily creating an ethnic difference" (Freedman 1999:106). What we would call racism was addressed to co-ethnic status inferiors. Whereas nobles had "blue blood," peasants were "black": "Ham had two medieval roles: as the father of a number of peoples, including black Africans, and as the ancestor of European serfs" (Freedman 1999:93). Status inequality generated a quasi-racial discourse of distinction in premodern societies.

Biological distinction went well beyond blood and skin color. Status distinction was no less natural or primordial than racial distinction. In most preindustrial societies, it connoted significant height differences (Floud, Wachter, and Gregory 1990:1). Peasants literally came up short against landlords. The seemingly metaphorical markers of status differences— "looking up," "being looked down upon," or "high and mighty"—were in fact the case.

In general, social categories are given somatic expressions. Few today would insist on the reality of witches as conceived by seventeenth-century New Englanders, but we would be remiss to ignore their reality to their contemporaries. Writing in 1929, George Lyman Kittredge (1972:33) observed that witchcraft "was not merely an historical phenomenon, it was a fact of contemporary experience. Whoever denied the occurrence of witchcraft in the past, was an atheist; whoever refused to admit its actual possibility in the present, was either stubbornly incredulous, or destitute of the ability to draw an inference. . . . [Witchcraft was recognized by] the Bible, by all branches of the Church, by philosophy, by natural science, by the medical faculty, by the law of England." Witches could be identified by the devil's mark: "any unusual protuberance on the body that could conceivably be considered a supernumerary teat that the demons might suck in the form of familiars" (Russell 1980:81). Furthermore, as Robin Briggs (1996:24) argues: "One very powerful link did unite many of the accused; that of family and heredity. The idea that a 'race' was either sound or tainted was much employed." In fact, witches tended to be those "who lacked the proper sense of neighbourhood and community" (Briggs 1996: 23). Social marginality was racialized, and the regnant discourse confidently identified the race of witches (cf. Briggs 1996:21).

Social categories often claim biological foundations. Few today argue that caste, status, or class constitute distinct gene pools, but the prevalence of endogamy—indeed, the outright proscription on exogamy—make them functionally equivalent to race. Endogamous groups, such as South Asian subcastes (*jati*), reveal genetic differences (Dobzhansky 1962:234–238). Ironically, the assumed significance of racial and ethnic categories lead Indian researchers to focus on ethnic affiliation, rather than caste membership, in their population genetics studies (Singh, Bhalla, and Kaul 1994: 6). Similarly, although Emmanuel Le Roy Ladurie (1984:142) claims class endogamy in eighteenth-century Occitan, few today would hesitate to use Occitan as a unit of analysis. In this regard, mixed marriage traditionally referred to nuptials across status and religious boundaries. As late as the nineteenth century, mixed marriage or intermarriage referred to cross-status marriage in Italy (Cardoza 1992:177–181) and interfaith union in the United States (Rose 2001:121–128).

Class difference—though no one today will argue that it is a biological category—manifested itself as physiological differentiation. The 1840 British Royal Commission report on handloom weavers described them as "decayed in their bodies; the whole race of them is rapidly descending to the size of Lilliputians" (Floud, Wachter, and Gregory 1990:2). The average height difference between students at Sandhurst (an elite military academy) and those at Marine Society (with its plebeian membership) was in the order of 20 cm between 1760 and 1860: "Almost all the Sandhurst boys would have been taller than almost all the [Merchant Society] boys" (Floud, Wachter, and Gregory 1990:198). Class difference persisted in Britain to the 1980s. In one class classification scheme, those of the upper two classes were on average 3.2 cm taller than those of the lower two classes. In contrast, the maximum difference across regions was 3.8 cm (Floud, Wachter, and Gregory 1990:199,216).

If class was racialized, then what about people who are physically disabled or fat? The reluctance to classify them as races is not at all obvious. These highly visible somatic attributes possess a certain genetic propensity toward intergenerational reproduction. Furthermore, there exists considerable, albeit not universal, affinity based on, as well as discrimination against, each attribute. Heightism—systematic preference for taller people—is a significant social phenomenon. No one would doubt its heritability, and what little evidence that exists shows its considerable social salience (Economist 1995–96). Not only do stigmatized groups face systematic disadvantage in marriage and employment, they also form movements to eradicate discrimination and to establish a group identity. Some groups of physically disabled people share descent, contemporary commonality, and even engage in identity-based political mobilization (Oliver 1990:118–131). Yet these social groups are insistently distinguished from race. This is because race presupposes modern peoplehood, not all biologically defined groups.

Distinct appearance underlies and fortifies a variety of social categories, such as caste or class, but genetic evidence does not readily support the meaningfulness of any system of classification (Macbeth 1997:60). Plasticity and adaptation are powerful forces that constrain genetic determinism. Differences are gradual, intra-cluster variation is often greater than inter-cluster variation, and interbreeding occurs even if there are formal proscriptions. In the aforementioned Oxford village study, G. Ainsworth Harrison (1995:20) found genetic diversity among five social classes, but twenty generations previously, they shared 95 percent of common ancestry. Had biological science developed earlier, however, we might very well have seen the rise of class or status science akin to racial science. In fact, speculations abounded on the distinct origins of and natural differences among status groups and classes, but they tended to be articulated in religious, not scientific, discourse. The categorical emergence of modern peoplehood is necessary for racial science.

In summary, appearance is inadequate in and of itself to justify racial distinction. To the extent that we can identify race, we should look for genetic variation, rather than superficial morphological distinction.

In this regard, the received distinction between race and ethnicity is spurious. The modern sense of ethnic—"common racial, cultural, religious, or linguistic characteristics" according to the *Oxford English Dictionary*— stems from the mid-nineteenth century in contradistinction to the older usage denoting groups of heathens, individuals, and even animals (Chapman 1993:14–22). It became entrenched as a euphemism for race in the 1970s (Glazer and Moynihan 1975:1). Be that as it may, social scientists frequently seek to distinguish race and ethnicity. As Hubert Blalock (1982: 4) suggests: "The concept *race* in principle refers to biological character- istics, such as skin color, physical build, body hair, and skull measure- ments. In contrast, *ethnicity* refers to cultural characteristics of diverse types" (cf. van den Berghe 1978:9; Holt 2000:16). However, status and other social distinctions are given physical grounding, whereas biological groups, such as deaf people, are given cultural expressions. The natural and the social are enmeshed in the work of social classification.

6

Just as it is possible to apply peoplehood categories to past populations, it is possible to classify all manners of categorical prejudice and discrimina- tion as racism. The stereotyping of a racial minority may be similar to that of a religious or physically disabled group. However, racism is distinct from other biosocial forms of discrimination. Few today would regard witches or peasants as races. Although proto-biological rationales were given for their social marginality, they did not belong to the conceptual universe of modern peoplehood. It is only with the birth of modern peoplehood that race and racism emerge.

The modernity of racism is counterintuitive because expressions of group superiority are ubiquitous. Contempt or disdain, mixed with fear and hatred, for vaguely known outsiders is something of a cultural uni- versal, although it is not as pervasive as some believe. Xenophobia and xenophilia often go together. The foreigner or the stranger may be despised, but he may very well be a superior being, becoming at times a king or, precisely because of his alien status, a relatively autonomous servant to power (Coser 1972:580). Hellenistic Greeks were ethnocentric and xenophobic, but they also sought wisdom from the barbarians (Momigliano 1975:149). More mundanely, European explorer-missionary-pirates did not surprise—or generate negative sentiments among—Southeast Asians in mercantile regions because they were accustomed to people of diverse appearance (Reid 1994:271–276). Tahitians were famously hospitable to Captain Cook and his crew (Pagden 2001:115). Peasants may personify xenophobia, but they are also known for their hospitality to strangers. What begins in fear may end up in folly or feud, but it may just as likely end up in friendship.

Insofar as groups of people are deemed inferior, there are inevitably discourses about them that appear racist to modern sensibilities. Ancient Athenians assumed their superiority over barbarians, and the First Crusaders believed in the truth of their faith over Islam and Judaism. Concurrently, Athenians had disparaging things to say about barbarians, and Christians were withering in their contempt of infidels. Most individuals and cultures, past and present, have employed essentialized categories to denigrate other peoples and cultures. The claim of the civilized is notoriously smug and self-centered, although that of those called barbaric is probably no less so. Many cultures, after all, use the same term to refer to themselves and to human beings *tout court* (Lévi-Strauss 1969:46).

Distant lands inspire spectacular speculations that reveal abysmal ignorance. Monstrous races haunted the art and literature of medieval Europe (Friedman 1981); Isidore of Seville in the seventh century wrote of fantastic beings, such as Cyclops and Giants, dog-faced and noseless people (Hodgen 1964:54–59). Between triumphant imagination and blissful ignorance, stereotypes of distant others are dogmatically formulated, but they are usually lightly worn, to be shed at the first infusion of information. For most individuals, however, they are of little interest and therefore ignored.

Most instances of fearing, hating, or belittling others are expressions of ethnocentrism or xenophobia. As generalized sentiments about fear of the unknown, they apply to all outsiders, not just to categories of modern peoplehood. As we saw in Chapter 1, foreigners frequently denoted people outside of one's village or locality, rather than outside of one's kingdom or empire (cf. Geremek 1990:352–355). More significantly, most people's attention is fixed on internal or domestic affairs. For example, Martin Luther wrote scathingly of Turks and Jews, but he is more scathing about the Pope in the same texts (cf. Brecht 1993:iii,354). If the text is about the enemy far away, the subtext is about the enemy within.

Premodern European anthropology was fundamentally Christian and asserted the unity of humanity. To the extent that a discourse of the others existed, it used the language of religion and civilization: Christianity and civilization against Satanism and savagery. Two interrelated categories— non-Christians and barbarians—denoted the equivalent of our racial and ethnic others. Non-Christians included not only Jews, Muslims, and other heretics, but also lepers and witches. We can readily understand Jews and Muslims as adherents of rival faiths, but what of lepers and witches? "Leprosy was a disease of the soul, brought on by moral corruption and sin" (Nirenberg 1996:57). Hence, leprosy, as a sign of sin, rendered lepers as less than upright Christians. As William the Monk chastised Henry of Lausanne: "You too are a leper, scarred by heresy . . . bare-headed with ragged clothing, filthy garment; it befits you to shout unceasingly that you are a leper, a heretic and unclean, and must live alone outside the camp, that is to say outside the church" (Moore 1997:246). Witches practiced a non-Christian belief system. In fact, the accusation of witchcraft embraced all manners of social deviance, masking neighborhood quarrels and other conflicts (Macfarlane 1970:173–176). The barbarian had a pejorative connotation and referred to non-Christians, foreigners, and peasants (Borst 1992: 6–9). The church loathed heathens; royalty and nobility feared foreign political rivals; and landlords were wary of peasant unrest. In addition, villagers were suspicious of all outsiders. In other words, the barbarian was a mobile signifier of those who threatened one of the powerful institutions of medieval Europe.

Nonetheless, European colonial institution and imaginary appear irrevocably bound up in a particular complex of power and knowledge that can be summarized as racist. Thus, Howard Winant (2001:1) declares: "Race has been fundamental in global politics and culture for half a millennium," and Cornel West (1982:47) intones: "The very structure of modern discourse *at its inception*"—referring to the likes of Francis Bacon and René Descartes—"produced forms of rationality . . . which require the constitution of the idea of white supremacy." However, full-fledged racist articulations—influenced by Gobineau and others—had to wait until the twentieth century (Said 1979:230–236,306–328). European expansion generated negative stereotypes about non-Europeans, but racist discourse emerged with the rise of the modern state and modern colonialism. Before then, the language of religion, civilization, and status—not racism—justified conquest and plunder.

Early modern European intellectuals collated, synthesized, and generated ideas about non-Europeans, constituting the genres of cosmography and comparative ethnology (Pagden 1986:4; McGrane 1989:10–19). Often ethnocentric, occasionally brilliant, early European cosmographers specialized in epigrams and epithets to characterize peoples (Delft 1993:87–104). The discovery of the new world generated a dispute about its inferiority and immaturity (Gerbi 1955). But post-Columbian European discourses on non-European peoples were not inevitably xenophobic. Rather than unrelenting demonology, expressions of European inferiority—if only to hasten domestic reform—were common. It would be misleading to characterize European projections of their fantasies on the New World as racist (cf. Brandon 1986:47). Most educated early modern Europeans believed that they were living in a corrupt world, in one or another stage in a cycle (cf. Bury 1955:9,65–69). In contrast, the noble savage idea pictured prelapsarian idyll elsewhere. From Marco Polo through the Jesuits to Leibniz and Voltaire, China represented a superior civilization (Lach 1965:i,xii–xiii, ii,822–835, 1977:560–566). From the twelfth to fifteenth century, the assumed locus of the paradise was eastward, whether in the guise of Prester John's Christian Kingdom in Ethiopia or John de Mandeville's fabled utopia (Baudet 1988:13–20; cf. Boas 1966:138–164). From the sixteenth to eighteenth century—after the discovery of the New World—the promised land was usually located westward (Baudet 1988:32–35; cf. Delumeau 1995: 160–172). The early eighteenth century may very well be characterized as the age of xenophilia in Europe. In contradistinction to Christian intolerance and monarchal corruption, foreign cultures ranging from the sophisticated civilization of Persia (Montesquieu) to the primitive purity of Tahiti (Bougainville) captivated and enchanted Enlightenment intellectuals (Baudet 1988:50; cf. Becker 1932:110). Many eighteenth-century European writers presumed that "the most beautiful peoples on earth were to be found within the Ottoman Empire or further east, and the ugliest in the farthest north of Europe" (Bindman 2002:12).

If the idea of progress "reached its zenith" between 1750 and 1900 (Nisbet 1980:171), then the belief in decadence or decline was also "the gift of modernity" (Chaunu 1981:69). Only when the idea of progress became "a general article of faith" did the European confidence in its superiority spread (Bury 1955:346; cf. Nisbet 1980:171–178). However, until the nineteenth century—when the Darwinian worldview challenged the biblical belief in monogeny (cf. Bowler 1986:131–146; Pagden 1993:184–188)—climate and civilization offered the privileged explanation for human diversity. The biological concept of race had little airing. As Margaret Hodgen (1964:213) concluded: "Any effort to distinguish among the 'races' of mankind on either anatomical, physiological, or cultural grounds was relatively negligible. Racialism in the familiar nineteenth- and twentieth-century sense of the term was all but nonexistent." The languages of religion, civilization, and status superseded that of race. Early modern European discourse of status in particular approximated the modern language of race. Contemporary opinions of status inferiors stressed their "ignorance, irresponsibility, laziness, and general worthlessness" (Blum 1978: 45). The peasantry was the primary target of what we would call racial stereotyping.

The prism of modern peoplehood refracts reality inflected by modern categories. Yet the universe of modern peoplehood is not transhistorical and transcultural; people have been identified by a variety of classificatory schemes. We should not conflate all instances of ethnocentrism—expressions of group difference that almost inevitably connote superiority—to racism. It is, of course, anachronistically accurate to characterize the Athenian disdain of slaves or barbarians, or the Christian contempt of non-Christians, as racist. Yet we should be wary of a transhistorical and transcultural usage of racism to encompass all expressions of group calumny. Although cultural snobbery or religious-based persecution may very well be redolent of racism, few would wish to categorize insults against illiterates or persecutions of witches as racist. Is racism the same as status or class prejudice? Given the quasi-racial discourse of status hierarchy, should we call nobles' prejudices against peasants or urban professionals' descriptions of dangerous classes as racist? The framework of modern peoplehood rejects the categorization of lords and peasants in medieval France or bourgeoisie and lumpenproletariat in modern France as distinct races because they belong to the same group in modern classification. Few today would be willing to employ racism to denote status or class prejudice. However, when the status groups seem to consist of different peoples in the modern sense, then we transpose the framework and language of modern peoplehood. In any case, as I elaborate in Chapter 4, racism is almost always articulated against groups internal to society, who are nevertheless regarded as external to it. Precisely when universal citizenship and status equality describe the constitution of modern society does the language of race express categorical inequality in the idiom of cultural distinction.

7

Nonetheless, didn't racism emerge to describe, explain, and justify Christian plunder and conquest of non-Christians? It would be anachronistic to assume that early European explorers and conquerors, such as Christopher Columbus and Hernán Cortés, were brimming with racist sentiments. Racist though they may appear in retrospect, they were still steeped in the language and worldview of status society and Christianity. The classificatory scheme of modern peoplehood would have been alien to them. If nothing else, the first conquerors suffered from conceptual poverty, almost inevitably classifying the Americans they found in the Aristotelian-Thomist category of the barbarian or the Christian one of the heathen (Pagden 1986: 13). Familiar categories account for the unfamiliar, and stereotypes make sense of the strange. In other words, European expectations absorbed the shock of the new. Columbus, to his dying day, thought that the nature and people of the Caribbean and the Americas were familiar to him from his earlier readings and explorations (Pagden 1986:10; cf. Todorov 1984:50).

Consider the Castilian conquest of the Americas, the first extensive European incursion in the Americas. In 1519, Cortés and his entourage arrived at Cozumel, on the coast of Yucatán, and eventually reached Tenochtitlán, the capital of the thriving Tenochcha Empire. In his second letter to Charles V, Cortés described how Emperor Moctezuma II (Xocoyotzin) regarded him as an emissary of the feathered, or plumed, serpent Quetzalcóatl. According to Cortés (1986:86), Moctezuma II said: "And we have always held that those who descended from him [Quetzalcóatl] would come and conquer this land and take us as their vassals. So because of the place from which you claim to come, namely, from where the sun rises . . . we shall obey you and hold you as our lord." If we were to trust Cortés, then his appropriation of the role of "the symbol of the sanctification of authority, the paradigm of legitimate rule and order" (Carrasco 1982:106) was critical to the conquest of the vast stretches of Mesoamerica (Sahagún 1990:ii,219–222,954–957; cf. Orozco y Berra 1960:261–278). Skeptics regard the tale as fabulous and fabricated (Pagden 1990:102).

The encounter between the Castilian conquerors and the Nahua royalty is not unique in generating antipodal accounts. Intercultural contacts are rife with misunderstandings generated by linguistic barriers. In 1779, Hawaiians apparently regarded James Cook's appearance as the return of the Hawaiian deity Lono (Beaglehole 1974:657–660). Whether Hawaiians regarded Cook as a divinity, albeit a minor one, engendered one of the most engaging and entertaining North American academic debates of the 1990s (Obeyesekere 1992; Sahlins 1995). It may very well be the height of European arrogance to assume that the natives had regarded the explorers and conquerors as gods, but it may also be anachronistic, indeed Eurocentric, to deny and denigrate the contemporary accounts of native beliefs. My intention is not to adjudicate between these two parallel controversies, or many other intriguing, if ultimately inscrutable, accounts of cross-cultural contact after 1492. Endlessly fascinating though they may be, there are two major consequences of European exploration and conquest.

Perhaps the most dramatic was the demographic collapse of the non-European world. According to Sherburne F. Cook and Woodrow Borah (1979:1), the Mesoamerican population was 25.2 million in 1518, but declined to 6.3 million by 1548 and 1.1 million by 1605. From an estimated figure of 800,000 Hawaiians in 1778, the number dropped to 130,000 by 1832 and fewer than 40,000 by the 1890s (Stannard 1989: 45–49; cf. Crosby 1994:121–137). European expansion produced catastrophic, albeit often unintended, consequences. The inhabitants of Hispaniola in 1492—variously estimated from 100,000 to 8 million (Cook and Borah 1971:408; Arranz Márquez 1991:42–64; Cook 1998:21–24)—were virtually extinct by 1535. Similarly, 9 million people of Inca Empire declined to 1 million 50 years after the initial European contact and to 600,000 in another half-century (Cook 1981:114; cf. Spalding 1984:136). Although estimates vary wildly, no one disputes the dismal fact of demographic catastrophe.

Bartolomé de las Casas's (1974) impassioned chronicle of European violence and terror has spawned numerous discursive successors, who have emphasized the destructive impact of colonization. Most devastating, however, were the epidemics that caused massive mortality, ranging from smallpox to typhus, sometimes leading to 90 percent depopulation (Crosby 1986:196–216; Cook 1998:206–209). Biology is important in history (McNeill 1976:5), but not as race, although race may become important in modern historical reconstructions (Stannard 1992:13).

Few would hold European explorers and conquerors responsible for the epidemics, but they also wreaked havoc by desecrating religious monuments, plundering local treasures, and enslaving people. Post-Columbian European colonial history is a chronicle of crimes. However, would it be correct to call Cortés a racist? Did the Christians murder and plunder because they were racists (Stannard 1992:269–281)? Undoubtedly, Cortés believed in the superiority of Christian civilization, and found Nahua human sacrifice rituals reprehensible: "the most terrible and frightful . . . ever witnessed" (Cortés 1986:35). However, his characterizations of Mesoamerican civilization were far from derogatory, and he praised the buildings, markets, and people of various cities as "civilized" (Cortés 1986:67). A member of his expedition, Bernal Díaz del Castillo (1956:190), was overtaken by the sight of Tenochtitlán: "We were amazed and said that it was like the enchantments they tell of in the legend of Amadis. . . . And some of our soldiers even asked whether the things that we saw were not a dream. It is not to be wondered at that I here write it down in this manner, for there is so much to think over that I do not know how to describe it, seeing things as we did that had never been heard of or seen before, not even dreamed about. . . . I stood looking at it and thought that never in the world would there be discovered other lands such as these." He went on to lament that "of all these wonders that I then beheld today all is overthrown, and lost, nothing left standing" (Díaz del Castillo 1956:191). Cortés and Díaz had ample reasons to exaggerate their marvelous discoveries, and their appreciation of architectural wonders did little to halt their destruction of Nahua religious monuments. However, were they racists? Did racism play any role in their conquest?

Cortés and others did not explore, conquer, and pillage the Americas because of their racist convictions. To the extent that we can reconstruct their motivation, they sought to ennoble and enrich themselves, expand Charles V's domain, and convert Mesoamericans to Christianity (Parry 1981:19; cf. Elliott 1970:11). As Las Casas (1974:41) intoned: "Their reason for killing and destroying such an infinite number of souls is that the Christians have an ultimate aim, which is to acquire gold. . . . It should be kept in mind that their insatiable greed and ambition, the greatest ever seen in the world, is the cause of their villainies." Greed was notoriously difficult to justify, having to wait until the rise of laissez-faire economics in the nineteenth century, but the quest for gold was of paramount significance (Clendinnen 1987:13). As Montaigne (1991:1031) trenchantly observed in the late sixteenth century: "Whoever else has ever rated trade and commerce at such a price? So many cities razed to the ground, so many nations wiped out, so many millions of individuals put to the sword, and the most beautiful and the richest part of the world shattered, on behalf of the pearls-and-pepper business! Tradesmen's victories!"

Christianity and civilization provided more potent rationales. Beyond adventure, fame, and wealth—motivations that we moderns appreciate—we should not forget the centrality of Christianity. We may call Cortés Spanish or European, but he and his ilk referred to themselves as Christians (Seed 2001:116). If the expulsion of Jews and Muslims from Spain offered one terminus for missionary Christianity, then the Iberian explorers continued the crusades beyond Granada and Gibraltar (cf. Parry 1981:22–26; Lewis 1995:62). Symptomatically, the expulsion and Columbus's first voyage both occurred in 1492. Soon after Cortés, Franciscans in particular set out to preserve and transmit native beliefs, however Christianized their understanding and if only for the purposes of converting the natives (Elliott 1970:34; cf. Gruzinski 1988:239–261). The 1493 Papal Bull was important in legitimating Spanish conquest (Syme 1958:27). Interestingly, Castilians initially treated Mesoamericans as *aljamas,* or tribute-paying communities, revealing Islamic influence on Spanish political thought (Seed 1995:85).

My intention is not to condone the deleterious consequences of European exploration, but merely to point out that race- and racism-centered history misses the principal source of mass deaths and the major motivations of European conquest. Europeans made numerous negative comments about non-Europeans, replete with astounding misunderstandings, ethnocentric observations, and condescending judgments. However, Columbus and Cortés did not plunder and conquer because they were racists, just as much as their contemporary counterparts did not become pirates and buccaneers because they were convinced of their racial superiority. Many Castilians probably regarded the Nahua as primitive, but they held "the same attitude toward non-Castilian Europeans (including peripheral Iberians) and other Old World peoples" (Lockhart 1992:444). In turn, "the Nahuas had always had a similar attitude toward non-Nahuas" (Lockhart 1992:444). Ethnocentrism, as I noted, is well-nigh universal. Yet intermarriage was common, and some conquistadores believed they were engaged in hypergamy by marrying Mesoamerican nobles.

Colonial rule was justified by religious and cultural superiority (Hanke 1974:82; cf. Chaunu 1969:396–400). Juan Ginés de Sepúlveda argued that the Indians "require, by their own nature and in their own interests, to be placed under the authority of civilized and virtuous princes and nations, so that they may learn from the might, wisdom and law of their conquerors to practise better morals, worthier customs and a more civilised way of life" (Parry 1981:312). Here, the natural justification of slavery, following Aristotle, was based not on physiological or biological as much as on moral and psychological grounds (cf. Hanke 1970:27; Pagden 1986:27). In fact, it was not so much right and justification but duty and obligation to care for the heathen barbarians (Pagden 1986:3). Enslavement was part of missionary work, as a means to convert slaves, who, it was conveniently reasoned, hailed from African slave society in any case (Baudet 1988:29). Similarly, Juan de Matienzo legitimated the Castilian conquest of the Inca Empire by arguing that "we give them religious instruction [doctrina], we teach them to live like men, and they give us silver, gold or things worth [them]" (Stern 1982:73).

Even if initial conquest did not depend on or develop racism, didn't colonialism rely on, or at least generate, racist ideas? In seventeenth-century Mexico, Castilian colonizers monopolized privileged roles, whereas colonized Indians, African slaves, and people of mixed descent were plebeians in the sistema de castas (cf. Seed 1988:21–25). There is an overlap between the modern analysis of race and the premodern category of status, as we will also see for slavery in the antebellum U.S. South. However, the colonizers were not operating in the universe of modern peoplehood but in the world of premodern status hierarchy. The language of blood and lineage distinguished the nobility from the rest. Distinction concerned honor and status (Seed 1988:134–146; Gutiérrez 1991:177–180). In the Americas, the Spaniards became hidalgos (nobles). In the first postcolonial generation, they did not hesitate to marry natives or grant inheritance to whom we would call mixed-race children. The chief concern was not racial status, but the legitimacy of marriage and of offspring (Cope 1994:14; cf. Gutiérrez 1991:199). The category of mestizos referred to illegitimate children, or extramarital offspring (Cope 1994:18). In Spanish Peru around the same time, 95 percent of mixed-race children were illegitimate; legitimate mixed-raced children, however, could and did inherit property and privileged status (Lockhart 1994:188). Race and racism became more important in the nineteenth century (Gutiérrez 1991:285–292).

The sistema de castas was an elite ideology of status ordering that distinguished the ruling elite from the rest. Among the non-privileged, there was little evidence of inter-casta prejudice, as multiracial households and casta status change were common (Cope 1994:76,162; cf. Seed 1988:155). The very category of Indians did not become a political identity until the twentieth century, as the largest category that indigenous people used were their *altepetl* (local state), or what Castilians called *pueblo* (Lockhart 1991:9,54, 1992:14). Most identified themselves with their villages, which preserved their boundaries into the twentieth century (cf. Taylor 1979:170). In addition to their narrow territorial identity, status remained critical (Lockhart 1992:94–102). As Alonso de Molina found when compiling the Nahuatl-Spanish dictionary in the sixteenth century, there was no Nahua word for human beings *(hombre)*; there were only status categories, such as *pilli* (noble) or *macehualli* (commoner) (Lockhart 1992:94,114).

The belated emergence of racism can be seen also in the case of American Indians. Like their counterparts elsewhere, European contact with the native populations of North America led to a demographic collapse. Yet Puritans or Catholics did not initially generate racist discourses. Beyond the classic dichotomy of civilized against barbarian (Jennings 1976:6–11), Europeans employed categories at hand, such as Africans, Wild Irish, and savage (Axtell 1992:67–70; Seed 2001:131–134). "From the days of earliest colonization to King Philip's War, the Puritan remained convinced that the Indians were probably Jews and that all Indians were born white" (Vaughan 1995:20). Rather than race, religion remained primary in Puritan—or, for that matter, Catholic—understanding of the native peoples of North America (cf. Vaughan 1995:lii–lix). Christian anthropology stunted racial science (Lafaye 1976:39–42). Rather than asserting racial difference, European intellectuals sought a suitable genealogy for Americans. Some British writers claimed that Indians, like Irish, descended from cannibalistic Scythians (Rawson 2001:79). Thomas Thorowgood (1660:5) conjectured that American Indians are "Jews, or descended from them," while Jean François Lafitau's 1724 treatise claimed that "the Huron and the Iroquois were descended of the Spartans and the Lycians" (Pagden 1986:203). Thorowgood and Lafitau may have regarded American Indians as inferior— as they did of their domestic status inferiors—but they neither drew racial distinctions nor used biological explanations.

Until the nineteenth century, European colonialism entailed tributary relations and symbolic dominance. Colonial relations were governed by power, greed, and prestige, and justified by the language of religion, civilization, and status. Only in the nineteenth century did Europeans begin to transform colonized people into imperial subjects. Whether for profit or prestige, Western Europe, the United States, and Japan conquered nearly every landmass. Having achieved territorial integration and cultural unification at home, the modern colonizers sought the cultural integration of colonial subjects as well. As I argue in the following chapter, colonial authorities employed the categories of modern peoplehood to make sense of the colonized. Only then did racism become a correlative force of conquest and colonialism. Social Darwinism and other manifestations of racial science legitimated colonial rule, and racist practices, such as a ban on miscegenation, proliferated.

Nonetheless, colonial ideology was not uniformly racist even in the nineteenth century. Whatever the distorting and degrading impact modern colonialism had, its ideal justification was not so much racism but rather progress—the rehabilitation of the civilization argument—and imperial-national integration. In the high tide of colonial rule, we find simultaneous but antithetical movements toward exclusion and integration. The British rule in India, for example, initially saw its mission as bringing civilization, including Christianity, to South Asia, as Britain had earlier done for Ireland (Metcalf 1994:30). Furthermore, the British rule over India was analogous to the rule over people in Britain; the status elite lording over the status inferior (Cannadine 2001:8; cf. Hechter 1975:39–43). As *homo hierarchicus,* British rule extended domestic hierarchy to its colonies (Cannadine 1999: 126,145). After the 1867 Reform Act that greatly expanded male suffrage, colonial ideology enhanced the role of racism: "No longer was it possible . . . for Englishmen to conceive of the lower classes at home as in some measure equivalent to colonized peoples overseas" (Metcalf 1994:55). The problem with scientific racism was that Indians were part of the Aryan race (Metcalf 1994:83). More generally, British rule needed Indian collaborators (Metcalf 1994:185–199). Though racist sentiments against Irish or Indians existed (Lebow 1976:40), the British elite sought to justify colonial rule as part of imperial integration. That is, Britannia, like Romanitas, was open to the peripheral aspirant.

European expansion—as Montaigne presciently appreciated—wreaked havoc nearly everywhere. However, its cause was not racism. In general, unsavory acts generate ad hoc justifications that rely on a repertoire of available and accepted tropes. One does not need to think of others as alien to steal from or to kill them, as the story of Abel and Cain suggests. Racial ideology became increasingly important in the nineteenth century, but we would be remiss to neglect other practices and ideas that sustained colonial rule before then and even during the heyday of modern European colonialism.

8

Wasn't American slavery based on racism? Status categories were often racialized and slaves were often conquered people. The correlation between slaves and ethnoracial groups seems inescapable.

Racism did not cause slavery; slavery did not imply race (cf. Davis 1984: 33). In classical Rome, even as the Stoics stressed the humanity of slaves, what mattered was the deeply entrenched hierarchy (Bradley 1994:173). Slaves constituted a status category independent of their linguistic, religious, or cultural background. Once freed, their erstwhile status did not bar them from becoming a famous philosopher (Epictetus) or even an emperor (Pertinax, the son of a freed slave) (Brunt 1990:118). Outside of its entwinement with status hierarchy, racial inequality was not necessarily freestanding. After all, of 55 slave societies, three-fourths of them enslaved members of the same racial group (Patterson 1982:176). Today, race is largely irrelevant for the estimated 27 million slaves around the world (Bales 1999:8–11).

Even in North America, where slavery and race overlapped most powerfully, servitude, whether black slave or white servant, was relatively color blind in the seventeenth century (Jordan 1968:44–48; Morgan 1975:313). Slavery was a matter of status, not race. The search for slave labor initially targeted American Indians and white Europeans (Williams 1966:7,18). As Eric Williams (1966:19) argued: "White servitude was the historic base upon which Negro slavery was constructed." Furthermore, African slaves and European, principally British, indentured servants "seemed to be remarkably unconcerned about their visible physical differences. They toiled together in the fields, fraternized during leisure hours, and, in and out of wedlock, collaborated in siring a numerous progeny. Though the first southern white settlers were quite familiar with rigid class lines, they were as unfamiliar with a caste system as they were with chattel slavery" (Stampp 1956:21). In Britain, slavery before 1730 was not racially identified (Colley 2002: 63). British colonizers were color blind in their ferocious treatment of Irish and Caribbean islanders, treating poor whites and blacks equally abysmally (Morgan 1975:325; Allen 1994:31–35).

In short, race, slavery, and African Americans should not be conflated for all times and places. In the notorious article of the Constitution, it is to slaves, not to African Americans, that the three-fifths metric applies. Slave law was not the same as race law given "problems in determining race when it mattered, miscegenation on a scale large enough to complicate line-drawing, and manumission with its concomitant creation of an underused, but apparently ineradicable, class of free blacks" (Tushnet 1981:43).

Rather than race, slavery was a status category; rather than racism, it was primarily justified by religion. "Enslavement was captivity, the loser's lot in a contest of power. Slaves were infidels or heathens" (Jordan 1968:56). Conversely, conversion provided a potent rationale for manumission (Fredrickson 1981:70–74). Symptomatically, the principal literary representation of the African slave in the late seventeenth century, Aphra Behn's *Oroonoko* (1688), depicted the tragic fate of an African prince. Redolent though it was of the noble savage stereotype, Behn's characterization would hardly qualify as racist.

Slavery and race began to be equated in the late seventeenth century. The influx of British migrants declined by the 1680s when the availability of African slaves was at an all-time high (Galenson 1981:153). The labor market situation and the unfettered power of the planter class closed the possibility of acculturation or conversion (Elkins 1976:47–52,63), which allowed the language of race to inflect the discourse of slavery (Morgan 1975:313; Oakes 1990:51–56). The ideas of white supremacy and black inferiority mutually reinforced racial identities. By the rise of abolitionist agitation in the U.S. North in the 1830s, the institutions and ideologies of race-based slavery became entrenched in the South (Faust 1981:4; cf. Berlin 1998:358).

Assaults on slavery generated justificatory discourses in the South, which did not rely on racism. Not biology but the Bible underpinned the Southern proslavery argument (Faust 1981:10; cf. Davis 1975:523). If the Northern abolitionists condemned slavery as a moral evil, then the Southerners replied that "slavery was a positive moral good—a necessary arrangement sanctioned in Scripture and thus by God Himself" (Elkins 1976:36). In the 1860 compendium, *Cotton Is King*, Albert Taylor Bledsoe (1860:273) wrote that slavery "is in accordance with the will of God and the designs of his providence, is conducive to the highest, purest, best interests of mankind." Insofar as slavery was justified by Christianity, the manifest argument was not racist. John Henry Hopkins (1864:21) observed that "the highly privileged Anglo-Saxon . . . now stands at the head, although our ancestors were heathen barbarians only two thousand years ago." In other words, racial inequality in and of itself did not legitimate slavery. Fred A. Ross (1857:6) exclaimed: "*God never intended the relation of master and slave to be perpetual. Let him give up the theory of Voltaire, that the negro is of a different species. Let him yield the semi-infidelity of Agassiz, that God created different races of the same species.*" That is, the biblical argument was inimical to racial or racist argument because it asserted human monogeny.

Beyond the Bible, the principal Southern justification for slavery was to defend its way of life. Slavery was inextricably intertwined in the economic and social life of the antebellum South. The Reactionary Enlightenment—what Louis Hartz (1955:176) called "the only Western conservatism America has ever had"—was an impassioned defense of the Southern way of life, and particularly the Southern form of slavery (cf. Wyatt-Brown 2001:142). One of the first books with sociology in the title to appear in the United States, Henry Hughes's *A Treatise on Sociology* (1854:227), proposed and defended warranteeism, or paternalistic society, as a superior form of social life. "In the United States South, warrantees are persons who have all their rights. . . . Their slavery is nominal only; and the name, a wrong to the warrantee States." Another pioneering sociology title, George Fitzhugh's (1965:244) *Sociology for the South* (1850), assaulted the capitalist North: "The sordid spirit of mammon presides over all, and from all proceed the sighs and groans of the oppressed." In contrast, Southern slavery society is "the best form of society yet devised for the masses" (Fitzhugh 1965:162): "We provide for each slave, in old age and in infancy, in sickness and in health, not according to his labor, but according to his wants. . . . A southern farm is the beau ideal of Communism" (Fitzhugh 1965: 244). Echoing the moral imperative of Marx's critique of the Gotha Program, Fitzhugh (1960:201) offered a robust sociological defense of slavery, "a benign and protective institution," as a quasi-communist utopia (cf. Ashworth 1995:228–246).

In effect, Reactionary Enlightenment thinkers envisioned the South as a status society, with whites constituting various degrees of nobility and blacks being plebeians. Slave status was about honor and status, not race and class (cf. Wyatt-Brown 1982:362; Fehrenbacher 2001:306). If honor was associated with freedom, dishonor was equated with slavery (Oakes 1990:16). It was not racism in and of itself, but rather status society and slavery as its central institution that buttressed Southern intransigence. In this regard, the principal audience of proslavery arguments may well have been non-slaveholders in the South, as slaveholders sought status alliance with non-slaveholders (Oakes 1990:129–133).

Racism, to be sure, played a role in the Southern defense of slavery. In contradistinction to ancient Athenian or Roman or modern Brazilian slaves (Degler 1971:88–92), the slave status in the South had become permanent and intergenerational (cf. Oakes 1990:31–35). By the early nineteenth century, the modern idea of racial hierarchy complemented the traditional notion of natural inequality (Genovese 1974:1–7; Oakes 1990:130–134). Josiah C. Nott (1844), who translated Gobineau's chief work into English, attempted to ground slavery on the ethnological inferiority of African Americans (cf. Dain 2002:227–237). Racial science was most explicitly applied in the slave trade. The technology of differentiating human commodity, not unlike veterinary science for domestic animals, revealed the modern face of the peculiar institution (cf. Johnson 1999:146–161). But the science, at least in retrospect, seems merely a fantastic legitimation of slavery. For example, S. A. Cartwright (1860:727) argued that the prognathous race, or Africans, welcomed punishment: "A remarkable ethnological peculiarity of the prognathous race is, that any deserved punishment, inflicted on them with a switch, cowhide, or whip, puts them into good humor with themselves and the executioner of the punishment."

The Southern racist argument was careful not to contradict Christianity and echoed the paternalistic conservatism of the Reactionary Enlightenment. Race was peripheral because racial science in particular and science in general were subservient to biblical discourse. Monogeny was a dogma. Polygeny was very much a minority view, bordering on the heretical. Biology eventually superseded theology, as the American School, including Samuel George Morton and George R. Gliddon, challenged the belief in monogeny on a more scientific and empirical basis. Because many of them were abolitionists and anticlerical to boot, their argument was inimical to the dominant Southern view (Bachman 1850:287; cf. Stanton 1960:193). Consider in this regard that John Scopes—usually depicted as a progressive hero battling Southern prejudice—used a "Darwinian" textbook, A Civic Biology (1914), by George Wilken Hunter, who wrote of the Caucasian race as "the highest type of all" (Gould 1999:168).

The demise of slavery as an institution and a status unbound racism from the language of status and honor. The failure of Reconstruction led to the rise of racial segregation and racist ideology (Foner 1988:588–601).

The post-Reconstruction South accentuated the simplification and strength of the color line that at once denied the reality of cross-race relations and intra-race tensions (cf. Scott 2000:79–83). The one-drop rule of defining African Americans—usually taken as a unique characteristic of U.S. slavery—became dominant (Degler 1971:101–105). Legal disenfranchisement and racial segregation reached their height between the 1890s and 1910s (Woodward 1974:97) when lynching symbolized the sheer dominance of white over black (Williamson 1984:183–189). While miscegenenation was common in antebellum South, interracial sex became taboo in the Jim Crow era (Genovese 1974:413–431; Williamson 1984:39–42,307). Exemplified by Thomas Dixon's *The Leopard's Spots* (1902) and *The Clansmen* (1905), as well as Ulrich B. Phillips's *American Negro Slavery* (1918), the late nineteenth century and early twentieth century represenatations of and writings on slavery and African Americans, both in the South and the North, assumed African American racial inferiority (Pressly 1965:266–272; Elkins 1976:10–13). As Ira Berlin (1998:364) writes: "Behind the most vicious assaults on the character of people of African descent during the first two hundred years of American slavery stood a firm belief that, given an opportunity, black people would behave precisely like whites—which was what made African and African-American slaves at once so valuable and so dangerous. The new racism rejected this logic." The emancipation of slaves liberated racism.

9

The category of race is thus modern. Its most common contemporary definition—"one of the great divisions of mankind, having certain physical peculiarities in common," according to the *Oxford English Dictionary*—dates from the late eighteenth century. Previously, race referred to all manners of great divisions, such as gender (the race of women as used by Spenser and Steele) or wine (the race, or flavor, of wine) (cf. Conze 1984:137–141).

The very idea of human racial classification is usually traced to Johann Blumenbach's 1775 treatise, *De generis humani nativa varietate* [On the Natural Variety of Human Beings] (cf. Plischke 1937:71–74), although François Bernier and Immanuel Kant, among others, compete for the dubious distinction of inventing the concept of race (Conze 1984:142–150; Bernasconi 2001:12–16). Blumenbach proposed a fourfold classification of human beings, but he noted that "when the matter is thoroughly considered, you see that all do so run into one another, and that one variety of mankind does so sensibly pass into the other that you cannot mark out the limits between them" (Blumenbach 1973a:98). In addition to the gradual, quantitative nature of human variations, he argued that environmental factors affect physiology, such as skin color or head size (Blumenbach 1973a:121). By the third edition of 1795, Blumenbach (1973b:264) proposed five principal varieties of human beings, but he remained steadfast in his environmentalism, and stressed the biological unity of humanity (Blumenbach 1973b:276). Although he suggested that Caucasians are the most primeval of the five varieties and wrote of people in Georgia as "the most beautiful race of men" (Blumenbach 1973b:269), he countered the nascent racist ideas of the time by asserting "the perfectibility of the mental faculties and the talents of the negro" (Blumenbach 1973c:308). Quite clearly, Blumenbach was neither a racist nor a racial scientist in the modern sense.

In eighteenth-century Europe, the unity of the human race was taken for granted, whether because of the Enlightenment belief in universal human nature or the biblical belief in human monogeny (cf. Burrow 1966: 52; Glacken 1967:620). As Edmund Burke (1968:11), often taken to be the father of conservatism, wrote in 1757: "On a superficial view, we may seem to differ very widely from each other in our reasonings, and no less in our pleasures. . . . It is probable that the standard both of reason and Taste is the same in all human creatures." Environmental factors explained human variability, exemplified by Montesquieu's De l'esprit des lois [The Spirit of Laws] (1748) (cf. Wheeler 2000:21–26). Buffon, for example, argued that human "variations were in any case slight, and they might disappear in time: blacks transplanted to Denmark would regain the original whiteness of the species" (Roger 1997:466).

Race was reified as a biologically based descent group, or a permutation of modern peoplehood in the nineteenth century (Stepan 1982:109). Philology laid the basis of racial science, stressing kinship and genealogy and downplaying theology and Christian universalism (Trautmann 1987:229; Olender 1992:136–142). The decline of Christianity and status society and the coeval rise of evolutionary theory enhanced the prestige of racial science (cf. Burrow 2000:103). What had been explained by climate or culture came to be explained by innate differences.

Nonetheless, as late as the early twentieth century, the lay usage of race continued to refer to any large human grouping based on geography or religion, class or color (cf. Barkan 1992:2). Symptomatically, the dominant meaning of anthropology in the nineteenth century was the study of what unites human beings. It is only in the twentieth-century connotation that it became the study of what separates human beings.

What promoted racial discourse was the modern state and biopolitics. Modern European states extolled their nationals and denounced their enemies in the language of race and racial destiny. Symptomatically, the precursor of *Foreign Affairs* was entitled *Journal of Race Development* (1910). Nationalist myths were often articulated as racial myths. Herein lies the cause of the proliferation of races in the late nineteenth century. Fueled by and fused with nationalism, the hitherto unified Caucasian race splintered into nation-based races (cf. Kevles 1985:46; Gossett 1997:345). The racial science of Blumenbach or Linnaeus was useless in claiming, for example, France's supremacy over Germany because it conflated them. After all, the aristocratic ideology of France—the Franks conquering the Gauls—made the German barbarians the true ancestors of French people (Geary 2002: 20). At the same time, European states seized racial science to justify colonial domination. Karl Pearson (1937:31), for example, found scientific legitimation for "the race of white men" to rule over nonwhite races. European conquests were retrospectively emancipated from their Christian mooring to rest on the biologistic notion of European superiority. Race became a pan-European discourse that at once articulated national greatness and justified colonial domination.

Racial science became salient as part and parcel of biopolitics or the effort to forge normal or normative citizens, as I elaborate in Chapter 4. Most systematically, eugenics—coined in 1883 by Francis Galton—promised to be a true science, with practical applications. Experts on race and eugenics focused almost exclusively on inequality within. That is, they became concerned more with status or class than with race in and of itself. In the course of the twentieth century, however, race referred increasingly to incompletely nationalized people, or racial minority. Racial science supplanted the discourses of status and religion to emerge as a dominant discourse on inequality. Its horrific apotheosis was in the extermination politics of Nazi Germany, which I examine in Chapter 5.

Gobineau offers an exemplary and intriguing instance. Celebrated or vilified as the founding theorist of racial inequality, he (1966:25) provided in the 1853–55 treatise *De l'inegalité des races* [The Inequality of Races] a universal history of the decline or degeneration of nations. Although he asserted the existence of three races (black, yellow, and white), he found the same three races in France (Biddiss 1970:119). That is, his specific concerns focused on national groups and nonnational status inequality. Gobineau (1966:25) exhorted: "The man of a decadent time, the *degenerate* man properly so called, is a different being, from the racial point of view, from the heroes of the great ages." Who were the "heroes of the great ages"? "Everything great, noble, and fruitful in the works of man on this earth, in science, art, and civilization, derives from a single starting-point, is the development of a single germ and the result of a single thought; it belongs to one family alone, the different branches of which have reigned in all the civilized countries of the universe" (Gobineau 1966:xv). In other words, conquering aristocrats and conquered hordes are distinct races that inter-mingled over time (cf. Voegelin 1997:170). Not only was he antidemocratic and antiegalitarian, he was also antinationalist because of the nationalist neglect of status differences (Biddiss 1970:172). He retained the transna-tional ethos of aristocracy, and was anti-patriotic in our sense, as he shifted his enthusiasm from France to England to Germany (cf. Voegelin 1997: 220). While he was a pioneer of racial theory, he remained ensconced in the world of status hierarchy that was in decline during the nineteenth century (cf. Lukács 1980:679–682). In other words, he remained an un-reconstructed aristocratic elitist.

Gobineau's concern with the masses can be found in the most developed strand of racial science: the eugenics movement that flourished in the early twentieth century. The idea of selective breeding synthesized the idea of heredity, the practice of animal breeding, and the politics of mass unrest (cf. Stepan 1991:22–26). True to its proximate inspiration in animal breeding, the positive program was to breed better citizens. Galton (1909: 36) declared: "The aim of Eugenics is to represent each class or sect by its best specimens" (cf. Davenport 1911:1). The stress was on class, not race (cf. Galton 1892:312). Galton (1909:24) encouraged high-class offspring: "An enthusiasm to improve the race would probably express itself by granting diplomas to select class of young men and women, by encouraging their intermarriages, by hastening the time of marriage of women of that high class, and by provision for rearing children healthily." Insofar as he sought national improvement, he advocated "the policy of attracting emi-nently desirable refugees," noting "how large a proportion of the eminent men of all countries bear foreign names" (Galton 1892:346). He did not assume the natural superiority of the English.

Eugenics seeks to promote the reproduction of the best and the brightest.

If one believes in traditional aristocracy, then the inescapable conclusion would be to promote aristocratic sexual activity. In this line of reasoning, Frederick Adams Woods (1906:284) sought to prove Galton's law of ancestral heredity. In his study of European royalty, he observed: "The two fields of activity in which royalty have most distinguished themselves, have either been military leadership, or leadership in affairs of state." Hence: "The very formation of royal families was thus a question of selection of the most able in government and war" (Woods 1906:302), though the royalty have traditionally achieved their preeminence by dint of their genius to be born into the right pair of parents. The royalty gave Woods (1906: 303) hope for the future of humanity: "We have found among royal families the morally superior surviving, and in the inheritance of mental and moral excellence we see ground for a belief in the necessary progress of mankind." Ironically, in modern genetics textbooks, European royalty exemplifies the ill effects of inbreeding, such as the prevalence of hemophilia in the House of Windsor (cf. Ritvo 1997:118).

Eugenics reflected the Social Darwinist mindset. In promoting racial renewal and combating racial degeneration (Pick 1989:11–27), the positive project of eugenics became predominantly preventive and prophylactic, or dysgenics. The fear of the dangerous classes in late nineteenth-century European societies or the anxiety about national survival after a military defeat (France after the Franco-Prussian War or Germany after World War I) generated widespread worries about racial, or national, capacity (Pick 1989:222; Weindling 1989:305). As Charles Féré wrote in 1888: "The impotent, the mad, criminals or decadents of every form, must be considered as the waste-matter of adaptation, the invalids of civilization" (Pick 1989:32). In Ludwig Gumplowicz's *Der Rassenkampf* (1928:207–212), first published in 1883, the race struggle is between what we would call class or status groups. As I have emphasized, its most common premodern articulation denoted distinct status groups. Or as Madison Grant (1916:49) put it in *The Passing of the Great Race*: "The most practical and hopeful method of race improvement is through the elimination of the least desirable elements in the nation by depriving them of the power to contribute to future generations." Over time, then, the negative project of eliminating class or status inferiors became paramount. That is, eugenics entailed the study of "what classes of the community are reproducing themselves fastest," in order to avoid "the threatened growth of lunacy and pauperism" (Whetham and Whetham 1909:208,210).

In the United States, the negative program of elimination dominated.

Samuel J. Holmes's *The Trend of the Race* (1921:267) was concerned less with other races or racial mixing and more with intra-racial, or class, inequality. "An ignorant and poverty-ridden proletariat will multiply rapidly through sheer lack of restraint" (Holmes 1921:382). In order to prevent the inferior sorts from reproducing rapidly, he appealed to the "eugenic conscience." "Those who have been most fortunate in the possession of heredity gifts should feel that upon them rests an unusual obligation to see that their qualities are not allowed to perish from the earth" (Holmes 1921: 383). In contrast, dysgenic reproduction was to be discouraged (cf. Davenport 1911:8). In this vein, the sociologist Frank H. Hankins (1926:275) argued: "But the present tendencies toward dysgenic reproduction are certain in the course of a few generations to draw out of the population and destroy much of its hereditary and potential genius. This is not a question of preserving the Anglo-Saxon stock. Much of that stock is utterly worthless and should be sterilized at the earliest possible date. Nor it is a question of drawing racial lines and cultivating a sense of racial caste. This increases social frictions and reduces social efficiency." Although Hankins (1926:ix) did not believe in racial equality, he wrote favorably of "mixed racial ancestry."

Thus, eugenics followed the mandate of the modern state and biopolitics. This explains, in part, the international appeal of eugenics in the early twentieth century (Adams 1990:217). Where science in general and biopolitics in particular established legitimacy and supremacy, eugenics soon followed from intellectual centers. From Galton's England, eugenics spread not only to Europe but also to Asia and the Americas (Stepan 1991:4–9). Although eugenics and racial science expressed racist sentiments, and eugenics at times focused exclusively on racist policies—such as in Nazi Germany and early twentieth-century United States and Latin America (Kühl 1994:70–76; cf. Kevles 1985:74)—the racist focus was a subset of a more general concern with biopolitics and state power. Racial science in pre-Nazi Germany focused more on class than race (Pine 1997:11; cf. Weindling 1989:499–503). Only retrospectively has eugenics become racial science par excellence, when it had frequently regarded race and nation interchangeably, and, more interestingly, highlighted the significance of status and class (cf. Haller 1963:150; Searle 1981:217).

Eugenics and racism should not be conflated; race or racism is not necessary for eugenics. In the near future, we may very well see social groupings based on an individualized notion of genetic fitness. Advances in reproductive technology and genetic engineering may facilitate social selection that allows for a personalized eugenic. Instead of status or race, future bioengineers may very well present what they will regard as a truly objective ground for social identification and distinction, along the line of Aldous Huxley's novel *Brave New World* (1932) or Andrew Niccol's film *Gattaca* (1997).

10

In the early twenty-first century, the popular category of race enmeshes itself in nature: the realm of the objective, immutable, and necessary. Racist discourse expresses itself in the language of permanence or destiny, which echoes the pioneering theorists of race. As Gobineau (1966:151) declared: "Thus the human groups are unequal in beauty; and this inequality is rational, logical, permanent, and indestructible." Or as Robert Knox (1850: 90) put it: "Race is everything; literature, science, art—in a word, civilization, depends on it." Given its foundation in biology, racial characteristics are immutable and transhistorically valid. Albert Gehring (1908:4) stated that the "fundamental distinction between the arts of the races, distinctions which in a general way are valid for all times and nationalities. . . . Graeco-Latin art-works tend toward clearness and simplicity, Germanic ones toward complexity." No one has demonstrated that characteristics that human cultures, past and present, have valued—morality, intelligence, or beauty—are unevenly distributed among different races. Or, for that matter, no one has proven the viability of racial classification and categorization. Nonetheless, whether in terms of differences in intelligence or character, racial science insinuates itself in the work of social distinction. Scientifically discredited, it survives as folk wisdom.

Certainly, much of the evidence and conclusions of racial science seem fanciful in retrospect, and what are repugnant to contemporaries are easy to castigate, whether on scientific or moral grounds. Yet it would be misleading to regard past discourses and representations in the light of contemporary concerns and values, or to lump all racial scientists and to condemn them simply as fanatics and ideologues. For one thing, we would miss some of the animating impulses of racial science, including, paradoxically, the relative lack of interest in race, as we saw for eugenics.

The temptation to treat race and racism as transhistorical and transcultural concepts is beguiling. Yet race is a social and, hence, historically transient category. As we have seen, repeated efforts to justify racial ontology have failed against the recalcitrant reality of variation, hybridity, and history. Although it seeks to anchor itself in the realm of biology, its putative natural foundation does not distinguish itself from many other important social categories. The epistemic work of social distinction highlights the natural in the social. Insofar as we restrict the range of racism to beliefs about racial inequality, the search for its manifestation in antiquity or the age of European expansion (Delacampagne 1983:297–300; Geiss 1988:16–20) would distort our understanding of the past. Whether in inchoate forms by early European cosmographers or in more systematic manners by nineteenth-century biologists, race sought scientific grounding. However, race became salient precisely when it was nationalized, or articulated along or against the discourse of modern peoplehood. As I elaborate in Chapter 4, the establishment of modern racial discourse depended in part on the displacement of categorical inequality—status distinction and discrimination—onto the plane of horizontal distinction. Only then did race enter national political discourse from its previous perch in speculative anthropology.

Racial science has been the target of righteous indignation by contemporary scholars (Appiah 1996; Gilroy 2000). In concert with the civil rights movement in the United States, the 1960s witnessed an efflorescence of counter-racist writings (Livingstone 1962:279; Washburn 1963:531). It would be misleading to see the mid-1960s cascade as the culmination of scientific progress and moral uplift. The post–World War II international organizations, such as UNESCO, underscored the biological and moral unity of humanity (Barkan 1992:341). In the United States, many scholars had written eloquently against the race myth before World War II (Radin 1934; Barzun 1937; Snyder 1939). Although the Nazis probably did more than any book or movement to forestall racial science, the popularity of eugenics had generated powerful counterblasts against racial science before the Nazi seizure of power (Hertz [1928] 1970:14–17; Hogben 1931:122–127; Huxley and Haddon 1935:106–109). Darwin had provided an argument against racial classification. Indeed, the earliest articulations of anti-racism—here limited to the assertion that human beings cannot be divided into biological races—are as old as racial science itself. In the germinal period of racial science—the mid-eighteenth century—there were well-reasoned critiques by Herder and Rousseau, as well as Alexander von Humboldt and Wilhelm von Humboldt (Montagu 1965:37). Racist and counter-racist writings are coeval.

Why does racial science have such regenerative power in spite of its intellectual shortcomings? Whence the will to classify human beings and to ground it in nature? The impulse toward racial classification rests on the phenomenology of human variety that is simultaneously a naturalizing ideology. Categorical divisions are consequences of power relations, institutions, and discourses that sustain them, and categories become enmeshed in our understanding of reality. As I elaborate in Chapter 6, racial science is an instance of a more general effort to ground human difference in nature, transmogrifying contigent perception into primordial essence. In the era of religious wars in Europe, God was an indispensable hypothesis. Just as theology was inevitably called on to define and defend Christians from non-Christians, biology since the nineteenth century has been used to define and defend racial differences. Better science will not expunge the category of race or cognate categories of peoplehood because modern peoplehood is the indisputable hypothesis in the era of the modern state.

Modern State / Modern Peoplehood

"Do you know what the proletariat is? Masses of men who collectively love peace and abhor war," asked and answered Jean Jaurès in July 1914 (Haupt 1972:11). He believed in proletarian pacifism and socialism as the fulfillment of *la patrie* (Jaurès 1931:292). Gavrilo Princip's bullet shattered these ideals mere days after his speech, and Jaurès himself was murdered in the same month. The allegiance of the Second International—"the most important anti-militarist political force in the world" (Haupt 1972:1)—shifted from international socialism to patriotic nationalism. V. I. Lenin (1964: 123), who derided "the defence of the fatherland" as "a capitalist fraud," was able to achieve a socialist revolution in only one country, thereby casting socialism in the crucible of the modern state.

World War I proved patriotic nationalism as a potent unit of political identification and military mobilization. Stefan Zweig (1987:173) recalled the euphoric unity forged by the Great War: "As never before, thousands and hundreds of thousands felt . . . that they belong together. . . . All differences of class, rank and language were flooded over at that moment by the rushing feeling of fraternity." The protection of individual freedom became inextricable from the ideal of national self-determination, the reigning principle of the Treaty of Versailles. The sanctity of national borders manifested itself in the tragedy of trench warfare. Millions were said to have died for the sake of their nation, and nationalism was frequently cited as the single most important cause (Taylor 1958:527; cf. Hinsley 1963:289–308).

In this chapter, I explore the formation and dissemination of modern peoplehood in Europe and its spread to the non-European world. Although contingent causes, parameters, and tempos differ across each polity, I focus on their significant similarities. Geopolitics ultimately shaped national borders, and the modern state was crucial in forging and disseminating peoplehood identity. The infrastructural development of the modern state nationalized the population, superseding subnational (e.g., village) and supranational (e.g., religion) sources of identification. The democratic revolution destroyed status hierarchy and hastened the aristocratization of the masses. Modern peoplehood, in short, is the product and predicate of the modern state, becoming a regulative ideal that governed political, intellectual, and scientific discourses. Modern colonialism spread it to the non-European world, and by the middle of the twentieth century, it had become a dominant way to classify and identify human beings. Everywhere a population (a geographical or administrative category) transformed into a people (a self-conscious entity).

2

The boundaries of the modern state provided the proximate mold of peoplehood identity. Cultural integration accentuated national commonality over local variation. By intensifying and expanding its dominion, the complex of organizations that we call the state developed rapidly. Indeed, the development of state institutions—education and judiciary, military, and welfare—simultaneously constituted and integrated the polity by unifying language and law, culture and currency. The territory of the state thereby defined a significant and substantive space that differentiated itself from outside. Status integration created formal equality, which superseded status or qualitative inequality. Most people within a polity came to share an inclusionary identity. The congruence of the state and peoplehood went hand in hand with the racial, ethnic, or national isomorphism of the rulers and the ruled (cf. Gellner 1983:1). Modern state making and the democratic revolution, in other words, transformed people in itself (population) to people for itself (peoplehood). The modern state is the objective correlative of modern peoplehood.

The modern state monopolizes political and military power within a delimited territory. It is distinct from premodern polities in combining the cohesive city-state ideal of republican virtue and the expansive rule of empires (cf. Strayer 1970:10). This presupposes a new conception of political space. The realm of the early modern European state or empire was geo-

graphically indeterminate and historically fluctuating. Much of the periphery constituted frontiers where central rule was nominal in character.
Ecclesiastical and local authorities competed with royal power. Linguistic
and cultural variation reigned. Wars led to a radical redrawing of maps. As
late as the eighteenth century, the Habsburg Empire acquired a greater part
of Hungary from the Ottoman Empire and southern Netherlands from
Spanish rule, while France annexed Lorraine, Naples, and Sicily, and the
Russian Empire gained Estonia and Livonia from Sweden. Eighteenth-
century European diplomats partitioned without qualm what their
twentieth-century counterparts would have regarded as integral polities
(Schroeder 1994:vii). Beyond territorial reconfiguration, people came and
went without official tags of territorial belonging. The term foreigner frequently referred to everyone outside of one's locality (cf. Noiriel 1988:76).

Modern state boundaries are definite and determinate. After the Treaty
of Westphalia, the state emerged as the fundamental unit of sovereignty
(Smith 1989:35–41), characterized by control over contiguous territory.
By the late nineteenth century, Frederick Jackson Turner (1963:28) described Europe as a place where "a fortified boundary line [runs] through
dense population," in contrast to frontiers—"the meeting point between
savagery and civilization" (Turner 1963:28)—that still remained in the
United States. In modern polities, frontiers disappear, boundaries are
meaningful, and border surveillance is the norm (Prescott 1987:12; Sahlins
1989:186–192). The state reigns as the sole political and military authority
and supersedes ecclesiastical and local political powers. It defines and ad-
ministers a space that is integrated by communication and transportation
networks (cf. Alliès 1980:146–167). Modern geography and cartography
inscribe exact borderlines, inventing the very idea of territoriality as a classified, bordered, and controlled area (Sack 1986:28). Territorial rights become grounded in history, often claimed from time immemorial, so that
wars are fought over a symbolic stretch of no-man's-land. Irredentism—a
reconfiguration of the Christian missionary ideal—and secessionism
emerge as serious issues, leading a contemporary scholar to wonder why
"neither Plato, Hobbes, Locke, Rousseau, Hegel, Marx, nor Mill devoted
any serious attention to secession" (Buchanan 1991:vii). The integrity and
independence of states become sacrosanct (Schroeder 1994:800). People
cannot come and go as they please without state-sanctioned mechanisms
of identification and permission. The term foreigner comes to refer to nonnationals or noncitizens (Torpey 2000:158–167).

In addition to cultural integration, status integration occurs. In terms of politics, sovereignty—"a final and absolute authority in the political community" (Hinsley 1986:1)—shifts from the divinity and the personal rule of the monarch to the people and the impersonal rule of the bureaucracy. Medieval Europe lacked a conception of sovereignty (Hinsley 1986:60–69), albeit the idea of reason of state had emerged as early as the thirteenth century (Post 1964:301–310). The classical conception of Jean Bodin or Thomas Hobbes championed monarchal rule, and sovereignty remained close to its etymological meaning denoting superiors, as in Augustin Thierry's idea of "great chain of duties" (Jouvenel 1957:171). Bodin (1962: 84,98), the pioneering theorist of sovereignty, defined it in the late sixteenth century as "the most high, absolute, and perpetuall power," which allows the sovereign, or the king, to promulgate "laws vnto the subiects in generall, and without their consent." Although Hobbes (1996:121,120) argued that "the Soveraigne Power is conferred by the consent of the People assembled," they should "conferre all their power and strength upon one Man, or upon one Assembly of Men." In both conceptualizations, sovereignty denoted royal power and jurisdiction over subjects, and not over a delimited territory (Febvre 1973:213).

Furthermore, nation or people referred principally to privileged, not to all, denizens (Dann 1988:4,75). Bodin (1962:68) took status hierarchy for granted. Subjects were voiceless (Poggi 1978:67–71), and in a sense were not even people. According to Hobbes (1998:95): "Prior to the formation of a commonwealth a *People* [*Populus*] does not exist, since it was not then a person but a crowd [*Multitudo*] of individual persons." Not surprisingly, Bodin and Hobbes bypassed race, ethnicity, and nation in discussing the sources of sovereignty (d'Entrèves 1967:170). The Treaty of Westphalia presupposed "sovereignty as belonging to the ruler rather than the people" (Shaw 2000:31). As Marshall Ignacy Potocki, one of the putatively enlightened fathers of Poland, put it as late as 1789: "Our programme refers only to the nation and its citizens, but in fact the nation is the First Estate, and the citizens are the nobility" (Geremek 1996:168).

The modern conception of sovereignty, exemplified by Rousseau and expressed in the 1776 Declaration of Independence and the 1789 Déclarations des droits de l'homme et du citoyen, rests on an inclusionary ideal of the people. The decline of kingship and religious authority occurred in tandem with the rise of the people (Bendix 1978:5–9). In the modern ideal of popular sovereignty, citizens constitute the ultimate authority (Hinsley

1986:156; cf. Rousseau 1994:140). The republican notion of citizenship is not a matter of ethnic or cultural distinction, but rather an expression of status or vertical integration. It refers to the people, the commoners, or the Third Estate, with antimonarchal and antiaristocratic overtones (Dann 1988:8; cf. Talmon 1960:283). Represented though they may be in governance—representation itself is a modern idea (Pitkin 1967:2)—people or nation rules. While premodern empires or absolutist states did not rely on popular legitimacy, the modern state, whether authoritarian or democratic, must cultivate it. Already by 1749, Bolingbroke (1965:87) had to justify monarchy by arguing for "a Patriotic King at the head of an united people." Royal patriotism transmogrified into popular nationalism; the object of loyalty shifted from the sovereign (king) to the state (people). The transfigured royalty, however, frequently served as the symbol and proof of national antiquity and continuity.

Status integration underlies the modern ideas about society, culture, and peoplehood. The rise of popular sovereignty is coeval with the emergence of civil society as a key arena of politics (Poggi 1978:77). The creation of the public sphere is part and parcel of the democratic revolution (cf. Habermas 1962:28–41). While the European notion of society—the French *monde* or the German *Sozietät*—referred to the upper echelon as late as the eighteenth century, the modern idea of society—the French *société* or the German *Gesellschaft*—embraced the whole populace (Wolf 2001:323–326). In so doing, the idea of the people loses its pejorative connotation as rabbles or masses, and joins the hitherto restricted realm of high society. Simultaneously, national boundaries circumscribe and define society and culture. Indeed, the very idea of the population emerges in the eighteenth century as the state defines the social (cf. Le Bras 2000:347).

The epistemic shift is clear in high philosophy. In spite of his impeccable Enlightenment credentials, Kant (1964:658) divided *Volk* (*populus*) into two groups: *Nations* (*gens*) and *Pöbel* (*vulgus*). The vulgar masses are "uncivilized" and therefore excluded from the laws. G. W. F. Hegel (1991:340) defined "the people" as "that category of citizens *who do not know their own will*," and continued to discuss estates, although his ideal of popular sovereignty approximates the modern notion of an inclusionary and involuntary peoplehood (Hegel 1991:318–321). Not coincidentally, the state forms the people in Hegel's view. The gradual attenuation of status hierarchy ushers in the universe of modern peoplehood, which is articulated for example by Elisha Mulford (1971:61) in 1887: "The people in its organic unity, constitutes the nation. It is not a sum or an aggregate of men . . . it is not a mob, but a people; not a vulgus but a populus." Between Kant and Mulford, then, we witness the transition to the conceptual universe of modern peoplehood.

The transformation in territoriality and sovereignty cannot be told apart from the development of the modern state. The expansive and efficient bureaucracy—with its patrol and passports, control and customs—transmogrified monarchal realms and frontiers into state territories and boundaries. Institutions and ideologies of governance, very much in concert with the presumed unity of the nation, operated under the cultural understanding of the singular, reified state. The state projected itself as a unitary subject, a legacy of monarchal and imperial rule, as Leviathan. In controlling chains of command that diffused throughout the realm, however, the state in fact operated as Hydra. From education to the economy, the state was the supreme institution (Shennan 1974:107–111). The philosophy of Leviathan was also Erastian. The state replaced the church and secularized institutions and ideologies (Schmitt 1985:36). Pastoral duties and metaphysical ideas—the idea of good and evil, the custodial right over life and death—became the suzerainty of the state.

The possibility of national integration depended on the modern state's distinct capacity and conception of power. Early modern European states and empires were nominally absolutist. Yet, as much as they cultivated and wielded sovereign or despotic power, their institutional or disciplinary power was limited (cf. Mann 1993:59). The nineteenth-century Prussian jurist Felix Eberty believed as a child that "the king could cut off the noses and ears of all his subjects if he wished to do so" (Behrens 1985:41), but Frederick William had trouble filling positions with qualified bureaucrats and lacked systematic and effective means of exacting taxation (Behrens 1985:44,68–78). That is, the sovereign could summarily execute a subject, but could not collect taxes. Public finance reflected the monarch's needs in premodern Europe, and personal solicitations often amounted to a "begging tour" among local notables (Jouvenel 1957:178). State offices were bought, leading Jean-Baptiste Colbert to remark that the value of venal offices was greater than that of all the land in France (Behrens 1985:50). Expensive dynastic wars and opulent royal displays thrust most royal treasuries near the precipice of bankruptcy. The French Revolution, for instance, cannot be considered apart from the fiscal collapse of the ancient regime (Hobsbawm 1962:24).

In contrast, the development of the modern state was coeval with the growth of systematic tax collection (cf. Schumpeter 1991:108–116). By the eighteenth century, some state bureaucracies were professionalized toward Max Weber's celebrated ideal type (Fischer and Lundgreen 1975:560). If the modern state could not exist without systematic taxation, then tax collection could not exist without popular legitimacy. The ideal of no taxation without representation was not restricted to the American revolutionaries. It was the chief obligation of state membership, the price of popular sovereignty (Ardant 1975:234; Braun 1975:324). The modern practice of taxation, such as income tax, relies on effective bureaucracy and popular acquiescence (Webber and Wildavsky 1986:300–304).

Taxation was necessary because of warfare, perhaps the chief preoccupation of modern nation-states. To be sure, Thucydides (1.23) observed that war and state go hand in hand (cf. Herodotus 1.1), and Otto Hintze (1975:181) declared in 1906: "All state organization was originally military organization, organization for war." Organized life and warfare are inextricable. Although military expenditure frequently accounted for three-fourths of government revenues in premodern Europe (Behrens 1985:41; cf. Mann 1993:373), there was a military disjunction between state and society before the eighteenth century. Many premodern European wars focused on quelling internal dissidence, and the military doubled as the police (Zagorin 1982:ii,1–8). War was largely a matter for dynasties and other authorities, such as lords and churches, but not peoples (Best 1982: 16; van Creveld 1991:39). Early modern states relied on transnational nobles, foreign mercenaries, and the poor and the marginal in their domain (Kiernan 1965:121–133; Guerlac 1986:65–68). The warrior class equated honor and nobility, sharply demarcating the elite from the masses (Vagts 1967:68). Aristocratic values of status and honor permeated cosmopolitan officers (Best 1982:24–28).

In contrast, military and society became increasingly intertwined in the nineteenth century (van Creveld 1991:39). The militarization of society occurred simultaneously with the industrialization of war. Not only did the state monopolize the means of violence in its domain—as suggested in Weber's influential definition of the state—but also wars were fought in the name of, by, and for the people (cf. Luckham 1979:232–235). The nation, not the divinity or the royalty, became the ultimate justification for war. Rather than the poor, the marginalized, and the mercenary, the modern military relied on citizen soldiers (Parker 1988:46–52). The national isomorphism of officers and soldiers became the rule (Best 1982:53–59). The nationalization of previously supranational officers severed transnational ties that had tempered the intensity of warfare.

Mass militarism, exemplified by the postrevolutionary French *levée en masse*, emerged as a normative practice that saw its catastrophic consequence in the two world wars (Vagts 1967:116–128). Conscription became compulsory in most modern nation-states (Paret 1992:72), as the distinction between soldiers and citizens became blurred in modern warfare (Wright 1964:73). Military obligation was a crucial component of citizenship by the late nineteenth century (Paret 1992:49), when European education provided the physical and psychological preparation for patriotic warfare (Howard 1983:26). Mass conscription contributed to democratic citizenship in the form of extending male suffrage (Janowitz 1975:70). The expectation and experience of war entrenched the meaning of the nation at the popular level; warfare and propaganda promoted national consciousness. Nobles and masses alike became nationals, citizen soldiers. No longer the monopoly of the nobility, honor became the virtue of the whole nation. The modern military transformed into a professional and disciplined organization, an integral yet distinct part of the modern state, which in turn contributed to the making of the civilian government (Tilly 1990:122–126; cf. Mann 1993:438).

Needless to say, concrete changes were crepuscular, but it is useful to contrast the preceding night from the day of the modern state. Premodern states had neither the capacity nor the will to instill a common political-cultural identity. They lacked institutional power and infrastructural means, whether mass communication or universal and compulsory education, to instill a common identity over a large territory. More significantly, the dominant ideology of premodern polities was the superiority of the rulers over the ruled. Even if premodern rulers were capable asserting the identity of the rulers and the ruled, they would have had little interest in doing so. Given the lack of capacity and conception, national identity remained largely latent.

In contrast, the modern state defines a space where, ideally, a people share a single language, legal system, currency, and way of life. It claims its rightful rule over natural boundaries (geography) in the name of the people (society). In order to fight wars with citizen soldiers and to achieve popular legitimacy, citizenship becomes an expression of territorial belonging, grounded in history and nature. The modern state seeks to align language, religion, and culture with its territory, which in turn forms the basis of an involuntary identity. In short, it promotes national integration and disseminates national identity. Nationalism—the congruence of the boundaries of the state with the extent of the people, who are in turn sovereign—becomes a powerful ideal and a substantial reality of modern Europe.

3

The modern state is neither a unitary entity nor an autonomous power. Variation in state apparatus results from a confluence of political and bureaucratic struggles. Yet Tocqueville's (1955:57–60) observation that the state intensified and expanded its rule after the Revolution is true of non-French polities. In other words, state institutions and sovereignty, social-cultural integration, and the idea of an inclusive peoplehood developed in tandem. The causes of this trend can be seen in the fundamental forces of nineteenth-century Europe. Geopolitical competition forced all polities to enhance their war-making capacity by promoting taxation and conscription, which heightened the need for popular legitimacy and, hence, peoplehood identity. Another revolutionary force, capitalist industrialization, accelerated national integration. Popular upheaval demanded political participation and generated nationalized politics.

Nationalist, irredentist, and secessionist claims notwithstanding, military and diplomatic struggles shaped European political boundaries. Although the Treaty of Westphalia established the ideal of external noninterference and nonintervention, the reality of international politics since then has underscored the hypocrisy and strength of powerful states (Carr 1946:87; Krasner 1999:20). That is, territoriality is a negotiated outcome of interstate alliances and national conflicts. For example, the French revolutionaries reckoned the natural limits of France to include Savoy and Belgium, but they did not become part of France because of military defeats and diplomatic agreements (Woolf 1991:13). Similarly, the geography of the United States was far from fixed: "The natural boundaries at the west had been, in the closing years of the American Revolution, the Mississippi. In 1803 they had become, for Jeffersonians, the Rocky Mountains. In the 1840's they had become, for those who had vision, the Pacific Ocean; and for many, the continent, indeed, the hemisphere" (Merk 1966:33). It would have taken more than a devout belief in manifest destiny to discern the eventual extension of the United States in the early twenty-first century. Once established, however, territoriality seemed etched in stone, natural and obvious (cf. Alliès 1980:176–180; Foucher 1988:63).

Geopolitical competition facilitated the rise of the modern state. The medieval European ideal had projected the unity of Christendom that entwined politics and religion, whether in Dante's *Monarchia* or Marisilus of Padua's *Defensor Pacis* (Hinsley 1963:14–20). Monarchs and nobles paid scant attention to the subjects in their realm. Religious and monarchal ideals overshadowed any nascent appeal to the people. If the Treaty of Westphalia divorced religion from politics—the modern states system depended on the decline of Christendom (Rosenberg 1994:75)—then the Thirty Years War indelibly impressed on every potentate the imperative of military prowess. From the seventeenth century, modern nation-states proved their superiority in war making over empires and city-states (Tilly 1990:30; cf. Spruyt 1994:29–33). City-states or principalities were often unable to defend themselves against larger polities, whereas empires frequently failed to achieve successful military mobilization. The amalgamation of smaller units (city-states and principalities) or the differentiation of larger political entities (empires) transformed the map of Europe into a congeries of contiguous nation-states. While roughly two hundred autonomous polities existed in Europe around 1500 (and up to five hundred depending on the definition), only twenty-five or so states existed by the end of World War I (Tilly 1990:45).

Long-term trends were clear at least by the Treaty of Westphalia, but the French Revolution was the definitive landmark. The postrevolutionary French military success demonstrated and the Napoleonic victories proved the power of citizen soldiers and the efficacy of military nationalization (Vagts 1967:130–136; Brown 1995:121). The French military conquered neighboring territories and spread its revolutionary and republican ideals (Godechot 1988:18–26). Most European regimes attempted to restore the old dynastic order and to squelch the revolutionary ideals, but the successful states emulated, rather than resisted, the French model. Every state depended on citizen soldiers by the beginning of World War I. The dynamics of escalating obligations on subjects, especially conscription and taxation, required reciprocal privileges, such as political participation and social recognition. States sought not only to instill political loyalty from above, but also to incorporate the subject population by sharing sovereignty. Popular loyalty and political legitimacy went hand in hand. Post-

Napoleonic European states were the consequence of postrevolutionary geopolitics.

The states system imposed the imperative of state- and nation-building (cf. Wallerstein 1974–89:iii,170). Success in the new states system rested less on dynastic alliances and artful diplomacy and more on military and economic prowess. The 1815 Congress of Vienna, which featured Castlereagh, Metternich, and other diplomats to restore a European balance of power (Gulick 1967:301–309), was the last hurrah of transnational, dynastic politics. In the age of borders and barricades, territorial struggles and popular upheavals converged in being both about the nation. Diplomats shed their cosmopolitan and aristocratic garb and donned the uniform of nationalistic bureaucrats. By the 1860s, the diplomats of Prussia, the Italian states, and the Habsburg monarchy, who had been communicating in French, wrote to their home offices in their respective national languages (Taylor 1954:xxiii). In turn, the masses—whether from combat or education—began to differentiate friends from enemies, nationals from non-nationals. By the 1918 Treaty of Versailles, the ideal of national self-determination had become one of the reigning principles of international politics. As Henry Kissinger (1958:145) described the dramatic transformation of the European commonsense: "It would have occurred to no one in the eighteenth century that the legitimacy of a state depended on linguistic unity. It was inconceivable to the makers of the Versailles settlement that there might be any other basis for legitimate rule" (cf. Osiander 1994: 331).

Military and diplomatic competition was not the only force to promote state development and national integration. The quest for power necessitated the search for wealth, which by the nineteenth century clearly pointed to the dynamics of industrialization. The mechanization of war, if nothing else, demanded the industrialization of the economy. Wealth and technology highlighted the importance of merchants and industrialists, who sought to expunge tolls and other impediments to interregional trade and to achieve the standardization of weights and measures, currencies, and mercantile laws and regulations. The French state, for example, intervened aggressively in the economy, erecting infrastructures and exacting taxation (Tombs 1996:155–161). In turn, capitalist industrialization accelerated national integration. Capitalist industrialization and technological transformations were instrumental in developing the railroad and the telegraph (Kahan 1967:28), which made possible the shrinking of space and the quickening of time—the experiential foundations of modern life—and the construction of dense national networks (Schivelbusch 1986:36–39). Whether in Marseille or the Var, political and economic changes of the nineteenth century integrated localities into national polity and economy (Agulhon 1982:295–298; Sewell 1985:313–316). Capitalist industrialization promoted urbanization and pulverized tradition, leaving in its wake the ever encroaching stated-based identity whether for military mobilization or political legitimation.

If capitalist interests supported infrastructural development and economic integration, the state in turn relied on economic development to alleviate fiscal problems and geopolitical threats. Just as a premodern polity made an alliance with the dominant religious institution, the modern state collaborated with the dominant economic institution. The state intervened directly and intensely in economic and social spheres, and structured education, media, and other institutions that at once articulated with capitalist industrialization and penetrated and constituted civil society (cf. Tilly 1990:114–117). Modern politics became inextricably intertwined with capitalist industrialization.

The modern state and capitalist industrialization both contributed, in turn, to the stirring of popular upheavals. Polities required greater popular legitimation as they faced resistance to higher taxation and wider conscription. The convergence of political and economic demands manifested itself in the campaign for political participation and social recognition, exemplified by the European-wide rebellions of 1830 and 1848. Both waves of rebellions asserted the place of the people in the polity, especially the urban middle classes, and 1848 in particular symbolized the initial articulation of popular demands against both the modern state and capitalism (Sperber 1994:230–240). While the eighteenth-century collective violence in France was predominantly defensive, such as tax and food riots, by the mid-nineteenth century the struggles had become offensive, such as for suffrage and class interests (Tilly, Tilly, and Tilly 1975:44–55). Henceforth, the modern state faced a choice between incorporating popular demands or facing a constant threat of rebellion.

In this context, politics became resolutely national. The barricades in the class wars of nineteenth-century France no longer divided monarchists and republicans as two races but as two parties within the same nation. Even the idea of monarchy was nationalized. While Louis XV could proclaim in 1766: "It is in my person alone that sovereign power resides"

(Behrens 1985:25), both Napoleon and Louis Philippe ruled in the name of the nation (Zeldin 1958:5; Furet 1992:252,351–359). The equality of citizens mandated the destruction of regional and local privileges and liberated religious minorities, such as Protestants and Jews. Electoral participation expanded (Hunt 1984:125). Cosmopolitan nobles, along with town dwellers and rural agriculturalists, became citizens.

Furthermore, the deleterious consequences of capitalist industrialization mobilized workers to seek higher wages and better working conditions. The state became the ultimate forum and mediator of capital-labor conflict, and "offered a fulcrum on which people could fight out their social conflict with others" (Tarrow 1994:191). Social movements, whether in terms of categories of identity or repertoire of collective action, became nationalist (Tarrow 1994:191). Even labor organizations that advocated proletarian internationalism were organized nationally (Hobsbawm 1987:127). The expansion of the welfare state and the entrenchment of social citizenship insinuated state power in the very constitution of society and peoplehood. Who spoke of politics increasingly spoke of national politics (te Brake 1998:183–188).

If political elites mimicked the innovations of French mass mobilization and infrastructural development, popular movements idolized and emulated the political ideals of the French Revolution. The nationalization of politics, in other words, went hand in hand with the diffusion of political ideals and techniques. There was something of a revolutionary international in nineteenth-century Europe. As Tocqueville (1955:157) memorably narrated: "Revolutionaries of a hitherto unknown breed came on the scene: men who carried audacity to the point of sheer insanity; who balked at no innovation and, unchecked by any scruples, acted with an unprecedented ruthlessness. Nor were strange beings mere ephemera, born of a brief crisis and destined to pass away when it ended. They were, rather, the first of a new race of men who subsequently made good and proliferated in all parts of the civilized world, everywhere retaining the same characteristics." Limited though it may have been to the educated, revolutionary ideas and activists infiltrated every corner of Europe. The idea of national liberation was a transnational movement. Herder inspired pan-Slavic nationalists (Kohn 1960:ix–xii), German Romantics stirred the Young Turks, and Michelet's lectures at the Collège de France mobilized Romanian nationalists (Gildea 1987:74).

Needless to say, modern politics drew on premodern, proto-national consciousness and condition. There is considerable truth to the idea that modern peoplehood refers to descendants of those who once obeyed the same king. Because the past inevitably shapes the present—and nothing is created ex nihilo—there are inevitably precursors and continuities (Bromley 1978:12–15; Smith 1981:134, 1986:13–18). Expressions of political loyalty and therefore political identity are coeval with the birth of a polity. Aided by print technology, national vernacular promoted proto-national consciousness in early modern Europe, especially among those who thought, traveled, traded, or fought. Yet, as I noted in Chapter 1, cultural integration was limited in premodern Europe. Village, local, or regional belonging superseded national identity. When identity was not local, it was often supranational, whether as Christians or nobles. More critically, the limitation of status integration narrowed the circle of national identification. Because status-based societies—if we can even call them societies in the modern sense, as "society" implied elite membership—depended on the existence of qualitatively different types of people, the very ideal of integral polity was at best inchoately intuited. As late as 1848, the putatively nationalist revolutions lacked the support of and the nationalist consciousness of the peasant majority (Rosdolsky 1979:143).

Modern nation-building may benefit from prior linguistic, religious, or cultural integration, but geopolitics, not proto-national consciousness, determined the concrete contours of modern peoplehood. The claim of antiquity and continuity is almost always important (Smith 1986:231), but the stubborn fact is that competing narratives can always be told. National history, like personal genealogy, has manifold and ever widening ancestral or antecedent influences. To take one example, Greek, Bulgarian, Serbian, and Macedonian origins of Macedonia have been claimed in the twentieth century (Karakasidou 1997:14–18). The triumph of a particular nationalist narrative depends not so much on historical accuracy but on politics. The assertion of an end point reconfigures the narrative of nationhood, but the telos is ultimately a contingent outcome of political and military conflict. Nationalist ideals and movements were important by the mid-nineteenth century, but military and diplomatic struggles shaped the political map of Europe.

The primacy of geopolitical competition and the vagaries of state-building ensured that the extent and tempo of cultural and status integration differed for each nation-state (cf. Hroch 1985:pt.2; Breuilly 1994:pt.3). Whether France or Finland, Germany or Greece, however, the polity had to assure territorial integrity. That is, the modern nation-state became all but inevitable as the dominant political form of modernity. If geopolitical struggles established political boundaries, then the modern state sought to construct a permanent national space. Even if a polity should remain nominally a monarchy, in substance it promoted national and status integration, everywhere usurping and reproducing modern peoplehood as a dominant identity and ideology.

Consider in this regard Germany where the cultural yearnings of unity were ubiquitous by the mid-nineteenth century (Schulze 1991:66; Vick 2002:208). The spread of literacy bypassed the aristocratic Francophone circle and cultivated the middle-class German ideal of *Bildung* (Rosenberg 1966:182–192). Popular forces, especially in urban areas, agitated for republican and national ideals, representing the impulse of the French Revolution against the inertia of the nobility. Proto-national professional and civic associations emerged (Hamerow 1969–72:ii,22–26). Merchants and industrialists hankered for economic integration, seeking a common system of weights, measures, and coinage, as well as lower trade barriers and greater political influence (Hamerow 1958:274). Urbanization and industrialization stressed regional and national networks over local ones (Tilly, Tilly, and Tilly 1975:205).

The mid-nineteenth century German political unification failed because of the geopolitical rivalry between the Habsburg Empire and Prussia. German unification had to await Prussia's victorious wars against Denmark in 1864, the Habsburg Empire in 1866, and France in 1870–71 (Meinecke 1977:chap. 3). If the opposition of the European powers had prevented German unification in 1848, then Prussian power ensured it in 1871 (Mearsheimer 2001:288–297). Prussia, which was outside of the Holy Roman Empire and occupied present-day Poland, ruled over disconnected realms in the eighteenth century when regional identities superseded Prussian identity (Paret 1992:15). Its bureaucracy ultimately prevailed over the Junkers and the *Ständestaat* (Rosenberg 1966:221–228). Prussia's eighteenth-century ascent was largely due to its military prowess (Vierhaus 1988:136–140). Germany emerged in 1871 as Prussia writ large.

A similar phenomenon can be seen in Italy. As Owen Chadwick (1981: 90) remarks: "Few thought about Italy. They thought of Lombardy, Venezia, the Papal States, Naples, Sicily, the duchies. Turin was psychologically not remote from Paris. Milan was near to Vienna. Naples was psychologically and politically much nearer to Madrid. Palermo felt to be near nowhere." If cultural integration was lacking, so too was status integration. The road to Italian unification was paved by the military and diplomatic successes of Piedmont, which emulated Britain and France (Tilly, Tilly, and Tilly 1975:87). Cavour's diplomatic and military successes, rather than Mazzini's high ideals, established the modern Italian state. Like Prussia, Piedmont achieved geopolitical success in no small part due to its state capacity. The Piedmontese alliance with Prussia against the Habsburg Empire in the Austrian-Prussian War of 1866 ensured the success of the Risorgimento. Just as Germany was Prussia writ large, Italy was Piedmont writ large.

The consolidation of western European states transformed kingdoms and amalgamated smaller polities. The primacy of geopolitics mandated the establishment of nation-states, which in turn squelched other forms of polity. Whether Prussia or Piedmont, or Hanover or Sardinia, struggling polities appealed to larger political-cultural unity and drew on language, religion, and culture to forge political-cultural solidarity. The general pattern in the east featured the collapse of empires—most notably the Habsburg and the Ottoman—and the ensuing establishment of successor states, usually based on former administrative units (cf. Breuilly 1994:123). To be sure, western European states were also successor states, though of older empires, whether Roman or Holy Roman. Breakaway states often trumpet nationalist rhetoric, but their success also depended on geopolitics.

Consider Greece and its celebrated struggle for national liberation. In the early nineteenth century, the basis of Greek peoplehood was fundamentally religious, distinguishing themselves from Armenians, Jews, and other confessional communities in the Ottoman Empire (St. Clair 1972:8). To be sure, Greek nationalists sought to institute a standard national language, culture, and history in the early nineteenth century (Clogg 1992: 2). Yet it was not the factious anticolonial forces that led to Greek independence, but the intervention of external powers—most importantly, Britain, France, and Russia—that sought to weaken the Ottoman Empire (Ternon 2002:130–136). Symptomatically, Greek people did not participate in the 1832 independence treaty, a Bavarian teenager became the king of Greece, and the external powers effectively ran the country in the 1830s (Krasner 1999:162). As the British minister to Greece, Edmund Lyons, noted in 1841: "A truly independent Greece is an absurdity. Greece can either be English or Russian, and since she must not be Russian, it is necessary that she be English" (Clogg 1992:57). Because less than a third of ethnic Greeks lived within the Ottoman Empire, the idea of Greater Greece motivated expansionist efforts well into the twentieth century (Beaton 1988:94). The Greek-Turkish War of 1919–22, which ironically became the Turkish war of independence, extinguished Greek imperialist ambition (Clogg 1992:101). Had Greek independence been foiled, the Greek Diaspora—stretching from Amsterdam to Odessa, nominally united by the Orthodox Church—may well have simulated the situation of the pre-Israel Jewish Diaspora.

As historians come to write national history and stress the significance of national consciousness and movement, successful cases are naturalized as obvious and inevitable. Switzerland traces the origin of *Eidgenossenschaft* to the 1296 Rütli oath, which is roughly the story told in Friedrich Schiller's *Wilhelm Tell* (1804), but the myth ignores discontinuities (Im Hof and Capitani 1983:i,197; Kästli 1998:378–382). Switzerland remains a congeries of perhaps three thousand *Talgenossenschaften* (valley communities), characterized by local particularism (Braun 1990:104; Steinberg 1996:8–9,18). Sovereignty has resided in cantons, rather than Swiss people *tout court* (Kutter 1995:133). The very idea of the nation frequently refers to the locality (Schorske 1994:5). Furthermore, the fundamental status difference between citizens and subjects existed in the nineteenth century (Arlettaz and Arlettaz 1996:259). Rather than a long tradition of Swiss unity or a modern nationalist movement, modern Switzerland survived because the three powers that could make plausible territorial claims—France, Germany, and Italy—were unable to impose hegemony. Given that Switzerland's survival depended in part on the prowess of the Swiss army, it is not surprising that the Swiss army provided the principal meaning of a true Swiss identity *(rechter Schweizer)* (Steinberg 1996:234–248).

Consider in contrast the European Union. Although the idea of European integration may seem absurd to committed nationalists, the future state of Europe has some claims to nationhood, such as the legacy of the Roman Empire or Christendom (Geremek 1996:73–94). No less an authority than Ernest Renan asserted the unity of European civilization (Olender 1992: 60–63), and even Mazzini was favorable toward a European union (Mack Smith 1994:220). Yet, as Federico Chabod (1991:33–47) argued, the equation of Europe and Christendom is misleading. European unity has been articulated against the Turks (or Saracens) or the Russians (Neumann 1999: 60–63,107–112), and any concrete history cannot bypass Islamic or Byzantine influences. Thus, Tony Judt (1996:60) argues that " 'Europe' is too large and too nebulous a concept around which to forge any convincing human community." Yet if China, with a greater population and larger territory, can make a nationalist claim, then why can't Europe? Political unity generates a common consciousness, which may take only a few generations to ground its existence from time immemorial. Then Europeans may find Nietzsche's (2001:242) pronouncement prophetic: "We who are homeless are too diverse and racially mixed in our descent, as 'modern men', and consequently . . . we are *good Europeans,* the rich heirs of millennia of European spirit."

Failures are either forgotten or dismissed as pipe dreams. Few tears are shed for suppressed proto-nationalist identities. Hence, only the idealistic minority would regard Savoy or Osnabrück, or Rumelia or Ruthenia, as a plausible peoplehood identity. Who now remembers Cisalpine or Cispadane, or Lemanic or Ligurian Republic? But if Holland is an indisputable nation, then why isn't Hanover? Bismarck feared that it would be "hard to swallow" Hanover (Pflanze 1990:ii,100), but successful swallowing vanquished Hanoverian proto-national consciousness. Who now remembers Budweisers, at once the nonnational and supranational identity between Czechs and Germans, save perhaps as a brand of American beer (King 2002:2)? The Illyrian movement of the mid-nineteenth century seems unreasonable today because Illyria has fragmented into Bulgarian, Slovenian, Serbian, and Croatian nations (cf. Lampe 2000:41–45). Yet the survival of the Illyrian nation-state would have made Illyria as meaningful as Switzerland. Similarly, the collapse of Yugoslavia prompted scholars to pronounce its artificiality when most of them in the 1950s "simply assumed that the country would and should continue to exist" (Lampe 2000:4).

What exists has a prima facie air of plausibility; what does not seems merely fanciful. The discourse of modern peoplehood is intensely Whiggish. The inevitability of the present is assured by delineating a deterministic path from the past. If the end point should shift, then so too can the triumphalist narrative. Modern peoplehood depends on proleptic, post hoc theorizing.

4

The consolidation of modern peoplehood was gradual. Nineteenth-century European polities were predominantly monarchal, the nobility remained the preponderant group, the church continued to be influential, and most people were farmers. In short, preindustrial and pre-bourgeois elements of nineteenth-century Europe should not be ignored (Mayer 1981:17; cf. Charle 2001:pt.1).

French people, for example, did not suddenly become patriotic nationalists after the Revolution. During the revolutionary wars, many regions were indifferent, if not hostile (Forrest 1996:302). Napoleon's *Grande Armée*—and Napoleon himself—remained less than half French (Finer 1975:146). Indifference, resistance, and desertion characterized the revolutionary and Napoleonic military (Forrest 1989:18). The process of political-cultural integration faced resistance from the start, centralization and nationalization penetrated rural France slowly (Weber 1976:241–247), and regional differences remained acute throughout the nineteenth century (Planhol 1988:534). Conservative reaction—the very word being a product of the Revolution—sought to restore the legitimacy of monarchy and religion (Levillain 1992:163–170). As late as the 1830s, less than 2 percent of French people were able to vote (Walicki 1989:6). France remained fundamentally hierarchical until the 1840s (Pinkney 1986:3), and Legitimists, such as Chambord and Belleval, openly defended status hierarchy into the 1860s (Hazareesingh 1998:144–147).

The dominant trends went the other way, however. While merchants and industrialists struggled for national integration, republican and popular forces fought status hierarchy. The monarchy and the church declined in significance, along with the rural population. Serfdom was extirpated, while suffrage expanded. Modern nation-states were democratic and secular, industrial and urban. In this regard, World War I proved to be a fatal blow to the old order, which Francis Ferdinand personified: "He was not only a haughty aristocrat, arrogant absolutist, proud Austro-German, fervent Catholic, and imperious militarist; as an integral reactionary he was also an aggressive antidemocrat, anticapitalist, antilibertarian, antisocialist, anti-Magyar, anti-Slav, anti-Semite, and antimodernist" (Mayer 1981:328). Rather than empires and other forms of nonintegrated polities, the nation-state emerged as the principal model of an integrated polity. Symptomatically, states that had been called powers were called nations after World War I (Parker 1998:59).

If military and diplomatic struggles defined territoriality, then the modern state sought political, economic, linguistic, and cultural integration that promoted national identity and loyalty. Economic integration, state formation, and nation-building went hand in hand (Watkins 1991:121–

129). The national-level integration of language, religion, and culture superseded regional or local identities and differences. The true achievement of nation-building was to erase the reality of contingency and construction and to paint the patina of antiquity and continuity. Structural amnesia that is nationalist historiography remembered the past as an inevitable foreboding of the present. The nation as an institution and an imaginary circumscribed and differentiated inside from outside, us from them.

The modern state wielded esemplastic powers in transforming population into peoplehood. Nominal identity became substantial through nationalized education, economy, or culture (Gellner 1983:140). That is, abstract categories became institutionalized networks and meaningful identities. The state shaped social life, making the nation the privileged unit of identification (Girardet 1966:198). Demarcated by state territoriality, civil society emerged as a nationally specific field. National boundaries came to denote the symbolically and materially significant space of polity, economy, and society. Wars in particular promoted national identification (cf. Colley 1992:1–5). In France, the revolutionary army was a premier school of republican patriotism; the citizen soldier "heard everywhere the great words Liberty and Equality, the Republic and the Nation, the rolling thunder of the 'Marseillaise' and the lighter strains of the 'Carmagnole.' He saw the tricolor every day at his barracks" (Palmer 1969:80). From the postrevolutionary wars to the two world wars, the idea of French peoplehood was mobilized constantly against external enemies (Paret 1992:44). State policy instituted a national language and culture and exerted control over education and mass media, labor market and military conscription, public health and social welfare (cf. Mann 1993:378–381). A compulsory, secular, and free education system accelerated linguistic and cultural unification. As Mazzini (1907:15,87) put it: "Education . . . is the great word which sums up our whole doctrine. . . . Without National Education, from which alone a national conscience can issue, a Nation has no moral existence." Universal and compulsory education became a European norm by the beginning of the twentieth century, constituting one of the chief obligations of the state (Sutton 1965:57). Other welfare benefits—in part to forestall the march of socialism—accrued to citizens. In the course of the nineteenth century, the nationwide system of commerce and finance became well established, and interregional transportation and communication improved (Weber 1976:218,486). Economically, trade and the labor market privileged domestic over foreign interests. Transportation and communication—epitomized by the railroad and the telegraph—constituted national networks that contributed to national integration. Badges of national belonging, such as state-issued identification papers, readily separated people of one nation from another. Politics became nationalized, penetrating everyday life with national networks of law and judiciary. Universal manhood suffrage spread to virtually all European polities by 1914 (Hobsbawm 1983b:267). The chief carriers of class politics—socialism and communism—were also nationalized.

The nationalization of the masses and the aristocratization of the nation occurred simultaneously. In attempting to imbue the modern state with a specific and differentiating foundation of the sort that I discussed in Chapter 1, the state elite frequently provided the basis of national distinctiveness, and facilitated the nationalization of the masses (Hobsbawm 1992: 37). The educated middle class served as the promoters and guardians of peoplehood identity. The language and culture of the center disseminated throughout the country via a combination of enforcement and enticement. In effect, people joined society.

In the transformation from population to people, the crowd or masses elevated status and emulated the nobility in everything from valorizing genealogy to political participation. The vocabulary of pride, dignity, and honor that had been the privilege of the nobility became the property of the whole nation. Henceforth, everyone could take part in the symbolic glory of the nation, sharing in military victories, colonial conquests, and athletic triumphs. In France, a classic justification of monarchal or noble rule—the idea of monarch or nobility as a superior race that conquered indigenous people (Chaussinand-Nogaret 1985:18)—was turned upside down. As Abbé Sieyès (1963:60) exhorted: "Why should [the Third Estate] not repatriate to the Franconian forests all the families who wildly claim to descend from the race of the conquerors." Rather, "all races are mixed" (Sieyès 1963:60), and sovereignty resides with the people (Sieyès 1963: 119). According to Sieyès (1963:57), the nobility "is not part of our society at all," but the Third Estate is, in contrast, *"everything,"* constituting "a complete nation" (Sieyès 1963:51,56; cf. Sewell 1994:198). If the Revolution accomplished nothing else, it destroyed the legal rights and obligations of *société d'ordres* and founded a new nation based on status integration (Hunt 1984:26). In the language of the French Revolution, the nation represented the people and their emancipation (Godechot 1988:14–19), which was encapsulated in the slogan "Liberté, Egalité, Fraternité." As Rabaud de Saint-Etienne proclaimed in 1789: "The title of citizen is a new word in our language as the ideas for which it stands are new in this country. The title of citizen is now your glory" (Behrens 1985:23). Sovereignty and citizenship became fused (cf. Gauchet 1995:42–51). Although early modern peasants of Provence may have had nothing to do with the cultural glory of Paris, their descendants in Provence or Paris came to share equally in the newfound national heritage. That is, peasants of France claimed the grand tradition of French nobility, which shed its cosmopolitanism. Although they had been literally two distinct races, they became integrated into a common national identity, a community of character. That is, the privileges of birth and status that had been the foundation of aristocratic society spread to the masses. In particular, the middle classes, who were closely allied with the development of the modern state and staffed its expanding bureaucracy, achieved collective upward status mobility.

The works of cultural construction and distinction identified and celebrated modern peoplehood. Every European nation-state was defined by a peoplehood with a series of predicates: language, religion, literature, history, clothing and food, customs and mores—precisely the factors that I discussed in Chapter 1. For example, the bureaucrats and ideologists of the Third Republic, such as Jules Ferry and Ernest Lavisse, assiduously promoted French identity, and state bureaucracies instituted most contemporary symbols of French national identity: the Bastille Day, *La Marseillaise,* and the tricolor flag (Hazareesingh 1994:129; cf. Déloye 1997:69). As Léon Bourgeois put it, France was to become "a single army . . . marching in a single step, moved by the same thought, seeming to form one being" (Hoffman 1974:405). The production of national identity—asserting its distinction and differentiation from other nations—was a global industry. Every nation was to have a national flag, a national anthem, and even a national bird. Every country celebrated its anniversaries and holidays. The emergence of historic anniversaries in "postage stamps, that most universal form of public imagery other than money," occurred between 1896 and 1914 in the major European countries (Hobsbawm 1983b:281). The nation became the legitimate unit for everything from "politics and legal codes to weights and measures, language, *opinion publique,* currency, tariffs, trade, uniforms, ice cream, and the prospective bride of the 'prince royal' " (Higonnet 1994:120).

The prism of social classification and identification shifted. Christianity that defined the metaphysical universe of premodern Europe was superseded by the modern state and its predicate, modern peoplehood. Religion transformed into nationalized and sacralized politics. The language of the nation for Fichte or Herder was suffused by the rhetoric of Christianity (Balfour 2002:50,112). For Mazzini, Mickiewicz, or Michelet, however, the nation constituted the chosen people (Kramer 1998:67–70). As Mazzini (1907:29) declared: "God wills it—God wills it! is the cry of the People, O Brothers! It is the cry of *your* People, the cry of the Italian Nation." The secular state carried the burden of sacralized universe and unity. While status had been the main source of social division, racial, ethnic, or national grouping became salient. If the boundary of horizontal distinction was political and territorial, then its anchor was in the correlate discourse of modern peoplehood, whether grounded in biology, language, religion, culture, or history. Although these putative foundations did not create peoplehood, they provided its base retrospectively.

Intellectuals in particular contributed to creating a new metaphysics of peoplehood. They were particularly critical to the nascent "scholarly interest" in national culture, but continued to be important in the succeeding phases of "patriotic agitation" and "mass national movement" (Hroch 1985: 23). Whether out of idealistic aspirations or cynical desires, intellectuals served state interests in the name of the people. They created and contributed to the public sphere and national patriotism (cf. Giesen 1993:73). They synthesized the past and prophesied the future, providing a rational foundation for irrational construction. They fashioned themselves as secular priests, as engineers of the national soul.

The idea of human nature underwent a major transformation. Modern philosophical anthropology posits the primacy of peoplehood identity. In the eighteenth century, the enlightened opinions accepted universal principles and cosmopolitan history. By the twentieth century, human variety and national difference were taken for granted. As I suggested in the previous chapter, status distinction was the functional equivalent of race in premodern Europe. In the modern era, race denotes horizontal divisions among human beings. Henceforth, the idea of peoplehood signifies a closer affinity between German nobles and German peasants than between German and French nobles.

As an expression of national difference, history emerged as an important branch of the human sciences. Modern historiography is predominantly nationalist, and the nation-state is the privileged unit of analysis (White 1978:28,43; Geary 2002:29). In France and elsewhere, nationalist history played a critical role in the social and ideological controversies after the French Revolution (Kelley 1984:7; Caron 1995:54–58). By the mid-nineteenth publication of Michelet's *Le peuple* (1846), the idea of French peoplehood, expressed in the mandate for universal manhood suffrage or the popularity of folklore, was well disseminated (Agulhon 1983:9–14). C. A. Sainte-Beuve purveyed the conventional wisdom about history in his 1861 essay as "that task and aptitude of our age" (Kelley 1984:13). Indeed, the historian and the nation become inseparable, whether Michelet for France, Henri Pirenne for Belgium, Konstantinos Paparrigopoulos for Greece, or Manning Clark for Australia. As Amilcar Cabral (1979:143) wrote: "The foundation of national liberation lies in the inalienable right of every people to have their own history" (cf. Fanon 1965:180).

Like Locke's theory of personal identity, where memory provides the basis of continuity, history offered the heroic and mythical tale of the origins and continuity of a community (cf. Lowenthal 1996:128). Rather than dynastic or confessional chronicles, national history delineated an evolutionary progress toward the present nation-state. Extra-cultural and extra-regional events and influences—even if they may have been part of the polity in the past—were systematically purged. Depending on amnesia and anachronism, the past became always and already part and parcel of national history. The master trope chronicles the dormancy and awakening of a people (Gellner 1997:7). In so doing, national narrative made sense of the absence of past national identity as well as maintaining its continuous and teleological trajectory. Characteristically, national history begins with a description of the natural environment—geography and climate—and the isomorphism of the writer and the reader, the subject and the object. As Michelet (1973:3) grandiosely exhorted: "This book is more than a book; it is myself, and that is why it belongs to you." The purpose of history became a discovery of identity and its crystallization; a chronicle of homeland to which history marks both its symbolic return and future glory in a singular, continuous narrative. In so doing, nationalist history conjured up the spirits of the past, restoring time-honored disguise and borrowed language. As secular theodicy, it responded to the question of fate and destiny and provided glimpses of the future and immortality. People looked to history, rather than the Bible, to decipher the human condition (cf. Arendt 1977a:68). Peoplehood identity congealed past and future.

Collective memory—usually articulated against and based on kinship, religion, and locality—became national (cf. Connerton 1989:36). Precisely when traditional agents of cultural transmission, such as grandparents and village elders, declined in significance, formal institutions of school and media promoted a shared national field of meaning and memory. That is, the unit of collective memory shifted from the village to the nation, informal oral transmissions to formal written legacy (cf. Wertsch 2002:6). Space and time became redolent of identity. From nature—mountains and rivers—to the built environment—buildings and landmarks—wonders were taken as symbols of the nation. Nature was nationalized; nation was naturalized. Whether the frontier in the American imagination or the Alps in the Swiss, landscape at once unified and differentiated a people (Zimmer 1998:648–652). Places and monuments were saturated with meaning, maps and museums celebrated national progress, and narratives and songs expressed common peoplehood. National heroes and demons populated the myth and ritual of nationhood. Culture was the site of national consciousness, as collective rituals and bodily practices were nationally defined. What had been the province of family, neighborhood, and religion became the domain of the state. The national imaginary colonized childhood, from songs and tales, and offered a potent sentimental basis of nostalgic national identity. From cognitive to emotive, visual to aural, public knowledge and symbols evoked primordial loyalty and identification. Modern peoplehood, grounded in geography and history, was thereby naturalized. And the state was at once the primary producer and disseminator of the master narrative. To be human meant to be nationalized; to be individual meant in some ways to represent the nation. As Mazzini put it: "Without a country you have no name, no vote, no rights, no baptism of brotherhood among the peoples . . . you are humanity's bastards." (Talmon 1960:291).

Thus, modern peoplehood became the foundational unit of social imagination. The very ability to imagine a society is coterminous with its rise as a nation. Under the guise of the state, society, nation, and people are mutually constituted in philology and archaeology, history and geography. Whether for scientific analysis or for policy prescription, the state was the bedrock of the social sciences (Parsons 1986:110). Statistics—true to its German origin—were state-based. In contrast to the Christian or classical universalism of her premodern counterparts, every modern pupil learned nationalist history, geography, and sociology. Archaeology as a science of national origins (cf. Trigger 1989:206), geography with its stress on borders and nations (Ratzel 1923:17–32; cf. Ancel 1936:7), political science with state and nation as the cardinal units of analysis (Favre 1989:315–319), and sociology with its focus on national society (Wallerstein et al. 1996: 18) were established in the late nineteenth century. National character studies of the culture-and-personality school exemplified the holistic approaches to the study of modern peoplehood, which in turn instilled a belief in its naturalness as a unit of social classification and identification. For peoples who have not reached the evolutionary stage of the nation-state, the category of tribe made sense of their ur-peoplehood. The idea of modern peoplehood was the sine qua non of the modern social sciences.

The world was henceforth conceived as a society of societies. The couplet—national and international—became the bedrock of modern thinking about the world (Shaw 2000:29). The narcissistic inflation of minor differences governed the intellectual discussion of nations and international relations (cf. Hewitson 2000:3–11). Everything from the economy to sports became matters of international competition, and therefore yet another basis of peoplehood identity. Wars in particular promoted and aligned friends with fellow people and enemies as other nationals. In turn, the cardinal distinction between "us" and "them" transformed nonnationals within as enemies as within, as I elaborate in the following two chapters.

The institutional and epistemic universe of modern peoplehood was a systematic feature in Europe by World War I. Everywhere one looked or imagined, from mountains and rivers to the distant past, *nation* presented itself as the natural unit of identification. By then, the principle of national self-determination and the cognate idea of nationalism—one state, one people—were widely accepted (Osiander 1994:318). Once national integration occurred, nation-states were increasingly inimical to territorial fluctuation. Transformations in the twentieth century have resulted from military defeat or devolution, rather than amalgamation. Few challenged the principle that European polities should be based on modern peoplehood.

5

The primacy of thick identities—usually based on kinship or residential propinquity—is a cultural universal. Concrete ties of kinship and friendship, however, should not be mistaken for abstract relations among citizens of the modern state. Isaiah Berlin (1980:342) argued: "Perhaps the most compelling [reason] for holding a particular belief, pursuing a particular policy, serving a particular end, living a particular life, is that these ends, beliefs, policies, lives, are *ours.*" But why should what is "ours" be our nation's or people's? The elision between the concrete and the abstract is beguiling. In discussing Lloyd George's political view, John Maynard Keynes (1971:20) observed in 1919: "Nations are real things, of whom you love one and feel for the rest indifference—or hatred. The glory of the nation you love is a desirable end—but generally to be obtained at your neighbor's expense." Again, as commonsensical as the statement may seem, it ignores the difficulty of creating and sustaining "nations" as "real things." As I argued in Chapter 1, premodern European peasants thought of their neighboring villagers or nobles as "strangers" or "aliens." Why should their descendants come to think of millions of people whom they will never meet as "one of us," sharing particularistic ties of blood and land, history and culture? How does it come about that what Berlin and Keynes say seem so obvious?

The shift from lineage and locality to the nation, or the nationalization of popular consciousness, is a stupendous achievement of the modern state. To disseminate and sustain an abstract and expansionary identity, such as national consciousness, across great divides of space and status requires nothing less than a revolutionary transformation in social life. The political project entails convincing denizens of a particular territory to believe that they constitute a community of fate and character (cf. Bauer 1975:170). Contemporary political leaders well understood the need to make Italians or Poles after the establishment of the modern Italian or Polish state. Massimo d'Agelio memorably remarked after Italian unification: "We have made Italy, now we have to make Italians," and the liberator of Poland Józef Piłsudski said: "It is the state which makes the nation and not the nation the state" (Hobsbawm 1992:44). The artificial state was to transform into an organic nation; a population was to transmogrify into a people.

Whatever one may say about monarchy, its personal rule rendered it concrete. The monarch, clad in sartorial splendor, personified and symbolized the polity. In contrast, the modern state evoked machinery, at once gray and artificial (Poggi 1978:95–101; Haslam 2002:167). As late as 1862, Lord Acton (1985:412) observed in his celebrated essay that the theory of nationality "is the most recent in appearance" among the "subversive theories of modernity" (cf. Gentile 1960:121). The recent construction of the modern state was not lost on the great social theorists of the early twentieth century and explains, in part, their neglect of the problems of peoplehood (Stone 1985:19; cf. Schnapper 1998:chap. 2). If the modern state lacked divine justification like its premodern counterpart, then its membership—citizenship—also did not seem natural or necessary. What binds a large aggregate of people? What holds society together?

The modern state adorned the garb of the nation to elicit political loyalty and thereby nationalized political identity. Rather than an artificial, top-down idea, state membership became a natural, bottom-up notion. We can see the transformation from an artificial agglomeration into an organic entity in French thought. In *Encyclopédie,* nation refers to an aggregate of people who live in the same territory and obey the same government (Diderot and d'Alembert n.d.:ii,1003). For Renan (1990), writing a mere century later, it is invested with a soul. The equation of the state (an artificial entity) and the nation (an organic group) conflated and confounded the descriptive and the normative in referring to its constituent members. That is, the very discussion of national always and already entailed value judgments about who should belong to the polity.

The meaning of citizenship changed. In classical republican thought, civil religion and military discipline underscored the devotion to *patria* (Pocock 1975:203), but the object of patriotism was either one's locality or a larger political entity (Keohane 1980:124–129; Alter 1994:2). Furthermore, classical conceptions of citizenship, whether articulated by Aristotle or Machiavelli, denoted an elite characterized by land ownership or political participation. In civic republicanism, the performance of civic duties, exemplifying commitment to community, defined citizenship (Oldfield 1990:159). Romanitas was achieved, and we see its legacy in the French revolutionary-republican ideal of citizenship and peoplehood.

Modern citizenship synthesizes the classical conception of active, self-ruling citizens with the premodern notion of passive, governed subjects. It connotes not merely obligations but privileges, ranging from legal advantages and political participation to employment preferences and welfare benefits (Marshall 1964:74–83). The new ideal elides the distinction between national membership (nationality) and state membership (citizenship). To be sure, the particular parameters of citizenship varied across nation-states and historical periods. Yet even in the extreme case of the United States—in spite of the national self-identification as a land of immigrants—the idea of citizenship has frequently stressed the horizontal divides of race, culture, and nation (Smith 1997:198,408). Contrary to the abstract ideal of citizenship, state membership was often racialized and excluded minority groups, as I elaborate below, in part to forge the solidarity of the majority at the expense of the excluded. The modern citizen is a nationalized and naturalized subject.

The vocabulary of state membership assumed the language of naturalization. In part to counter its artificiality, citizenship became a largely ascriptive, involuntary status. The vertical ideal of status integration and self-determination shifted to the horizontal ideal of national self-interest. In other words, to square the circle of finding an identity among a large aggregate, nominal membership was claimed to represent a community with deep commonality. That is, the state as a community of fate required more than a community of ideal (Gesellschaft); rather, it was to be a community of character (Gemeinschaft), or even of nature based on blood and kinship (cf. W. Connor 1994:197). Society no longer denoted a voluntary group but an involuntary collectivity. Rather than people choosing, political loyalty was chosen as an a priori, ascriptive identity. Rather than the achievement of conscious citizenship, peoplehood identity is inscribed in name and body (cf. Isaacs 1975:31). Just as early baptism ensured the reproduction of the church, birth-based citizenship grounded it in the mantle of naturalness. The artificiality of state membership transformed into the primordial fact of national belonging. The ethical state and the Romantic *Volk* became the one and the same.

The nominal character of state membership facilitated the elision between citizenship (choice) and nationality (chosen). Local attachments were fused to cosmopolitan narratives. Rather than supplanting local loyalties, peoplehood identity incorporated them and became a master signifier. As the maximal identity, all infra-national attachments became appropriated in the name of the collectivity. Thick identities—family, lineage, village, or locality—were transposed on the thin identity of modern peoplehood; they came to express one and the same thing. Thus, *petit pays* became part of *grand pays* (Lebovics 1992:xii); *Heimat* no longer referred to locality but to the nation (Applegate 1990:13). Discussing Herder, Berlin (1976:163) noted: "What then is the right life for men? They should live in natural units, that is, in societies united by a common culture." Rather than the family or the Aristotelian community, "natural units" became nations in no small part because of the writings of Herder, Berlin, and others. Thus we find appeals to *Blut und Boden, la terre et les morts,* and kindred ideas that unite ancestry and territory. This mindset is exemplified by Charles Maurras (1937:252): "*La patrie* is a natural society. . . . Its decisive character is birth. One does not choose one's *patrie*—the land of one's fathers—than one chooses one's father or mother." The emotive resonance of thick identities was thereby projected on the abstract plane of imagined communities. As Michael Ignatieff (1993:9) notes: "Ethnic nationalism provided an answer that was intuitively obvious: Only trust those of your own blood." It took a particular education to expand the circle of blood ties from the family and lineage to the nation and race.

The civil religion of the state provided not only a metaphysic but also a particular ontology—a solidarity based on likeness, or mechanical solidarity—and a peculiar ethic whereby even savage murders came to be sanctified as honorable, selfless actions. The multitude of sins was absolved in the name of the people. The binary between purity and pollution or good and evil underpinned the visceral distinction between inside and outside. Greater international contact merely reinforced the salience of national distinction, as each individual became a diplomat and a missionary for her nation. Competition pitted one nation against another, most destructively in wars and most spectacularly in sports, such as the Olympics and the World Cup. National belonging became inescapable such that its absence provoked fear and revulsion, whether for the proverbial man without a country or Hitler's tirade against Jews as a people without a nation.

In the transition from the artificial state to the organic nation, European politics assumed their modern manifestations. The vector of early nationalists combined the impulses toward both horizontal and vertical integration, exhibiting the congruence of nationalism with universalism. Both the American and French Revolutions sought to extend their political message around the world. Thomas Paine (1995:5) wrote in *Common Sense* (1776): "The cause of America is in a great measure the cause of all mankind . . . not local, but universal, and through which the principles of all Lovers of Mankind are affected." In turn, Tocqueville (1955:10) noted: "The French Revolution aspired to be world-wide and its effect was to erase all the old national frontiers from the map" and to create in its stead "a common intellectual fatherland whose citizenship was open to men of every nationality and in which racial distinctions were obliterated." The French Revolutionary ideals pitted the people against the monarchy, nobility, and clergy. The nation denoted citizens who were against tyranny and oppression (Rudé 1959:232–239; Lefebvre 1973:202–209). The revolutionary "chant du départ" sang: "Tremble, enemies of France / Kings drunk with blood and pride" (Lynn 1984:48). That is, the enemies of the people are kings, not foreigners. The stress on status integration minimized the significance of horizontal distinction; "If not all those born in France were part of the French People in its full sense, foreigners who embraced the cause could become so" (Tombs 1999:121). Citizenship expressed a solidarity based on a constitutional and universal ideal, not racial, ethnic, or national identity. State membership—and ultimately national belonging— was accorded to those who shared the political ideal. It also accounts for the transnational character of nationalist ideals and resolves the paradox of nationalists fighting for other nations. As Mazzini (1907:41) declared: "Your first duties . . . are to Humanity." The 1792 National Convention decreed that France should "accord fraternity and aid to all peoples who want to recover their liberty" (Morgenthau 1974:57). Thus, there was nothing inconsistent in the actions of Thaddeus Kosciuszko, who fought for George Washington in 1776 and published a call for Polish nationalism in Paris in 1794 (Walicki 1989:94), or the rootless revolutionary Tom Paine who struggled in the name of the people across the Atlantic.

Late eighteenth- and early nineteenth-century nationalists stressed the populist, or vertical, dimension. The idea of the people, *pueblo,* or *narod* pitted the masses against the powerful or the establishment. Nationalism was anti-statist precisely because of the state's impersonal character and its association with royalty and nobility (Burrow 2000:133). Equating the nation and the people, the forces for democracy, nationalism, and socialism often overlapped. Mazzini himself stressed the basic liberties of the individual (Mack Smith 1994:220). Popular democracy and nationalism grew together in nineteenth-century Europe (Pomian 1996:92), representing common interests (people) against particular ones (elite) (Agulhon 1981: 181–189; Tombs 1999:116–123). The numerical symbolism of 1830, 1848, and 1871 identified the nation with republican and revolutionary ideals, developing class and national consciousness against the nobility throughout the nineteenth century (cf. Sewell 1980:277–284). "L'internationale / Sera le genre humain"; that is, the revolutionary republican ideal highlighted cosmopolitanism and universalism, not parochialism and particularism (cf. Girardet 1953:23).

In the course of the nineteenth century, the revolutionary impetus transmuted itself into socialism, communism, and other articulations of egalitarian political philosophy. Its liberal internationalist variant, most trenchantly embodied in Wilsonian idealism, sought liberties of all peoples (Morgenthau 1974:64). More true to the cosmopolitan heritage, socialist and communist movements stressed the vertical dimension of peoplehood. As Marx and Engels (1974:84) put it: "The working men have no country." They understood that the proletariat "must constitute itself as the nation . . . though not in the bourgeois sense of the word" (Marx and Engels 1974: 84) and projected that the future communist revolution would transcend national boundaries. The cosmopolitan spirit can be seen in the 1892 Erfurt Program of the German Social Democratic Party. As Karl Kautsky (1971: 205) argued: "The modern proletarian [is] a citizen of the world; the whole world is his home." Like Marx and Engels, he envisioned "an international amalgamation of great sections of the people of different lands" (Kautsky 1971:209). In spite of the alleged inability of Marxists to theorize nationalism (Nairn 1981:329), some of the pioneering analyses of nationalism were explicitly Marxist (e.g., Bauer 1975). Many Marxists were aware of the attractions of patriotic nationalism, and their political strategy was to prescribe one form of solidarity (class) over another (state) (cf. Benner 1995:93; Forman 1998:46–60). Certainly, Third World or postcolonial intellectuals embraced Marxism in order to be at once anticolonialist and nationalist, socialist and populist (Young 2001:167).

Conservatism arose against the republican and anticlerical impulse of the French Revolution. Insofar as it rejected the cosmopolitan universalism of the Revolution, it seemed to shroud itself in the garb of nationalism. Joseph de Maistre is often described as a nationalist, but the Savoyard who spent most of his life in the Piedmont-Sardinian Empire was far from being so in our sense. Rather, he was against secularism and republicanism. In his *Considération sur France* (1794), Maistre (1994:36) dismissed the nation as "a wonderfully convenient word, since one makes of it whatever one wishes." Rather than advocating nationalism, his polemic attempted to underscore "a satanic quality to the French Revolution," to show "the phrase *large republic,* like *square circle,* is self-contradictory," and to champion faith and patriotism, or "*submission* and *belief*" (Maistre 1994:36,109). Although he discussed "the national soul," he was not interested in the vast majority of the people, obsessed as he was with throne and altar (Maistre 1971:108). Faith and patriotism meant for him church and monarchy.

Rather than being nationalist in the modern sense, early conservatives were opposed to cosmopolitan ideals and status integration. Maistre famously claimed never to have met a man in general—only French and Germans—but the particularistic polemic should not be taken as an expression of modern nationalism. As I noted in Chapter 1, proto-peoplehood consciousness was often elitist, excluding the majority of the population. As Jacob Friedrich Fries wrote in 1815: "Love of German fatherland is and must remain first and foremost a cause for the learned, not the commoners" (Alter 1994:50). Konstantin Frantz, to take another pioneering conservative thinker, was neither nationalist nor racist (Pulzer 1988:72–75). The only thing worse than secularism for Fries and Frantz was revolutionary democracy or republicanism that promised status equality. Aristocratic—or reactionary or royal—nationalism resisted status integration.

The early conservative rhetoric of nationalism frequently expressed the dynastic desire for political power. In the case of Hungary, where the Magyar nobility held parliamentary meetings in Latin as late as the 1840s and the majority of them spoke German as the first language, its independent polity was for the Magyar nobility, not the people at large (Gildea 1987:71,104). The promotion of state power did not necessarily entail nationalism, as for example in the mid-nineteenth century British imperialism (Kahler 1984:70–74).

Conservatism became nationalist in the modern sense after the triumph of the modern state and modern peoplehood. Later expressions combined the left-wing impulse for status integration and the right-wing stress on state power. An alliance was forged between state power and capitalist interests. Even as the twin forces of modernity pulverized tradition and community, they legitimated themselves in the name of the people. As socialists and communists sought greater equality, conservatives stressed the principle of political-cultural distinction. Against the universalist and cosmopolitan ideals of the left—liberty, equality, fraternity, and peace—the right embraced national particularism and chauvinism (cf. Hazareesingh 1998:248–251). In stressing roots and belonging, family and home, state membership became saturated with emotional resonance. True to the original meaning of nationalism—coined by Abbé Barnel in 1798 to refer to antagonism toward foreigners (Gildea 1987:54)—conservatives focused their ire on foreign elements, such as Jews and immigrants, rather than on the masses.

The extreme articulation of conservative statism or nationalism was fascism, which was at once anticommunist and antidemocratic but populist and nationalist (Carsten 1980:49; Griffin 1991:4–8). It idealized a politics of purity, simultaneously stressing homogeneity and egalitarianism. The socialist element was explicit in Mussolini and Hitler. Japan, in contrast, was fascist by imputation because of the Axis alliance (cf. Payne 1995:335). In this regard, racism is not a critical element of fascist rule (Griffin 1991: 26; cf. Brooker 1991:297). Rather, fascism accepted status integration but stressed cultural distinction.

The belated conservative appropriation of nationalism can be gleaned from the shifting relationship between nationalism and militarism. Most eighteenth- and nineteenth-century republican and nationalist thinkers, blaming militarism on nobility or feudalism, had envisioned international peace after the victory of the people (Hinsley 1963:109–113). According to early nationalists, national self-determination would engender national self-satisfaction and hence international peace (Waltz 1959:143). The people or the masses were against the state and the warring classes (Howard 1978:31). Carlton J. H. Hayes (1931:303), a pioneering historian of nationalism, argued that "altruistic longing for human peace and betterment is the explanation of the modern vogue of nationalism." In fact, modern nationalists were no more self-satisfied or pacifist than their predecessors. Just as the salience of nationalism was unanticipated, the particular turn toward militaristic nationalism was unforeseen by early nationalists. However, this should not be surprising given the convergence of state interests and nationalism by the late nineteenth century.

In response to the conservative articulation of nationalism, liberals—including the cosmopolitan left—systematically criticized the conservative, and in effect our, notion of nationalism. Nationalism thereby became severed from its earlier association with popular democracy and republican virtues. As the liberal political theorist John Dunn (1993:57) expatiates: "Nationalism is the starkest political shame of the twentieth century, the deepest, most intractable and yet most unanticipated blot on the political history of the world since the year 1900." Emotive and amorphous, nationalism became inimical to the liberal and rational temperament (cf. Miller 1995:103). Repeatedly belittled and condemned, patriotic nationalism became the whipping board of the high-minded, thereby escaping serious analysis and scrutiny.

The ideological shift manifested itself in individual national debates on the meaning of citizenship and nationality. In general, the very promotion of peoplehood identity conflated and confused the distinction between state and nation, citizenship and nationality (cf. Miller 1995:18). Broadly, territorial-based citizenship stresses the vertical dimension (everyone born in a territory is a citizen); blood-based citizenship emphasizes the horizontal dimension (genealogy, not accidents of geography, is what matters). The contrast is commonly articulated as citizenship based on *jus solis* (e.g., France and the United States) and that grounded on *jus sanguinis* (e.g., Germany and Japan) (cf. Schnapper 1991:34–51). As Rogers Brubaker (1992:1) puts it: "If the French understanding of nationhood has been state-centered and assimilationist, the German understanding has been *Volk*-centered and differentialist." Social-scientific efforts to disentangle them, and especially to construct a typology of nationalism—whether Eastern v. Western, political v. cultural, civic v. ethnic, good v. bad, Sleeping Beauty v. Frankenstein's monster (Snyder 1968:112–132; Hechter 2000:5–17)—have been influenced by the very rhetoric of national distinctiveness. These distinctions are specious given the primacy of politics. The idea of peoplehood is ultimately indivisible, interweaving political and cultural, as well as civic and ethnic, criteria.

As I elaborate in the following chapter, citizenship laws or peoplehood identities are far from fixed (cf. Brubaker 1992:13). If geopolitics, capitalist industrialization, and political and social movements shape the contours of modern peoplehood, then their impact changes over time. In post-revolutionary France, the significance of status integration—enshrined in its revolutionary republican ideals—mandated state membership to be open. As I noted, some argued for a purely voluntaristic criterion of citizenship, which finds echo in Renan's definition discussed in Chapter 1. Its nationality laws therefore facilitated immigration and naturalization. Yet the French laws have changed over time, and significant struggles have occurred on the meaning of French identity. The former French president Valéry Giscard d'Estaing, for example, identified *droit du sang* (right of blood) and *droit du sol* (right of soil) as the key components of French citizenship by the late twentieth century (Geary 2002:5). Similarly, U.S. citizenship and immigration laws have fluctuated over time. As I elaborate in the following chapter, nativist currents have sought to limit immigration and citizenship rights of minority groups by invoking the blood criterion (Shklar 1991:9; Gerstle 2001:5). That is, the lands of *jus solis* often incorporate and are sometimes dominated by the principle of *jus sanguinis*.

Many states seek political loyalty by stressing the familial character of the nation, thereby rendering citizenship law relatively impermeable to immigration and naturalization. Germany is often taken as the example par excellence of closed nationalism and the principle of *jus sanguinis*, but its citizenship laws have been far from stable (Kvistad 1998:54–58). During

World War I, for example, eighteen Poles and nine Danes served in the Reichstag (Dahrendorf 1979:67). Both conceptions of the nation were debated in post–World War II Germany (Müller 2000:266). By the early twenty-first century, its citizenship laws are closer to being based on the idea of *jus solis* rather than *jus sanguinis*. Japan, to take another example, had held an extremely expansionary definition of citizenship, granting it to colonial subjects during the heyday of the empire. The restrictive, blood-based laws of the post–World War II era face significant challenges in the early twenty-first century (Lie 2001:105–108).

Historical fluctuations and internal heterogeneity render typological explanation problematic. Like racial distinction, typological classification may express a modicum of truth at any particular place and time. Yet the political or territorial definition and the ethnoracial or blood criterion rely on the same emphasis on ancestry and descent (Stevens 1999:60,149). The very definition of citizenship, in any case, is neither stable nor indivisible. Citizenship is a bundle of rights, privileges, and obligations that can be changed in bits and pieces. Furthermore, social reality may be far different from what the typological characterization suggests. Post–World War II West Germany may have been a classic case of *jus sanguinis*, but its actual population had a very high proportion of non-Germans.

In general, explanations based on national character or cultural tradition are readily refuted by historical transformations. Carl von Clausewitz (1992:260) wrote in 1807 that "the Frenchman . . . is more easily pressed into a uniform whole, more amenable to the aims of government, and hence a generally superior political instrument to the German, with his boundless spirit, his manifold originality and individualism, his inclination to reflection, and his ceaseless striving toward a higher, self-imposed goal." A century later, most people would have reversed the contrast: the intellectual and romantic French against the political and militarist German. Having proffered a cogent explanation of German dictatorship in 1945, a social analyst faces the seemingly irrevocable reality of German democracy in 2003 that looks as robust as the Third Reich did in 1939. The inevitable backward glance of historical explanation renders it ripe for an ad hoc and anachronistic account. As the object of explanation changes, so too does the explanation itself, which is reasonable except that it proves problematic to the scientifically ambitious. Although each reiteration may be convincing, fluctuating reality demands a more systematic account, which ironically must take seriously geopolitics and other exogenous and macrosociological factors in the formation of national politics and culture in general and citizenship laws in particular.

6

The concept of modern peoplehood spread around the world via European expansion. Precisely when empires were crumbling within Europe, some nation-states engaged in imperial expansion. The late nineteenth-century scramble for Africa and Asia divided the world into European-administered territories. Colonial authorities imputed the modern conception of peoplehood to the colonized. Just as importantly, anticolonial movements emulated European political practices and ideologies and organized and integrated themselves on the basis of colonial divisions. The dialectic of colonialism and anticolonialism engendered distinct peoplehoods.

Precolonial Africa lacked the institutional equivalent of the modern state and the ideological equivalent of modern peoplehood. Although there were kingdoms, empires, and warring states (Coquery-Vidrovitch 1988:66–74), their cultural consolidation was limited and status hierarchy was well established. Perhaps the most complex of premodern African polities, Kuba Kingdom, numbered only 120–160,000, who were divided into five distinct groups with little internal cohesion (Vansina 1978:66). Precolonial Africans were also far from static in their allegiance to their chief or clan, guild or religion (Ranger 1983:247–250). Although village identities were important, villages were neither self-contained nor egalitarian (Iliffe 1995: 231).

In the last decades of the nineteenth century, Britain, France, Italy, Germany, Portugal, and Belgium conquered much of the African continent. What had been a geographical concept for Europeans until the 1870s turned into a land that signified prestige and profit (Sanderson 1985:99). Though the parameters of colonial rule differed, colonizers imposed boundary lines instead of frontiers and zones that characterized precolonial African polities. Colonial boundaries did not follow natural or political regions (cf. Hance 1975:74), and colonizers frequently flouted their artificiality. As the British Prime Minister Lord Salisbury characteristically exaggerated after the 1890 Anglo-French Convention: "We have been engaged in drawing lines upon maps where no white man's foot ever trod; we have been giving away mountains and rivers and lakes to each other, only hindered by the small impediment that we never knew exactly where the mountains and rivers and lakes were" (Anene 1970:3).

Once boundaries were delineated, they defined the space of political, economic, and cultural consolidation. Transportation and communication networks, as well as language and commerce, followed colonial contours (Hodgkin 1957:29; Boateng 1978:49–53). To be sure, the extent of European rule was limited; to take one measure, there was one European civil officer for every 2,900 square miles and 45,000 Africans (Mamdani 1996: 73). Not surprisingly, then, European powers pursued indirect rule (Young 1994:149–154). In so doing, they used the European notion of peoplehood to make sense of and administer Africans.

European administrators and anthropologists alike believed in the existence of African peoplehood in the form of tribes, which were imposed on overlapping networks of environments, languages, religious practices, customs, and cultures (Colson 1967:204; Young 1994:234). They at once transposed the Romantic nationalist idea of modern peoplehood to Africa (cf. Colson 1967:203; Mamdani 1996:80), and stressed biology in the form of kinship (cf. Fabian 1983:80–87; Kuper 1988:5). In this view, a tribe was the undeveloped form of a nation, and tribal people lacked the capacity for self-governance, which was the fundamental justification for colonial rule in the first place (cf. Plamenatz 1960:176). By identifying predicates of peoplehood, such as distinct languages, religions, and customs (Ranger 1983:252), anthropologists and missionaries contributed to classifying natives into convenient ethnolinguistic groups for the purpose of control or conversion (Coquery-Vidrovitch 1988:99). In other words, the idea of tribe at once justified and facilitated European rule.

Africans in turn borrowed European institutions and ideas and reified received categories and identities (Lonsdale 1985:700). As the Negritude poet and Senegalese president Léopold Sédar Senghor (2001:145) reminisced: "As I have been taught by Marcel Mauss and Paul Rivet . . . each ethnic group, each people, has its own civilization, which is the succulent fruit of the geography, but also of the history and language of the race; in short, of life in society." He not only learned about Africa from European social scientists, but he was also influenced profoundly by the integral nationalism of Maurice Barrès (Vaillant 1990:121–126). Senghor is not unique; tribal identification was not only a matter of ideological acquiescence. Rather, African leaders organized their "people" as tribes to achieve European recognition and to influence political or economic matters (Iliffe

1995:231; Cohen 1969:2). Anticolonial resistance also hewed closely to colonial boundaries and categories. In other words, tribalism and nationalism emerged against colonial encroachment and imposition (Colson 1967:201).

Consider Tanganyika/Tanzania. "Early nineteenth-century Tanganyika was not inhabited by discrete, compact, and identifiable tribes, each with a distinct territory, language, culture, and political system" (Iliffe 1979:8). German and later British administrators entrusted governance to tribes, which they believed lay at the foundation of African social organization. "Tribes were seen as cultural units 'possessing a common language, a single social system, and an established customary law' " (Iliffe 1979:323). If tribalization was insisted from above, it was constituted from below as well. Primarily led by the powerful and the educated, tribal organization mirrored the colonial imagery (Iliffe 1979:325–334). In addition, rapid urbanization supplanted rural kinship and village networks and contributed to the salience of tribal organization as an urban political and social entity (Iliffe 1979:384–395; cf. Mitchell 1968:44).

Influenced by the emerging nationalist movements in neighboring African countries, ambitious, European-educated Tanganyikans formed the Tanganyika African National Union (TANU) in 1954–55 (Iliffe 1979: 487,513–523). As TANU's leader and the first president of Tanzania, Julius Nyerere (1966:271) acknowledged: "Until we were colonised this 'nation' did not exist. . . . It was the colonial power which imposed a common law and maintained it by force, until the growth of the independence movement put the flesh of an emotional unity on to the skeleton of legal unity." The anticolonial, independence movement sought status integration in the colonial-defined territory; the call for *uhuru* (freedom) was synonymous with the ideal of equality (Maguire 1969:362–365). The colonial unit was the basis of Tanzanian peoplehood.

Kenya provides another instance. The nineteenth-century spread of agricultural settlement consolidated linguistic and cultural differences among Kamba, Gikuyu, Meru, and other groups (Ambler 1988:9). However, they did not live with neat and rigid boundaries, singular and homogeneous identities, or stable and exclusionary consciousness. Identities were, rather, intensely local, characterized by diverse and overlapping allegiances (Ambler 1988:31–36). British authorities imposed administrative divisions along the tribes they identified and imputed ethnonational characteristics to them (Berman and Lonsdale 1992:330; Ambler 1988:152). In spite of

its basis in ignorance (Mungeam 1966:4), native leaders appropriated colonial categories in order to compete for state resources and to promote
individual and community interests (Ambler 1988:154). The logic of
modern peoplehood spread even when the authorities did not identify or
establish tribes. Whereas people from Mombasa hinterland were essentialized as the Mijikenda in the 1930s in the course of rapid urbanization,
predominantly town-dwelling Muslims became Swahili (Willis 1993:6–
7,106–110). Far from being rural, premodern, and primordial identities,
Mijikenda identity served new urbanites who mobilized social networks to
secure employment and other benefits (cf. Epstein 1958:231). The logic of
colonial administration and anticolonial resistance reified Kenyan identity
(Lamphear 1982:276). The most rapidly and thoroughly colonized groups,
such as Gikuyu people, constituted the principal anticolonial force (Tignor
1976:10). The Kenyan national movement emerged from the British colonial unit.

As the cases of Tanzania and Kenya suggest, colonial divisions provided
the proximate bases of anticolonial independence movements to form new
nations, new peoplehoods. Tribes and nations emerged together in the
course of colonialism and anticolonialism, although some were predated
by European missionary and economic contact. The modernity of European invention was, however, denied as most European scholars insisted
on the primordial character of the tribe (Apter 1963:12; Hance 1975:10).
Contemporary Africans also argued for the ancient provenance of their
tribe. Jomo Kenyatta (1953:309) was not only Kenya's first president, but
also a pupil of the anthropologist Bronislaw Malinowski. Influenced by the
contemporary wisdom of British anthropology, Kenyatta (1953:309) declared that "the key" to Kenyan culture was "the tribal system." The Ahfao
in Ghana offer another example: "Citizens would say without equivocation
'I am an Ahafo' " (Dunn and Robertson 1973:31), but two-thirds of the
Ahafo population were born outside of the area, mainly in the neighboring
Ashanti region, and 16 percent more hailed from present-day Burkina Faso
(Dunn and Robertson 1973:11). As a chief admitted: "The white man
showed us our boundaries" (Dunn and Robertson 1973:16). In this regard,
the anthropologist Elizabeth Colson (1967:204) writes: "In the 1940's, I
found the rural people in the southern province of Zambia largely indifferent to questions of tribalism or nationalism. Only the school boys
recently returned home from the secondary school which served the territory were ardent advocates of the development of local culture and the

rights of the local language as against other African languages." These children, in turn, would provide the nucleus of the educated African common sense that valorized tribe and nation by the 1950s (Ranger 1989:145; Vail 1989:1).

The liberation of people simultaneously disseminated peoplehood identity. As colonial societies unshackled themselves from metropolitan rule, the combination of geopolitical concerns and anticolonial organizations led them almost always to follow colonial administrative boundaries. Anticolonial independence movements were typically led by European-educated leaders, schooled in the idea of national liberation and of modern peoplehood. As they attempted to achieve status integration, many of them borrowed the European discourse of nationalism and modeled themselves after a European nation-state (Mazrui and Tidy 1984:373–381).

The dialectic of colonialism and anticolonialism was not restricted to the African continent. The colonial administrative unit was the crucible of a new nation even in the unlikely case of Indonesia. Stretching 3,000 miles and comprising 13,000 islands, with a myriad of languages, religions, and cultures, Indonesia is about as far from the ideal of the nation-state as one might imagine. Nonetheless, Dutch East Indies transmogrified into Indonesia. Colonial boundaries defined later national divisions. For example, the southern part of Borneo, which belonged to Dutch East Indies, became Kalimantan, a part of Indonesia, but two of the northern British protectorates became part of Malaysia and Brunei Darussalam, an independent nation-state.

The Dutch territory was the template of future Indonesia, within which the Dutch-educated native elite forged a new national consciousness (Drake 1989:31–36; Anderson 1991:116–123). A new language, Bahasa Indonesia, became the lingua franca and the basis for a national literary tradition by the 1930s (Ricklefs 1993:185). Nationalist leaders established standards of national identity and authenticity (cf. Siegel 1997:9). Competing against the modern Muslim revival and the communist movement, Sukarno proposed a program to achieve cultural and status integration in 1933: "We shall . . . attain independence . . . by waging a struggle in which all the people participate"; the new nation "has no aristocracy, no bourgeoisie, no classes, no capitalism" (Sukarno 1975:246). He did not deny the existence of ethnic and tribal differences, but, as in the cases of Tanzania and Kenya, these categories congealed in the dialectic of colonialism and anticolonialism. In central Borneo, "groups with the same name might speak different languages, while groups with distinct ethnic names seemed to be identical" (Rousseau 1990:1). Dutch anthropologists, missionaries, and explorers, however, attempted to classify the overlapping and fluctuating networks of people in Borneo (Rousseau 1990:43). Many ethnonyms are of recent vintage, as ethnic identity was important in modern politics (Rousseau 1990:11). Although religion divided people in Borneo (King 1993:31), anthropologists continued to assume the primacy of ethnic identity (cf. Tsing 1993:7).

In some areas, the category of caste replaced the language of tribe and ethnicity. Quite simply, tribe is a category for preliterate peoples and therefore is inappropriate for any civilization that Europeans deemed more advanced. In Bali, the precolonial history of slavery and warring kingdoms was superseded by the romanticization of village life and caste society (Robinson 1995:22–32). From Margaret Mead and Gregory Bateson to Clifford Geertz, Western anthropologists reified the contingent particulars of the locality and ignored the dynamics of Dutch and Japanese colonialism and collaboration or the fluidity of village and caste boundaries (Boon 1977: 146; Robinson 1995:5–9). Rather than tribe as in Africa, Bali was seen through the prism of caste that imputed territorial integrity and an unbroken and holistic tradition and religion, neither of which existed. Eventually Bali transmogrified into a paradise (Vickers 1990:184–194).

The acknowledgment of civilized status precluded tribal classification for South Asia. British bureaucrats and scholars employed instead the categories of religion and caste. The very idea of caste, however, became dislodged from its grounding in religion in the twentieth century (Béteille 1996:155–159). The British authorities were critical in this process (Dirks 2001:14–18). The nineteenth-century European theory claimed prehistorical racial subjugation as the source of immutable caste hierarchy (Bayly 1999:126–138; cf. Inden 1990:56–84). Simultaneously, the British presumed the sedentary and timeless character of Indian village life and even conducted historical research to prove the thesis (Irschick 1994:192–195). British rule divided the colony into convenient regions for administrative purposes and assigned religious and caste categories to the population. In fact, as Anil Seal (1973:28) argues: "In the towns and villages, men of different religions, castes and occupations worked promiscuously together, heedless of the categories of the census and legislation." In dealing with the British, the permissible categories of organization were villages, regions, castes, and religions. Ambitious political leaders asserted them in order to promote their interests (Seal 1973:16–22). The structure of the Raj, with its assumptions of Indian peoplehood, thereby provided the crucible of Indian political mobilization and social categorization. Educated Indians, like their counterparts in Africa and elsewhere, eagerly appropriated the European notion of peoplehood. As M. N. Srinivas (1966:85) observes: "Indian nationalism was fed by the study of European history and English literature." Symptomatically, Bakimchandra Chattopadhyay—"one of the first systematic expounders in India of the principles of nationalism" (Chatterjee 1986:54)—was versed in European literature and social sciences, while Gandhi was not only educated in England but also spent many years abroad, gradually formulating the idea of *swaraj* (self-rule) during diasporic peregrinations (Brown 1994:209–231).

European categories of peoplehood have colored Indian self-understanding (cf. Robb 1995:70–76). Postindependence political mobilization transformed castes into ethnoracial groups (cf. Béteille 1996:168–174; Bayly 1999:268–291,355–364). Dalits (Untouchables) identify themselves as a quasi-racial group and victims of racism (Human Rights 1999).

The vagaries of geopolitics and the strength of the political elite saved some polities from European colonialism. Although premodern Japan exhibited some linguistic, religious, and cultural commonality, it would be a gross exaggeration to insist on its social homogeneity or national consciousness. Feudal powers sustained regional diversity and rigid status hierarchy. The emergence of modern Japan entailed geographical expansion and consolidation, as well as the eradication of status-based order (Lie 2001:chap. 3). In the process, the modernizing elite emulated European political models, ranging from militarism to imperialism. The Meiji state extirpated feudal political authorities, annexed Hokkaidō, a frontier without a well-recognized sovereignty, and Ryūkyū Kingdom (contemporary Okinawa), and intensified political control of the territory, solidifying border control and superseding local authorities. Furthermore, the state sought to instill national loyalty under the emperor in order to create an organic family-state. Japan also became an imperial power, colonizing much of East and Southeast Asia. In so doing, it sowed the seeds of modern peoplehood in its colonies, such as in Korea (Lie 1998:Appendix).

The case of Japan may suggest the significance of national consciousness, but neither modernization nor national integration was necessary for political survival. Geopolitics, rather than national consciousness, makes possible the existence of modern states and the eventual development of modern peoplehood. Located between British Burma and Malaya and French Indochina, Siam benefited from playing off Britain against France as well as undertaking administrative reforms in the nineteenth century (Wyatt 1984:208–222). Boundary making provided the crucible of Thai identity (Winichakul 1994:164–170). However, it remained a kingdom with limited status integration until the politically and economically nationalist leadership of Luang Phibunsongkhram in the late 1930s (Wyatt 1984:252–256). Similarly, Ethiopia escaped European colonialism by an alliance between the Abyssinian elite and European powers (Holcomb and Ibssa 1990:388–389). As a premodern polity, however, it failed to achieve substantial territorial or status integration until the late twentieth century. Geopolitics, rather than national consciousness, is the proximate cause of political independence.

Most Latin American countries remained politically independent under U.S. hegemony. The ideal of modern peoplehood diffused slowly and remained restricted to the educated elite (cf. Nugent 1997:312). Mexico, along with much of present-day Latin America, was an administrative unit of Castile (Stein and Stein 1970:69). Territorial identification was nominal. Mexico stretched from the arid plains of present-day California and New Mexico to the swamps and forests of Yucatán. Indigenous cultural traditions persisted throughout Mexico (Chevalier 1963:313). In this context, loyalty was resolutely local (*patria chica*) (Lafaye 1976:9). Mexican unity before the twentieth century rested largely on the *haciendas,* or feudal estates that were consolidated in the seventeenth century (Chevalier 1963: 288). Although *criollos,* Europeans born in the Americas, distinguished themselves from *peninsulares* (born in Europe) soon after colonization, the elite differentiated themselves from *castas,* including indigenous people and African slaves (Liss 1975:152–157). The European elite excluded the *mestizo* population, barring them from churches, fiestas, and barrios, as well as their wearing European clothes (Reed 1964:20). The Indians were exploited but excluded (Lafaye 1976:14–17). In sum, neither cultural nor status integration occurred in the eighteenth century.

The political independence of Mexico in 1810 occurred as *criollos* and *castas* made an alliance against Spanish rule (Stein and Stein 1970:110–119). Nonetheless, as the Porfiriato—the long reign of Porfirio from 1876 to 1911—demonstrated, the new Mexican polity was based on patron-client relationships that simulated the European absolutist states (Wells and Joseph 1996:21–27). During the 1910 Mexican Revolution, the provincial local elite promoted a form of economic and political nationalism (Hart 1987:373). In the mass mobilization that marked the revolution, however, there was little in the way of a well-articulated group identity. Neither campesinos nor Mayan people exemplified a unified consciousness (Wells and Joseph 1996:241–247,291). In the early twentieth century, most peasants evinced local and religious identities (cf. Becker 1995:67). As late as the 1960s, anthropologists were still seeking to solve "the problems involved in drawing peasant peoples into effective participation in national life" (Foster 1988:5; cf. Clarke 2000:161–165).

By the 1960s the dominant way to understand the world mandated it as an international society: a family of nation-states (cf. Shaw 2000:51–57). In other words, the nation-state defined world politics (cf. Badie 1992:108–115). From the United Nations to the Olympics, the world came to comprise nation-based peoples and societies.

Instead of the overlapping networks of mobile individuals, natives were ensconced in the self-contained and unchanging category of peoplehood, whether as tribe, caste, ethnicity, or nation. Area and national studies emerged to make sense of recently liberated countries (Cooper and Packard 1997:13–18), as well as of tribal and ethnic populations (cf. Sharpless 1997:184). Although European social sciences frequently misrecognized local realities (Hill 1986:46–69), European-educated intellectuals promoted Eurocentric categories and concepts. The imperialism of European peoplehood followed political imperialism and disseminated and institutionalized modern peoplehood. The very idea of the nation-state was European, and European-educated elite realized it, albeit in their own idiom, whether for the Paris-educated Ho Chi Minh, the Cambridge-educated Jawaharal Nehru, or the London-educated Kenyatta.

The vocabularies and institutions of modern politics, whether law or political party, were indelibly European (Badie 1992:pt.2). Non-Europeans frequently took the European conception of peoplehood very seriously, including their historical and biological grounding. European origin did not imply sameness, however. No two nations are exactly alike; each nation has its own distinctive articulation of the same formal discourse, which I elaborate in the following chapter. However, operating in the same geopolitical universe of modern states, the idea of modern peoplehood was the normative ideal against which differences were articulated.

The new nations faced problems in transforming an artificial unit into an organic entity. While European nation-states were well established, postcolonial states engaged in nation-building. After all, European colonial authorities imputed the categories of modern peoplehood on populations that had no such inklings. As Edward Shils (1963:22) wrote: "The constituent societies on which the new states rest are, taken separately, not civil societies, and, taken together, thereby certainly do not form a single civil society. . . . The sense of identity is rudimentary. . . . The sense of membership in a nation-wide society [is] not great" (cf. Geertz 1963:109; Deutsch 1966:177–181). The inescapable irony is that Shils could have been describing the Europe of less than a century ago. The postcolonial state stripped ahead of civil society in much of the Third World, but European national integration had taken well over a century. Putatively tribal societies and identities were far from being traditional or primordial and were, in fact, modern constructs. As the nationalist idea waned in Europe, it continued to wax in the non-European world. The postcolonial afterlife of an old European idea became yet another proof of the primitive and primordial nature of non-Europeans.

The Paradoxes of Peoplehood

The triumph of patriotic nationalism was far from total by World War I. The very memory of popular enthusiasm is in part a tendentious historical reconstruction (Verhey 2000:6). The ideals of liberty, democracy, and pacifism (Marwick 1970:47–50), as well as the youthful desire for adventure and heroism (Langer 1965:xviii), were just as, if not more, important mobilizing ideals as the love of the country. Once at the war fronts, the delight in spectacle or the demand of comradeship entrenched many soldiers (Gray 1970:28). The high rhetoric of duty to and glory of the nation effaces the differential experience by generation or gender, class or religion (Becker 1977:574).

The cauldron of combat forged a generational identity (Wohl 1979:203–217), characterized alternatively, or even simultaneously, by patriotic fervor, this-worldly despair, and plain indifference. The protagonist in Ernst Jünger's (1929:315) *Im Stahlgewittern* [In the Storm of Steel] (1922) was "gripped by the sad and proud feeling of being more closely bound to my country because of the blood shed for her greatness," but his counterpart in Frederic Manning's (1979:25) *The Middle Parts of Fortune* (1929) nowhere mentions national greatness in a war where "honor . . . had become a fugitive and cloistered virtue." This is not necessarily a matter of national difference. The narrator of Erich Maria Remarque's (1958:12) *Im Westen Nichts Neues* [All Quiet on the Western Front] (1929) recalls that "they taught duty to one's country [as] the greatest thing" but "we already knew that death-throes are stronger." Returning home, he no longer feels that he "belong[s] here any more, it is a foreign world" (Remarque 1958: 104).

Patriotic pride, once transmuted into foolhardy adventurism, destroyed its own delusions. Whether propagated by literature or life experience, the nightmare of mass killing alienated many people from the ideal of the nation (Leed 1997:213; cf. Becker et al. 1994:pt.4). As Ezra Pound (1990: 190) memorably rhapsodized in "Hugh Selwyn Mauberly" (1920): "walked eye-deep in hell / believing in old men's lies . . . / then unbelieving." The Great War itself became an international cultural memory that promoted antimilitarist and counter-nationalist ideals.

Having outlined the making of modern peoplehood in the previous chapter, I delineate its limitations and paradoxes in this chapter. The language of blood and soil, geography and history, biology and culture crystallizes categories of modern peoplehood as natural units of social classification and identification. Because the modern state is everywhere marked by the historical contingency of its boundaries, however, there is no transcendental standpoint from which to define peoplehood. Indeed, the ideal of nationalism is impossible. I also explore the discourse of modern peoplehood, stressing its negative capability. The formal and nominal character of peoplehood identity enables it to account for distinct and disparate realities. If modern peoplehood is a product of cultural and status integration, then incomplete integration accounts for nonnational identities, usually expressed as racial, ethnic, or national minorities. Normative and deviant, or majority and minority, identities are relationally constituted. The incomplete integration of peoplehood is the structural source of racism.

2

The idea of modern peoplehood presumes an inclusionary identity over a delimited territory. As the early twentieth-century American Gino Speranza (1925:163) declared: "We know that a republic is possible only to men of homogeneous race." However, nowhere has it reached this condition. Indeed, the ideal of one state, one people is unattainable.

Why? As I argued in Chapter 1, premodern polities were horizontally and vertically disintegrated. The correspondence between political boundaries and peoplehood distributions is never perfect. Morever, the very effort to build a modern political economy implies economic expansion or labor influx in the sense that Niccolò Machiavelli (1970:281) intoned: "Those who plan to convert a city into a great empire should use every available device to fill it with inhabitants." Massive migration characterizes major civilizations (McNeill 1986:14). Powerful polities are often imperialist, annexing contiguous or distant areas. Consequently, the expansionary state usually does not promote racial or ethnic homogeneity. Conversely, a stagnant state may appear more homogeneous but at the cost of limited national integration. Polities everywhere face the recalcitrant reality of ethnic mixture. Chiaroscuro characterizes not only political boundaries but also polity *tout court.*

Consider the most fanatic effort to achieve a monoracial or monoethnic ideal. Nazi Germany sought to secure a living space (*Lebensraum*) and to forge a national community (*Volksgemeinschaft*). The slogan "ein Volk, ein Reich, ein Führer!" epitomized its commitment to extreme nationalism. As I elaborate in the following chapter, the Nazi regime systematically slaughtered people who did not fit into its vision of a national community, including Jews, Gypsies, homosexuals, leftists, and other community aliens.

If the Great Depression contributed to the Nazi seizure of power, then the economic upswing of the mid-1930s was crucial in sustaining its rule (cf. Barkai 1990:1). By 1937, the German economy faced an acute labor shortage (James 1986:413–418). A potential solution was to transform farmers and women into industrial workers. However, farmers constituted "the ideological darling of official Germany in 1939" (Schoenbaum 1966: 153). Seeking agricultural autarchy, they were the *Blutquell der Nation* [bloodwell of the nation] (Hardach 1980:67). The Nazi regime also discouraged women's participation in the public sphere, including paid work (Koontz 1987:398). The Nazi propaganda—"Kinder, Küche, und Kirche" ("Children, Kitchen, and Church")—envisioned women as wives and mothers (Bridenthal and Koontz 1984:33), and the patriarchal family as the foundation of Nazi society (Mason 1995:203). There was only a 1 percent increase in female labor force participation between 1939 and 1944 (Rupp 1978:75; cf. Bock 1994:121).

Growing labor demand was largely met by non-German workers, as was the case during World War I (Herbert 1990:118). Blatantly contradicting Nazi racial policy, exigencies of war led to German racial heterogeneity (Homze 1967:299–308; Herbert 2001:154–159). Rather than a massive rural exodus, there was a steady influx of foreign workers, principally from Italy and East Europe. By 1944, 22 percent of agricultural workers in Germany were foreign (Noakes and Pridham 1988:909), and 21 percent of the industrial labor force, and one-fourth of the overall labor force, were non-German (Kershaw 1983:297; Herbert 1990:153). Foreigners manufactured a fourth of German military goods (Pfahlmann 1968:232).

The pursuit of nationalism and racial dominance transformed Germany into an ethnically heterogeneous society. A paradoxical consequence of Nazi rule was the relative homogenization of neighboring countries. After the war, the massive expulsion of Germans from Poland and Czechoslovakia occurred (Naimark 2001:131). Consequently, the population of 3 million Germans declined to fewer than 200,000 in Czechoslovakia by 1955 (Lumans 1993:258).

The promise of nationalism—the congruence of a polity and a people—has tempted many governments to pursue the asymptotic condition. The 1922 Treaty of Lausanne is an egregious case. In order to follow the principle of nationalism, 1.2–1.5 million Anatolians and 300–400,000 Aegean Macedonians were forcefully relocated to their putative homelands (Naimark 2001:54). In so doing, they were uprooted from their linguistic, religious, and cultural communities. Relocation created not only a refugee problem but also new minority identities and ethnic antagonisms that last to this day. That is, the effort to effect ethnic homogeneity generated dislocation and diversity.

Indeed, the ideology of nationalism underpins the massive refugee problem of the twentieth century (Marrus 1985:3). It became a major issue after World War I with the formation of new nation-states (Skran 1995:31). The modern idea of the refugee is dependent on the idea of the nation-state, with its presumed isomorphism of territoriality and peoplehood. Wars are fought in order to align territoriality and peoplehood—irredentism or ethnic cleansing—but they in turn generate massive displacement. The refugees are excluded from the presumptive universal of state belonging.

In spite of the inevitable ethnic heterogeneity, some states nonetheless declare themselves to be ethnically homogeneous. Taiwan is one such instance. Since the seventeenth century, the Netherlands, a rebel regime from the Chinese mainland, Qing China, and Japan colonized the island, which generated a diverse population mix (Shepherd 1993:7). After Guomindang (Nationalist Party) conquered the island in 1949, it promoted Mandarinization, mandating a unitary Chinese identity (Mendel 1970:44–55). It proclaimed its rule over all of China and projected Taiwan as a homogeneous island of Mandarin speakers and Han Chinese people. The assumption of monolingualism contradicted the reality of numerous Taiwanese, Japanese, and Hakka speakers (Cheng 1994:363). Distinct streams of immigrants, with distinct dialects and identities, arrived from the mainland (Tu 1998: 88). Furthermore, indigenous peoples articulated their pan-ethnic identity as *yuanzhumin* (aborigines) by the 1980s (Hsieh 1994:411). At the same time, Taiwanese consciousness, which defines itself against mainland China, emerged (Wachman 1994:107–110). Ethnic identity and conflict are rife in contemporary Taiwan (Rubinstein 1999:495).

Similarly, the state of Israel has often proclaimed itself as a land of Jews. Even before the state of Israel existed, Jewish immigrants to Palestine had imagined an empty landmass. A character in Yosef Chaim Brenner's novel recollects: "Before going to Palestine, the country . . . appeared in my imagination as one city inhabited by non-religious Jews surrounded by many fields, all empty, empty, empty, waiting for more people to come and cultivate them" (Morris 1999:42). The founding of Israel in 1948 generated some seven hundred thousand refugees (Morris 1993:410). It also symbolically effaced non-Jewish peoples in Israel (Flapan 1987:102–108; Sternhell 1998:43–47). "[U.S. Secretary of State John Foster] Dulles said in the 1950s that the Palestinians would disappear, and Golda Meir spoke in 1969 as if they had disappeared, going so far as to declare that they had never existed in the first place" (Khalidi 1997:209), when a million Palestinians constituted nearly a fifth of Israel's population. The Palestinian past was expunged by tendentious scholarship (Bowersock 1988:186; Whitelam 1996:234–237). Palestinian and Arab political movements have engaged in the politics of recognition to claim Palestinian peoplehood (Khalidi 1997:177–209; Rubin 1999:197–201; cf. Sayigh 1997:46–57).

3

The development of the modern state generates the reality of modern peoplehood. Because the modern state is grounded in neither natural boundaries nor a ready-made nation, the normative idea of peoplehood shifts over time and remains contested. On the one hand, pan-racial or pan-cultural identities represent expansionary visions of peoplehood, which may hark back to the territoriality of a putative precursor, such as a premodern empire, or project a glorious future. While pan-Turkism and pan-Slavism recall the splendor of Ottoman and Russian Empires, pan-Africanism and pan-Aryanism look forward to future unity. Expansionary polities frequently claim a maximal definition of peoplehood. The Soviet Union, for example, sought a pan-Slavic unity (cf. Kohn 1950:235). The problem is that it risks being hollow. Thin identity offers slim support for solidarity because artificiality is manifest. On the other hand, states may seek a thicker identity, thereby pursuing particularism and purity, authenticity and homogeneity. The devolution of the Soviet Union, for example, created ostensibly organic nation-states such as Russia and Ukraine but neither was in any sense ethnically homogeneous (Hosking 1998:461; Liber 1998:187). The search for thick identity is a receding ideal that can only be approximated in the suffocating intimacy of family or village life.

Put in institutional terms, powerful states tend to be expansionary and therefore face the challenge of national integration. This is especially so as the age of the nation-state overlapped with the era of modern colonialism. That is, nationalism was often imperial nationalism. The search for the primordial essence, in contrast, chases a diminishing population, which may inspire secessionist and devolutionary movements and the increasing likelihood of geopolitical demise. There is a perpetual tension between a grand and gargantuan vision and a little and lilliputian ideal of peoplehood.

This dialectic can be see among Germans, who are, according to Isaiah Berlin (1980:350), "the first true nationalists." The Holy Roman Empire included non-Germans by all but the most expansive definition (cf. Breuilly 1994:97). Over three hundred states and nearly fifteen hundred lordships existed in a predominantly agrarian area characterized by extensive serfdom, as well as linguistic, confessional, and cultural diversity (Walker 1971:1; Hughes 1988:30–37). The purported unity was language, but dialectal diversity was significant, and the nobility spoke French (Lowie 1954:5–14; Hagen 1980:17). Therefore, few regarded German-speaking areas as a unit (Epstein 1966:243; Gagliardo 1980:125), and those who did expressed devotion to the Holy Roman Empire (Krüger 1993:48–53). As C. M. Wieland wrote in 1793: "I see Saxon, Bavarian, Württemberg, and Hamburg patriots, but German patriots, who love the entire Reich as their fatherland . . . [W]here are they?" (Sheehan 1989:373). Bavarians, Saxons, and other populations were themselves not so much ethnic groups as political-administrative units (Schulze 1998:15; cf. Green 2001:60).

In eighteenth-century Germany, the nation denoted a princely domain, which was not linguistically or ethnically homogeneous (Müller 1989:43). *Heimat* at the time referred to locality or township (Walker 1971:110; Applegate 1990:4). The very idea of *Volk* had pejorative connotations well into the nineteenth century (Sheehan 1978:107; cf. Müller 1989:43). This should not be surprising in a rural country dominated by the landed nobility (Sheehan 1989:125–132) and the local-minded peasantry (Hamerow 1969–72:i,275). Expressions of patriotism until the early nineteenth century referred to local states or the nobility (Schulze 1998:56). The *Vaterland* in Thomas Abbt's *Vom Tode fürs Vaterland* [From Death for Fatherland] (1761) or Josef Sonnenfels's *Ueber die Liebe des Vaterlandes* [On the Love of Fatherland] (1771) implied local, not pan-German, patriotism (Beiser 1992:21). If *Vaterland* meant one's own state, then other "German" states were foreign (*Ausland*) (Bruford 1935:297). Justus Möser's counter-Enlightenment particularism manifested itself in a history of Osnabrück (1768), not of Germany (Knudsen 1986:99; cf. Meinecke 1970:26). It was also aimed at princes, not ordinary people (Gagliardo 1980:57; cf. Epstein 1966:334). Before expanding his notion to incorporate all German speakers, Herder's *Vaterland* was Riga, which is located in present-day Latvia and had been part of Swedish and Russian empires (Sheehan 1989: 165). As Mack Walker (1971:259) trenchantly summarized: "*Volksgemeinschaft* is a contradiction in terms: a whole people cannot have community: *monstro simile*."

In contrast to local patriotism and regional or status identity, initial articulations of German peoplehood were universalistic. The French revolutionary ideals galvanized the leading philosophers, such as Fichte (Buhr 1965:27–41) and Hegel (Ritter 1982:43–47). German Romantics were universal humanists (cf. Toews 1980:110). "[Kant, Herder, and Schiller], as for Lessing, Klopstock and Hölderlin, it is the word 'humanity', not 'nation', that is invested with the fullest meaning" (Bruford 1935:306; cf. Lowie 1954:37–42). They may have idolized Goethe, but they also lionized Shakespeare, Napoleon, and other non-German figures. In fact, they almost always stressed cosmopolitan themes that harked back to classical antiquity (Bruford 1935:306–310), and classical Greece remained the ultimate ideal (Butler 1958:332–336). That is, Germany was linked to the cultural glory of classical Greeks, not to their ethnoracial ancestors, barbarians. Those who rejected the universal humanism of classical Greece embraced the Christian universalism of the European Middle Ages (Beiser 1992:273–278). As Novalis wrote: "The German character is no more limited to a particular state than Roman, Greek or British. . . . German nature is representative of genuine humanity and is therefore an ideal" (Meinecke 1970: 55). The prophet of the *Volk*, Herder, is no exception; his stress on national particularism does not deny the ideal of cosmopolitan universalism (Bruford 1962:190; cf. Gadamer 1941:17). Following the revolutionary stress on equality, nation or people was defined against the nobility, not France or Britain. Herder prized the nation against the state, stressing status integration more than patriotic nationalism (Beiser 1992:211). Written during Napoleonic invasion, Fichte's (1997:670) putatively nationalistic *Reden an die deutsche Nation* [Addresses to the German Nation] (1807) did not argue for political unification, but rather for the education of the *Volk* (cf. Meinecke 1970:81–87).

The initial stirring of German patriotism conjoined anti-French feelings with pro-Catholic sentiments during the Napoleonic Wars (Schulze 1991: 48–53). Anti-French sentiments were more antirevolutionary than nationalist (Blanning 1983:220–224,249–253; cf. Sheehan 1992:56). German conservatism—anti-Revolution, counter-Enlightenment, and anti-egalitarian—defended status hierarchy and traditional religion (Beiser 1992:281–288). As I argued in the previous chapter, early conservatives were concerned not with modern nationalism but rather with premodern status hierarchy and religion. Particularistic loyalties superseded pan-Germanic sentiments (Hamerow 1969–72:i,381).

Once the idea of German unification was in the air, the debate was over *gross* (great) or *klein* (little) Germany (Schulze 1991:131–138). The logic of linguistic or cultural sphere of influence suggested a vast swathe of Europe to be part of Germany. Ernst Moritz Arndt, an ardent German nationalist and the author of *Germanien und Europa* (1802), initially regarded himself as Swedish but later incorporated Scandinavians among Germans (Sheehan 1989:381). Because of local and regional variation, as well as the mixture of religion and culture, Germany demonstrated neither an obvious unity nor a clear boundary. In contrast, the idea of Little Germany placed Prussia as Germany's cohesive core (Sheehan 1989:847–852). Prussia was an unlikely heart of Germany, being outside of the Holy Roman Empire. Only the pragmatic and political underpinning of linguistic or cultural nationalism made possible the idea of Little Germany.

The Prussian unification of Germany left the definition of Germanness unresolved. Although Bismarck declared that his "highest ambition is to make the Germans into a nation" (Pflanze 1990:ii,95), there was a great deal of confusion as to what exactly constituted and identified it (Müller 1989:43–58; cf. Longerich 1990). Bismarck himself noted in 1864: "There must be some special magic in this word 'German.' One can see that each person calls 'German' whatever it suits him and whatever assists his party standpoint. Thus the use of the word changes according to requirements." Bismarck's Prussianization efforts (Pflanze 1990:ii,111–126) did not squelch conflicting visions of Germanness (Repp 2000:315–327; cf.

Hughes 1988:156). The *Kulturkampf* underscored the centrality of confessional divisions (cf. Blackbourn and Eley 1984:263). Although territorial struggles against France and Poland enhanced German consciousness (James 1989:15–19), they generated new questions about the Germanness of people in Alsace-Lorraine or in the Ruhr region. The sense of local identity long remained salient (Green 2001:320–326). As I have emphasized, *Heimat* referred principally to locality, with significant anti-Prussian and anti-elite connotations (Green 2001:330–334). As the most powerful socialist party in Europe, the German Social Democrats framed the idea of *Volk* as a nonnational class identity (Lidtke 1985:199). "The 'Volk' did not include the capitalists, just as, before the [Great] War, the 'nation' did not include the proletariat" (Speier 1986:115). Migration in and out of Germany continued (Bade 1992:chap. 4). The difficulty of defining Germanness can be gleaned from the belated emergence of the nominal category and national symbols (Schulze 1996:100). The German national flag was established in 1892, and the national anthem was decided only after World War I (Craig 1978:58).

Germany's aggressive foreign policy went hand in hand with patriotic nationalism. Yet, in the heyday of Imperial Germany, an influential conception of Germanness went far beyond the boundaries of Great Germany (Wehler 1985:464–485). In line with its imperialist ambitions, the domain of Germany stretched far beyond the widest notion of language or culture, leading some to regard Mt. Kilimanjaro as the "highest German mountain" (Schulze 1998:186). More grandly, Friedrich Naumann wrote in 1897: "What is nationalism? It is the urge of the German people to spread its influence all over the globe" (Dehio 1959:72). The Great War unleashed the ideal of German nationalism as the exemplar of European civilization (Fischer 1974:17). Max Scheler's 1917 treatise *Der Genius des Krieges und der deutsche Krieg* [The Genius of Wars and the German War] (1982:139) argued for a European unity under German leadership. Germany's defeat in World War I and the end of German colonialism stunted supra-German identity, but the Third Reich revived it. While Nazism appeared to favor a narrow version of German identity, its imperialist ambitions championed a truly expansionist definition. Hitler sought Aryan unity, which was tantamount to a pan-European—indeed, pan-Eurasian—identity, which harked back to the medieval understanding of Germania: "the region beyond the Rhine and the Danube," which encompassed "Goths and Lombards in Italy, West Goths in Spain and southern France, Anglo-Saxons in Britain, Burgundians and Franks in Gaul" (Schulze 1998:4).

After the Nazi debacle, the idea of German peoplehood continued to resist facile consensus (Fulbrook 1999:1). Over forty years of territorial division generated distinct state loyalties and social characteristics (Dahrendorf 1979: chap. 26; James 1989: chap. 8), and the gulf between *Wessis* and *Ossis* remained significant well over a decade after reunification. More importantly, massive immigration—foreign workers constituted nearly a tenth of the West German labor force by the early 1970s (Fulbrook 1991: 199)—questioned the very basis of German identity (cf. Herbert 2001: 286–296). While neo-Nazi racist rumblings exist, Jürgen Habermas and others call for constitutional patriotism and post-national identity (Müller 2000:93–98).

Similar tensions can be seen in England/Britain. The confusion over British identity begins with the persistent equation of England and Britain. A. J. P. Taylor (1965:v) observed: "When the *Oxford History of England* was launched a generation ago, 'England' was still an all-embracing word. It meant indiscriminately England and Wales; Great Britain; the United Kingdom; and even the British Empire." The domain of British history has fluctuated over time from England; England and Wales; England, Wales, and Scotland; England, Wales, Scotland, and Ireland; to the British Empire *tout court* (cf. Cannadine 1995:22–25). There was no conception of the British national; British nationality usually implied "some sort of personal bonding between subject and monarch" (Colls 2002:159). For some, Britain was associated with the state; English with the nation or the people (Marquand 1996:63). The confusion should not be surprising for a domain ruled by a succession of foreign rulers. In the language of modern peoplehood, French (Plantagenets), Welsh (Tudors), Scots (Stuarts), Dutch (House of Orange), and Germans (Hanoverians) have ruled the British Empire (Anderson 1991:83).

By the eighteenth century, British identity was widely disseminated but so was regional identity. Industrialization, especially in the guise of improvements in communication and transportation, promoted national integration, but it also crystallized regional identity that frequently superseded English identity (Evans 1995:233; cf. Levine 1986:73). For example, nineteenth-century Lancashire retained a distinctive dialect and celebrated its regional difference (Joyce 1991:279–292). The same can be said for the major British nations or races. For example, two-thirds of people in Wales spoke Welsh as the first language as late as 1870 (Evans 1995:240). Many in Ireland began to consider themselves as members of the Irish race (Colls 2002:95–99).

More strikingly, colonialism generated a supranational consciousness by the eighteenth century (Armitage 2000:196). Arthur Young's (1970:1) *Political Essays Concerning the Present State of the British Empire* (1772) provides an early expression of colonial universalism: "The British dominions consist of Great Britain, Ireland, and divers colonies and settlements in all parts of the world: there appears not any just reason for considering these countries in any other light than as parts of one whole. . . . [T]he clearest method is to consider them all as forming one nation, united under one Sovereign, speaking the same language and enjoying the same liberty, but living in different parts of the world." British imperialism made the British into "a world-wide people" (Marshall 1995:221). Migration throughout the empire promoted pan-British identity (MacKenzie 1999:212). As Lord Acton (1985:432) observed: "These states are substantially the most perfect which, like the British and Austrian Empires, include various distinct nationalities." Colonial universalism articulated well with the gentlemanly ideal. Aristocratic or upper-class culture was not nationalist but cosmopolitan in the eighteenth century (Newman 1987:11–14).

The Commonwealth ideal, albeit saturated with the discourse and practice of status hierarchy, projected a nonracist vision of the empire (cf. Rich 1990:54). Some intellectuals, to be sure, promoted racist ideology—though inflected by the language of religion and status—such as Thomas Carlyle's "The Nigger Question" (1849) and Robert Knox's *The Races of Man* (1850). However, in spite of what may seem like a straightforward racial hierarchy, the dominant state ideology claimed racial equality (Constantine 1999:184). The 1914 British Nationality and Status of Aliens Act defined British citizens as "any person born within His Majesty's dominions and allegiances" (Constantine 1999:163). The imperial character of Britain, like the Roman Empire, emphasized civilizational identity that existed alongside status hierarchy (cf. Mandler 2000:229–233). Although the expansive British identity may be a convenient ideology to justify colonial rule, more than a few subjects eagerly subscribed to it (Anderson 1991: 92). Although some regarded the idea of the gentleman as rooted in the biological meaning of breeding—blood and race—others upheld the sociological sense of breeding where "individuality becomes the essence of humanity" (Letwin 1982:12).

The fluctuating parameters of peoplehood can be seen in the unlikely case of Japan (Lie 2001:chap. 5). In spite of particularistic nationalist currents, Japanese colonialism generated a utopian vision of Asian unity in the early twentieth century. While the early Meiji leaders envisioned Japan as a family state, the reality of the empire incorporated Koreans, Chinese, and others as younger siblings in the family. In fact, imperial ideology postulated the common ancestry of Japanese and Korean people. If World War II had dealt a massive blow to Japanese imperialist ambitions and ushered in an era of a small Japan—with a strong belief in its monoethnic character—post–World War II Japanese economic growth engendered a much grander vision by the 1980s.

We can see a similar dynamic even in countries without any imperialist inclination. Given the tremendous diversity of languages, religions, and cultures, TANU, and Nyerere in particular, espoused both narrow and wide visions of Tanzanian peoplehood. On the one hand, Nyerere (1966:170) sought to build Tanzania on the idea of *ujamaa* (familyhood). Kinship is an elementary human association, offering the narrowest basis of Tanzania. On the other hand, he expressed both pan-African ideals and universal humanism in terms of "uhuru" (freedom): "All the time that TANU has been campaigning for *Uhuru* we have based our struggle on our belief in the equality and dignity of all mankind" (Nyerere 1966:139). Between *ujamaa* and *uhuru,* Nyerere covered the narrowest and widest possible foundations for human association. In a similar spirit, Kwame Nkrumah (1997:99) simultaneously advocated Ghanaian nationalism, African unity, and universal humanism, and Senghor sought Senegalese independence, pan-African socialism, and universal humanism (Vaillant 1990:267–271).

If each nation failed to reach a consensus on the concrete contours of its peoplehood, then it should not be surprising that few could agree on the abstract definition of nationhood or peoplehood. As Hugh Seton-Watson (1977:4) quipped: "Most definitions have in fact been designed to prove that, in contrast to the community to which the definer belonged, some other group was not entitled to be called a nation." John Stuart Mill (1977:549) blithely dismissed the legitimacy of many would-be nations: "Nobody can suppose that it is not more beneficial to a Breton, or a Basque of French Navarre, to be brought into the current of the ideas and feelings of a highly civilized and cultivated people—to be a member of the French nationality . . . than to sulk on his own rocks, the half-savage relic of past times, revolving in his own little mental orbit, without participation or interest in the general movement of the world." While Mill and Mazzini discredited the nationalist aspiration of Ireland because of its small size, it is precisely the smaller units that have clamored for national independence in the twentieth century (Hobsbawm 1992:31).

Being in thrall of territorial fluctuation and ideological contestation, the idea of peoplehood is at once descriptive and prescriptive. Rather than seeking to order the chaos by definitional fiat or static typology, we need to grasp the source of its protean manifestations. Thus, it is to the state and the idea of political belonging, rather than to predicates (language, religion, or culture) or to principles (race, ethnicity, or nation), that we should trace the concrete manifestations of modern peoplehood. By focusing on the reality of power politics, we can better appreciate the wide swing in the parameters of peoplehood identity.

4

Charles de Gaulle's (1971:3) memoir begins: "France has emerged from the depths of the past. She is a living entity. She responds to the call of the centuries. Yet she remains herself through time. Her boundaries may alter, but not the contours, the climate, the rivers and seas that are her eternal imprint. Her land is inhabited by people who, in the course of history, have undergone the most diverse experiences, but whom destiny and circumstance, exploited by politics, have unceasingly molded into a single nation. . . . [T]his human amalgam, on this territory, at the heart of this world, comprises a past, a present and a future that are indissoluble. Thus the State, which is answerable for France, is in charge, at one and the same time of yesterday's heritage, today's interests, and tomorrow's hopes." De Gaulle's certain idea of France is rooted in nature and history. As a "living entity," everything that changes—most obviously, national boundaries—is ephemeral and therefore epiphenomenal. What is essential is France, which was, remains, and will be France. Geography and history, people and the state are one and the same. If de Gaulle's notion of France seems peculiarly Gallic, then replace France with England or Egypt, Indonesia or Iran, Austria or Australia in his Francophile testament. It would take no great leap of imagination to see that, far from being unique to France, he could have been talking about any country.

As I argued in the previous chapter, the claim of peoplehood is made plausible by geopolitical success, and made convincing by the nationalization of the masses. In addition to the substantive realization of cultural and status integration, the discourse of peoplehood renders peoplehood identity as natural, inevitable, and ineffable. Deductively asserted, the idea of modern peoplehood possesses extreme negative capability. It is nominal in that the category absorbs empirical complexity and historical transformation. It is formal in that the same means are used to describe and differentiate peoples. It is essentialist in that it posits a homogeneous identity. And there are no particular essences to the category except its essentialization and differentiation.

The nominal character of peoplehood identity allows it considerable flexibility. Although the premodern idea of French peoplehood applied largely to the French nobility, the modern idea of French peoplehood traces a seamless continuity and identity with the elite past. *Patria* may have referred to locality in the past, but it can be invoked to justify a continuous tradition of national patriotism. Similarly, in Germany the nationalized *Heimat* of the twentieth century appropriated the nineteenth-century meaning of locality (Applegate 1990:13). The discourse of modern peoplehood systematically misrecognizes diversity and rupture in articulating nominal homogeneity and continuity. In so doing, it absorbs the emotional intensity of thick identity—family or village—in the abstract sponge of thin identity.

Peoplehood categories are formally isomorphic, relying on the same means to describe them. That is, Chinese and Belgians, or French and Sudanese belong to the same order of entities and are characterized using the same panoply of predicates. Just as each member of the United Nations receives one vote—whether the state has 1.2 billion or 1.2 million citizens—each entity has a territory, a history, symbols, rituals, and other attributes of nationhood. That is, everyone has an ancestral homeland, a story of descent, and a way of life. As I noted in the previous chapter, the transnational diffusion of peoplehood identity ensures that the same set of attributes, tropes, and predicates is found in all nation-states. In particular, language, religion, and culture emerge as indisputable marks of distinction. They arise belatedly—largely coeval with the development of the modern state—but they are asserted as the organic basis of peoplehood. It is not because of language, religion, and culture that peoples are different, but it is because nation-states exist that they assert their own language, religion, and culture.

Peoplehood categories are essentialist. Boundaries define and differentiate groups and presume the significance of inter-group differences over intra-group differences (cf. Barth 1969:15). Although nobles and peasants may have constituted distinct races, they are retrospectively essentialized as a single and singular people. Peoplehood is personality writ large, described in reified and stereotyped characteristics. In other words, it is an expressive totality, in which each person is a bearer of the category. It is a form of mechanical solidarity, or a unity based on likeness. Essentialist formulations are frequently lapidary, however much worse they may be for the facts of the matter. Changes and differences are often negated by definitional fiat. If some characteristics change or do not seem to exemplify essences, then transforming or heterogeneous elements are said to express a yet deeper uniformity. Otherwise, they are inessential or epiphenomenal.

Finally, the discourse of peoplehood differentiates. In insisting on categorical distinction, it leads to a hypertrophy of distinguishing attributes. Like modern individuals, what is unique or different is what characterizes national identity. As the state forges the nation, it asserts the naturalness and necessity of its contingent construct. In creating this identity, the inventors and guardians of peoplehood identity become bricoleurs, cobbling together various salvages from the past that demonstrate its difference, and preferably uniqueness, from others. Nietzsche (1999:131) quipped: "It is characteristic of the Germans that they can never exhaust the question, 'What is German?' " What country doesn't? Japanese have numerous theories of Japanese uniqueness (Nihonjinron) (Lie 2001:150–159), Americans engage in endless disputes about American exceptionalism (Bell 1980), Greeks generate obvious and obsessed writings on Greekness (Gourgouris 1996:171), and Thais presume the uniqueness of Thainess (Winichakul 1994:3). Every country is a rugged individualist, rebelling against some norm to which all others are said to conform. The discourse of peoplehood is inevitably an assertion of its essence and identity, difference and uniqueness.

Thus, peoplehood identity is a mobile signifier. Given the inevitable historical dynamism and contemporary diversity, there are many plausible predicates. Hence, the discourse of modern peoplehood is protean and is a palimpsest on which many contradictory things can be delineated. It follows the oneiric logic of Treppenwitz; predicates of peoplehood are post hoc claims that resist logical or empirical refutation. The distinguishing quality of Frenchness may be revolutionary or republican ideals, such that liberty, equality, and fraternity stand for France. If nearly all the advanced industrial countries share a similar set of ideals, then one may say with Lavisse (1918:30) that "humanity loves France because France loves and serves humanity." If the Vichy regime finds them problematic, then the slogan changes to "travail, famille, patrie" (Larkin 1997:90). If the national motto resembles that of Nazi Germany, then the tricolor flag can stand for

French distinction. Never mind that all nation-states have a flag of their own, many of which look suspiciously similar. Indeed, differences come to resemble one another. Sacred symbols and characteristics change, but they only need to differentiate one from another. The dialectic of distinctions is a play of synchrony, not diachrony. The archaeological deposits of distinction, in turn, constitute the knowledge of which demonstrates the mastery of peoplehood identity.

Consider in this regard the role of language in the discourse of peoplehood. The nominalist assumption leads some people to assume that Americans speak American and Brazilians speak Brazilian. Because every language is unique, language serves as a ready-made *differentia specifica* of peoplehood, although there are no fundamental obstacles to anyone learning any language. Furthermore, every member of peoplehood is assumed to speak the same language. Finally, language differentiates one group from others, whether to claim the beauty and clarity of the French language or to stress the inimitable and inscrutable grammar of the Japanese. If, as in the case of Switzerland, a people should have several different national languages, then it is taken as yet another mark of uniqueness.

History plays an equally critical and constitutive role. Every people has a myth of origin—usually from time immemorial or when there are no written records to verify or falsify—that asserts the ethnocentric assumption of the group's significance, often as the chosen people. The master narrative of difference is teleological, retrospectively locating the convenient origin that leads to the contingent present. Thus, archaeology and mythology are significant in the discourse of peoplehood. Although narratives of national development may be suspiciously similar, each peoplehood has a unique history by definitional fiat. German historiography long insisted on its particularity (*Sonderweg*) (Steinmetz 1993:252–257), even though it did not even emerge as a political unit until the very assertion of its particularity. Although the substantial plurality of contemporary French citizens may have hailed from present-day Germany, Italy, or Portugal, it is not the heterogeneity, but rather the organic unity and development of the French nation that matters (Noiriel 1992:61–65). The idea of hybridity may be used as yet another distinction of a particular people, as in the case of the twenty-first century United States. In other words, something can always be adduced to prove the categorical distinction of one people from others. The idea of modern peoplehood is an empty signifier; there is nothing essential except essentialization and differentiation.

The artificiality of peoplehood is especially obvious for non-European societies where the putative ideal diverges starkly from the reality. For Indonesia or the Philippines, Nigeria or the Congo, the very newness of the state casts doubt on the naturalness and necessity of peoplehood. However, the same was true for European nations. It was in Austria, according to H. Munro Chadwick (1973:5), "that modern nationalism seems first to have shown itself." In the eighteenth century, however, Austria signified the dynasty (Klingenstein 1997:442). As the core of the Habsburg Empire, Austria, or more accurately Vienna, was a cosmopolitan center in music, architecture, and literature. Squeezed between traditional religious identity and modern class allegiance, Austria had no obvious national identities (Jelavich 1987:129–145). When Austria became independent in 1918, Vorarlberg sought to join Switzerland, Tyrol attempted to become independent, and others wanted to join Germany (Bluhm 1973:1). The opposition of France and Italy prevented the *Anschluss* in 1918 (Jelavich 1987:156). In effect, the League of Nations sustained Austria. No wonder then that most people were confused about the meaning of Austrianness. Only in the 1920s was Austrian identity—"der österreichische Mensch"—articulated by the Jewish poet Anton Wildgans (Bluhm 1973:31). However, his and other early expressions of Austrianness were usually supranational and universalist, the product of cosmopolitan Vienna. Lacking a distinct national identity, the 1938 *Anschluss* therefore did not generate any significant opposition, and even after 1945, most Austrians hoped to remain part of Germany (Bluhm 1973:48–52). The contemporary Austrian identity is a product of denazification, defining Austria against Germany (Bluhm 1973: 130–134).

Belgium provides another case. The impulse to secede from the United Kingdom of the Netherlands in 1830 came principally from the Catholics, especially in Flanders. The Dutch isolation in geopolitics enabled Belgium to be independent (Kossmann 1978:154–160). Belgium remains a predominantly Catholic country, but the religious orientation provides a poor source of distinction. Although Flemish speakers constituted the majority in the nineteenth century, the state was associated with French speakers. As a Flemish nationalist put it in 1918: "Belgium is an invention of diplomats! Flanders is God's creature!" (Schaepdrijver 1999:291). The Flamingants, who were linguistically and culturally close to Dutch, could not constitute the heart of Belgian identity, which depended on its distinction from the Netherlands as well as France. The search for an answer to the question, What is Belgium? remains a national obsession, the very interest in which defines Belgian identity.

Peoplehood categories are assumed to exist as static essences; as trans-historical facts, they remain to be discovered. How do we know what a German or a Japanese is? Although there are no pre-given meanings or essences, signifiers abhor vacuum and unleash the hermeneutic urge. Peddlers of peoplehood identity answer the dubious ontological question and generate epistemic constructs that constitute the shared common sense that becomes yet another marker of peoplehood identity. That is, every category begets its narrators, who generate learned disquisitions. Intellectuals identify the primary predicates of peoplehood. They are neither instrumental nor ideological in the narrow sense. However, nationalist intellectuals almost inevitably work in the national field that constructs and constitutes the discourse of peoplehood (cf. Suny and Kennedy 1999:411). Though they may import the very idea of the nation or people, they seek its particular and peculiar articulation that has at least some tangential connection to local reality.

The project entails identifying essences or axial principles of peoplehood (cf. Jaspers 1949:18). Architects of peoplehood retrieve shards of meaning from the treasure trove of the past. They construct an intellectual sandcastle that would withstand the elements. As Nietzsche discerned, people speculate endlessly and obsessively on the meaning of peoplehood. The intellectual game seeks to identify differentiating predicates. The primacy of intellectuals does not mean that their writings are logical, rational, or rigorous. The unkind remark that nationalist thinking attracts second-rate minds is alas too often true. Rather, they must shroud peoplehood identity in the aura of naturalness to convince the nationalizing masses of the continuity and reality of modern peoplehood. In convincing or deluding others, they must first convince or delude themselves. Therefore, anything smacking of the eternal is prized, such as geography, language, and history. Tacitus may have written *Germania* to hold a mirror for his fellow Romans, but German humanists and nationalists took his description seriously (Schulze 1998:46–49). Living memory has to be transcended before a nation can claim its growth from time immemorial. The discourse of peoplehood needs a gestation period to achieve discursive density, or the fog that masks its newness and artificiality. Only then can the claim of peoplehood, whether Austrian or Belgian, Filipino or Indonesian, achieve a measure of obviousness and naturalness.

The cogency of peoplehood is grounded not so much on empirical evidence, but, to paraphrase Renan's famous quip, on forgetting or getting facts wrong. While regional diversity had stunted national consciousness, Louis Marin, Charles Maurras, and Maurice Barrès identified it as the real France (*pays réel*) (Lebovics 1992:138) that became the ideology of roots that fueled modern French racism (Lévy 1981:122–125). It is not so much the accuracy of each empirical claim that matters, but the very mode in which claims are articulated, which is typological. Rather than thinking in terms of populations—actually existing aggregates that are in flux—the typological mindset presumes a homogeneous and static group with essential attributes that differentiate themselves from others. Heterogeneity or hybridity is ruled out. Because typology is defined a priori, it is immune to empirical refutation. Reified in books and pamphlets, discourses of peoplehood often experience renaissance, as proponents of peoplehood identity seek grounding in history.

The discourse of modern peoplehood is often encapsulated as modern, secular catechism. Though banal or tautological it may be, people are taught a vague sense of what constitutes Germanness or Swissness, or Thainess or Taiwanness. Against the infinitude of ignorance, the light of knowledge—however dim—becomes yet another proof of the distinguishing quality of peoplehood. The stock of narratives or practices may be historically transient and culturally marginal, but no matter: Whether language or a food item, history or geography, the inevitable difference provides a potent ground for distinction and conviction. At times, there are literal catechisms, such as the 1808 Spanish one (Schulze 1996:177). Mass education and mass communication ensure the universal literacy of peoplehood identification and differentiation. Education in the tawdry trivia of peoplehood functions as the primary intellectual differentiation of peoples. As Roland Barthes (1972:153) put it: "Myth economizes intelligence; it understands reality more cheaply."

Being akin to belief or myth, the discourse of peoplehood convinces in the illative sense, or an assent based on totality (Newman 1947:289). As believers in a mythical or religious universe are unperturbed by logical inconsistencies or empirical failings, believers in peoplehood cannot be converted by reason or fact. The illative sense is skeptical of unbelievers, whose lack of faith is taken as yet another proof of their outsider status, their exclusion from peoplehood. Indeed, the sheer repetition of the category reveals the phatic function of the discourse, which affirms the very relations it claims to represent. Symbolic representations are of more importance formally than substantively. National flags and anthems are drenched in sentimentality, requiring only a generation to render them from time immemorial. Redolent of nostalgia, recent inventions and constructions come to stand for the unmovable metaphysical universe of peoplehood.

Combining history and biology, ethics and metaphysics, theodicy and cosmology, the discourse of peoplehood gained credence precisely when world religions receded in significance. Indeed, religion becomes incorporated as part and parcel of peoplehood. While the secular state and profane industrialization pulverized tradition and community, the discourse of peoplehood proffered an analytic of inside and outside, natural and foreign, pure and polluted, good and evil (cf. Douglas 1966:121). Rooted in the very imaginary of the physiological body, it fused the personal and the political: at once incorporating individuals into the body politic and inscribing peoplehood on individuals (cf. Douglas 1970:viiif). Indeed, the nation has two bodies: one that is eternal and teleological and the other that is merely mortal and contingent. The eternal national body is simultaneously the spiritual essence of the nation. Although functioning as a palimpsest, the discourse of peoplehood is *au fond* a pentimento in which the nominal category seeps through to shape the very horizon of vision and imagination. Predicates of peoplehood are chimerical not only in the sense of being mythical, but also in the literal sense of Chimerae being a concatenation of disparate parts.

To return to de Gaulle's paean, the discourse of peoplehood expresses a mythical universe in which even the stars and the mountains speak for peoplehood's past and present. It transforms quantitative and gradual changes into qualitative and sudden ruptures, rendering flows and processes into immobile and reified entities. This is the reason why de Gaulle's nationalist paean can be transposed to every people. Its fluctuating and elusive character renders it modular, but modules that are perforce substantively distinct. Therefore, all rhetoric of modern peoplehood is suspiciously similar but subtly different. The Japanese novelist Natsume Sōseki (1986:38) wryly remarked that there were few fools left in Japan who identified Japaneseness with Mt. Fuji. However, it is precisely such superficial yet irrefutable associations that sustain the mythical universe of modern peoplehood. Inculcated by parents and schools and reinforced by mass politics and the mass media, the presumption of modern peoplehood is nearly inescapable. As Lucien Febvre (1942:500) once argued about the impossibility of atheism in the mental universe of Rabelais, so it was nearly impossible to think about human classification and identification in the twentieth century without the categories of modern peoplehood. Modern peoplehood is an indisputable and indispensable hypothesis in the age of the modern state.

5

The predicates of peoplehood are categorically asserted rather than inductively proven. Being more prescriptive than descriptive, they propose and enforce what it means to be a typical or normal member. The political identity of the modern state fluctuates over time, but contingent norms are enforced and naturalized. In other words, the state and its associated institutions constitute people in their idealized image, exercising biopower that shapes society and citizens. Guardians of identity prescribe and proscribe actions and beliefs for their fellow people and even judge whether individuals belong to the people in the name of the people. The production of norms inevitably generates deviants. Hence, as much as modern peoplehood seeks to be an inclusionary identity, it excludes relationally defined minorities of the body and of the mind.

The modern state, as a powerful and ubiquitous institution of modernity, has a great deal of infrastructural power and normative impact. Like all institutions, it generates norms and mandates conformity. Nation-building is therefore at once person-building: Homo Sovieticus, the Aryan Blond Beast, and the Israeli Sabra have their counterparts in most polities. Those who fail or resist are defined as deviants. Being mutually and relationally constituted, the formations of majority and minority identities are coeval. Drawn predominantly from the educated middle class, bureaucrats and professionals devise and dictate norms of peoplehood. Recall here that the state was frequently the largest employer of literate workers in early twentieth-century Europe and post–World War II developing societies (Hobsbawm 1992:81). These state- and self-appointed custodians of the nation keep track of everything, including the birth and death of nationals, their sexuality and health, and the state of their minds and bodies.

Norm generators and enforcers frequently express deep-seated ambivalence about people in their care, who are fellow nationals but incompletely and inadequately so. Guardians of identity seek to assimilate or integrate them, which becomes yet another legitimation of their pastoral duties, and at times may seek outright exclusion and even destruction. Beyond the state, guardians of identity create para-state apparatuses to prescribe state-sanctioned norms and practices. Fraternal groups—often representing middle-class men—promote national norms and state loyalty (cf. Clawson 1989:33–38). Boy Scouts in early twentieth-century Britain, for example, sought to prevent British moral, physical, and military weakness by instilling "the supreme virtue of social conformity," such as submission, discipline, stoicism, and service (Rosenthal 1986:7). It championed the virtues of patriotism and militarism, which in the British case involved the defense of the empire (Rosenthal 1986:254–263).

Gender is an intriguing instance of the ambivalence of state membership. Although European history is not an unremitting chronicle of male oppression, patrimonial rule and patriarchal dominance have been the rule. The Enlightenment and the French Revolution inspired the modern articulation of feminism, understood as the right of women to participate in the economy, polity, and society (Fauré 1991:120–127). The modern state and capitalist industrialization generally favored the education and labor-force participation of women (Offen 2000:79–82). Just as the nation asserted its place against the nobility, women sought to unshackle "the tyranny of man" (Wollstonecraft 1975:318).

In spite of the seemingly invincible case for female integration, the nation was often envisioned as a patriarchal and fraternal collective. The martial nature of the modern state valorized men as citizen soldiers, championing the virtues of courage and camaraderie, manliness and masculinity (Elshtain 1987:198–202; Connell 1995:27–34,98–103). In so doing, it systematically devalued women, who were symbolically confined to the domestic sphere (Ogden and Florence 1987:63). Whereas male citizen soldiers won suffrage for defending the nation, women were excluded from both political and military affairs until the twentieth century. Politics in early modern Europe excluded non-nobles; modern European international politics and warfare proscribed women (Enloe 1990:11–15). The structural isomorphism between patriarchy in the household and in the state provided a potent justification for regarding women, along with children, as dependents. Male political philosophers envisioned citizenship as a patriarchal category, idealizing the classical ideal of citizen soldiers and of republic as fraternity (cf. Pateman 1988:112–115). Emasculation is the touchstone of numerous national and anticolonial struggles, which tacitly

seek to defend dependents, such as women and children, as part of patriarchal and patrimonial duties. Nationalism, as Cynthia Enloe (1990:44)
characterizes it, springs from "masculinized memory, masculinized humiliation and masculinized hope." Hence, nationalism long remained patriarchal nationalism.

The political inclusion of women occurred principally in the twentieth
century. For instance, women gained the right to vote in 1902 in Australia,
1920 in the United States, and 1944 in France. Like early nationalists,
pioneering feminists stressed status integration. The mid-nineteenth century transnational movements for female suffrage were inspired in part by
the revolutionary demands of 1848 (Anderson 2000:17–27). Following the
nationalization of politics, feminist politics also became nationalized (Offen
2000:221). In struggling for inclusion, women's movements were often
nationalist, often partaking in colonial efforts or racist exclusions (cf. Wildenthal 2001:201).

Non-European feminists either emulated or reacted against the European
example. While European feminist ideals were disseminated around the
world (Jayawardena 1986:3–8), anti-colonial struggles mobilized women
as part of nationalist movement (Mies 1986:194). Both influences contributed to the national integration of women.

In spite of their ambivalent place in peoplehood, no one can deny
women's centrality in reproduction. The state of reproduction is the key
to the reproduction of the state. Biopolitics fuses the glorious past and the
bright future. In the course of the nineteenth century, birth and child
rearing came under state custody in most European polities (Weeks 1981:
122–138; Murphy-Lawless 1998:158–167). In particular, the state intervened in biological reproduction (Ginsburg and Rapp 1995:2–5). Racial
renewal was a common European concern in the late nineteenth century,
which, as I argued in Chapter 2, was almost always about people of the
putatively same race. German pronatalism, despite its Aryan rhetoric, was
not concerned about British people, who are descendants of the same
Aryan, indeed German, stock. Beyond birth and children, biopolitics fostered public health, combating contagion (Baldwin 1999:556–563) and
monitoring mortality (Seale 1998:81). As the welfare state expanded its
reaches from cradle to grave, the state superseded the church as the sovereign institution over life and death.

The concern with reproduction accompanied sexual regulation. Norms
and deviations in sexual practices were largely under religious jurisdiction

in premodern Europe (Ariès 1985:64–67). Sexuality came under state surveillance in the nineteenth century as a barometer of national health and morality (cf. Rubin 1984:310). In Britain, state regulation was established on obscenity in 1857, prostitution in 1885, indecent advertising in 1889, and homosexuality in 1898 (Weeks 1981:83). If the sexual norm of the nation-state is heterosexuality, then all other forms of sexual liaison become antinational and deviant. The definition of the homosexual as a distinct identity became a matter of legal and scientific concern in the nineteenth century (Weeks 1981:102–105; cf. Ariès 1985:68). Beyond the terrain of law and science, the very definition of homosexual identity was imbricated in state policy (Rayside 2001:51), occasionally even posing as a national security risk (D'Emilio 1992:62).

Along with sexual norm, body norm appeared. The state prescribed everything from ideal body size to body comportment. In so doing, it inscribed society on individual bodies, rendering body and nation homologous. While variations in body size and shape characterize all social groups, an ideal of what it means to be a member of a people was propagated from the late nineteenth century. Social Darwinism informed discourses on eugenics, degeneration, and public health that sought to separate the fit from the unfit.

Disabled people constituted a quasi-race. While deformity was widely discussed in the eighteenth century, the categorical unity of the disabled did not emerge until much later (Deutsch and Nussbaum 2000:2; cf. Whyte 1995:284). Physical deviance was indexed and classified, defining deficient citizens (Stiker 1982:95,149) with circumscribed citizenship rights (Oliver 1996:46–49). At worst, they suffered involuntary sterilization and euthanasia to prevent their reproduction (Galler 1984:167). In spite of the ideal of rehabilitation in the twentieth century, disabled people continued to be a distinct identity (Zola 1982:235; Murphy 1987:135). The same is true for mental capacity. At the height of biopolitics in the early twentieth century, modern European states practiced sterilization and other eugenic measures against mentally disabled people (Field and Sanchez 1999:10). Mental disability, such as Down's syndrome, which was racialized as Mongolism, transmogrified into an ethnoracial anomaly (cf. Jenkins 1998:2).

In addition to body norms, state-sanctioned belief norms emerged. While religious institutions defined the permissible range of conduct, character, and cognition in premodern Europe, the modern state, especially through educational institutions, became the warden of national morality.

The discourse of peoplehood articulates the ideal of manifest destiny or chosen people and identifies enemies of the state and therefore of peoplehood. While heretics were the chief enemy of the church in medieval Europe, secular atheists—nonbelievers in the modern state and modern peoplehood—posed threats to the state. During World War II, the Japanese state propagated the category of *hikokumin* (nonnationals or noncitizens), which included Christians, Marxists, pacifists, and all those who opposed the state-mandated war effort. Cold War anticommunism stipulated the identification and exclusion of un-Americans (communists) from American life. In contrast, communists in Europe often became a quasi-ethnic identity, combining the claims of common descent and contemporary commonality (Shore 1997:42–47).

In denying the legitimacy of the modern state, anarchists were perhaps the most deviant. The black flag of anarchism flew prominently in the late nineteenth and early twentieth centuries (Romein 1978:161), but it has been associated above all with terrorism as a threat to the very foundation of civilization. This is not surprising because of the resolutely antinationalist and antistatist tenor of anarchist thought (Marshall 1992:32–35). As Leo Tolstoy (1935:553) mercilessly criticized the state and guardians of identity: "The more patriotic an official is, the more he prospers in his career. . . . The more every writer, teacher, and professor preaches patriotism, the more secure is he in his place."

The modern state projected norms about peoplehood identity ranging from gender and sexuality to body and belief. In so doing, it generated a motley crew of deviants—dependents and enemies of the state—as distinct categories. The homosexual, the disabled, and the communists are given a measure of national belonging, but they remain incompletely integrated. Needless to say, significant historical and cultural variations in the classification of nonnational deviants existed, but biopolitics became a crucial correlative force of the modern state.

6

The distinction between insiders and outsiders, or the established and newcomers, is a generic feature of social life (Elias and Scotson 1994:xixff). Whether for dogs or human beings, priority implies—at least initially—primacy. Xenophobia or ethnocentrism is universal but it is usually articulated locally, applying just as well to those in the next village as to those in the next continent. At the national level, however, the meaning of insiders was hollow to the vast majority in premodern societies as they did not in any substantive sense belong to the polity. In contrast, the modern state promotes cultural and status integration and practices a politics of inclusion and exclusion. Insiders, or citizens, are given systematic advantages over outsiders, or noncitizens, in political participation, labor market, welfare provisions, and other public-sphere activities.

If modern peoplehood is a product of cultural and status integration, then racism is part and parcel of incomplete integration. The source of racism is exclusion from national norm on the basis of peoplehood identification. Precisely when horizontal and vertical integration replaces regional diversity and status inequality—when people are identified by their involuntary and inflexible categorical belonging—does racism arise. Incompleteness is, as I suggested, inherent in a polity. Exclusion is endemic. As cultural integration disseminates a common identity, those who deviate from peoplehood norms constitute minority populations. In turn, racism accentuates the solidarity and integration of the majority. Inclusionary and exclusionary identities are relational constructs; peoplehood identity and racism develop hand in hand.

Racism identifies outsiders within, rather than outsiders *tout court*. Just as conflict is a form of sociation, racism must at least imagine interaction. To put it simply, genuine outsiders—people who live far away—almost never matter very much. Germans may consider themselves superior to Turks, but contemporary German racism targets Turks and their descendants in Germany, not Turks in Turkey. Nazi Germany may have trumpeted Aryan superiority, but it was quick to retract it when the Japanese government protested (Hilberg 1985:i,68). In the 1950s United States, racial prejudice was rife against African Americans, but the attitude toward Africans was largely one of ignorance and indifference (cf. Bohannan and Curtin 1971:5; Staniland 1991:35). When the future United Nations Secretary-General Kofi Annan needed a haircut in the United States in 1961, the white barber retorted: "We don't cut niggers' hair." When Annan replied that "I'm not a nigger, I'm an African," the barber said: "That's O.K., come on, siddown," and he cut his hair (Gourevitch 2003:61). The black Briton Gary Younge (1999:39) found that: "Race in America is everywhere . . . you cannot get away from it," yet when he visited a racially segregated white church in the South, he was welcomed as an Englishman (Younge 1999:153). Ethnocentric stereotypes of people far away disseminate widely only in times of international conflict. Because the claim of modern peoplehood is never universal—no leader in modern times has seriously contemplated world dominion—there will always be outsiders. The extreme articulation of racism—ethnic cleansing—seeks to exclude outsiders from within, but not to exterminate outsiders *tout court.*

Racism is polymorphous in appearance, but there are two main expressions: structural and symbolic. The former refers to institutionalized exclusion or inequality. The latter refers to ethnocentric expressions of exclusion or inferiority, which I elaborate in Chapter 6. Structural racism, in turn, manifests itself as horizontal, political racism, or vertical, economic racism. The former sanctions categorical exclusion, whereas the latter legitimates categorical inequality. Racism is robust when distinction coincides with hierarchy.

Cultural or national integration identifies a core peoplehood that renders others as outsiders. Formally the cardinal distinction is between citizens and noncitizens, which is often articulated as that between nationals and nonnationals. Yet just as women or disabled people are incompletely integrated into normative national identity, some citizens are regarded as incomplete nationals or even nonnationals despite their formal citizenship. Antimiscegenation laws, for example, at once define and discriminate against the excluded minority (cf. Moran 2001:99). Some groups are not integrated in terms of language, religion, or culture and are therefore identified by their own peoplehood identity. This is especially true when past political independence characterizes a region that maintains contemporary distinction, such as the Chŏlla region in South Korea (Lie 1998:162) or Scotland and Wales in Great Britain (Nairn 1981: 213). Relatedly, when a polity colonizes a contiguous, or, for that matter, distant, territory, it willy-nilly incorporates people living on the land. Although successful integration may expunge memories of difference and marks of distinction, it may take generations. The tendency toward exclusion is acute when other nation-states can make competing claims on an incompletely integrated population. In particular, immigrants, exiles, and refugees are outsiders not only by virtue of belated arrival but also their identification with another polity.

Political racism is most potently targeted against literal outsiders: immigrants. Predicates of distinction—language, religion, culture, and physical appearance—often clearly demarcate natives from newcomers. In this regard, refugees are frequently perceived as a national security threat, not just as potential saboteurs but also as subverters of national boundaries (cf. Malkki 1995:7).

Because the very definition of peoplehood fluctuates, so too does that of the excluded. Racism is historically fluctuating as it responds to political struggles and economic changes. The expansionary conception of peoplehood or the stress on status equality promotes an inclusionary notion of peoplehood. The 1948 British Nationality Act, for example, expressed the commonwealth ideal. Conversely, the collapse of the empire and economic downturn fueled anti-immigration movements. By the 1981 British Nationality Act, *jus sanguinis* had become the principal criterion of British citizenship (Rich 1990:211). Similarly, the Japanese conquest of Korea promoted the ideal of the racial homogeneity of Japanese and Koreans. The end of the empire stripped citizenship rights of Koreans and excluded Korean residents from Japanese life (Lie 2001:105–109). In France, anti-Semitism, most emblematically in the Dreyfus Affair, questioned the possibility of Jewish assimilation into the body politic, but the republican and universal ideals have encouraged their integration into mainstream French social life (Marrus 1971:120; Benbassa 1999:124; cf. Birnbaum 1993:103–114). Indeed, the very idea of France as an immigrant nation is alien, though a fifth of French citizens in the late twentieth century had at least one parent or grandparent who was an immigrant (Noiriel 1988:20, 1992: 50–58; Schnapper 1991:13). The legacy of the revolutionary ideal celebrated the ultimate integration of the diverse multitude into the ideal of French peoplehood (cf. White 1999:147–150; Thompson 2000:77–84). Yet France in the early twenty-first century features a significant racist movement, especially against colonial immigrants.

Two factors in particular intensify exclusion. First, war draws a sharp line between insiders and outsiders. The struggle against enemies without heightens the search for enemies within. In modern politics, foreign policy becomes a matter for the masses, inviting their manipulation by militaristic jingoism and tawdry patriotism. Thus the vicissitudes of political racism are frequently linked to international affairs. Consider something as seemingly internal as the U.S. government treatment of African Americans. The fear of their alliance with Japanese, communists, or anticolonial movements promoted racial integration (Borstelmann 2001:43). The Soviet propaganda about U.S. racism and the U.S. effort to promote allegiance among postcolonial societies facilitated the civil rights legislation of the 1960s (Dudziak 2000:249–252). Relatedly, the democratic revolution—

expressed as universal (male) suffrage—heightened the role of electoral competition. Whether facing secessionist movements, border disputes, economic competition, or other forms of international conflict, fabricating the phantom of enemies within becomes a convenient, albeit limited, way to forge political solidarity and support. Political racism aligns politics from above with xenophobia from below.

Political racism also facilitates the integration of the included by identifying the excluded. If the Other is entailed logically to define self-identity, then agreeing to hate the Other offers a sociologically primal bond. Just as nationhood or peoplehood is forged by cultural and status integration, the excluded is generated by the same processes. In other words, forging the majority depends in part on identifying the minority. Constructing peoplehood identity simultaneously racializes the excluded. In this regard, it is misleading to assume the ontological primacy of races in the sense that Pierre van den Berghe (1978:13) does: "The most important necessary (but not sufficient) condition for the rise of racism is the presence in sufficient numbers of two or more groups that look different enough so that at least some of their members can be readily classifiable." After all, the excluded do not share a common identity. Though prior commonality may facilitate the identification of "us" v. "them," they can be created out of a myriad of potential divisions.

Consider the contrast between anti-Semitism and anti-Catholicism in Imperial Germany. Bismarck's nation-building defined Germanness in part by defining non-Germans. If wars identified enemies without, they also contributed to locating enemies within (Jeismann 1992:76–95; Korinman 1999:61–77). Anti-Semitism was a negative expression of nationalism, highlighting the commonality of the majority (Pulzer 1988:221–228). Anti-Semitism became a focal point, along with antimodernism and antiliberalism, for those who sought "a new national religion that would bind all Germans together" (Stern 1961:xii). Thus, political anti-Semitism highlighted the commonality of the majority. Retaining the appeal of populist nationalism that demanded status equality (Eley 1980:349–353), the political right sought to dominate the language of the nation. The Pan German League was not only a premier organization of German nationalism but also of anti-Semitism (cf. Stern 1961:167–170).

The role of anti-Semitism in modern German history should not be exaggerated, however. Anti-Semitism was not a major issue for mid-nineteenth-century German nationalists (Vick 2002:210). More significantly, racial anti-Semitism was never a major movement in Imperial Germany (Tal 1975:259–279; Rürup 1991:93). Our view of Imperial Germany exaggerates the role of anti-Semitism because of the Holocaust. In fact, anti-Semitic parties were small and ineffectual (cf. Pulzer 1988:288). Anti-Semitic politics of pan-Germanism, led by Georg Ritter von Schönerer, was much more popular in Austria in the late nineteenth century (Whiteside 1975:307–317). The Nazis became a mainstream electoral party when it shrouded its fanatical anti-Semitism and promoted populist and nationalist agenda, as I argue in the following chapter.

The significance of state-centered nationalism can be seen in the anti-Catholic campaign during the *Kulturkampf*. Catholics constituted roughly a third of the 1871 Reich population (Blackbourn 1987:145). "The consciousness of being a minority—a "born minority"—was part of the innermost self-understanding of Catholics in the new German nation state of 1871; it lay at the very core of the classification by which the political and journalistic spokesmen of Catholicism defined themselves" (Altgeld 1999:100). The persistence of religious identity challenged the primacy of German identity.

The German culture war—far from being principally an anti-Semitic campaign—was an intense state-led persecution of Catholics. Bismarck sought to establish the primacy of the state over all other institutions and called Catholics the "enemies of the Reich" (Blackbourn 1987:143 cf. Ross 1976:15). "By the end of the 1870s . . . more than half of Prussia's Catholic episcopate was in exile or in prison, nearly a quarter of all parishes were without pastors, and a third or more of all religious houses and congregations had been suppressed" (Ross 1998:7; cf. H. Smith 1995:42–45). State-led persecution extended well beyond the religious realm. By the late 1870s, "numerous newspapers were confiscated, Catholic associations and assemblies dissolved, houses searched and individuals expelled or interned" (Altgeld 1999:115). They were systematically excluded from prestigious civil service and university positions (Altgeld 1999:115). Catholics were persecuted for their deviant religious belief, and for constituting a separate nation within Germany. They were *Volksfremde* (alien) and *Nationalfeind* (national enemy) (Altgeld 1999:113). Anti-Catholic sentiments probably superseded anti-Semitic feelings in the late nineteenth century (cf. Clark 1999:144) and persisted well into the twentieth century (H. Smith 1995:146–154).

Why didn't anti-Catholicism develop into full-fledged racism? From the racialized perspective of modern peoplehood, the answer would be obvious: Catholics and Protestants were both Germans. The answer begs both the savagery of anti-Catholicism in the late nineteenth century and the strong corporate identity of Catholic Germans. Rather, the ruling elite was not unified against Catholics, the state's infrastructural power was relatively limited, and the late nineteenth-century Reich did not face a military or political crisis. Most importantly, the political alliance between the Center Party—the fountain of Catholic power in Germany—and conservative rule promoted the national integration of Catholics (Ross 1976:132; Blackbourn 1987:160). The Center Party highlighted Christian unity and attempted to replace anti-Catholicism with antiforeign sentiments against Poles and Jews (H. Smith 1995:209). Electoral solidarity ended the state-led persecution of a deviant religious group and prevented its transformation into an ethnonational or ethnoracial group. The mandate of power politics prevented the racialization of Catholics.

In spite of the contemporary shibboleth about the United States as an immigrant nation, political racism was rampant in its history. By the 1830s, the dominant American identity implied Anglo-Saxon origins (Horsman 1981:4). Although there was a relatively open policy on immigration until 1875 (Konvitz 1946:1), already by the 1850s the American Party, or Know-Nothingism, articulated an anti-immigrant sentiment. Nativism expressed nationalism; natives sought to exclude and excoriate newcomers. John Higham (1974:6–11) identified three major targets of nativist attacks in the 1850s: Catholics, political radicals, and non-Anglo-Saxons. In other words, the norm of Americanness was to be Protestant, politically moderate, and Anglo-Saxon. The excluded included religious others (Catholics and Jews), political others (subversives), racial others (non-Anglo-Saxons), and other deviants from the biopolitical norm: "all idiots, insane persons, paupers or persons likely to become a public charge, persons suffering from a loathsome or contagious disease, persons who have been convicted of a felony or other infamous crime or misdemeanor involving moral turpitude, polygamists" (23 Stat. 332). Racism captured distinct dimensions of non-Americanness of various groups. Italians "bore the mark of Cain . . . the deed of impassioned violence" (Higham 1974:90), with affinity to Africa (Foner 2000:147). Not only were they racially undesirable, they were predominantly Catholics, and included politically undesirable people, such as Sacco and Vanzetti, and incorporated racial, or "Negroid," features (Solomon 1956:167). Similarly, Jews represented religious, political, and racial others (cf. Jaher 1994:245–248).

The definition of natives shifted rapidly. Given the fluidity of horizontal integration, despised newcomers transformed into staunch defenders of American nativism in a generation. Irish immigrants were worse off than blacks in Boston, and some even talked of Black Irish (Roediger 1990:145), but the Catholic Church and the Democratic Party integrated Irish immigrants into the native majority (Roediger 1990:140–143). Only by aggregating people of European descent as white people did the master race ideology make a fundamental distinction between white and black workers.

Once established, immigrant groups often vented their racist fury on later arrivals. As a descendant of the group that "bore the mark of Cain," Gino Speranza (1925:103), put it: "The Jew, in America as elsewhere, holds tenaciously to this racial and special culture. . . . He can, of course, be politically a citizen of any state . . . but he cannot . . . be culturally and in regard to the national-spiritual, anything but Jewish." Irish Americans, who had been reviled as unassimilable and even black in the mid-nineteenth century, led the campaign against Chinese immigration in California in the 1870s (McClain 1994:10). Ultimately anti-black racism superseded anti-immigrant racism in the United States. As Ralph Ellison (1995:583) trenchantly put it: "One of the first epithets that many European immigrants learned when they got off the boat was the term 'nigger'; it made them feel instantly American."

To be sure, others continued to represent the old American stock—privileged Anglo-Saxon Protestants—who formed the core of the Immigration Restriction League established in 1894 (Solomon 1956:102). Rather than focusing on horizontal distinction, the elite anti-immigrant sentiment explicitly combined the dislike of foreigners with the disdain of lower classes (cf. Solomon 1956:22,208). The most intense phase of the turn-of-the-twentieth-century anti-immigration movement coincided with the nadir of the anti-African American movement (cf. Smith 1997:369–372).

Nativist, anti-immigration sentiments continued to combat newcomers in the early twentieth century. Taking on the language of eugenics and racial science, anti-immigrant ideas combined horizontal and vertical distinction. The patriotic fervor associated with World War I generated a campaign against "hyphenated Americans" (Higham 1974:195–204). The self-proclaimed "100 per centers" sought national conformity and loyalty. Given that the United States was fighting Germany, German Americans were objects of nationalist opprobrium. In addition, the "Big Red Scare" sought to combat political radicals. The popularity of the Ku Klux Klan (KKK) in the 1920s and the 1924 immigration act highlighted the three elements of American nationalism. The KKK represented Protestant, conservative, white supremacy, and attracted three million members at its height in 1923 (Higham 1974:297). Its demonology included not only racial others, such as African Americans, but also religious minorities, such as Catholics, and political deviants, such as radicals (Higham 1974:287). The 1921 Quota Act (42 Stat. 5) was the first to institute racial restriction on groups other than Asians. The 1924 immigration act imposed national origins quota, which minimized the influx of non-Nordic Europeans (Higham 1974:322). The stress was not only on race but on class as well. Although the father of eugenics, Galton, welcomed able refugees as we saw in Chapter 2, American eugenicists were vehemently opposed to lower-class and inferior-race immigrants, such as Jews, justifying their exclusion on the basis of their low IQ scores (Ludmerer 1972:95–113).

Political racism is a common byproduct of political nationalism and modern state making. Incomplete horizontal integration provides a basis for identifying and excluding linguistic, religious, and other groups that deviate from national norm. Especially in times of military mobilization, the link between a foreign enemy and its descendants provides a potent basis for political racism. Electoral competition also encourages the identification of enemies within. Political racism provides a convenient cover for expressing ethnocentric and xenophobic attitudes and actions.

7

Because cultural integration is inevitably incomplete, racism is ubiquitous. Though potentially everywhere, racism in fact faces constant entropy. The structural and ideological barrier against horizontal integration erodes over time. That is, national exclusion is not as intransigent as it appears. Although *jus solis* may not be universal, naturalization, or formal integration, is possible everywhere. Given that most modern states seek maximally possible suzerainty, the general tendency is toward assimilation or integration. The infrastructural capacity of the state promotes—and popular culture ensures—cultural integration over generations. Generational transition is corrosive; familiarity may breed contempt, but it also eviscerates exclusionary claims. Racist parties have been unsuccessful insofar as they have focused solely on racism and succeed to the extent that they proffer populist-nationalist appeals that go beyond a gospel of hatred. Seemingly immobile, racism is in fact quite mobile.

Political racism is entropic because pure difference is inadequate to sustain it. Expatriates, sojourners, or temporary residents may very well achieve the status of honored guests, replete with privileges ranging from extraterritoriality to symbolic allure. This is especially true when they hail from richer countries, wielding the might of money or the lure of culture. Expatriates may experience ethnocentric slights and symbolic exclusion from natives, but it would be difficult to call them victims of racist oppression. In general, there is a high correlation between the status of minority peoplehood and the stature of the associated nation.

Inequality is important in sustaining a sense of superiority. While horizontal differences erode over time, vertical hierarchy tends to persist. That is, minority groups reproduce themselves because not only are they different (horizontal) but they are also inferior (vertical). They suffer simultaneously from exclusion and inequality—or political and economic racism (cf. Fredrickson 2002:9). This is true for conquered or colonized people, who in settler societies are variously called indigenous or aboriginal people (cf. Rex 1983:163). In modern colonial-settler societies, such as the United States and Australia, indigenous or aboriginal people are both excluded from and deemed inferior to their conquerors. Conquest, as I discussed in Chapter 2, is not necessarily motivated by racism, but the survival of native peoples generates racist discourses to justify past conquest and present inequity. Native Americans, for example, were considered at first to be lazy and savage, and later to be a vanishing, dying race (Dippie 1982:10). Immigrants and refugees similarly are not only different but also inferior, whether because of poverty or lack of education. If nothing else, ignorance of local language or culture renders them as racial or cultural inferiors.

Colonial migrants almost always suffer from political and economic racism. Owing to colonial-era relations, a large number of low-waged labor from the colonized periphery emigrate to the colonial metropolis. They face a double burden: the historical memory of inferiority and the current reality of poverty. Colonized people are, after all, also conquered people, whether for nineteenth-century Native Americans or Mexicans in the United States (Saxton 1990:41,293; Almaguer 1994:73,149). In the late twentieth-century United States, "the most widely denigrated immigrant population [was] Mexicans, a group highly associated with poverty, manual labor, low education, and dirt" (Mahler 1995:227). Refugees are also racialized qua refugees with a mixture of pity and prejudice (cf. Marrus 1985: 1–5).

Economic racism manifests itself as a redoubt of categorical inequality. As I have argued, modern state making abolishes status hierarchy. In most cases, premodern low-status groups shed their distinctiveness; peasants become ordinary Germans, poor though they may remain. Class and other categories make sense of remnant inequality. In some instances, however, a low-status group persists in occupying a distinct niche. Although modern peoplehood is an inclusionary identity that denotes qualitative equality among people within a delimited territory, the robustness of inequality may express itself as distinct peoplehood categories. Economic racism defines and defends group inequality amidst the formal equality of citizens.

Categorical inequality at once expresses and reproduces distinct occupational groups or class cultures. Thus, just as peasants are a distinct kind of people in agrarian societies, working-class people may be regarded as distinct in industrial societies. Conversely, a previously privileged class identity can become disadvantageous in socialist society, such as the Soviet Union under Stalin or Cambodia under Pol Pot, as I argue in the following chapter. Yet, because modern peoplehood presumes status integration, class inequality is understood as intra-peoplehood inequality. In order for categorical inequality to sustain itself in modern societies, it must bear the mantle of horizontal distinction.

Whereas political racism concerns citizenship and national belonging, economic racism is about stratification. Given the inevitable association between industrialization and modernization, the economy emerges as an important sphere in modern life. Even in the realm of suffrage, property ownership long remained a major qualification. In spite of the stress on individualism and meritocracy, employers may exploit existing group inequalities, whether in order to legitimate low pay or to preempt worker solidarity (cf. Balibar and Wallerstein 1991:33). Workers, in turn, may demand differential treatments, such as to protect their marginal advantage both in material and symbolic benefits vis-à-vis inferior groups.

The labor market everywhere features inequality in wages and working conditions. These bases of discrimination encompass a myriad of categories, such as gender and generation, region and religion. As in the case of political racism, however, economic racism refers only to discrimination based on plausible categories of modern peoplehood. Racism in this sense fills the ideological vacuum left by the demise of formal status hierarchy. Rather than the language of class, vertical hierarchy is justified as a matter of horizontal distinction. That is, in the name of cultural distinction, inequality is sustained. The racially stratified labor market may draw on hitherto existing status distinctions and accentuates them (cf. Bonacich 1972: 549). More commonly, the sheer magnitude of population movement generated by industrialization provides a potent basis of distinguishing types of workers. Conversely, there is a great deal of truth in W. Arthur Lewis's (1985:44) proposition that "the most effective destroyer of discrimination is fast economic growth." That is, the weakening of vertical inequality simultaneously undermines the robustness of horizontal distinction.

Consider the trajectory of Burakumin—descendants of premodern outcastes—in Japan. Before the Meiji Restoration, the future Burakumin comprised numerous low-status groups, ranging from leather and funerary workers to lepers and the handicapped to the homeless and the poor (Amino 1991:80–145). The 1871 Emancipation Decree transformed them into "new commoners" (*shin heimin*) (Kobayashi 1969:69–75). Rather than rigid status distinctions that proscribed occupational mobility and interstatus marriage during Tokugawa rule, the Meiji state guaranteed occupational mobility, residential freedom, the right to surnames, and other features of formally egalitarian citizenship.

The nascent nationalist ideology in Japan pitted ordinary Japanese against a variety of social inferiors, including Burakumin. The very fact that the family registry system (*koseki*) distinguished *heimin* (commoners) from *shin heimin* (new commoners) allowed a simple documentary basis for differentiation. The residentially segregated new commoners were racialized as a breed apart from mainstream Japanese. In the early twentieth century "popular notion," Burakumin had "one rib-bone lacking; they have one dog's bone in them; they have distorted sexual organs; they have defective excretory systems; if they walk in moonlight their neck will not cast shadows; and, they being animals, dirt does not stick to their feet when they walk barefooted" (Ooms 1996:303).

The Meiji state destroyed the legal basis of discrimination as well as legal protective measures, such as monopoly over several occupations that had sustained the livelihood of Burakumin ancestors. Burakumin therefore lost their principal sources of livelihood and were forced to cultivate meager plots of land; engage in low-waged crafts, such as footwear and matches (Akisada 1993:60–77); or work in the secondary labor market, especially in construction and coal mines (Yoshimura 1986:30). Poverty, geographical segregation, and social stigmatization characterized Burakumin life. In the 1930s, Burakumin households earned income perhaps one-half of the

national average, and experienced poorer living conditions than mainstream Japanese (Neary 1989:148). In short, Burakumin held the worst
jobs and housing of modern Japanese society; legal discrimination was
replaced by economic competition and class reproduction.

In the post–World War II period, Burakumin continued to occupy a
distinct niche in Japanese society, characterized by residential segregation,
low educational attainment, low income, and high welfare dependency
(Fukuoka et al. 1987:18,26). Not unlike the Jim Crow U.S. South, Burakumin day laborers in rural areas had separate and substandard facilities
for dining and sanitation (Neary 1989:3). In spite of legal equality, they
were excluded from prestigious corporate jobs and marriages with mainstream Japanese people (Upham 1987:114). The Japanese people John Cornell (1967:347) interviewed in the 1960s regarded Burakumin as "rough
in speech, crude or brutal in relations with each other, having a low boiling
point, quarrelsome, highly sensitive to insult, born traders, and relatively
much more cohesive than any other community." In the classic language
of otherness, Burakumin were "darkly disreputable, mysterious, and substantially unknown" (Cornell 1967:348).

Burakumin, who had been a distinct race with speculations about their
distinct racial origins from mainstream Japanese, became part of Japanese
peoplehood by the end of the twentieth century. The phenomenal economic growth since the 1960s and active state policy of integration have
transformed the status of Burakumin in contemporary Japan. Both mainstream Japanese and Burakumin have rescinded the claim of racial or ethnic
otherness (Lie 2001:88).

Racialization—the process by which a group is endowed with racial
characteristics—is possible in a society with significant inequality. That is,
racism at times literally constructs races. In this regard, because class exists
to the extent that it is recognized, its very recognition entails a degree of
racialization. Though they are not known to be biologically or sociologically distinct from other residents of Shanghai, Subei people are regarded
as a distinct group. They are Subei because they are, above all, poor (Honig
1992:1,36,58–62). That is, class consciousness is functionally equivalent
to peoplehood identity.

Indeed, class is often indistinguishable from race. In spite of the stress
on equality, status hierarchy remained salient long after the French Revolution. Even Abbé Sieyès—the great champion of the Third Estate—observed that any "great nation" is composed of two peoples (or two status

groups) and went so far as to suggest "the production of new species of 'anthropomorphic monkeys' to accomplish the 'passive labors,' to be supervised by 'negroes' " (Sewell 1994:155). French urbanites regarded peasants as "another race" throughout the nineteenth century (Weber 1976:7). Ironically, when farmers were unambiguously rooted, they neither considered themselves nor were considered by urbanites as really French. As peasants became urbanites, class emerged as a category of social distinction that combined horizontal and vertical differentiation. Eugène Buret, the foremost chronicler of nineteenth-century French workers, was far from being alone in calling them "barbarians" and "savages," accentuating their "biological traits and physical characteristics" (Chevalier 1981:290–299). As Louis Chevalier (1981:296) wrote of the early nineteenth century: "Nothing was more familiar to the Parisians of the time than the regional origin of large groups of workers. They could always be recognized at sight by their dress, dialect, general behavior and, even more easily, by the trades they plied and the districts and streets they lived in." In other words, their otherness was overdetermined. It is no wonder then that they "were universally described in terms of what we should nowadays call racial or ethnic differentiation" (Chevalier 1981:301).

The racialization of class identity also occurred in Britain. Roy Porter (1982:16) describes eighteenth-century England as "unabashedly hierarchical, hereditary, and privileged." The ideal of the cosmopolitan gentleman and the reality of the transnational nobility stunted the development of national consciousness (cf. Cannadine 1990:21–25,602–605). "Society" referred to the upper class, and there was little in the way of a common national culture (McKibbin 1998:22–37,527). The claim of two nations, rich and poor, belied the national integration of England or Britain (Himmelfarb 1983:498–503). In the early nineteenth century, William Cobbett noted: "the labouring Classes as a *distinct cast.* They are called, now-a-days, by these gentlemen, *"The Peasantry."* . . . It means . . . a *distinct and degraded class of persons,* who have no pretensions whatever to look upon themselves, in any sense, as belonging to the same *society,* or *community,* as the *Gentry*" (Snell 1985:8).

With the onset of industrialization, the language of orders, ranks, and estates gave way to the language of class (Briggs 1985:23; cf. Langford 1991:457–461,505). By the end of the nineteenth century, few would gainsay the place of farmers or workers among the rank of English or British people in the sense that Matthew Arnold (1993:107) wrote in 1869: "The

working class . . . is now issuing from its hiding-place to assert an Englishman's heaven-born privilege of doing as he likes." The enhanced integration of the working people manifested itself not only in terms of expanded educational opportunities and voting rights, but also in terms of
religious convergence between the classes (cf. Taylor 1965:170). Forster's
1870 Education Act and the 1885 and 1919 Reform Acts extended primary
education and suffrage, and Britain achieved theoretical democracy by
1928 (Taylor 1965:262; Cannadine 1995:14). The Fourth Reform Act of
1918 enfranchised most adult men, and national consciousness was widely
dispersed.

Nonetheless, class remained the fundamental language of distinction in
Britain. To begin with, there was a persistent consciousness of the division
between "us" versus "them" (Hoggart 1958:72–91). The notion of the class
war was common in the twentieth century (Cannadine 1999:136). In turn,
the people—previously known as the poor—were a politicized group
(Himmelfarb 1983:297–302), and industrial workers remained class conscious and deeply solidaristic well into the mid-twentieth century (Hoggart
1958:104; Goldthorpe et al. 1968:75). Class membership determined popular cultural activities, whether sports, reading, or music, in the early twentieth century (McKibbin 1998:528). Given the widespread awareness of
differences from "manners of speaking" to clothing, middle-class and
working-class Britons constituted distinct subcultures (Hoggart 1958:20).
Middle-class prejudice was such that residential and other forms of segregation were common (McKibbin 1998:99). In other words, class segregation was as distinct, and vigilantly enforced, as racial distinction in racist
societies.

After World War II, the reality and discourse of class gradually dissipated
(Marwick 1970:300–305). By the end of the twentieth century, class-based
subcultures that expressed status hierarchy waned in significance. Even
conservatives ceased their allegiance to status hierarchy (Cannadine 1999:
162). The Oxford-educated prime minister at the turn of the century went
by the demotic name "Tony," speaking in the common Estuary tongue (cf.
Cannadine 1999:189–193).

As I have emphasized, modern peoplehood is *au fond* about horizontal
distinction. Because of the primacy of geopolitics and territoriality, cultural
or racial distinction is the master signifier of social divisions. Status integration occurs over time as a response to popular legitimation that makes
it difficult to deny moral inclusion. That is, categorical inequality must be
expressed in the language of horizontal distinction to be politically viable.

Thus the racialization of the working class was most pronounced among those with regional identification, such as Irish and Welsh, who experienced both regional underdevelopment and working-class identity (cf. Nairn 1981:290). More important, however, was the influx of immigrants, predominantly from the former British colonies after World War II. Powellism identified the nation with the British race, and thereby rendered all nonwhite immigrants as non-British (Gilroy 1991:44–51; Paul 1997:180). Powellism cast black immigrants as at once the enemy of the British and the cause of imperial decline (cf. Solomos 1988:227–233; Smith 1994:140–169). As I noted, colonial relations combined difference and inequality. Not surprisingly, colonial migrants were targets of virulent racism (cf. Balibar and Wallerstein 1991:62).

As I have stressed, horizontal distinction erodes over time as acculturation, intermarriage, and political integration—in short, assimilation—occur. Vertical hierarchy tends to persist but in most societies working-class or poor people become part of the polity. Because racism is ultimately about horizontal distinction—exclusion from national norm—it tends to erode as excluded groups become integrated. Those that persist are those who occupy the bottom rung of society, such as African Americans or Burakumin. Racial domination is frequently a combination of political racism and economic racism (cf. Marx 1998:178–190). That is, racial hierarchy reproduces itself because of economic inequality. Others, whether defined by their class or status position, may experience endogamy and intergenerational immobility and even constitute a distinct class culture, but they do not become a people unless they are racialized as nonnational others.

When political and economic racism fuse as a matter of explicit national policy, such as in the postbellum U.S. South, Nazi Germany, or South Africa under apartheid, we have a modern recrudescence of status society or racist society. Racist society tends to be unstable, however, because it stands against the dominant forces of modern life. An inevitable fact of racist society, which depends on violence to sustain itself, is its militarization. Combining instability and violence, it often wreaks havoc during its short reign, as we will see in the following chapter.

8

In spite of the analytical distinction between political and economic racism, the discourse of racism is indivisible. Not only do the excluded minority constitute the same order of grouping as the included but they are also mutually constituted as counterimages. The essentialist binary distinguishes the included from the excluded as pure v. polluted, good v. evil, virtue v. vice, healthy v. ill, God's people v. devil's people, and so on. The logic of inclusion and exclusion assumes the form of antipodal contrast. If one group is moral, intelligent, and beautiful, then the other isn't. Binary essentialization affirms categorical distinction. Racism defines an antipeople. That is, the poetics of racism draws on the epic of peoplehood.

Just as peoplehood identity is essentialist, racism reifies and naturalizes the multifarious and multivalent quality of human beings into an essence. As Aristotle wrote in *Politics* (1252b5–7): "But among barbarians no distinction is made between women and slaves, because there is no natural leader among them: they are a community of slaves, male and female." The barbarians in fact made numerous distinctions among themselves (cf. Amory 1997:38). That is, the premodern "them" were no more likely to exhibit common consciousness than the civilized "us." The unity is imposed by racism. As Malcolm X (1973:284) asked "one particular university's 'token-integrated' black Ph.D. associate professor": " 'Do you know what white racists call black Ph.D's?' He said something like, 'I believe that I happen not to be aware of that'—you know, one of these ultra-proper-talking Negroes. And I laid the word down on him, loud: *'Nigger!'* " People who may all have been Jewish to Nazi thugs in Auschwitz were for Charlotte Delbo (1995:5) a wide array of Europeans:

> Some came from Warsaw wearing large shawls and with tied-up
>   bundles
> some from Zagreb, the women their heads covered by scarves
> some from the Danube wearing multicolored woolen sweaters
>   knitted through long night hours
> some from Greece, they took with them black olives and loukoums
> some came from Monte Carlo
> they were in the casino

Women or men, fat or thin, tall or short, kind or mean, rich or poor, beautiful or ugly, literate or illiterate, old or young—attributes that matter in everyday life—are rendered insignificant, all subjugated to racial ontology.

The essentialized minority provides the mirror image of the essentialized majority. Yet the racist mirror does not reflect truly but generates contrasting images of the ideal and the non-ideal. That is, insofar as racism projects a *Schreckbild* or the horrible image of the excluded, it constitutes the dark underside of the positive, convenient, sanitized, and wished-for image of the included. This is precisely why racist discourse provides tantalizing clues into what the norm or, more likely, the fantasized ideal of a racist society is. Thus, Herodotus's claims about Scythians say more about the Hellenic conception of themselves than about the purported subject (cf. Hartog 1988:209; Nippel 1990:25). Ethnocentrism characterized British (Curtin 1964:ii,479) or French (Cohen 1980:283) views of Africans, but they reveal more about themselves than about the putative subjects of their discourses. As Paul de Lagarde famously characterized it, the Gray International constituted an alliance of rootless, Godless, and capitalist forces, in contradistinction to the rooted and rural, Christian, and agricultural and craft forces (Pulzer 1988:78). In Hitler's view, Jews combined the horror of hybridity and statelessness (Hitler 1943:296,305; cf. Chamberlain 1968:327). Not surprisingly, Hitler envisioned racial purity and a powerful polity for Germany.

The mirror of racism, moreover, refracts distinct images. That is, predicates of the discriminated fluctuate widely and may even be contradictory. Jews, for example, came to stand for all the putative ills of modernity in Imperial and Weimar Germany (Mosse 1981:92,130). A strong component of anti-Semitism expressed an anticapitalist mentality (Adorno and Horkheimer 1979:173–176), which prompted the saw—attributed among others to August Bebel (*der Sozialismus des dummen Kerls*) (Pulzer 1988: 252) and Ferdinand Kronawetter (*der Sozialismus des blöden Mannes*) (Whiteside 1975:89)—that it was the socialism of fools. Yet Jews were associated not only with capitalism, but socialism and Marxism as well, which, as I elaborate in the following chapter, constituted one of Hitler's major complaints against them.

One reason for the disparate and often contradictory nature of racist discourse is the essential ambivalence that undergirds it. The fact of incomplete integration cuts both ways. The stranger in the midst—if she is a complete stranger who is transient, then she may be an honored guest—becomes a problem because she threatens to stay and pollute the presumed purity of the integrated majority. The discriminated in this sense constitute a liminal group, all the more polluted for that reason. Yet they inevitably sow doubts that the excluded may in fact share the virtues of the normative group. Similarly, though the discourse of racism insistently attributes inferiority to the discriminated, it cannot always sustain the unquestioned belief in the majority's superiority. Finally, the very fact of exclusion may generate counter-attraction. That is, the claim of aesthetic blight may repulse some but it may attract others if only by the seduction of the forbidden. The robust tradition of black aesthestic inferiority never quelled erotic fantasies. Indeed, it redounds as a psychosexual danger, such as the fear of black masculine sexuality in the postbellum U.S. South. The paternalist protection of women seeks to safeguard at once status hierarchy and cultural boundary.

In spite of historical and cultural variation, the discourse of racism shows remarkable similarity. Though formal, it does not differentiate. It draws on available tropes formulated against other groups in the past. That is, racist discourse is part of a generic rhetoric that differentiates "us" from "them." One can exchange one group for another and still find the same litany of complaints about inferior intelligence and lax diligence, sexual excess and moral deviance, poor etiquettes and sordid hygiene, and so on. In the early centuries of Christian history, Christians were "accused of clandestine rites involving promiscuous intercourse and ritual meals in which human flesh was eaten" (Wilken 1984:17). Several centuries later, medieval Europeans accused heretics of "sexual promiscuity, massive genital endowment and skill in seduction" (Moore 2000:175). If anti-Semites accused Jews of being boorish, dirty, cowardly, and simultaneously powerful and powerless, Jews can transpose the anti-Semitic discourse on Arabs as being boorish, dirty, cowardly, and simultaneously Semitic and anti-Semitic (Morris 1999:43). We find echoes of antiquarian fulminations in modern racial discourse, seemingly all the more powerful because of its antiquity. Scythians—the barbarians par excellence—have been singled out as the ancestors of despised groups ranging from Irish to Indians (Rawson 2001:211).

Racist discourse travels in time and space. Books and other media products resurrect long-forgotten, mad scribblings about racial others. Hence, racism often exists independent of races. What Norman Cohn (1967:232–250) calls the Antisemite International has propagated numerous ideas and representations about Jewish people in such tracts as *Protocols of the Elders of Zion*. Transnational flows of racist discourses and ideas beget a façade of deep-seated anti-Semitism in Japan, a purely imaginary threat in a country with virtually no Jews (Goodman and Miyazawa 1995). One of the reasons that racism appears so robust is that it is difficult to extinguish its utterance and recrudescence.

Oral transmission complements written knowledge. In particular, rumor—"the process by which a collective historical consciousness is built" (Vansina 1985:6)—facilitates the bottom-up transmission of clichés, stereotypes, and idiomatic expressions that have often been disseminated from the metrople (Allport 1979:63; cf. Vansina 1985:88). Face-to-face communication functions as a communal database of racist memory and knowledge (cf. Fine and Turner 2001:65–69). Racist knowledge is usually encapsulated in nicknames, epithets, and jokes (Allen 1983:10–13), providing a loose metaphorical understanding of a group. However, few locals generate full-fledged discourses of racism. They are not spontaneously generated but are usually disseminated from centers of learning. Codified knowledge is critical in unifying localized xenophobia with cosmopolitan racism.

As in the classic liberal response to nationalism, most antiracists find it difficult to take racism seriously: "There is no way to overestimate the amount of ignorance in the racist movement. Many of the players are working with only the scrappiest of educations. . . . The white racist press is filled with foolishness" (Ezekiel 1995:312). Yet racists and racist movements frequently stress the significance of ideas (cf. Ezekiel 1995:xxiv). Derided racist ideas are often survivals or revivals of old, respected, even scientific ideas from polite societies of the past. More significantly, as the underside of peoplehood identity, a racist worldview convinces in the mythical, illative sense. Getting facts or footnotes wrong is immaterial to ideas that separate the pure from the polluted, good from evil. If inclusion to peoplehood basks in the warm glow of emotional comfort and familial love, then exclusion receives the cold blast of visceral rejection. In asserting the isomorphism of personal body and body politic, a logical terminus of modern peoplehood identity resists contagion and infection, or whatever is unfamiliar and different. Hence, as much as ideas are important, racist discourse expresses itself as a fear of infection and pollution.

Racism's emotional resonance should not deny the importance of racist ideas. Just as racial, ethnic, and national belonging offers a master explanation of an individual's ancestry and future, racist discourse exists as popular sociology and metaphysics, or a theory of history and society (cf. Balibar and Wallerstein 1991:128). Racist leaders ranging from Marr and Maurras to Hitler and Powell have proffered master explanations of social life. The correlation between imperial decline and black immigration, or that between black immigration and increased criminality almost begs to be connected (cf. Gilroy 1991:109). Scapegoating or displacement falls on the excluded others of modern peoplehood's imagined social relations. The contingent fact of otherness and poverty or other social ills are naturalized and explained by racist knowledge, which offers a cogent set of answers in the form of epithets about character flaws ranging from stupidity to sloth to sexual deviance. In this regard, racial divides in opinion buttress the very racial divisions and categories (cf. Kinder and Sanders 1996:33).

The polarity between the discourse of peoplehood and that of racism is in fact mutually symbiotic and parasitic, providing unverifiable and unfalsifiable—and therefore all the more powerful—explanations of the social world. Hence, the scapegoated group is almost always a source of the inevitable ills of life. Thus, racism is especially robust in times of crisis. In particular, there is an affinity between racism and conspiracy theory, or what the historian Richard Hofstadter (1996:29) called the paranoid style: "a vast and sinister conspiracy, a gigantic and yet subtle machinery of influence set in motion to undermine and destroy a way of life."

The sociological underpinning of racism underscores the generalization that racism is robust precisely when horizontal and vertical divisions overlap. Racist knowledge is reproduced in a racist society. If the majority of the excluded are poor and ill educated, then the correlation provides a seemingly irrefutable ground for racist rhetoric. Insofar as class inequality is aligned with cultural distinction, racism remains potent as the very reality people experience, providing proof of racist propositions. In other words, racist stereotypes express kernels of truth, often expressed as sociological generalizations. Howard Odum's pioneering study of African Americans, *Social and Mental Traits of the Negro* (1910), offers an unremittingly negative portrait of Southern blacks, characterized by filth, ignorance, and immorality. It would be facile to excoriate him as a racist or as a specimen of "the car-window sociologist" (Du Bois 1986a:469). However, Odum could not have changed the early twentieth-century reality that African Americans in the rural South suffered from poverty and other attendant ills. Some victims may even embrace racist discourse. The classic instance of Jewish self-hatred exists in part because of Jewish intellectual disdain for their indigent, unassimilated counterparts (Gilman 1986:4).

Thus, sociological generalizations may merely buttress the convictions of racists, whether of the disparaged group's intellectual attainment or moral worth. Sociological generalizations teeter close to stereotypes, misrecognizing the contingent reality of residential pattern, educational attainment, or occupational distribution as irrevocable facts about a group. One consequence is over-racialization; everything becomes a racial matter (cf. Patterson 1997:3). In the contemporary United States, for example, there is an inevitable equation of poverty and race, however laudatory the intention to ameliorate a social problem (cf. Wilson 1996:pt.1). The critical question is how one would explain this state of affairs (cf. Loury 2002: 104–107). Social scientists wishing to avoid racist generalizations must presuppose a nonracist world, recognizing that even strict heritability is not a proof of racist generalizations. The stress on individual attributes captures the consequence of racial inequality, which may be generated by the structure of economic opportunity (Lieberson 1980:363–383; Stier and Tienda 2001:218–237). They must also go beyond racial or racist generalizations to consider the confluence of cultural exclusion and economic inequality that dooms groups to the vicious cycle of discrimination and poverty (cf. Myrdal 1962:75–78). The consequence of contingent contexts should not be mistaken for deep dispositions.

The fundamental challenge to the discourse of racism requires critically considering categorical distinction. All the predicates of racist discourse ultimately function to heighten and entrench the racial boundary lines, fueling at once the moral and other forms of superiority of the majority and the oppression of the impure and the inferior (cf. Lamont 2000:57– 60; Moore 2000:129–133). Chasing the predicates misses the cardinal importance of categorical essentialization and distinction that generate them in the first place. It is not because Jews were communists or capitalists that Hitler reviled them; Hitler hated them and therefore associated them with other things he disliked.

Just as the focus on the logical consistency or the empirical adequacy of racist knowledge is misplaced, the stress on the psychology of racists is potentially misleading. Attitudes and opinions often transform rapidly. Consider the case of interracial marriage in the United States. When the actress Kim Novak dated Sammy Davis, Jr., in the 1950s, her agent told her: "[my] career would be over if I continued to see Sammy. Some of my friends wouldn't even return my telephone calls" (Kashner 1999:408). When the Swedish actress Mary Britt married Davis in 1960, Twentieth Century Fox canceled Britt's contract, which ended her career (Kashner 1999:408). A half-century later, such reportage merely becomes yet another proof of the bad old days.

Racial attitudes not only fluctuate rapidly, but they reveal little about what actions they inspire. Although the authoritarian personality (Adorno et al. 1964:ii,971–976), "free-floating aggression" (Dollard 1957:445), or "fear of the human condition" (Sartre 1948:54) may exist, it does not illuminate the political background that is so crucial to the rise of racist movements. There are few convinced racists as such, and they are usually relatively powerless to boot. For example, there were rabid racists among Afrikaners, but racism long remained secondary to anti-imperialism. Only after the Afrikaner National Party's electoral victory in 1948 did apartheid become a state policy with horrid repercussions (Thompson 1985:40–45; cf. Fredrickson 1981:249).

Psychological inquiries on racists are interesting and important, but they say little about the rise and fall of racist movements, which remain fundamentally enmeshed in political, economic, and social struggles. What makes racists dangerous is their alliance with political power. As I elaborate in the following chapter, racism in and of itself does little to explain the most dreadful tragedy of racism: genocide.

5

Genocide

In his heartfelt meditation on the Shoah, Primo Levi (1988:87) predicted that "a mass slaughter is particularly unlikely in the Western world, Japan, and also the Soviet Union: the Lagers of World War II are still part of the memory of many, on both the popular and governmental levels, and a sort of immunizational defense is at work." A mere decade later, Europe—and the rest of the world—was awash with reportage of concentration camps and ethnic cleansing in former Yugoslavia. David Rieff (1995:33) was not alone in sensing "a genuine stupefaction that what was going on was oc-curring *in Europe*. People kept asking how it could be happening here." Why should it be in Europe—after the breakdown of communism and the resurgence of democracy—that the Lagers, however diminished in scale and cruelty, should reappear? For that matter, why should the genocide have taken place in Germany—the land of Goethe and Beethoven, Kant and Lessing?

Beginning with the massacre of Armenians and the butcheries of World War I and ending with a paroxysm of killing sprees in Sri Lanka and Sudan, Bosnia and Rwanda, the Shoah is but the most ghastly in a series of mass murders that maimed millions of lives. The previous century may very well be remembered as the century of genocide. In a popular line of reasoning, group hatred, or racism, causes interracial or interethnic conflicts, ranging from quotidian squabbles to mass murders. The motivating sensibility of genocide is a recrudescence of the primordial, rooted in our bestial biology or horrible history. Against unimaginable horror, the ready-made response is to underscore the unfathomable evil of human nature or the long ge-nealogy of savage hatred. Thus, we read that two thousand years of anti-

191

Semitism led to the Shoah, ancient ethnic hatreds fueled the Balkan tragedy of the 1990s, and primordial tribal conflict resulted in the Rwandan massacre. In the cognitive universe of modern peoplehood, the salience of racial, ethnic, and national identity is taken for granted, presuming in-group solidarity and out-group hatred. Particularistic attachments and xenophobic sentiments, whether grounded in biology or history, describe and explain interracial, interethnic, and even international conflicts.

If I have been broadly right thus far, then the causal priority of racism and the permanence of inter-peoplehood conflict should be questioned. Far from being expressions of primeval savagery or interethnic hatred, racism and genocide are inextricably intertwined with the development of modern politics in particular and modernity in general. A centuries-old rivalry turns out to be a recent squabble adorned in the garb of antiquity; what appears deep and profound is shallow and empty. Genocide cannot be considered apart from its entanglement with the institutional and ideological power of the modern state. Political struggles create and destroy distinct groupings of modern peoplehood.

2

Genocide, according to the 1948 United Nations Convention, refers to "acts committed with intent to destroy, in whole or in part, a national, ethnical, racial or religious group," which has "at all periods of history . . . inflicted great losses on humanity" (Chalk and Jonassohn 1990:44; cf. Lemkin 1973: 79). Ethnic cleansing, a cognate concept, signifies the removal, not necessarily the destruction, of bodies and memories of a group (Naimark 2001: 3). Both seek the asymptotic goal of racial homogenization. Although there have been numerous efforts to exterminate enemies throughout history, genocide is a modern phenomenon and a consequence, however perverse, of modernity and modern politics. What makes genocide possible is the modern state's technological and bureaucratic capacity to execute industrial killing. In my view, genocide is categorical killing of people identified by a regime in power as its enemy. The conventional definition of genocide as the destruction of modern peoplehood constitutes a subset of a larger category: enemies of the state, though usually couched as enemies of the people. The widespread potential of an internal total war is rendered real by a militant regime in crisis. In order to substantiate my claim, let me consider the Shoah at some length.

The Holocaust, or the Shoah, is widely regarded as the paradigmatic instance of genocide, and some regard it as sui generis. The German *Historikerstreit* of the 1980s revolved around its absolute and unique status (Maier 1988:66–99). The painful testimonies of the survivors and the desolate images of the Lagers are unforgettable and render all dispassionate discussions somehow heartless. The refrain of "never again" accompanies the moral prohibition to explain the inexplicable or to compare the incomparable and instead highlights its singularity and uniqueness (cf. Clendinnen 1999:10–16). In this line of reasoning, the genocide as radical evil defy human comprehension and therefore reside in the realm of memory, not history or other human sciences (Friedländer 1984:122; cf. Benz 1987: 33). In this spirit, Elie Wiesel declaims: "Auschwitz defies imagination and perception; it submits only to memory" (Marrus 1987:2; cf. Levi 1961:5). Nonetheless, there is an implicit explanatory model in this moral view, which highlights anti-Semitism. That is, German anti-Semitism gave rise to Nazism, and the Nazis destroyed Jews.

Did anti-Semitism lead to Nazism? Hitler was anti-Semitic, anti-Semitism remained a master idea in Nazi worldview, and anti-Semitic sentiments facilitated the Nazi seizure of power. A German barber told Daniel Guérin (1994:110) in the early 1930s: "The Jews? [W]e should have got rid of that ilk a long time ago. They're responsible for our misfortune. They came here to steal our bread." The existence of anti-Semitic sentiments in Imperial and Weimar Germany and the fact of the Holocaust tempt us to castigate and demonize Germans and Germany: "German Jews became the victims of a uniquely powerful culture of racism" (Weiss 1996:viii). The presumption of German anti-Semitism leads even a sober-minded historian to lament that less than 3 percent of full professors at German universities in the early twentieth century were Jewish (Mosse 1985:13), when the Jewish proportion of the total German population was less than 1 percent. Because National Socialism and the Shoah color all reflections on modern German history and culture, Germans and everything German are presumed guilty.

In spite of racist sentiments, Jewish Germans in the early twentieth century were successful in many professions. By the early 1930s, 11 percent of doctors and 17 percent of lawyers in Germany were Jewish (Noakes and Pridham 1984:522). "The story of German Jewry may well constitute one of the most spectacular social leaps in European history" (Stern 1987:105). By 1933, 44 percent of Jews married non-Jews, and this figure excludes those who converted before marriage (Gordon 1984:17). As Joseph Roth

(2001:12) wrote in 1937: "Many years ago . . . there was no active problem affecting the Jews of Western Europe. What mattered to them was to persuade the Jews and non-Jews of Western Europe to grasp the tragedy of the Eastern Jews—and especially in the land of unlimited opportunity, by which of course I mean not America but Germany."

Given virulent anti-Semitism in neighboring countries, Franz Neumann's sally that Germany was the least anti-Semitic country in Europe may not be far off the mark (Gay 1998:31; cf. Volkov 1989:36–39). The historian Peter Gay (1998:62) recalls his Gymnasium days in Germany in the mid-1930s: "I was never ridiculed, never harassed, never attacked, not even slyly, to the best of my recollection" (cf. Gilbert 1988:98). The reluctance of some Jewish Germans to leave Germany after 1933 suggests not so much an irrational attachment to Germany as a reasonable assessment, however catastrophically wrong it was in hindsight (Dippel 1996:xxii; cf. Benz 1990: 134–144). Certainly, it makes sense of Jews in eastern Europe who chose to be in territory controlled by the Third Reich over the Soviet Union (Pinchuk 1990:118–121). Although ridicules, harassment, and attacks on Jewish Germans and anti-Semitic sentiments clouded Weimar Germany (Kauders 1996:190), anti-Semitism focused on recent Jewish immigrants from eastern Europe, Ostjuden: a prejudice shared by assimilated Jewish Germans (Aschheim 1982:4; Mommsen 1991:174).

Rather than rabid anti-Semitism, we should stress the evil of conformity and the indifference of non-Jewish Germans. Christopher Isherwood (1976:122) wrote of Germany in 1933: "People sat in front of the cafés listening to [the Nazis]—cowlike, vaguely curious, complacent, accepting what had happened but not the responsibility for it. Many of them hadn't even voted—how could they be responsible?" As Leo Baeck recalled the 1933 boycott of Jewish merchants: "in history the day of the greatest cowardice: Without that cowardice, all that followed would not have happened" (Baker 1980:156). But indifference cut both ways. Although the Nazi-instigated boycott was not resisted in 1933, it also did not generate popular anti-Semitic outbursts that the Nazis had hoped for (Kershaw 1983:231–246). In general, Nazi rule did not elicit mass mobilization and enthusiasm for anti-Jewish terror (Peukert 1987:198–207; Bankier 1992: 14–29). Perhaps the most enthusiastically received measures were those that benefited non-Jewish Germans, such as the purge of Jewish Germans from civil service and the professions or the Aryanization of Jewish-owned businesses (Bankier 1992:69). However, hysterical propaganda or hooliganism failed to stir active expressions of mass anti-Semitism. Although written after the war, Rudolf Höss's (1959:144) assessment of the notorious anti-Semitic journal, *Der Stürmer*—"far from serving serious anti-Semitism, it did it a great deal of harm"—is probably not inaccurate, and he even goes on to accuse that "a Jew edited the paper" (Hoess 1959:144; cf. Schumann 1991:29). Tepid popular anti-Semitism accounts in part for the relative secrecy of the Final Solution (Gordon 1984:179–197; Hilberg 1985: iii,962–967).

Most Germans were passive though complicit in Nazi rule (Stern 1972: 15–25; Gellately 2001:261), but some Germans resisted it (Large 1991; Geyer and Boyer 1994). Numerous non-Jewish Germans were imprisoned and even killed for their resistance (Hoffmann 1996:xiii,16). Carl Goedeler, Claus von Stauffenberg, and other plotters of the 20 July 1944 assassination attempt on Hitler were conservative and even pro-Nazi, but they were motivated in part by their opposition to Nazi Jewish policy (Hamerow 1997:381–385). If we belittle German *Widerstand* and celebrate French *Résistance*—which was no more effective than its German counterpart in overthrowing the Vichy regime or the Nazis—we should not forget that German resisters found no outside support (von Klemperer 1992:432–437) and operated in a terroristic polity (Gellately 1990:179–184).

Anti-Semitism was a master idea in Hitler's worldview, and the anti-Semitism learned in Karl Lueger's Vienna was present from the beginning of his political quest (Hitler 1943:55; cf. Hamann 1999:347–353). For Hitler, Jews stood for all the things he loathed, such as democracy, communism, pacifism, and internationalism (Jäckel 1981:100). Ardent anti-Semites constituted a significant number of early Nazi sympathizers, but some early Nazi adherents were repelled by Nazi racism (Abel 1986:163). In fact, National Socialism initially attracted some Jewish supporters: "Hans Joachim Schoeps headed the German Vanguard, the German-Jewish followers of Hitler. Max Naumann, the head of the Association of German National Jews, ardently solicited support from the Nazi party after Hitler had come to power" (Gordon 1984:47). They may have been self-hating Jews, but the paradox of Jewish Nazis resulted from the appeal of extreme nationalism and the muted Nazi rhetoric regarding Jews (Kershaw 1999: 290). Rather than eliminationist anti-Semitism, Nazi leadership in the 1930s espoused extreme nationalism (Lepsius 1966:37–40; cf. Kroll 1998: 309–313).

Hitler's early political popularity relied on promises to achieve economic recovery, restore national pride, construct a *Volksgemeinschaft* (people's community), and provide charismatic leadership, not to expunge Jews (Abel 1986:137–146; cf. Stern 1975:187). Whether to avenge the humiliation of the Treaty of Versailles or to construct a Great Germany, Hitler and his followers pounded on nationalist themes, and Hitler himself sought to symbolize the nation (Kershaw 1987:48–82; cf. Pélassy 1983:287–299). Joseph Goebbels (1979:11) noted in the early 1930s that "the people are the beginning, middle and end of all our endeavours," which expressed the fundamentally nationalist appeal of the Nazis that quenched the thirst for community that was prevalent in Weimar Germany (Fritzsche 1990:7). In the words of Hitler (1943:336): "The [National Socialist] movement must first accomplish the nationalization of the masses," and "*The German Reich as a state must embrace all Germans*" (Hitler 1943:398). According to Hermann Göring (1934:147): "the most important thing . . . Hitler has [achieved in his first year in office was that he] made one united people." The ideal of *Volksgemeinschaft* proved to be popular across the social divides of Germany (Peukert 1987:236–240). In contrast, mainstream parties failed to capture the nationalist bloc of voters. The socialist part of National Socialism represented an effort to eliminate class or status hierarchy. The promise of a *völkisch* community was at once a signal to achieve cultural and status integration, however unsuccessful the Nazis were in the latter aim (Kater 1983:238; cf. Burleigh 2000:246–251). In fact, Nazi rule resulted in the reverse of what they intended: seeking to support small business, capital concentration intensified; hoping to champion rural life, urbanization intensified; desiring income equality, inequality exacerbated. About the only point of egalitarianism was the Allied bombs that fell on the German population without discrimination (Schoenbaum 1966: 278,288).

More than any ideology, the dominant impulse in the National Socialist movement was to seize, exercise, and expand state power. Hitler's reigning motive was to control the Party, which was to dominate Germany, and which in turn was to create a Great Germany (Bullock 1964:130). Far from being ideologically doctrinaire, Hitler focused on wielding power and constructing a dictatorship in the first few years of his rule (cf. Mayer 1988: 448). The number two Nazi, Göring, declared that he "joined the party because [he] was a revolutionary, not because of any ideological nonsense" (Fest 1970:71). Echoing Carl Schmitt (1976:26), his political philosophy divided friends from enemies: "All principles which tend to further the recovery and the position of Germany we alone recognize as points in our programme; all other things which may be damaging to our country we condemn and they are to be destroyed" (Goering 1934:58). The mass murder of communists, Jews, homosexuals, Gypsies, Poles, Russians, and others became at once the cause, explanation, and justification for Nazi rule (cf. Schoenbaum 1966:278). The Nazi regime's raison d'être was power.

After becoming the chancellor in 1933, Hitler and his coterie consolidated their rule (Neumann 1966:47–51). Initially, they silenced political opposition by terror. The Storm Troopers (SA: Sturmabteilung) assaulted communists, social democrats, and trade unionists (Bessel 1984:98–105). "The Gestapo's primary task was to destroy political and clerical opposition" (Burleigh 2000:183). By July 1933, fifty thousand communists, social democrats, pacifists, and other political opponents were sent to concentration camps (Burleigh 2000:198–205). As Göring (1934:119) put it, the first task of Nazi rule was to "overthrow and crush Communism." In the early years of his rule, extreme anti-Marxism marked Hitler's speeches (Kershaw 1987:231–239; cf. Meinecke 1963:77–81). In this regard, anti-Semitism and anti-Marxism fueled one another (Mosse 1985:68; cf. Mayer 1988:107). "Our chief accusation against the Jews is that it was they who provided the Marxists and Communists with their leaders" (Göring 1934:131).

Besides communists and social democrats, political opponents included all potential threats to Hitler's regime. In June 1934, Hitler liquidated a challenge from within, namely Ernst Röhm and the SA (Bessel 1984:139–146). Afterward, no one seriously challenged Hitler's supremacy as political parties were banned outright (Broszat 1981:84–92). The SS (Schutzstaffel; elite guards) and the Gestapo formed the fulcrum of a terror state. The policy of *Gleichschaltung* (coordination) enforced uniformity and homogeneity, and squelched dissent and deviance among the populace (cf. Wette 1990:89–95). The Nazis centralized rule from above (Neumann 1966:55) and organized associations from below (Koshar 1986:246–250).

Hitler's popularity or Nazi legitimacy was, however, far from complete (Kershaw 1983:viii). Beyond a core of fanatical supporters, Nazi rule depended on tacit support and political indifference (Allen 1984:301). Most German workers remained principally preoccupied by their wages and working conditions (Kershaw 1983:198; Mason 1993:278). Neither farming villages (Rinderle and Norling 1993:164) nor big business (Turner

1985:340–349) expressed enthusiastic support for Nazi rule. Beyond terror and indifference, the administrative machinery of the state served Hitler's fiats and directives (Mommsen 1991:170–173). The economic upswing of the late 1930s shored up Nazi rule, but most Germans showed little enthusiasm for the September 1939 campaign against Poland until military triumphs promoted popular support (Steinert 1970:91; Bartov 1991:179). Thereafter, Hitler's enhanced popularity bound Nazi rule and German society.

3

If the actions of the Nazi regime were ultimately about retaining and expanding power, its worldview articulated an apotheosis of modern peoplehood: racial supremacy and national greatness. As Hitler (1943:687) emphasized, the struggle was between "the great united front of those who are really true Germans at heart against the common front of the enemies of our people." "True Germans at heart," of course, were true Nazis, and the goal of the state was "the preservation and advancement of a community of physically and psychically homogenous creatures" (Hitler 1943:393; cf. Rosenberg 1970:192). That is, Nazi rule attempted to remake the nation in its idealized image.

The Nazis sought to shape normative Germans, and to depopulate deviant others: promoting the fit at the expense of the unfit. Biopolitics imposed standards of normality on everything from sexuality and marriage to childbirth and child rearing (Koonz 1987:100–106,185–189,288–292), as well as ideals of masculinity and femininity (Proctor 1988:119–125). In particular, the SS fashioned itself as the racial elite, imposing somatic standards on its members (Ziegler 1989:52–58).

The Nazi self-fashioning of the racial elite was unsuccessful for the putatively normal, fit, and ideal. The project was doomed if we look at the leadership. The Austrian Hitler, who did not become a Reich citizen until February 1932 (Bullock 1964:142), was described by the leading racial hygienist Max von Gruber as: "Face and head bad racial type, crossbred" (Fest 1970:30). Indeed, persistent rumor of Jewish ancestry dogged Hitler (Rigg 2002:174). A *Gauleiter* (regional party authority) said of Heinrich Himmler: "If I looked like him, I would not speak of race at all" (Breitman 1991:4). Reinhard Heydrich, the brain behind the SS and the Final Solution who was called the "Blond Beast," had Jewish ancestry, and the racial ideologue Alfred Rosenberg was a Russian emigré with a Jewish mistress (Fest 1970:99–103). In spite of these deviations from the idealized Aryan and German norm, Nazi leaders and their followers defined and naturalized themselves as racial Aryans and Germans. As the SS faced difficulties in recruiting pure racial specimens, it enlisted people who lacked "as many as six molars, [had] tooth decay, and varicose veins, not to mention bad posture, bone abnormalities, and poor muscular coordination, and were often below height and weight standards" (Ziegler 1989:56). The failure of the ideal was not restricted to the Nazi elite. Most imperfections among ordinary Germans escaped the exacting racial gaze. Ordinary Germans did not become taller, healthier, or more Aryan in appearance.

Having stalled on perfecting the Aryan race, the Nazis were more scrupulous and zealous in dealing with the deviant others. While the Nazis promoted pronatalist policies to spawn racially pure Germans (Rupp 1978: 15), they were more intent on antinatalist measures to prevent the reproduction of racially impure and inferior Germans (Bock 1986:94–103; Grossmann 1995:149–153).

The establishment of *Volksgemeinschaft* entailed the designation of *Volksfeind* (people's enemy) and *Gemeinschaftsfremde* (community alien) (Mason 1993:278–281). Community alien was a mobile signifier that sought to ensure conformity and obedience among the people (Peukert 1987: 215,221). The category comprised, as one Nazi definition put it: "One whose personality and way of life renders him incapable of fulfilling the minimum demands of the national community through his own efforts" (Aly 1994:52). Jews were but one, albeit very important, group among many of the enemy of the *Volk*. As Nazi biopolitics mandated racial renewal and racial purification, the SS and the Gestapo assumed leadership in imprisonment and deportation, sterilization and euthanasia, and concentration camps and extermination camps. The privileged Nazi method of dealing with deviance was elimination.

The initial concern of the regime was to squelch resistance. As I noted, the vast majority of the arrests in 1933 targeted communists, Hitler's principal enemy at the time (Broszat 1968:402–408). Until the late 1930s, the Nazis primarily persecuted political opponents, who populated concentration camps (Kogon 1958:30).

After repressing resistance to Nazi rule, the focus shifted to "asocials" (*Asoziale,* or *Volksschädling* [people's pest]) (Sofsky 1997:33–37). Beggars, vagrants, alcoholics, homosexuals, Jehovah's Witnesses, and others were regarded as "harmful to the nation" (Wette 1990:146). They were racialized as people with potentially hereditary defects (cf. Friedlander 1995:17). Not only were they unfit, but they were also said to pose biohazard. Already in the first year of its rule, the Nazi regime had begun to arrest beggars and homeless people (Ayass 1988:212).

Nazi biopolitics systematically eliminated the biologically deviant. Following the Führer, biologists, anthropologists, and moralists sought to dictate desire and to proscribe unauthorized expressions of sexuality (Müller-Hill 1988:30). Hitler was a virulent homophobe (Noakes 1998:392–395). Homosexuality was deemed a crime against nature and antithetical to the regime's pronatalist policy. In 1937, Himmler summarized simply: "Homosexual men are enemies of the state" (Stümke 1996:159). Some were castrated (Grau 1993:310–323) and many more were sent to concentration camps. They often occupied the lowest rung of the prison hierarchy (Stümke 1996:162), and the Nazis killed proportionally more homosexuals than they did political prisoners or Jehovah's Witnesses (Lautmann 1990: 203). Nonetheless, many homosexuals had impeccable German networks to help them. Of the Nazi estimate of 1.2–2 million homosexuals, fewer than 50,000 were eventually convicted (Plant 1986:148; cf. Jellonek 1990: 328).

Other categories of the biologically unfit fared less well. As Hitler (1943: 404) noted: "Those who are physically and mentally unhealthy and unworthy must not perpetuate their suffering in the body of their children. In this the folkish state must perform the most gigantic educational task." The pedagogical project entailed imprisonment, sterilization, and elimination. The broad category of *Geisteskranke* (spiritually ill) included mentally ill patients, as well as blind, deaf, and other physically disabled Aryans (Friedlander 1995:xif; Biesold 1999:160–164). Fear of degeneration motivated the sterilization and extermination of Germans deemed unworthy of life (Bock 1986:104–116). In this regard, Nazi Germany merely continued, albeit in an intensified fashion, a eugenic policy that had significant consensus between the welfare state and scientific elite (Weindling 1989: 450–457; Hong 1998:264–276). Over time, the execution of eugenic policy shifted from welfare-related bureaucracies to the police and the SS (Peukert 1987:233; Hong 1998:269). In the first year of Nazi rule, sterilization law for the hereditary ill was passed. The domain of hereditary illness was expansive (Burleigh 1994:58–61). For example, schizophrenia was regarded as a hereditary disease (Müller-Hill 1998:110), and tuberculosis, which was known to be infectious, was thought to be partially hereditary and hence a possible basis for sterilization and extermination (Proctor 1988:215). Vagrants and other asocial people were also sterilized (Ayass 1988:227). Between 1934 and 1939, four hundred thousand Germans were sterilized, and many women suffered enforced abortion (Müller-Hill 1998:106; cf. Bock 1986:233–246).

After 1939—the year declared by the Nazi regime as "the duty to be healthy"—euthanasia superseded sterilization and forced abortion as the primary means of dealing with "life unworthy of life" (Proctor 1988:114–117). By September 1939, Hitler authorized Aktion T4 (Dressen 1993:15). In addition to biopolitical concerns, institutional and economic demands, such as the need for hospital beds, contributed to its implementation (Burleigh 1997:123). Aktion T4 made mentally ill and physically disabled Aryans the first victims of Nazi gas chambers, where 70,000 racial Germans were killed (Burleigh 1994:160; cf. Sereny 1974:363). "Doctors bestrode the wards . . . as self-styled 'soldiers' for whom the patients . . . had literally become 'the enemy' " (Burleigh 1994:3). Christian protests ostensibly stopped the operation in August 1941 (Nowak 1978:129; Dressen 1993: 32–37), but the personnel, institutions, and techniques deployed in Aktion T4 were transferred en masse to Auschwitz and other extermination camps in the early 1940s (Burleigh 1997:126). Yet the killing of physically disabled and mentally ill children, as well as those in concentration camps, continued (Burleigh 1997:141). When the state shifted its extermination apparatus to other victims, the task of eliminating the unfit devolved to individual hospitals (Proctor 1988:192). Many died from mass shooting (Burleigh 1994:130), and one hundred thousand mental hospital patients were intentionally starved (Müller-Hill 1988:65). In total, the Nazi regime was responsible for the death of two hundred thousand physically disabled and mentally ill Germans (Burleigh 1994:i).

The fundamental deviation in Nazi Germany was to be non-Aryan. The 1935 Nuremberg Laws stipulated a second-class status for non-Aryans, which applied not only to Jews but also to "Gypsies, Negroes, and their bastard offspring" (Friedlander 1995:259; cf. Adam 1972:125–144), including Slavic minority groups (Burleigh and Wippermann 1991:128–135). Given the low number of African Germans, there was no explicit policy against them, but about five hundred *Rheinlandbastarde*—mostly children of black French soldiers and German mothers—were some of the first victims of Nazi sterilization (Pommerin 1979:77–85). The valorization of racial purity implied the castigation of *Mischlinge* (people of mixed descent). Debated from the early days of German colonialism in Africa (Ehmann 1998:123), they faced shifting definitions and treatments (Grenville 1998:318–325; H. Smith 1998:117). A popular rationale of anti-Semitism was the belief that Jews were "a 'hybrid' between the Negro and the Oriental" (Proctor 1988:114). The 1935 Nuremberg Laws proscribed not only miscegenation but also even sexual intercourse across Nazi-defined racial groups (Proctor 1988:131–136).

Gypsies—the two primary groups being the Roma and Sinti—numbered approximately 26,000 in early 1930s Germany (Lewy 2000:15) and faced visceral and virulent prejudice (Lewy 2000:49–52). Until 1939, the Nazi campaign against the racial others focused on them, who were regarded as at once racially impure, asocial, and criminal (Thurner 1998:11–23). By 1935, the problem generated a "total solution" *(restlose Lösung des Zigeunerproblem)* (Hohmann 1981:99–102), which led to their enforced sterilization and imprisonment (Bock 1986:360–365). Regardless of their exact racial classification (Zimmermann 1996:156–162)—because they were believed to have hailed from India, they were in one sense Aryans (Burleigh and Wippermann 1991:119)—German territorial expansion brought more of them under Nazi control. They suffered mass shootings in 150 recorded sites of massacre (Długoborski 1993:2) and perished in gas chambers (Rose 1993:xiif), including 20–23,000 in Auschwicz (Milton 2001:226). The Nazis killed an estimated 200,000 Roma and Sinti (Benz 1995:99; cf. Longerich 1998:571).

In spite of fanatical anti-Semitism, Hitler and other Nazi leaders were slow to arrive at the Final Solution. The Shoah was by no means preordained: "No bureaucrat in 1933 could have predicted what kind of measures would be there in 1938, nor was it possible in 1938 to foretell the configuration of the undertaking in 1942" (Hilberg 1985:i,53). To be sure, anti-Semitic measures intensified over time: the 1933 Civil Service Law that banned non-Aryans from state employment; the 1935 Nuremberg Laws that prohibited intermarriage; the 1938 decree that forced the names Sara or Israel on Jewish Germans; and the 1941 rule that required Jewish Germans to wear a Star of David (Hilberg 1985:i,83–154; Kwiet 1988:596–613). In short, Nazi rule gradually stripped citizenship rights from Jews (cf. Krausnick 1968:4). Nazi racial science generated scores of studies on Jewish biomedical pathology (Hödl 1997:233–274). Yet, from the 1933 boycott to the 1938 *Kristallnacht,* Nazi efforts to foment popular anti-

Semitism were never successful (Kershaw 1983:257–277; Schleunes 1990: 88–91). Each failure, however, provoked renewed, and more radical, measures (Krausnick 1968:23–59; Schleunes 1990:251–262).

Between 1935 and 1939, the preferred solution to the problem of creating a Germany free of Jews (*Judenrein*) was to evict them (*Entfernung*) (Schleunes 1990:182). Thus the Nazis pursued ethnic cleansing and even espoused Zionism (Arendt 1977b:58). Himmler's May 1940 memorandum noted: "I hope to see the term 'Jew' completely eliminated through the possibility of a large-scale emigration of all Jews to Africa or to some colony" (Noakes and Pridham 1988:932; cf. Poliakov 1979:33–52). As late as 1941, there were plans to relocate Jews to Madagascar (Noakes and Pridham 1988:1074–1079; Longerich 1998:273–278), and Hitler even suggested sending them to Siberia (Jäckel 1984:53). As Christopher R. Browning (1992a:ix) observes: "If the Nazi regime had suddenly ceased to exist in the first half of 1941, its most notorious achievements in human destruction would have been the so-called euthanasia killing of seventy to eighty thousand German mentally ill and the systematic murder of the Polish intelligentsia."

Several developments transformed what would have been a Jewish refugee problem into the Shoah. The process was incremental, not teleological. The context of war and imperial conquest offered greater autonomy to the militarized regime. Hitler invaded Poland not in order to capture Jews, but to create *Lebensraum* and Great Germany (Mayer 1988:11). A consequence of German military success was that the Jewish population under German control rose rapidly. While there were about five hundred thousand Jews in Germany when Hitler assumed power in 1933, the 1939 conquest of Poland and the 1941 invasion of the Soviet Union had increased the Jewish population under German control to over seven million (Hilberg 1985:i,189,291). True to the Nazi propaganda, the enemy within turned out to be at once elusive and everywhere (Bartov 2000:108–111). As I noted in the previous chapter, the road to racial homogeneity leads to racial heterogeneity.

The Nazis faced difficulties in deporting the ever increasing number of Jews (Browning 1992a:22). The 1939 attempt to relocate them to the Nisko region failed because of transportation problems (Safrian 1993:68–81). The Madagascar Plan was doomed by British naval dominance (Breitman 1991: 121–135; Aly 1995:139–160). At the same time, many Jewish Germans, identifying themselves foremost as Germans, were loath to leave Germany, although about 150,000 had left by 1938 (Schleunes 1990:199). After the *Kristallnacht,* many more were eager to escape Nazi terror, but Allied countries were reluctant to accept them as immigrants or refugees, whether out of indifference or their own anti-Semitism (Breitman and Kraut 1987:249; cf. Yahil 1990:543–652). "The British Government . . . took the lead in barring the escape routes from Europe against Jewish refugees" (Wasserstein 1979:345). American Jewry, without unity or leadership, achieved little (Arad 1997:201). Even Zionist leaders of the Yishuv were more interested in creating the Jewish state in Palestine than in rescuing European Jewry (Wyman 1984:160–177). The Jewish Agency, to be sure, could not even claim to represent the Yishuv, much less world Jewry, but many in the Yishuv expressed "disdain for the Diaspora's passivity" until 1943, advocating "selective immigration" that favored those "trained for life in Palestine" over "just any Jew" (Porat 1990:245).

The Nazi regime banned Jewish emigration by October 1941 (Barkai 1989:153), but it did not completely foreclose emigration and expulsion until very late in the war (Bauer 1994:253). In this regard, the Rosenstrasse protest in spring 1943 saved 1,700 Jewish Germans married to Germans from deportation (Stoltzfus 1996:258). In contrast, European powers from Norway to Romania actively collaborated with the Nazi authorities to deport Jews to death camps (Hilberg 1985:ii,543–554; Longerich 1998:545–570). The Vichy regime in France, for example, conscientiously obeyed Nazi anti-Semitic policy (Paxton 1982:173–185; Rochebrune and Hazera 1995:650–654). Ian Kershaw's (1983:277) influential formula—"The road to Auschwitz was built by hate, but paved with indifference"—should not exculpate the indifference and complicity of non-Germans (Laqueur 1982: 196–208; cf. Geras 1998:17).

Contingent factors contributed to the colossal human tragedy. The war against the Soviet Union, which consolidated the Nazi identification between anti-Semitism and anti-Bolshevism, intensified the anti-Jewish campaign (Kershaw 1987:247; Noakes 1998:496). Jews—already blamed for Germany's defeat in World War I—became at once the internal and external enemy (cf. Adam 1972:333). Simultaneously, the SS achieved autonomy and gained resources to pursue its radical measures in Nazi-occupied territory. Nazi territorial expansion had resulted in political fragmentation that endowed the SS and Gestapo with a significant degree of freedom (Mommsen 1997:83). In the context of wartime mobilization, the radicalization of the SS and Gestapo led to the Final Solution between spring and autumn 1941, transforming the goal of a Germany free of Jews into the destruction of European Jewry (Browning 1985:37; Aly 1995:358–362).

The mass deaths of the early 1940s assumed three principal forms. First, many enemies of the people, from Jews to prisoners of war, perished in the Lagers, ghettos, and in transportation because of terrible conditions (Hilberg 1985:i,215–239; Scheffler 1989:824). In the ghettos of Warsaw, Łódź, and elsewhere, famines and epidemics killed hundreds of thousands (Hilberg 1985:i,266–269).

Secondly, beginning in Poland in 1939, mass shootings of communists, "Asiatic inferiors," Gypsies, and Jews occurred, focused initially on ideological opponents (Krausnick 1981:14,32–51). As Heydrich declared in 1939 after the Polish campaign: "The nobility, the clerics, and the Jews must be killed" (Noakes and Pridham 1988:929; cf. Browning 2000:3). *Einsatzgruppen*—gangs of mass shooters—murdered anti-Reich and anti-German elements, including physically disabled and mentally ill Germans (Friedlander 1995:140; Longerich 1998:324–345). As the *Einsatzgruppen* tactic of mass shooting proved to be injurious to soldiers' psyche, other means of mass murder were used or deliberated, such as mobile gas vans and dynamites (Hilberg 1985:i,322–334; Breitman 1991:210–221). In 1941 in Buchenwald, for example, 85,000 prisoners of war were serially shot on the nape of the neck (Sofsky 1997:37).

The Nazis soon seized on the idea of combining concentration camps and gas chambers. Aktion Reinhard—named after the death of the Jewish Nazi Heydrich—transformed militarized genocide into industrial killing that focused on Jews (cf. Bartov 1996:4). Especially after 1942, Judeocide dominated the Nazi campaign to eliminate enemies of the regime. In particular, Polish Jewry was the target of deportation and liquidation (Sandkühler 1996:368–387). Between 1942 and 1943, the extermination camps at Belzec (550,000 dead), Kulmhoff (150,000), Sobibor (200,000), and Treblinka (750,000) killed mostly Jews (Hilberg 1985:iii,893). After 1943, Auschwitz (and Auschwitz II, or Birkenau) was the main plant of industrial killing. In summary, about 6 millions Jews died: 1.5 million from poor conditions in the ghettoes, 1.5 million from mass shootings, and 3 million in the extermination camps (Benz 1991:15; cf. Hilberg 1989:170).

In spite of the centrality of Judeocide after 1942, the workings of extermination camps and of mass murders rested less on the ideology of anti-Semitism and more on the dull compulsions of bureaucratic rule and group conformity. The camps depended on an extensive division of labor to organize mass killing (Sofsky 1997:263–275). As Primo Levi (1988:36–69) suggested, the gray zone between culprits and victims was crucial in the everyday workings of the camps. Jewish *Sonderkommandos* performed the ghastly work of operating the crematoria, degrading Jews into Nazi operatives (Levi 1988:50–60). Christopher Browning's (1992b:142) study of a police battalion—numbering fewer than 500—that killed 83,000 Jews in Poland emphasizes the pull of group conformity that made the massacre possible. Conversely, lack of group conformity characterized many of the Polish rescuers of Jews. According to Nechama Tec (1986:152), the rescuers came from a variety of class, religious, educational, and other backgrounds. They were not motivated by friendship or expected rewards. Indeed, some claimed to be anti-Semitic (Tec 1986:152–159). Rather, it was "their inability to blend into their environment" that accounted for their heroism (Tec 1986:164; cf. Levine 1996:259).

The Shoah, however central and atrocious, was not the alpha and omega of Nazi atrocity. As we have seen, *Untermensch* (inferior people) included not just Jews, but the biologically unfit and Gypsies, Africans, and people of mixed descent, as well as Poles, Russians, and Asians (Breitman 1991: 178–181). Foreign workers, as racially undesirable people, suffered enforced abortion, sterilization, and infanticide (Burleigh 1994:255).

Most astoundingly, Hitler envisioned that "conquered peoples were to be expelled or exterminated" (Weinberg 2003:28). That is, ethnic cleansing or genocide was the potential fate of all non-Germans in Europe. The Nazis sought *Volkstumskampf* (ethnic struggle) and *Sanierungsarbeit* (cleaning work) in Eastern Europe (Kershaw 2000:243–246). Hitler told the *Wehrmacht* commanders in 1939: "I have sent to the East only my 'Death's Head Units' with the order to kill without pity or mercy all men, women, and children of Polish race or language. Only in such a way will we win the vital space that we need. Who still talks nowadays of the extermination of the Armenians?" (Breitman 1991:43). Nazi Germany cultivated anti-Slavic racism (cf. Burleigh 1988:155–186). Himmler planned to reduce the Slavic population by thirty million (Poliakov 1941:268). The 1940–41 General Plan East projected over 80 percent of Poles to be removed from Nazi-occupied territory, as well as 50 percent of Czechs, 65 percent of Ukrainians, and 75 percent of Ruthenians (Gellately 1990:218; cf. Benz 1990:72–82). As Michael Burleigh (2000:441) writes: "The thought of deporting or killing the entire Polish population also certainly crossed the minds of several Nazi officials, some of whom countenanced the bizarre thought of relocating the Poles to Brazil or western Siberia." After their use as helots, the Nazis planned to destroy Poles (Scheffler 1989:810). They suffered over six million deaths, over half of them Christians (Lukas 1990:90). Soldau— the first concentration camp dedicated to extermination—began in 1940 by killing Polish prisoners of war (Breitman 1991:93). The Nazis also destroyed Polish cultural monuments and bearers of Polish tradition (Noakes and Pridham 1988:987–999). In short, the Nazis sought the ethnic cleansing of Poles.

Operation Barbarossa pursued *Lebensraum,* anti-Bolshevism, and anti-Semitism that led to the mass killing of the Soviet population (Forster 1998: 1245). Between 5.5 and 7 million Ukrainians (600,000 Jews), about two-thirds of whom were civilians, perished (Hunczak 1990:123). Of 5.7 million Red Army soldiers captured, 600,000 were shot outright and 3.3 million died in German custody (Bartov 1991:83; cf. Jacobsen 1968:531). Compared to 4 percent of British and American prisoners of war who died in World War II or 5 percent of Russian prisoners of war who died in World War I (Burleigh 1997:60), 57 percent of Soviet prisoners of war died in World War II in German custody (Streit 1991:128–190). Of 20 million Soviet war deaths, 7 million were civilians (Noakes and Pridham 1988:874).

The grim accounting of Nazi torture and murder must include many others. Cruelty extended to racially pure Germans as well. Ernst Jünger, for example, executed numerous German deserters point blank, finding the activity "a higher form of curiosity" (Engelmann 1986:239). As I have discussed, many "normal" Germans were killed: "The circle of victims grew in the last months to include any Germans who stepped out of line" (Gellately 2001:263; cf. Aly 1994:91). More generally, World War II resulted in 50 million deaths, which included 50–70 percent civilian casualty (Mayer 1988:13). Combat deaths are feted or mourned, but what of 25–35 million civilian deaths?

The racialization and nationalization of the Holocaust, which became the dominant interpretation in the United States and elsewhere by the late twentieth century, contributes to the relative neglect of non-Jewish victims of Nazi terror (cf. Cole 1999:144). Yet the Shoah figured neither in the initial articulation of Israeli state identity (Shapira 1997:78) nor postwar Jewish American identity (Novick 1999:103–107). As the religious legitimacy of the Israeli state foundered, the Shoah emerged as a powerful rationale: "the primary political myth of Israeli society, the symbol of Israel's present condition and the one which provides Israel with legitimacy and the right to its land, Israel" (Liebman and Don-Yehiya 1983:137). Given the Zionist emphasis on the Jewish state in Palestine and the simultaneous neglect, even disdain, of the Diaspora, there is something troubling in the transformation of the Shoah—suffered by the Diaspora—as the foundation of the Israeli state. As the Israeli historian Idith Zertal (1998:274) argues, the Zionist understandings "sanctify the victims of the catastrophe and tarnish them at the same time" (cf. Claussen 1987:60). It may be one thing for the collective memory of the Holocaust to be the foundation of Jewish German identity (Rapaport 1997:253–259; cf. Brenner 1997:142–157), but it is another to learn that it "has become a symbol central to the identity of American Jewry" (Bernbaum 1990:3; cf. Young 1993:pt.iv). Some Jewish Americans with no discernible links to the genocide wantonly associate contemporary Germans with Nazism, and even condemn Jewish Germans for their irrational attachment to Germany (cf. Neiman 1994:259; Kaplan 2001:90).

A politics of the past valorizes the memory of victimhood and vanquishes revisionism (Vidal-Naquet 1987:chap. 5). Yet the sacralization of victimhood may assume its own sanctimonious dynamic that stifles others. The incantatory repetition of "never again" bypasses the proliferation of mass killings since the Holocaust (Novick 1999:14; cf. Boltanski 1999:191). It also ignores the proper memorialization of the Roma and Sinti, for whom restitution was long denied (Benz 1995:99; Lewy 2000:202). If we focus solely on anti-Semitism and Judeocide, we cannot make sense of the massacres of political enemies, the biologically unfit, Gypsies, and others (cf. Marcuse 2001:353). The racialized view bypasses not only the variety of victims, but also the central institutional culprit: the modern state, albeit an extremely savage one. Karl Jaspers (1946:56) was closer to the mark in advocating a break with the nation-state, rather than dwelling simply on German racism.

The Nazi regime was anti-Semitic, but anti-Semitism was far from being the singular factor that explains the rise of Hitler or the Holocaust. The Shoah was unprecedented in the modern state's effort to extirpate a people, but the Nazis sought to expunge not only Jews but also all enemies of the state. The enemies were in fact of the regime but were exterminated in the name of the people. More than primordial racism, the Nazi regime depended on the bureaucratic capacity of the modern state to undertake categorical killings not only of Jews, but also of Gypsies, the mentally ill, and many others. By emphasizing the institutional source, we can make better sense of Primo Levi's (1988:199) warning that the Holocaust "happened, therefore it can happen again."

4

Genocide is conceived and executed by a militarized regime, which inflicts a total war on an internal enemy (cf. Horowitz 1976:18–21; Harff 1992: 27–30). That is, the state and allied organizations engage in categorical killing. The modern state has the capacity to achieve mass murder because it monopolizes legitimate violence and preempts external intervention by invoking sovereignty. The militarized regime instills the motivation. States and wars are coeval, to be sure, and all states seek to squelch armed resistance to their rule. Human history is replete with spectacular examples. Certainly, the Second Punic War as described by Livy (22.49.15), or, worse, Polybius (3.117), was ghastly. However, premodern wars, whether against external entities or internal bodies, were waged with limited means of destruction and little incentive to extirpate enemies completely.

The worst slaughter of Jews in medieval Europe occurred during the First Crusade, destroying Jewish religious communities in Worms, Mainz, Köln, and elsewhere. Pope Urban II decreed a holy and just war, or a Christian jihad, to recover Jerusalem (Peters 1998:25–37). The Crusaders may have had a myriad of motives, but their initial decision rested on religious enthusiasm (Riley-Smith 1997:12–22; Tyerman 1998:10). On their way to Jerusalem, various armies attacked Jewish communities (Heers 1995:89–93). As Guibert of Nogent put it: "We wish to attack the enemies of God in the East. . . . However, before our very eyes are the Jews, and no people is more hostile to God than they are" (Chazan 1987:76). That is, Jews were enemies of Christians, although they were by no means the only victims of crusader violence (Siberry 1985:156).

Two factors distinguish the Crusaders from the Nazis. First, as atrocious as it seemed to contemporary observers, the violence in 1096 was "neither general nor wide-ranging" (Chazan 1987:63). At most, three thousand Jews died at the hands of the First Crusaders (Katz 1994:81). Secondly, Christian soldiers allowed conversion (Chazan 1987:73; Langmuir 1990:292). In contrast, Nazi genocide attempted to eliminate an incorrigible people; their fault was not a matter of religion (choice) but of biology (destiny).

Because massacres are coeval with human history and categorical killing is at least as old as the Athenian slaughter of Melians (Thucydides v,116), some scholars stress the antiquity of genocide, presenting an unsavory pageantry of human butcheries (Kuper 1981:11–14; Chalk and Jonassohn 1990:32–40; cf. Ternon 1995:267–270). Far from being a continuation or a recrudescence of savage atavism, genocide entails modern capacities and conceptions. Improvements in military technology underlie the cruel effectiveness and efficiency of mass killing. The damage inflicted by *Einsatz-gruppen* would not have been possible without automatic rifles, and the Nazi camps relied on modern transportation and communication networks (Hilberg 1989a:121–124). The death factories depended on the mass production of Zyklon B, which was invented in 1923 as a pesticide and disinfectant (Weller 1993:206). Modern technology, in other words, made possible three million deaths in three years. In contrast, the Melian massacre numbered in the hundreds. Spanish conquistadors may have inflicted mass deaths in the New World, but the vast majority died from diseases, as I argued in Chapter 2.

Just as important as modern technology were organizational innovations. Savage hatred may have motivated industrial killing, but its execution relied on planning and coordination (cf. Breitman 1991:249). The German civil bureaucracy played a critical part in identifying, tracking, and deporting Jews (Hilberg 1985:i,56–62). Extermination camps depended on municipal bureaucracies, local police forces, industries, and railroad officials to transport the victims (Mommsen 1998:219). In other words, the Final Solution relied not on ill-educated, racist Germans but on well-educated, presumably genteel medical scientists, lawyers, and other professionals to identify and indemnify the Jewish race (Bartov 1996:67). Nazi doctors selected and supervised inmates, making the all-important decision to triage them (Lifton 1986:186–192). As the Nazi doctor Fritz Klein said: "Of course I am a doctor and I want to preserve life. And out of respect for human life, I would remove a gangrenous appendix from a diseased body. The Jew is the gangrenous appendix in the body of mankind" (Lifton 1986:16). Although the Holocaust was neither conceived nor ordered by middle-level bureaucrats and scientists, they engaged in normal bureaucratic calculations and ordinary organizational struggles to realize the Final Solution (Aly and Heim 1991:488–492). In fact, inter-bureaucratic rivalry may very well have enhanced the efficiency of administrative murder (Hilberg 1985:iii,1003–1007). Bureaucratic rationality facilitated the dehumanization of victims (Bauman 1989:102). That is, instrumental rationality and other bureaucratic thought processes overcame many officials' scruples and inhibitions (Hilberg 1985:iii,1012–1029). In fact, many Germans blamed the bureaucracy, and not Hitler, for the excesses of the regime (Steinert 1970:544–564). They were right insofar as it was not Hitler's rabid racism in of itself that inflicted millions of murders, but his ability to command the bureaucracy. The banality of evil surely does not exculpate the banal functionaries (cf. Arendt 1977b:22–27).

Beyond technological and organizational advances, modern conceptions were critical. The concept of total war framed economic and ideological mobilization. It also expanded the definition of the enemy from just soldiers to all citizens, thereby justifying the comprehensive destruction of the enemy (Shaw 1991:20). As Raphael Lemkin (1973:80) argued, this is "the antithesis of the Rousseau-Portalis Doctrine [which] holds that war is directed against sovereigns and armies, not against subjects and civilians." In other words, modern total war was waged on the modern category of peoplehood. Here we should recall that colonial conquests, such as the German massacre of the Herero, put into practice not only the technology and logistics of mass murder but also the modern ideologies that justified extermination. Racial science and Social Darwinism contributed to the primacy of biopolitics and the vision of total destruction. The First Crusade made room for conversion, but in the Nazi racial universe the biologically unfit and the racial others were incorrigible.

Finally, we should not ignore economic interests and psychological factors. Mass killing offered material benefits not only to weapons merchants but also to soldiers and citizens. In addition to war booty, the promise of newly vacated land or jobs dampened the desire to defend their former friends or neighbors. The Nazi regime also fostered a culture of violence. The state and the military frequently tapped the violent and the vicious and encouraged killing sprees. Yet working at extermination camps was far from prestigious and the burden of inhuman acts fell on criminals and the lowest strata. Far from relishing in their savagery, many of them sought transfer or solace in alcohol (van Creveld 1991:160). Not surprisingly, the Jewish *Sonderkommandos* executed the ghastliest operations in the extermination camps.

5

Armenians in Ottoman Empire, Jews in Nazi Germany, Bosnian Muslims in ex-Yugoslavia, and Tutsi in Rwanda are commonly described and explained as victims of genocide. As important as racist sentiments or ethnoracial feuds may seem in retrospect, the agent of genocidal violence is the modern state, which simultaneously has the capacity and the will to engage in a total war against its enemies. Extremely nationalist and militarist regimes deploy racism in order simultaneously to promote regime legitimacy and internal cohesion and to exclude and expunge nonracial or nonnational others. More specifically, the regime in power mobilizes military and bureaucratic power to inflict mass murder. Potential or actual challengers are liquidated in the name of the people. Far from neighbors spontaneously killing neighbors, the regime's paramilitary and military forces plan and execute mass killing, abetted by state apparatuses ranging from the police to the mass media. Rather than racism, the analytical focus should be on power struggles.

The Armenian genocide of 1915–18 is frequently compared to the Holocaust (Boyajian 1972:309–314; Melson 1992:256) and is often taken to be a consequence of anti-Armenian racism (Astourian 1999:40). Just as pogroms preceded the Final Solution, the 1894–96 massacres that claimed some two hundred thousand lives preceded the genocide (Naimark 2001:22).

Despite claims of long history and ancient territoriality (Miller and Miller 1993:32–35), Armenians were far from achieving the conditions of modern peoplehood until the late nineteenth century. Migration, conquests, conversions, and intermingling characterized the geographical area around Mt. Ararat (Suny 1993:7), and status hierarchy precluded a widespread dissemination of an Armenian ethnonational identity. Armenian was largely a confessional identity.

By the 1908 Young Turk revolution, inclusionary Ottoman nationalism had transmuted into exclusionary Turkic nationalism that asserted Turkish superiority and purity (Ternon 2002:272–279). The Committee of Union and Progress (CUP) took its ideological inspiration from racist and nationalist pan-Turkism after the 1913 coup (Hovannisian 1986:24). In addition to religious intolerance, the CUP sought to suppress all expressions of political dissent (Zürcher 1993:115). It mobilized anti-Armenian sentiments by rendering them as not only scapegoats and traitors, but also as the religious enemy. Precisely when the meaning of Turkish nationalism was hollow to most would-be Turkish subjects, the CUP created an enemy that would fan political cohesion and religious support (cf. Hovannisian 1986:24). What had been a religious community became a proto-racial group and national enemy.

The 1915–18 genocide occurred as the Ottoman polity sought to squelch a dissident political, religious, and regional movement (Maleville 1988:59–63; Dadrian 1999:126–129). Beginning with the April 1915 deportation and detention of Armenian leaders, the CUP, in conjunction with the military and the Interior Ministry, waged a total war—a doctrine imported from the Prussian army (Reid 1992:29–33)—against Armenians. Their massive deportation relied on the modernizing military and bureaucracy, and their mass death was justified by Armenians being the enemies of the state (Reid 1992:42–45). It should be noted, however, that the Armenian genocide did not rely completely on racist categories. Because of the strong religious overtone, many Armenians who converted to Islam were saved (Naimark 2001:35). In spite of efforts to rescue Armenians (Hovannisian 1992:197), the world remained largely indifferent to their plight (Zürcher 1993:121). Between 600,000 and two million Armenians died, or as many as one-half of the total Armenian population in Turkey (Hovannisian 1999: 15; Karsh and Karsh 1999:156).

The Balkan tragedy of the 1990s, especially the ethnic cleansing of Bosnian Muslims in 1992, was often regarded as a consequence of ancient ethnic hatred. Serbian nationalism aroused some ethnic Serbs in Bosnia-Herzegovina to commit genocidal acts, but it would be misleading to highlight the role of distant historical events, such as the fourteenth-century Battle of Kosovo or the Yugoslav civil war during and immediately after World War II (cf. Judah 2000:1–8).

Yugoslavia emerged after the collapse of the Habsburg and Ottoman Empires following World War I. Linguistic differences, confessional cleavages, and cultural hybridity characterized the country. Bosnia-Herzegovina, marked by boundary shifts and population transfers throughout the nineteenth century, did not generate its own regional or nationalist movement and existed principally as an administrative unit (Bringa 1995:32). Although the people Engels called *Völkerabfälle*—literally, refuse of peoples— had been clamoring for various articulations of nationhood in the region since the late eighteenth century (Banac 1984:11,75–82), their dominant identity was confessional in the nineteenth century (Lampe 2000:22). In any case, the most prominent nationalist movement in the nineteenth century was the Illyrian movement (Lampe 2000:43–46).

Confessional identities transformed into regional and ethnonational identities in the twentieth century. Bosnians of Orthodox Christian persuasion identified themselves as Serbians and those of Catholic faith as Croatians. Tito's policy of national autonomy strengthened ethnic consciousness along with Yugoslavian identity (Lampe 2000:234–238). In contrast, Muslims lacked an ethnonational identification (Malcolm 1994:197–201). During World War II, for example, Muslims of Bosnia-Herzegovina fought on all sides, ranging from Germans to Partisans, Croatian Ustaša to Serbian Četnik (Malcolm 1994:192). However, Muslim identity eroded during Tito's rule, when Yugoslav identity began to supersede other substate national identities, especially in urban areas (Burg and Shoup 1999: 29). By the 1980s, about a third of marriages were mixed and Muslim identity manifested itself as flotsam and jetsam of the past, such as Muslim names, circumcision, and baklava (Malcolm 1994:221; Rieff 1995:168). Bosnia-Herzegovina was hardly seething with interethnic conflict (Bringa 1995:3).

Geopolitical situation—the waning Cold War and the loosening grip of the Soviet Union—facilitated political disintegration. Proximately, the economic crisis of the 1980s contributed to political devolution (Woodward 1995a:355–358, 1995b:15). Slobodan Milošević used the Serbian regional authority as the launching pad for Serbian imperialism by first conquering Kosovo (Judah 2000:54–60). Rather than being a racial ideologue, he sought to shore up his domestic support by promoting nationalism and racism (Doder and Branson 1999:138; cf. Mertus 1999:253). Serbia created an apartheid that favored Serbs over Albanians (Malcolm 1998:349). In particular, Serbia systematically purged the state bureaucracy, replacing Titoists, Yugoslavs, and others with Serbian nationalists (Burg and Shoup 1999:62–69).

During the Yugoslav civil war that began in 1991, Milošević's security and paramilitary forces led the campaign of ethnic cleansing against Bosnian Muslims (Malcolm 1994:251; Judah 1997:233–238). Invoking the tendentious history of Ottoman invasion and World War II–era massacres, the Serbian forces committed mass deportation and mass shootings, operated concentration camps, and destroyed cultural monuments (Cushman and Meštrović 1996:13–17). Although the principal killers were the Serbian forces, they elicited the participation of their co-ethnics in the region

(Burg and Shoup 1999:183). From one-third to two-thirds of the total Muslim population in Bosnia-Herzegovina were displaced (Burg and Shoup 1999:171). In spite of the Serbian state-initiated campaign of rape, torture, and massacre of Bosnian Muslims, the outside world viewed it as an internal matter (Barnett 1996:149–156).

Serbian nationalism and anti-Bosnian Muslim racism both contributed to the massacre of Bosnian Muslims, but it would be misleading to highlight only these two factors. Villagers, after all, did not engage in interethnic conflict until war came from outside. The effective cause was the Milošević regime's effort to secure more territory and its readiness to inflict savage violence. The invocation of ancient ethnic hatred not only makes a mockery of what had been a multiethnic Yugoslavia relatively free of interethnic tension (Woodward 1995b:234), but it also exculpates the chief culprit of the genocide. In this regard, the oft-proposed solution of ethnic partition merely enhanced the ethnic divide that was fostered in first place by those who sought partition (Kumar 1997:167).

The massacre of Tutsi Rwandans was often reported to be a consequence of tribal or ethnic conflict between the Hutu and the Tutsi. The distinction—the former denoting farmers and the latter referring to pastoralists—was largely meaningless before Belgian colonization (Newbury 1988:10; cf. Marx 1997:60–68). In the process of colonial state-building, the Belgian authorities, with their belief in racial classification, identified the Tutsi as the superior caste (Chrétien 1997:13–17) and provided them with privilege and power (Newbury 1988:206–209). Colonial hierarchy was reversed by the November 1959 coup. By 1973, when Juvénal Habariyama assumed power, Tutsi people had become institutionally marginalized (Prunier 1995:73–85).

Rwanda in the 1970s and 1980s was widely regarded as one of the most homogeneous countries in the world, marked by the same language, religion, and culture (Destexhe 1995:36). By 1990, however, the Habariyama regime faced political discontent and economic downturn (Braeckman 1994:102). In the same year, the Rwanda Patriotic Front (RFP), led by those driven out of power in the 1959 coup, began armed resistance. Facing a legitimation crisis, Habariyama's regime attempted to identify the Tutsi as the enemy of the people, conflating the domestic minority with the external enemy (African Rights 1995:59; D. Smith 1998:746). The regime attempted to promote Hutu power by asserting Tutsi unity (Human Rights Watch 1999:73–79). As a Rwandan newspaper reported in 1993: "Rwandan fascists and their chiefs have decided to apply 'the final solution' to their fellow citizens judged enemies of the regime. This refers to their political adversaries and defenceless populations" (McCullum 1995:16–17).

Mass slaughter began in April 1994 after Habariyama's death. The new junta sought to eliminate potential enemies, including Habariyama's cronies, opposition politicians, senior civil servants, business elite, and critical journalists, many of whom were Hutu (African Rights 1995:172–178). In fact, many of the initial victims of Hutu violence were co-ethnics from rival regions (African Rights 1995:30–35). Soon thereafter, the extermination campaign focused on Tutsi people, the putative enemy of Hutu power. The regime monopolized the media, especially the radio, and disseminated propaganda about the complicity of Tutsi with international enemies (Chrétien et al. 1995:297–306). From April to June 1994, it mobilized the military, local government officials, teachers, business people, and others to participate in the killing of Tutsi people and those who opposed the genocidal campaign (African Rights 1995:117–120). Seeking direct and mass mobilization of accomplices, the regime disseminated rifles and grenades—in addition to the much-publicized machetes—and used existing institutions and media to promote a frenzy of killing (Mamdani 2001:5). As the state-run radio repeatedly called for racial extermination—the victims were *invenzi,* or "cockroaches that have to be crushed" (Destexhe 1995: 28)—ordinary civilians were encouraged to take part in the killing spree. The radio broadcast promised "the radio, the couch, the goat, the opportunity to rape a young girl" (Gourevitch 1998:115). In so doing, the mass mobilization unleashed petty personal feuds and crimes that allowed sadistic savagery and mundane looting. By creating a community of killers, genocide became a collective responsibility (African Rights 1995:1022; Gourevitch 1998:244). Resistance, although it saved numerous lives, could not stop the state-organized terror (African Rights 1995:1024–1061). In three months, five hundred thousand, or three-fourths of the Tutsi population in Rwanda, were killed, along with those who had opposed the genocide (Human Rights 1999:1; cf. Mamdani 2001:5).

Reports of neighbors slaughtering neighbors led many observers to highlight latent or manifest expressions of interethnic hatred. In spite of the colonial racial classification or the ensuing political struggles that invoked ethnic affiliation, the 1994 genocide resulted from the militarist regime's quest for power. The initial killings focused on enemies of the regime, many of whom were Hutu. The absurdity of the situation can be gauged by the need for an identification card to mark an individual for slaughter (African Rights 1995:642–649). Terror and violence were as shocking as the quietude of the church or the belated and half-hearted response of international organizations (Braeckman 1994:214, 1996:65–97; Chrétien 1997:215–244). The murderers, for their part, sought to extinguish evidence of genocide (African Rights 1996:3). The killing spree ended with the RFP's military victory, but not before the RFP itself had committed massacres (Human Rights Watch 1999:709–722).

War or regime crisis is the immediate backdrop of genocide. The militarized regime, often with revolutionary intent, conflates external and internal foes. Above all, it engages in war as a mode of politics. Domestic resistance, which can be found in all four cases, is overwhelmed by a terroristic polity, which monopolizes the means of violence and secures international legitimacy. Neighboring countries and international organizations bypass mass slaughter in silence, if not actually aiding it for their benefit (Power 2002:503). Exceptions almost inevitably involve geopolitical interests. For example, the Turkish slaughter of the Greek Orthodox, in contrast to the Armenian Christians, was minimized in part because of the Greek state's opposition, which garnered the support of the European powers. Not coincidentally, all four cases ended with the military defeat of the genocidal regimes. Finally, every regime sought to extinguish, and ultimately to deny, its crime. Although the state did not rely on popular participation in the Armenian genocide or the Holocaust, it did so in the case of Serbia and Rwanda. This occurred in part as a response to the Nazi war crimes trial, as the genocidal leaders sought to deny or diffuse personal guilt in crimes against humanity and to render it as a collective responsibility, or a crime of the people. To call it interethnic conflict misses the central dynamic and risks naturalizing the evil and absolving outsiders' indifference.

6

After 1983, the Sudan experienced a protracted civil war that killed over 1.3 million people in a decade (Human Rights Watch/Africa 1994:1). Reports of atrocities, ranging from summary executions to indiscriminate bombings, proliferated. Given the systematic effort to exterminate Dinka people (Human Rights Watch/Africa 1994:46, 1996:307–314), it would be correct to talk of genocide. Yet, in the context of indiscriminate killings of all Sudanese who were perceived as enemies of warring factions, there is something problematic in merely highlighting genocide. Because genocide is associated with peoplehood, there is a tendency to overlook other forms of mass murder. Yet non-peoplehood categories of people frequently become targets of systematic violence as enemies of the state. Let me consider one intriguing instance of categorical killing: class.

After the Bolshevik Revolution, the militarized party-state transformed the polity in the name of the people. The Bolsheviks centralized state rule and sought to institute the norm of the new socialist man—Homo Sovieticus—a crucial component of which was a working-class identity. By the 1920s, class was a state-defined category, and popular discourses and social categories were class based (Fitzpatrick 1999:11). Workers were favored over "class aliens" in education and the labor market (Fitzpatrick 2000: 26). "There were stigmatized, 'untouchable' groups in Soviet society in the 1920s: kulaks, Nepmen, priests, and *byvshie* ["former people," or the bourgeoisie]. People in all these stigmatized groups were *lishentsy*—that is, they shared the common legal status of disenfranchisement and the civil disadvantages that flowed from it" (Fitzpatrick 2000:28). In particular, the late 1920s effort to collectivize farms targeted kulaks (Tucker 1990:139). Kulaks—defined as the class enemy of the people and the revolution in general and of forced collectivization in particular—were deported en masse. There was no precise definition of kulaks, which came to refer to anyone with an enviable living. This Stalin-era joke gives a sense of the arbitrary character of classification during the Great Purge, during which an estimated five million people were arrested and six hundred thousand were shot: When a pack of camels sought asylum in another country, they reported that there was a mass arrest of all pigs in the Soviet Union. When told by the border guards that they are not pigs, the camels replied: "Trying telling that to the security police" (Medvedev 1989:455; cf. Rummel 1990: 130–135).

The 1936 Stalin Constitution mandated equality "regardless to race and nationality, religious creed" as well as "social origin, property status, and past activity" (Fitzpatrick 2000:30). Formal status integration, however, did not eradicate class-based discrimination. Indeed, class was racialized, becoming a form of hereditary characteristic. "The stigma of a dubious political past—membership of other political parties before the Revolution, membership of oppositions within the Bolshevik Party, disgrace as an 'enemy of the people' during the Great Purges—was similarly indelible"

(Fitzpatrick 1999:102). One's class position was even marked on the passport (Fitzpatrick 1999:12).

Stalin's "revolution from above" culminated in the Great Purge of 1936–38. His attempt to eliminate political opposition became fused with the state's struggle to liquidate class enemies. In the goal of building socialism and combating capitalism, all enemies of the state were deemed enemies of Stalin, the people, and the revolution (cf. Kotkin 1995:331). Led by Nikolai Ezhov, the People's Commissariat of Internal Affairs intensified the class war against managers, officers, and kulaks (Kotkin 1995:341–344). The regime sought to justify it by invoking internal and external enemies. As a 1935 *Pravda* article exclaimed: "One must not forget that our country lives in a capitalist encirclement. . . . Inside the country there are still no few accursed enemies of socialism, splinters of smashed classes hostile to the proletariat, concealed counterrevolutionary Trotskyists, White Guard scum, and Zinovievists" (Tucker 1990:311).

The Great Purge went well beyond the mass murder of a class to include virtually all potential enemies of Stalin's rule. Officially, the terror was a struggle between the people and the enemy of the people (Davies 2000:49). In reality, it decimated Stalin's enemies, beginning with party members (Hosking 1985:186–193). The Great Purge conflated anti-Soviet actions and individuals with anti-Bolshevik and anti-Stalin actions and individuals (cf. Tucker 1990:205). The involution of violence threatened almost all citizens. Beginning with the effort to extirpate Stalin's enemies— "Trotskyite-Zinovievite monsters . . . enemies of the people . . . spies, provocateurs, diversionists, white guards, kulaks" (Westwood 1987:318), the Stalinist terror generated a society-wide wave of denunciations and deportations that covered everyone from "ex-kulaks" and "former tsarist civil servants" to "socially dangerous elements" and "the families of enemies of the people" (Werth 1999:187; Getty and Naumov 1999:259). In addition to all enemies of Stalin, class, the revolution, and people, two hundred thousand "socially harmful and socially dangerous" elements, including prostitutes and beggars, were deported (Fitzpatrick 1999:125). The catchall category of class enemies or enemies of the people encompassed an ever-widening circle of individuals, including priests, the nobility, capitalists, kulaks, and political opponents (Fitzpatrick 1999:115). While the Bolsheviks had emphasized the category of class enemies (*klassovye vragi*) over enemies of the people (*vragi naroda*), the Stalinist regime increasingly emphasized the nationalist motif (cf. Brandenberger 2002:17,111).

Numerous people became complicit in the Great Purge as its implementation depended on popular accusations and denunciations (Conquest 1990:252–256; Fitzpatrick 1999:205–209). In the guise of fighting for the revolution, people pursued petty personal agendas. The civil and military hierarchy became staffed by younger bureaucrats and officers faithful to Stalin (Hosking 1985:196; Werth 1999:201). Resistance was minimal, as Nadezhda Mandelstam (1970:108) recalled: "We all took the easy way out by keeping silent in the hope that not we but our neighbors would be killed." The Great Purge eventually led to the dismissal, exile, or death of 70 percent of the Central Committee; more than half of the delegates to the 17th Party Congress; 90 percent of Red Army generals; the entire Polish Communist Party leadership; hundreds of thousands of kulaks, Christians, nationalists, and criminals; and, most poignantly, the leading Bolsheviks, such as Bukharin (Westwood 1987:313–316; Thurston 1996:59–62). It resulted in 3.5 million detentions and 1.5 million deaths (Getty and Naumov 1999:587–594; cf. Conquest 1990:484–489).

The Khmer Rouge provides another case. The intensive U.S. aerial bombardment from 1969 to 1973, the threat from Vietnam, and the loss of external support for the Lon Nol regime allowed the Khmer Rouge to seize power in 1975 (Chandler 1991:230–235). Inspired by ideological systems ranging from extreme nationalism to revolutionary Marxism, the Paris-educated leadership led by Pol Pot, born as Saloth Sar, sought to create a nationalist, anti-imperialist, and autarchic society (Jackson 1989b:39–45). The regime also divided the population into three principal classes: *penh sith,* who were given full citizenship rights; *triem,* who were candidates for citizenship; and *bahnheu,* who had no rights (Jackson 1989b:52). The Khmer Rouge members and their putative class allies, rural peasants, became the privileged group, in contradistinction to urban, presumably Westernized, Cambodians. Befitting the leader of the proletarian revolution, Pol Pot claimed to be a rubber plantation worker, but was in fact a Paris-educated elite (Chandler 1999:24).

Pol Pot's goal of building a new society entailed the elimination of the old. The Khmer Rouge's initial targets were the leaders of the Lon Nol government, as well as intellectuals and teachers (Quinn 1989:184–189). Beginning in April 1975, "the revolutionary elite emptied its cities, destroyed Western consumer goods, burned books and libraries, partially liquidated its Westernized elite, severed most of its diplomatic relations, abolished money, markets, and foreign exchange, established state control over all foreign and domestic trade, and cut almost all trade links with the outside world" (Jackson 1989b:45; cf. Chandler 1991:246–255). The evacuees were called the "new people" or the "April 17 people" (Chandler 1999: 1). After the abortive coup attempt in 1976, the regime purged plotters, imprisoning them in the Tuol Sleng prison camp (Quinn 1989:197–200). Many loyal party members were tortured and executed in the notorious S-21 (Chandler 1999:124–129). The Khmer Rouge renewed its effort to expel people from cities, forcibly marching them to various camps (Ponchaud 1989:159). Rural youths in particular took the lead in massacring urbanites (Ponchaud 1989:168). In addition to urbanites, people with ties to the earlier regime, intellectuals, professionals, religious people, and others were killed (Sliniwski 1995:75–79). Border disputes with Vietnam intensified the regime's campaign against enemies within. As Pol Pot noted in 1977: "We search for the microbes *(merok)* within the party without success. . . . As our socialist revolution advances, however, seeing in every corner of the Party, the army and among the people, we can locate the ugly microbes" (Chandler 1999:129). Of 2,680 Buddhist monks only 70 survived the Pol Pot regime (Kiernan 1994:197). People associated ethnic and tribal minorities, ranging from the Cham to Chinese, with the external enemy, such as those of Vietnamese descent and eastern Khmer people (Kiernan 1996:460–463). During forty-four months of rule, the Khmer Rouge killed 1 million–1.7 million (out of 8 million) nationals as enemies of the people (Jackson 1989a:3; Kiernan 1996:458).

Communist regimes do not have a monopoly in vanquishing class enemies. The Indonesian government in 1965 engaged in a sustained campaign against the Indonesian Communist Party, which at the time was the third largest communist party in the world. Led by the army, and supported by Muslim and anti-Communist youth groups, the extermination effort resulted in 500,000–1 million deaths (Mortimer 1974:387–392; cf. Törnquist 1984:234). In the context of the Cold War, the United States and other allies did not intervene against Suharto (Gittings 1999:258). What had been a vibrant and popular movement was eliminated almost overnight.

Just as many hypernationalist regimes are not merely attempting to eliminate racial others, revolutionary or reactionary regimes are not merely combating class enemies. As the cases of Stalin and Pol Pot make clear, threats of mass slaughter faced all enemies of the regime, albeit in the name of class or revolution, people or nation. That is, the target of state violence is the enemy of the regime in power. In this regard, less than a decade after crashing the communists, the Indonesian state engaged in a systematic effort to exterminate East Timorese. As East Timor sought to become politically independent after the end of Portuguese rule in 1974, the Indonesian military subjugated East Timor and in so doing committed mass slaughter. Over half of the East Timorese population was placed in military-controlled resettlement camps by December 1978 (Taylor 1991:88). As an Indonesian military garrison commander stated in 1990: "We Indonesian soldiers do not need Timorese. . . . We deal with the Timorese as we deal with pigs—we slaughter them whenever possible" (Taylor 1991:164). Between a tenth to a third of the population was killed by 1979 (Schwarz 1994:176–180; Dunn 1995:182), and human rights abuses, including arbitrary detention, torture, and murder, continued throughout the 1980s and 1990s (Human Rights Watch/Asia 1997:17). Indonesia shut off East Timor from the rest of the world until the late 1980s, and the international community largely averted its gaze from the genocide (Gunn 1994:10–15; Schwarz 1994:206). In the name of fighting communism, the "free world" supported the Indonesian state (Dunn 1996:310–321).

Class is not the same as peoplehood. Whereas peoplehood identity is regarded as unchangeable, class is presumably much more fluid and flexible. In this spirit, class functioned more like religion. That is, regimes often sought conversion rather than extermination. Although the Nazis were only interested in the victims' racial background, the Stalinist regime insisted on confessions of counterrevolutionary activities (cf. Tucker 1990:474–478). The Chinese Cultural Revolution provides an extreme effort to elicit mass confessions and conversions. The Maoist stress on the mass line (learning from the people) and the power of criticism and self-criticism generated the concept of mass criticism (Dittmer 1974:310–320). As Lin Biao put it in 1969: "Smash revisionism, seize back that portion of power usurped by the bourgeoisie, [and thereby] ensure that our country continues to advance in giant strides along the road to socialism" (Harding 1997:231). Conflating the personal and the political, Mao unleashed a war on his Communist Party and the state apparatus in part to sustain his hold on power and to retain revolutionary fervor (MacFarquhar 1997:465). The Cultural Revolution sought to achieve a thoroughgoing thought reform, ranging from attacks on Confucianism and the glorification of manual labor to the critique of elite and technocratic privilege (Dittmer 1987:154–169). The Red Guards attacked four olds (old ideas, old culture, old customs, and old habits) and, borrowing from Moscow's show trials, persecuted many people (Fairbank 1992:401–404). Many of the Red Guards hailed from privileged class background. Their revolutionary fervor stemmed in part from their desire to overcome their own class background, which put them at disadvantage (Harding 1997:183). The Cultural Revolution was successful to the extent that 60–70 percent of central party organs and 20 percent of the bureaucracy of 15–20 million officials were purged (Harding 1997:242). Although there were no systematic efforts to kill class enemies, many people were harassed and tortured (Harding 1997:243) and the cost in human lives amounted to 400,000–1 million people (Fairbank 1992: 387).

Class should not be equated with race, ethnicity, or nation, but it can play a functionally equivalent role. In particular, class and peoplehood are at times conflated. For example, the Stalinist Great Purge had a strong anti-Semitic current, as Jews stood for the bourgeoisie (cf. Tucker 1990:40). The Khmer Rouge focused on Vietnamese and other non-Cambodians as at once national and class others. However, we should not regard racial, ethnic, and national categories as foundational and natural. The Nazi regime spent considerable energy attempting to define who exactly Jews are (cf. Wildenthal 1997:265–281). The prevalence of intermarriage and cultural interaction blurred the distinction between Bosnian Muslims and their neighbors. As I mentioned, Hutu killers frequently resorted to checking people's identification cards to identify their victims. Furthermore, class is not simply an achieved category, but often becomes racialized and is tantamount to an ascriptive category. In the Soviet Union, the People's Republic of China, and Cambodia, class enemies, such as intellectuals, were readily identified by their appearance, speech, and mannerism. Although class is not quite a biologically heritable characteristic, records of class background haunted Soviet and Chinese bourgeoisie in the era of class massacre.

State-mobilized slaughter takes the form of categorical killing but is not in fact dependent on the particulars of categories. War generates its own terrifying dynamic of escalating violence that at once reifies victims and numbs perpetrators. Modern technology furthermore allows social distance and makes mass murder a matter of science, of precision and predictability. As *Homo necans*, we are capable of astounding atrocity. Although peoplehood categories may facilitate the mobilization of hatred, the warring states are usually extremely proficient, even if only momentarily, in generating mass hatred. That is, race hatred is not necessary to unleash savage killing. The enemy is an empty and floating signifier. The French revolutionary terror or the U.S. Civil War or the Korean War pitted people of the same group and did not rely on racial, ethnic, national, or class hatred. The victims were merely branded as enemies.

7

Far from expressing atavistic barbarism or ancient hatred, genocide is a modern phenomenon. The modern state's technological and military prowess and modern conceptions, ranging from instrumental rationality to total war, are critical background to mass murder. Many categories that constitute enemies of the state are also modern, including class, as well as justificatory ideas, such as racism and revolutionary socialism. The desire to slaughter modern peoplehood is the underside of the effort to construct modern peoplehood. The modern state constructs modern peoplehood; it attempts at times to destroy it. However common as targets, racial, ethnic, or national groups should not be taken as the sole victims of genocide. Genocidal states foment and mobilize racist sentiments to facilitate mass killings, but they also do so for class enemies. Enemies of race, class, or people are ultimately enemies of the state, defined by the regime or dictator in power. Genocide entails the intentional and systematic murder of categories of people identified as enemies of the state. The regime in or seeking state power is the ultimate agent of genocide.

Many authoritarian states are genocidal, but the question of intention, however difficult to adjudicate at times, remains critical. Consider China under Mao Zedong's rule, whose economic policy led to several severe famines. In particular, the 1958–62 Great Leap Forward was a massive policy disaster that led to an estimated 30–40 million famine-related deaths (Becker 1996:272). Jasper Becker (1996:274) calls it "Mao's famine" and argues that it constituted "a deliberate act of inhumanity." Yet, given that Mao was, at least to the best of our knowledge, not trying to kill farmers— in contrast to his effort to purge his political enemies—it is difficult to characterize it as an instance of genocide. Similarly, as murderous as Stalin's rule was, he did not intend to kill the estimated one million who starved to death in Leningrad during World War II (Moskoff 1990:226).

Most mass famines, however, entail the complicity of the state. In the 1932–33 famine in the Soviet Union, six million people died, imposing an especially heavy toll on Ukrainians (Werth 1999:159). Given that the Soviet Union was exporting grains while the citizens were starving, the state is surely partially responsible (Werth 1999:167; cf. Suny 1998:227). In the case of the mid-1980s famine in Darfur, Sudan, the cause of mass deaths was not principally a natural disaster that led to food shortage, but rather the poor distribution of basic food entitlements and preventable diseases, such as diarrhea and measles (Drèze and Sen 1989:262; de Waal 1989: 193). Powerful interests also exacerbated the famine by pursuing economic benefits for themselves (D. Keen 1994:211–215).

Consider in this regard the Great Irish Famine of the late 1840s, which is "the main event in modern Irish history, as important to Ireland as, say, the French Revolution to France" (Ó Gráda 1994:173). In what Cormac Ó Gráda (1994:174) calls "the populist-nationalist paradigm," the tragedy "was entirely, or almost entirely, due to a negligent government and cruel landlords." No bystander comes off well, and many callous comments were made: *The Economist* wrote that "it is no man's business to provide for another," and *The London Times* remarked that "something like harshness is the greatest humanity" (Ó Gráda 1999:6). Yet, according to Ó Gráda (1999:156), no one really benefited from or caused the famine. Although the government (whether local or British), Irish landlords, or others could have done more to alleviate the calamity, the Great Irish Famine was caused in large measure by "a tragic ecological accident" involving the deadly *phytophthora infestans* (Ó Gráda 1995:68).

A priori analytical or moral conclusions do not work well in social life. Something as seemingly simple as mass starvation requires an empirical investigation that perforce assigns causal weight to various agents and factors. Although it would be tempting to single out a transhistorical and transcultural culprit, it can only be done at the cost of misunderstanding. Nature is hardly ever the only culprit, but there is no good reason to exculpate it either. Human history is the annals of human cruelty, but we should be careful to distinguish passive from active misdeeds, misfortunes from injustices. Empirical understanding is necessary for ethical judgment. It would be easy to denounce the dominant group, whether peoplehood or class, or the state because most dominant groups and states have been negligent regarding the desperate straits of the less fortunate. However, misunderstanding may merely redound as reverse racism or empty sloganeering. For example, Iris Chang's 1997 screed on the Nanjing massacre— when Japanese troops raped and massacred Nanjing citizens in 1937—

became a best-seller in the United States. Subtitled "The Forgotten Holocaust," Chang (1997:5) claimed that the "rape of Nanjing" was "one of the great evil deeds of history" and "one of the worst instances of mass extermination." Although the Japanese military committed numerous acts of atrocity during World War II, and the Nanjing massacre was certainly a ghastly incident of Japanese militarism run amok, it is hyperbolic to compare it to the Holocaust. Even more problematically, Chang (1997:15) asserted the "collective-amnesia—even denial" of the event in post–World War II Japan. Given the proliferation of books on the Nanjing massacre in Japan (e.g. Honda 1993), the argument is tantamount to claiming that contemporary Germans have forgotten and denied the Holocaust. Necessary evil governance and sinful the lot of humanity may be, but to condemn a people or a regime in toto commits the same conceptual error.

We should be wary, however, of most efforts to exculpate the state. Apologists readily cite the condition of civil war to justify, or at least to exonerate, mass murders. Genocide, after all, almost always occurs in the context of war or revolutionary upheaval. One of the emblematic truths of modernity is that revolution, total war, and terror go together, exemplified by the French revolutionary terror of 1793–94 (Hobsbawm 1962:67; cf. Melson 1992:258). Revolutionary regimes almost always come into power on the basis of violence; it is not surprising then that violence should remain one of the privileged means to secure the regime and to squelch the enemy. There is a kernel of truth in the claim of dictatorial and authoritarian regimes that they face enemies within and without. The paranoid, as the cliché goes, are not necessarily without enemies. The crimes of the Holocaust would not be expiated if the defenders of the Nazi regime made a compelling claim that Jews were indeed the enemy within. Some Armenians collaborated with the Ottoman Empire's enemies, and Tutsi people were involved in the RFP's war against the Rwandan regime. Genocide is seen as a righteous vindication for disloyalty, however disproportionate the punishment is to the alleged crime.

The principle of nationhood seeks always and already to justify state sovereignty, and, with it, crimes of the state. Few, if any, states are without the proverbial skeleton in their historical closet. Most successful nation-building efforts entailed mass murders, including colonial conquest and ethnic cleansing. Violent but successful state making ultimately erases past atrocities. Probably the single most deadly civil war in history, the Taiping rebellion in mid-nineteenth century China, resulted in twenty million deaths, but few regard the Qing state's massacre of the rebels as genocidal (cf. Spence 1996:18). In fact, many of the most murderous events in the post–World War II world have been civil wars, such as in China (2 million dead), Korea (1.5 million), Vietnam (2 million), Nigeria (2 million), Ethiopia (1.7 million), Mozambique (400,000), and many others (Brogan 1998: 643–646). Since World War II, there have been more civil wars than interstate wars, and the former have been more deadly than the latter (Shaw 1991:57–62; Brogan 1998:viii). The genocide of Bosnian Muslims in the 1990s or the slaughter of Serbs, Croats, and Bosnian Muslims during World War II are widely discussed, but few recall Tito's armed struggle for power during 1945–46 that resulted in 250,000 deaths, involving "mass shootings, forced death marches and concentration camps" (Malcolm 1994:193; cf. Lampe 2000:227). The cherished claim of state sovereignty contributes to the quietude of the international community; almost all nation-states avert their gaze from their neighboring states' crimes against civilians, except when the occasion suits them to condemn and to intervene. It is not just out of anti-Semitism that the Allied powers ignored the fate of European Jewry. Most countries supported Indonesia in its conquest of East Timor, but not because they were racists (Dunn 1995:66). Indifference, if not complicity, greets the atrocities committed in the name of combating atrocities (cf. Delacampagne 1998:211–222). Supranational and nongovernmental organizations have sought to combat genocidal acts in the name of humanity. The emergent global civil society clamors for humanitarian interventions (cf. Shaw 1996:156–161). Yet these countervailing forces pale in comparison to the power of modern states.

What makes categorical mass killing genocide is that it is a total war waged against internal enemies of the state. As a total war, it is planned and intentional. Michael Howard (1983:12) observes: "However inchoate or disreputable the motives for war may be, its initiation is almost by definition a deliberate and carefully considered act and its conduct, at least at the more advanced levels of social development, a matter of very precise central control. If history shows any record of 'accidental' wars, I have yet to find them." To be sure, plans and intentions often go awry, and wars have their unpredictable, unintended, and dangerous dynamics. Empty rhetoric may become reality. As W. B. Gallie (1991:36) writes: "Observers of war as different as Thucydides and Tolstoy have pointed out that it eventually drives men to do things which beforehand they would never have dreamed of doing."

Total war and genocide are techniques in the repertoire of militarized regimes. Bureaucratic learning accumulates methods of genocide; a radical regime in crisis instills the necessary savagery to execute them. Modern dictators are frequently history buffs, and learn from one another. Hitler reportedly said on 22 August 1939: "Who, after all, speaks today of the annihilation of the Armenians?" (Bardakjian 1985:1). Although the Nazis regarded Armenians as Aryans (Lewis 1998:45), few tears were shed for their massacre. Even at the beginning of the twenty-first century, the memorialization of the Armenian slaughter is deeply contested (Mazower 2001:19). Presciently Franz Werfel's *Vierzig Tage des Musa Dagh* [Forty Days of Musa Dagh] (1933) portrayed the Armenian tragedy and portended the Nazi danger. While Werfel's poignant warning gathered dust in the library, despots honed their tools of naked power. Although Hitler focused on race and Stalin on class, Robert Conquest (2000:xii) is surely right to remark that "without feeling the Holocaust one cannot feel, or understand, Stalinism." In turn, Pol Pot emulated Stalin's purges (cf. Chandler 1999: 123). And all of them learned the art of official denial (Cohen 2001:101–112).

We should not, however, overemphasize charismatic leadership. Charisma is in part a figment of the propaganda apparatus. Before his death in 1936, Maxim Gorky noted in his diary that "if a miserable flea were magnified so many thousandfold, the resulting creature would be the world's most awful beast, beyond human control" (Tucker 1990:364). The flea becomes an unmitigated evil not because of its charisma, but because of its ability to mobilize the state apparatus. Certainly, it is not because the dictator is one with the people. Just as Hitler was not German (Austrian) and Stalin not Russian (Georgian), Stalin, Mao, and Pol Pot could not claim proletarian background.

Like charisma, it is tempting to see interethnic conflict as transhistorical and transcultural (cf. Esman 1994:1). The nascent discourse of genocide highlights the workings of primordial group hatred and atavistic racism everywhere (Horowitz 1985:3–6; Snyder 2000:352–362). In so doing, we reify and essentialize groups and potentially mistake effect for cause (cf. Horowitz 2001:540–545). Neither cultural animosity nor the contact hypothesis—the idea that greater interaction would lead to greater harmony—is true in and of itself (cf. Forbes 1997:203–211). Neither madness nor evil explains genocide. Rather, we need to look at concrete dynamics of political struggles, rather than reifying the categories and identities that crystallize in the process of conflict. There is nothing like violence and murder to clarify one's status. Though Jews in Weimar Germany may have fancied themselves to be Germans, they were unlikely to do so after the Holocaust. The memory of victimization lies at the heart of many modern identities ranging from Armenian to Bosnian.

The theoretical stress on racism and peoplehood conflict occludes the primacy of power struggles. Though it may provide the symbolic key to understanding, ethnic or tribal hatred in and of itself does not explain genocide (cf. Luckham 1971:196). The pursuit of dignity and the expression of resentment are potentially everywhere and can be generated against racial, religious, class, and other groups (cf. Greenfeld 1992:487; Petersen 2002:265). Post-hoc theorizing rewrites the past.

One of the reasons that the Holocaust causes emotional shudder is the perverse idea that the state should kill its own people. As an internal matter, outsiders are told to mind their own business (cf. Cohen 2001:161–167). Few raise eyebrows when massacres are committed against nonnationals, especially if they are done in the course of warfare. Just as most states condoned Indonesia's mass murder of East Timorese, hardly any raised any complaint against the December 1941 Japanese invasion of East Timor that led to the death of roughly 14 percent of the population (Taylor 1995:32; cf. Dunn 1996:19–23). The very effort to question the distinction between the internal and external enemy is summarily dismissed, as if it would question the foundation of civilization.

The conditions that facilitate genocide make industrial killing possible and justify indiscriminate killing in total war (cf. Shaw 1988:32–39). Bombings of civilians and other massacres of noncombatants fall under the rubric of state terror that seeks to eliminate enemies completely. "Through the two world wars . . . total war became literally genocidal. Warfare had to be, could be and was directed against the peoples themselves, since their productive capacity and ideological morale were essential military factors" (Shaw 1991:21). This is indeed the logic of National Socialism, which sought to racialize the masses (cf. Lemkin 1973:80). Relatively innocent civilians are killed as part of the enemy nation. For example, the March 1945 bombing of Tokyo targeted overwhelmingly residential areas that caused one hundred thousand civilian deaths (Markusen and Kopf 1995: 175–179). General Thomas Power, who was in charge of the mission, called it "the greatest single disaster incurred by any enemy in military history" (Selden 1989:xvi). In the atomic bombing of Hiroshima (100,000 dead) and Nagasaki (70,000 dead), most victims were also civilians (Sherwin 1977:232–237). The survivors—*hibakusha*—even became a category of people because of their physical suffering and social stigmatization that have both proven to be hereditary (Lindee 1994:9). Given U.S. racism against Japan (Dower 1986:pt.2)—13 percent of Americans in December 1944, for example, "urged the extermination of all Japanese" (Alperovitz 1995:428)—what would differentiate the mass killing of civilian Japanese from that of civilian Jews except that the former was an external enemy whereas the latter was an internal one? The use of the atomic bombs was, after all, probably not necessary to defeat Japan (Alperovitz 1995:627–636).

How does one make a qualitative distinction between the intentional killing of civilians—albeit enemy civilians—and the intentional killing of enemies—albeit internal enemies? What unites total war and genocide is the indiscriminate massacre of citizens as a form of categorical killing (cf. Markusen and Kopf 1995:55–62). They both seek to defend the nation-state and to vanquish its enemies. While the proportion of civilian deaths in World War I was only 5 percent of all deaths, it had become 66 percent by World War II and 80–90 percent by the wars at the end of the twentieth century (Hobsbawm 2002:16). As in genocide, each occurrence of total war occasions the cry of "never again," the refrain heard at least since the Napoleonic wars (Gallie 1991:38). If total war implies total annihilation that elides combatants and civilians, then why is the distinction between external and internal enemies so zealously sustained in discussing geno-cide? The distinction in part helps hide the killing of indigenous peoples, or peoples without a nation (cf. Totten, Parsons, and Hitchcock 2002:66). Just as the modern idea of peoplehood restricts the domain of applicability of genocide, the sacrosanct nature of state sovereignty justifies the murder of external enemies, even if they are civilians. Why the ethical and emo-tional callousness toward outsiders? Why do we systematically misrecog-nize human beings with reified categories? To sacralize genocide while ignoring other acts of mass slaughter naturalizes the very conditions that make genocide possible.

I began this chapter by asking, why Germany? The answer is, in part, where else? The existence of an efficient bureaucracy and militarized regime initiated a total war against external and internal enemies. Monopolizing the means of violence within a delimited territory and protected from out-side by the claim of sovereignty, the modern state is the most likely agent of committing genocide. As an extremely nationalist measure, the genocidal state seeks to eliminate racial, ethnic, and national others and class enemies. The category of the enemy depends on the nature of the regime in power, but the action of mass killing inevitably depends on the infrastructural capacity that only the modern state can wield. If the modern state has shaped modern peoplehood, it has also tried to destroy it.

Identity

"The problem of the twentieth century is the problem of the color-line,"
declared W. E. B. Du Bois (1986a:372). The most quoted line in the vast
literature on U.S. race relations, this lapidary sentence surely connotes and
denotes more than merely declaring the bold boundary line that defines
and distinguishes white and black Americans. After all, as he noted in his
autobiographical *Dusk of Dawn* (1940), Du Bois, like many African Americans, could point to a rather complex family genealogy. His ancestors
included, to use the language of modern peoplehood, Europeans, Africans,
and Native Americans—across the presumably impassable color line (Du
Bois 1986b:630–636). Beyond his "mixed" racial origins, he grew up in
Great Barrington where "the racial angle was more clearly defined against
the Irish" because "income and ancestry more than color" was salient (Du
Bois 1986b:563). Furthermore, Du Bois (1986a:372) glosses "the problem
of the color-line" as "the relation of the darker to the lighter races of men
in Asia and Africa, in America and the islands of the sea." Clearly, he alludes
to the global phenomenon of colonialism.

Du Bois's intellectual trajectory almost always transgressed the simple
color line. At his Fisk University commencement speech in 1888, he lionized Bismarck as a man who "made a nation out of a mass of bickering
peoples" (Zamir 1995:30) and went on to advocate elite leadership encapsulated in the idea of the "talented tenth." In spite of its black nationalist
veneer, *The Souls of Black Folk* (1903) is very much a work influenced by
German Romanticism in using the folksong as the expression of peoplehood and highlighting the idea of "double consciousness" (cf. Rampersad
1990:42–47; Zamir 1995:113–116). Later, he became a Marxist and a pan-

Africanist, increasingly concerned with the problems of what we call the Third World. As Arnold Rampersad (1990:292) summarized: "He was a product of black and white, poverty and privilege, love and hate. He was of New England and the South, an alien and an American, a provincial and a cosmopolite, nationalist and communist, Victorian and modern."

The complexities and contradictions of Du Bois are hardly unique. The Harlem Renaissance—"a spiritual Coming of Age" of Negro identity (Locke 1968:16)—was led by people of mixed descent: Jean Toomer and Countee Cullen, Langston Hughes and James Weldon Johnson (Zack 1993:103). The same can be said about many great African American philosopher-politicians from Frederick Douglass to Malcolm X. Du Bois's contemporary, Alain Locke, was a renowned race theorist who declared: "There is, in brief, no 'The Negro' " (Locke 1989:210). They both studied at Harvard and Berlin, but what united them to their supposed brethrens in the South, who were mostly quasi-serfs? In this line of thinking, Harold Cruse (1967: 9) trenchantly criticized the Negro intellectual who often remained "socially detached from his own Negro ethnic world." Does the category of African American—variously expressed in the twentieth century as colored, Negro, or black—somehow capture the lives and minds of Du Bois and Locke? Locke was deeply concerned with what we would today call homophobia and heightism as well as with Baha'i faith (Harris 2001:338). Yet we remember him and Du Bois as black intellectuals.

In this final chapter, I return to the questions I posed in the Prelude. Racial, ethnic, or national identity is partially a product of institutional socialization and identification, but it is also a matter of epistemic classification and distinction. In Chapters 3 and 4, I stressed the majority identity, and in this chapter, I focus on the minority. In particular, I probe the essentialist construction of identity as well as the dialectic of racism and minority identity formation.

2

How does the question of "who are you?" become inextricable from that of "where are you from?" Why does a simple and ready predicate of one's membership in a racial, ethnic, or national group become constitutive of personal identity? A simple answer is that modern peoplehood is a dominant form of social classification and identification. That is, it has become the principal way in which we make sense of what kinds of people there are.

Classification is a crucial cognitive operation (Bruner, Goodnow, and Austin 1956:235). Classificatory schemes and categories reduce complexity and order the buzzing and booming confusion that we call reality. Indeed, we cannot think without them. They are eminently instrumental and practical, being ongoing efforts to define and relate words and things. Whether to distinguish between the edible and the inedible or friends and enemies, the correlative works of conceptualization, categorization, distinction, and identification are essential to our survival.

Being so good to think with, social classification is universal and inevitable in social life (Lévi-Strauss 1963:89). What is socialization but mastering the dominant system of classification? A critical test of group belonging is proficiency in using its categories, principles, and predicates. They are necessarily simplified, reflecting our cognitive limitation to process but a handful of them for a particular order of things (cf. Miller 1956). Furthermore, social limitations mark our ability to interact with the vast majority except as bearers of certain sanctified roles. Even if one lives in a small town, one cannot possibly know more than snippets about hundreds and thereby know little or nothing of thousands of fellow residents. Our impoverished sociological imagination seeks simplified schemas to make sense of people. In turn, our social identity perforce employs one of the readily available categories. Modern peoplehood reduces the complexity of social life to its least common denominators.

The universality of classification and categorization does not imply transcendental uniformity, however. Classifications of color, or plants and animals, exhibit a degree of commonality across cultures (Berlin 1992:31–35; cf. Ellen 1993:216–229). Yet modes of human classification vary widely across cultures and over time in spite of recurrent efforts to ground it in natural variation. Roger Bacon's (1953:188–193) thirteenth-century tract *Moralis Philosophia* divides humanity into six kinds ("Sarraceni, Tartari, Pagani, Ydolatre, Iudei, Christiani" [Saracens, Tartars, Pagans, Idolaters, Jews, Christians]) according to six ends of life ("voluptas, divicie, honor, potencia, fama, seu gloria nominis" [pleasure, wealth, honor, power, fame, God's glory]) and six major heavenly bodies. James Harrington's (1992:75) seventeenth-century treatise *The Commonwealth of Oceana* classifies people by "their quality, their ages, their wealth, and the places of their residence or habitation." Out of many plausible categories, only a few achieve widespread dissemination at any given time and place. Someone who follows Bacon's scheme in the early twenty-first century United States would be highly suspect, although Bacon would have found the conceptual universe of modern peoplehood bizarre. As we have seen, categories of modern peoplehood are historically inflected, sometimes undergoing dizzying transformations. They emerge, transmute, and even disappear. The meaning of and the membership in whiteness in the United States changed dramatically in the twentieth century. If the Soviet Union sought to construct Homo Sovieticus, the successor states in the 1990s attempted to fashion ethnonational identities.

Classificatory schemes and categories are not necessarily uniform within a given society. Different groups may use distinct and even conflicting systems of classification (Keil 1989:258–262). Professionals and children concoct idiosyncratic schemes (cf. Markman 1989:37; Bowker and Star 1999:293–300). More strikingly, individual variations, however molded they may be by social interaction and group identity, are common (cf. Ellen 1993:147). People routinely make mistakes. Furthermore, most classificatory schemes allow for a degree of strategy and choice in identification (cf. Patterson 1975:309). People do not slavishly follow a classificatory system or impute same meanings to it; they are strategic in identifying themselves and others. Given that most social situations allow for competing schemes and blurred boundaries, there is always a degree of choice and option in making sense and use of seemingly fixed categories and identities. When the Oxford-born anthropologist encountered a militant Breton during her fieldwork, her admission that her father is Welsh turned the militant's "accusation into acceptance" (McDonald 1989:121). When she said that her mother is Irish, she "was declared a 'Celt,' and, as such, united with the ranks of the oppressed" (McDonald 1989:121). That is, a British anthropologist can instantaneously transform from an imperialist oppressor to a colonized oppressed.

Why do classification schemes and peoplehood categories achieve systematicity and stability in social life? The anti-entropic force of institutional power and its correlative discourse sustains what would otherwise be fluctuating networks and evanescent identities. Institutions mandate a sense of belonging and loyalty. And the modern state is a dominant institution of modernity. If citizenship or nationality—the predominant expression of political, economic, and social belonging—shapes everything from domestic residence and foreign travel to political participation and employment preference, then it is not surprising that it should be valued so highly. Symbolic satisfaction often complements material benefits. Military victories or athletic triumphs bask individuals in the reflected glory of their peoplehood. Given the inducement of material and symbolic benefits, individuals naturalize received categories and identify with them. Indeed, nationhood comes to be seen as the very condition of possibility of human dignity. Belonging becomes an existential necessity, a cure for ontological insecurity. As Jean Améry (1990:84) claimed: "But you are a human being only if you are a German, a Frenchman, a Christian, a member of whatever identifiable group." Horror greets the idea of people without a country, such as Jews in Nazi Germany or blacks in Jim Crow South. The pathos of a man without a country—bathetically depicted in Edward Everett Hales's "The Man without a Country" (1865)—merely reinforces the necessity and naturalness of modern peoplehood.

The disciplinary power of the nation-state manifests itself in all media that shape individual consciousness throughout the life course, from the nationalist curricula of schools to the mass media of movies and television shows. Universal and compulsory schooling teaches the unity of the particular nation-state, whether in literature and the arts, geography and history, or sociology and anthropology. Popular music, sports, and the mass media all have powerful grounding in the nation-state. Transnational diffusion, as I outlined in Chapter 3, spread the principles and categories of modern peoplehood. The Western-dominated social sciences ensure their salience and scientificity. Once established, categories become reified and imbued with meaning by experts of peoplehood and guardians of identity. The very factors that I discussed in the first chapter align the polity and the people. From commemorative practices to collective rituals, the nation is the natural unit of identification. It becomes difficult to think or to leave one's country without it. Mehmet Akif was a merciless critic of Turkish nationalism, so much so that he went into exile. Yet one of his poems became the basis of the Turkish national anthem and we remember him as a Turkish poet, primarily in Turkey to boot. Modern peoplehood is significant because the modern world is inextricable from it and often meaningless without it.

3

Peoplehood classification and categorization provide the dominant matrix of perceptions, which in turn reifies social life and reproduces received categories and schemes. Research and reflection, however, reveal the complexity of self-identity and the recent dissemination of racial, ethnic, and national identities. Yet my answer surely fails to capture the pull of peoplehood identity, its obviousness and resonance. In spite of theoretical and empirical arguments against the reification of modern peoplehood, the common sense, the natural and the obvious persist in using categories, descriptions, and evaluations of modern peoplehood. That is, people are wont to insist on the naturalness of social differences, even when they may not have a sound riposte to the argument that I have advanced. The question remains: What is it about racial, ethnic, or national identity that seems so deep and inevitable, natural and necessary, that it seems so authentic and meaningful, ineffable and indivisible? The psycho-logic of naturalness belies the sociohistorical logic of construction.

The disjunction between expert and novice knowledge is pervasive in the modern world. Modern physics suggests that the globe is more or less round, a table is mostly empty space, and quarks exhibit baffling space-time indeterminacy; commonsense perceptions persist in picturing the earth as flat, a table as solid, and any object as occupying only one space at a time. In other words, lay perceptions often coexist with scientific propositions.

More generally, our cognitive disposition, which is broadly Aristotelian, presumes the permanence of categories and predicates. People may learn Newtonian physics, but they tend to consider momentum as a substance or internal disposition that dissipates over time. The Darwinian theory of evolution presumes species as evolving, but most people regard them as natural kinds that are fixed. Although the classical Aristotelian view of categories is philosophically and empirically inadequate, it remains regnant (Smith and Medin 1981:32; Gelman 2003:296–299). Natural kinds are imbued with essences that are not easily dislodged by statistical or other forms of scientifically cogent but experientially pallid evidence (Nisbett and Ross 1980:55–59). Contingent and situational characteristics are reconfigured as deep dispositions (cf. Ross and Nisbett 1991:125–133). The Aristotelian view or psychological essentialism is closely allied with our propensity to follow the law of small numbers and the dictates of peer pressure. The law of small numbers is the tendency to rely on unsystematic evidence to generate inductive generalizations or to buttress received ideas. Hearsay evidence or anecdotes have cogency even if they face systematic statistical refutation. As several classic social-psychological experiments (Asch 1955; Milgram 1974) suggest, obedience to peer opinions and authorities lead many people to deny the evidence of their sense or their conviction. People follow dominant categories and interpretations, often becoming somnambulists to the received wisdom.

The classificatory schemes and categories of modern peoplehood articulate with the Aristotelian mindset and are reinforced by external evidence and peer pressure. The imposition of characters, dispositions, and essences to contingent categories and objects is a common cognitive operation. Peoplehood categories are regarded as natural kinds, imbued with inward dispositions or essences and sustained by cognitive and social pressures. In other words, different peoples are seen as different natural kinds, just like dogs and cats, with distinct substance and essence. The phenomenology of naturalness renders all individuals as belonging to one of the natural kinds of peoples. As I discussed in Chapter 2, phenomenology provides the proximate grounding for naturalizing distinction. The popularity of animal metaphor suggests the deeply entrenched nature of group essentialism. People look different, which resonates with a classificatory system that makes sense of differences. Self-identification is experienced as intuitive and obvious. To argue that deeply felt identities are constructs, and recent constructs at that, militates against the full panoply of commonsense intuitions. As Freud (1999:569) confessed in 1930, though he does "not understand the holy language, [is] fully estranged from the religion of his fathers, [and] cannot share in the nationalist ideals," he nonetheless feels "his particular nature [*Eigenart*] as a Jew." Having abandoned all aspects of peoplehood [*Volksgenossen*], he remains ineffably Jewish.

The Aristotelian mindset or psychological essentialism is not dependent on peoplehood categories, however. As I discussed in the first two chapters, medieval Europeans imputed deep essence to status categories. Peasants, witches, or barbarians were said to possess somatic or spiritual substance. Similarly, Jérôme Rousseau (1990:57) reports that the Kayan of Borneo conflate Europeans and Japanese: "The Kayan are aware of the 'racial' similarity between themselves and the Japanese, because during the Second World War the Japanese emphasized the fact. The Kayan were not very impressed by this because of their radically different modes of life; Europeans and Japanese had to be grouped together because they were both able to build airplanes. The know-how to make complex technology is seen as an intrinsic feature of a people, not an acquired trait." Indeed, people often ascribe deep traits to randomly divided groups of people (Tajfel 1981:268–274). Recall that the Lilliputians divided themselves on the basis of which end of the egg they cracked first. That is, a formal attribution of categorical distinction—even if it is utterly arbitrary—generates a discourse of difference. The ubiquity of psychological essentialism accounts in part for the facility of transposing modern peoplehood categories onto past social relations. It also makes racial identification and distinction seem intrinsic, immutable, and therefore intractable (cf. Hirschfeld 1996:xi).

As peoplehood categories constitute natural kinds, phenomenology provides the most obvious way in which differences are naturalized. *Pace* modern biology, phenotype is the key to Aristotelian categorization. In spite of the shifting boundaries of racial identity, racial ontology endows epistemic certainty in racial identification. The quotidian work of distinction depends on our five senses. Smell is said to differentiate racial and ethnic groups (cf. Baker 1974:160–177). A traditional signifier of Jewishness, according to Sander Gilman (1991:10), is Jewish sound. Some people go so far as to use their sixth sense, becoming virtuosos of group identification and distinction. As a former Gestapo agent told Bernt Engelmann (1986:279): "After that training and a few months on the job I could recognize a Jew thirty feet away, no matter how he tried to blend in or how blond and blue-eyed he was. I had an unfailing instinct when it came to picking them out!" No wonder then that the sense of distinction, grounded as it is in the five senses, seems so natural, obvious, intuitive, and visceral. Yet, as I argued in Chapter 2, appearance is inadequate in and of itself to justify categorical distinction. Charles Johnson, a true believer in the flat earth, noted "that people should just look around and trust their own eyes. Reasonable, intelligent people have always recognized that the earth is flat" (Martin 2001:31). Racial distinction frequently necessitates formalized badges of identification, whether for Jews wearing the Star of David in Nazi Germany or Rwandans carrying ethnic identification cards during the genocidal mêlée.

Phenomenology is in turn grounded in metaphysics. The conceptual universe of modern peoplehood provides categories and narratives about their predicates and principles. In other words, the discourse of peoplehood offers a master explanation of social life, its ontology and epistemology. As I argued in Chapter 4, racist knowledge is essentialist, expressing itself in epithets and stereotypes. Because individual utterances are cogent in the illative sense, their falsification does not refute established categories and predicates. To put it another way, stereotype explains (cf.

McGarty, Yzerbyt, and Spears 2002:2–7). A well-meaning cosmopolitan guest to my house—having ascertained that my parents hailed from the Korean peninsula—decided that the dish I cooked was Korean when it was intended to be Italian. He identified the artworks on the wall—one by a New York Jew, another by a white Englishman, and the third by a French-speaking Swiss—as all Korean. Existing categories and predicates have re-markable hold in social life. Prejudice and stereotype are the dominant ways in which people are divided and identified in terms of peoplehood. Exceptions may be made, but in general strangers are given deep-seated dispositions (cf. Jaspars and Hewstone 1990:126). Thus the attribution of black criminality may persist despite consciously antiracist attitudes (Banaji and Bhaskar 2000:150–153).

More devastatingly, individual relations instantiate race relations. Just as people assume in-group solidarity, they also presume out-group animosity. Conflicts between individuals or groups are explained by racism or inter-racial hatred. Jonathan Rieder's (1985:29) ethnographic study of New Yorkers found that they "presumed that animosity between communal strangers was as inborn as the camaraderie of ethnic confreres." Or as Hitler (1943:285) said: "But you will never find a fox who in his inner attitude might, for example, show humanitarian tendencies toward geese, as simi-larly there is no cat with a friendly inclination toward mice." As we saw in the previous chapter, the master explanation of the Shoah focuses on or-dinary Germans and their garden-variety anti-Semitism rather than the rel-ative autonomy of the militarized state. Although the 1992 Los Angeles riots began in reaction to the perceived whitewashing of police brutality, pundits often stressed the conflict between African Americans and Korean Americans as its cause (Abelmann and Lie 1995:159). The presumption of an inter-group conflict may in turn become a self-fulfilling prophecy, ce-menting racist attitudes.

The Aristotelian mindset considers current social arrangements and cat-egories as natural and necessary, transforming the particular into the gen-eral and the contingent into the universal. In other words, it operates in the world of ideology. The narrow and negative way is to understand ide-ology as an idea that promotes specific interests or repels challenges to them. Experts, ranging from racial scientists to social scientists, political activists to state bureaucrats, have vested interests in reproducing received categories. Intentionality is not the issue here. Even if a social scientist wishes to challenge racism, she may very well accept the received racial categories for analysis and produce generalizations about them that are, at least formally, no different from racist pronouncements. As I queried in Chapter 4, was the sociologist Howard Odum racist because he delineated the impoverished state of poor Southern blacks? Would he have been an antiracist had he fabricated a utopian portrait of that community? The challenge to examine categories critically introduces unwanted complexities in scientific work and is therefore assiduously avoided. The widespread awareness of mixed-race people or the subjective nature of peoplehood identification does not prevent social scientists from persisting in using blunt, reified racial categories. In so doing, they retain their regnant status. This is the wider definition of ideology: it demarcates the very horizon of thinking.

The general process of ideology construction is to transform what is variable and contingent into something constant and fixed. Conventional though social categories and distinctions may be, they are grounded in history and biology. If they were not seen as natural kinds, then they would not be commonsensical. The psycho-logic of naturalism informs a metaphysics of identity whereby the individual is inextricably intertwined with the social and the natural.

Peoplehood categories are naturalized in part because they refract a social reality that existed from birth. Although infancy is not destiny, what we learn as young children has significant cognitive and emotional resonance. Our self-identification, which extends to our peoplehood identity, owes a great deal to caregivers and playmates (Mitchell 1994:88). In Zora Neale Hurston's *Their Eyes Were Watching God* (1937), one of the black children, reared by white parents, long considered herself white. This is far from unique to her: "When the infant is raised individually with members of a different species, it comes to prefer members of that species. . . . Apes reared with humans prefer humans to conspecifics, and since they also have self-recognition, they perceive themselves to be part of the human species and orient their social and sexual behavior exclusively towards humans" (Guyot 1998:514).

Infant memories—flotsam and jetsam from childhood—have emotional reverberation. Dick Diver, in *Tender Is the Night* (1934), captures the ensemble of petty concerns that made the patriotic nationalism of World War I possible: "This took religion and years of plenty and tremendous sureties and the exact relation that existed between the classes. . . . You had to have a whole-souled sentimental equipment going back further than you could remember. You had to remember Christmas, and postcards of the Crown Prince and his fiancée, and little cafés in Valence and beer gardens in Unter den Linden and weddings at the mairie, and going to the Derby, and your grandfather's whiskers" (Fitzgerald 1982:57). The stuff out of which tears are shed are incidental, albeit naturalized, infantile memories. Whether learned on grandparents' knees or at teachers' behest, childhood lessons transmute themselves into adult memory, nostalgia, and passion. Although emotions do not explain anything, they naturalize epistemic schemes and ontological affiliation. Phatic though its function may be, emotional resonance supersedes the logical and empirical shortcomings of social classification and identification.

The propensity to perceive peoplehood as a natural kind owes its ontological grounding to intimate kinship and household relations. That is, the institutional and emotional core of modern peoplehood is the family. In most families, common descent and contemporary commonality are rooted in the language of blood—faulty though it may be, as I noted in Chapter 2—and the phenomenology of family resemblance. The belief in the unity of a peoplehood group is ultimately a conviction about shared descent and family resemblance. That is, peoplehood—a community of descent and of character—is a form of extended kinship; peoplehood is an imagined family. As Horace Kallen (1924:200) said, nationality is "natural, organic" and "familial in its essence." In basing modern peoplehood in history and biology, individual-level ideas and experiences are expressed in terms of a reified understanding of human classification. As I suggested in Chapter 4, the nominal character of peoplehood allows the constant conflation of kinship and peoplehood or the elision of artificial categorical belonging and organic group identity. The basic binary—us v. them—animates the discourse of peoplehood.

Ideology is not destiny, however. Overcoming our Aristotelian heritage, many people embrace far more cogent schemes of describing and explaining the physical universe and the biological world. Similarly, we can aspire to do the same for the social world. As most moderns have jettisoned the essentialism of status or religious categories, many of us will one day expunge racial and racist categories. But just as the persistence of the Ptolemaic worldview was not a purely rational process of proofs and refutations, the same is true for the world of modern peoplehood. Institutional struggles, whether against the church or the state, remain critical. Knowledge and politics must change in concert.

4

State membership is the master signifier of belonging in the world of nation-states, providing, in turn, a bundle of privileges and a convincing answer to the question of identity. By the end of the twentieth century, however, patriotic and militaristic nationalism was clearly in decline; the very assertion of national pride came to be seen as somewhat archaic (cf. Howard 2000:96–101). Befitting the postmodern condition, the narrative of the nation was waning with other grand narratives of modernity. If modern peoplehood is the product and predicate of the modern state, then the decline of the modern state should lead to the dissipation of modern peoplehood.

Needless to say, the modern state continues to be a major institutional force in the contemporary world, though its parameters and intensities differ significantly. National and ethnic effervescence characterizes the post-Soviet successor states (Khazanov 1995:chaps. 1–2). Yet the dominant trend suggests the decline of modern peoplehood. The two world wars showed—and the Cold War confirmed—the impossibility of the nation-state as the sovereign unit of total war. Citizen-soldiers are declining in significance. Destructive wars, including genocides, have tempered the attractions of extreme nationalism.

Simultaneously, the economy and the mass media have superseded the boundaries of nation-states. Transnational capitalism is less beholden to the state and less dependent on peoplehood identity. Indeed, its hegemonic articulation is to foster individualization whether as petty capitalists or sovereign consumers. The decline of welfare programs and other egalitarian measures has begun to unravel status integration. Educated speech in rich countries, for example, unites the transnational elite and separates them from less-educated counterparts (Grillo 1989:217–221).

Transnational and supranational organizations intervene in hitherto sacrosanct national politics. Grassroots politics in turn seek transnational alliances. Counter-globalization movements cross national boundaries, whether in the guise of pan-Islam or environmentalism. The global movement of indigenous peoples articulates at once a politics of peoplehood recognition and of universal human rights (cf. Niezen 2003:193–197). In other words, there is a nascent global community comprising nongovernmental organizations and transnational networks (cf. Iriye 2002:202). The rising regime of human rights and individualism questions the sovereignty

of nation-states (cf. Soysal 1994:164) and the plausibility of racial classification (Banton 2002:215). Visionaries discuss the nascent concepts of
world or global citizenship and planetary or species consciousness (Morin
2001:chaps. 4–5). Indeed, people have *died* for these humanitarian causes
and supranational organizations.

Most fundamentally, massive migration has decisively destroyed the
once credible equation of polity and peoplehood. In brief, the alignment
of language, religion, culture, and other attributes of peoplehood are becoming decoupled from the state and the nation. Peoplehoods seem to be
devolving into populations.

More than the rise of supranational identification, such as pan-European
or pan-Islamic, the most potent expressions of peoplehood identity in the
post–Cold War era have been infranational, especially in rich countries.
That is, the problem of identity is most searchingly probed and most vi-
brantly articulated by people whose national belonging is ambiguous and
incomplete. In Chapter 4, I discussed some of these categories, such as
women, homosexuals, and disabled people. There are numerous causes for
the efflorescence of infranational identities. Economic and cultural globalization, the rise of universalist ideologies, and many other factors account
for the age of multiculturalism. Let me focus here, however, on the belated
efflorescence of minority peoplehood identity.

As I argued in Chapter 4, incomplete integration underlies structural
racism. Racism excludes and essentializes people, but the excluded do not
necessarily share common consciousness. Identity, rather, is achieved by
counter-racist mobilization. The dialectic of racism and counter-racism per-
forms the epistemic equivalent of horizontal and vertical integration.

Consider African Americans. As I argued in Chapter 2, race was not a
salient category until the eighteenth century in the United States (cf.
Johnson 1939:283). African Americans' common African origins belied the
diversity of language, religion, and culture (Berlin 1998:101). The distinction between Northern and Southern blacks or, more fundamentally, free
and slave stunted a common identification among African Americans until
the nineteenth century (Litwack 1961:viiif; Morgan 1998:442,457). Otherwise we cannot make sense of "the slender support given by free Negroes
to slave revolts, and . . . the willingness of some—in fact, of many in Louisiana—to side with the whites against the slaves" (Genovese 1974:411).
Furthermore, local identification remained strong (Morgan 1998:475). In
spite of proto-nationalist "race men," the predecessors of contemporary

African Americans constituted a population but not a people until the nineteenth century.

Similarly, until the nineteenth century, most migrants did not arrive in a new land with a strong sense of peoplehood identity and probably did not even think of themselves as migrants or transplants. We may speak of Polish immigrants to the United States or Irish immigrants to Australia, but their fundamental nexus was familial or local, not national. According to W. I. Thomas and Florian Znaniecki (1918–20:i,303), "all the peasant letters can be considered as variations of one fundamental type . . . to manifest the persistence of familial solidarity in spite of the separation." In a similar fashion, David Fitzpatrick (1994:615–620) describes Irish immigrants in Australia: "When Irish Australians spoke of 'home', they called to mind a social environment peopled by relatives or neighbours." Most Jewish immigrants to the United States in the late nineteenth century had a vague understanding of Jewish nationalism or Jewish identity (Howe 1994:69–72; cf. Glazer 1989:xxiv). East European Jews "identified themselves by town or region or by dialect" (Hannerz 1974:44). Needless to say, later immigrants arrived with stronger identities.

The lure of assimilation generates a common response to exclusion: inclusion qua individuals. In a racist world in which individuals by themselves are powerless to change, passing provides a potentially instantaneous solution. Given material and symbolic benefits of national belonging, the desire to partake in its privileges is not difficult to discern. Quite frequently, the ultimate test of belonging is a telltale sign, whether the foreskin that distinguished Jewish from non-Jewish Germans or the pronunciation of certain syllables (*pa pi pu pe po*) that separated Japanese from Koreans. Yet the sign can be veiled or transformed. The search for an indisputable mark is doomed because the classification of human beings is grounded in neither biology nor history. A feature as resistant to transformation as skin color cannot sustain the boundaries perfectly, owing in no small part to mixed ancestry. Even in the extreme case of the black-white divide in the postbellum U.S. South, Mark Twain's *Puddn'head Wilson* (1894) or James Weldon Johnson's *The Autobiography of an Ex-Colored Man* (1912), suggests the absurdity and ambiguity of racial distinction and the possibility of passing. Although fear of exposure may dominate the passer's life, many in fact succeed (Sollors 1997:280–284). As Walter White (1968:364) remarked in 1925, the number of blacks passing as whites "is very large—much larger than is commonly supposed" (cf. Myrdal 1962:129). The principle I noted in Chapter 1—act like a Roman, become a Roman—remains a possibility at all times and places.

More commonly, people who are excluded lack the capacity or opportunity to transgress a reigning division. For them, passing only occurs in the realm of fantasy. Because the excluded lack the essential attribute—be it a facial feature or a genital mark—they often desire that icon of distinction. This is the mindset in which a black girl wishes for blue eyes, as in Toni Morrison's *The Bluest Eye* (1970), or an Arab girl in Israel says: "I wished I was Jewish, I wished I was a man, and I wished I was rich" (Singer 2001:62). The fantasy life of the oppressed is often colonized by the somatic sign of privilege, which may realize itself in plastic surgery, whether to Aryanize the Jewish nose or to Occidentalize the Oriental eyefold. Beyond fantasy or surgery, hypergamy exists as another escape route from racist exclusion. As the female character in Mayotte Capécia's *Je suis Martiniquaise* (1948) described her white lover: "I loved him because he had blue eyes, blond hair, and a light skin" (Fanon 1967:43).

Some groups attain collective passing, which is the traditional terminus of integration or assimilation. Whiteness, or normative Americanness, was a major achievement of the melting pot. Randolph Bourne (1964:107) reported in 1916 that "vigorous nationalistic and cultural movements in this country [existed] among Germans, Scandinavians, Bohemians, and Poles," who were excluded from the Anglo-Saxon norm. Yet a few generations later, almost no one questioned their belonging in the category of white or normative American. Irish immigrants in the United States—those who were more discriminated against than blacks during Du Bois's childhood— sought to join the Anglo-Saxon majority through the Democratic Party, the Catholic Church, and labor unions. In striving to achieve whiteness, they in turn distanced themselves from and discriminated against blacks and later immigrants (Roediger 1991:140–156). Or consider *métèques* (foreign scums) in France. Before World War II, they referred principally to immigrants from Italy, Spain, and Portugal. After World War II, some children of pre–World War II *métèques* used the term to castigate Maghrebi and Indochinese immigrants (Hazareesingh 1994:127). That is, victims may transform into oppressors in a generation.

There is a strong element of denial in passing as the passer simply ignores the wider world of racism and leads a life of convenient and elaborate fiction. Successful passing does not alter the reality of legal discrimination or social ostracism. In any case, passing is not a strategy open to everyone or to every group. More concretely, people accept the racial hierarchy and seek advancement within one's own group. Like tribal leadership under indirect rule, ethnoracial leadership pursues political and economic interests and thereby gains vested interests in sustaining the status quo. Political competition (ethnic voting bloc or ethnic party) and economic interests (ethnic trading networks or ethnic-based trade unions) seal the material foundations of ethnic identity (cf. Cohen 1969:183–187; Tilly 1998:154). No one should underestimate the significance of instrumental rationality lurking beneath the emotional rhetoric of peoplehood identity. Booker T. Washington's idea for Negro advancement projected a vision of the black elite in the wider world of white superiority (Litwack 1998:374–378). The strategy of accommodation does not challenge the racist order and may in fact entrench it. In this regard, the privileged minority often reproduces the dominant norm. Thus, pale skin emerged as a mark of the black elite (Litwack 1998:30–33).

If the strategy of accommodation does not alter the racist reality, neither does the path of exit, which presumes racial incompatibility. Less radically, it manifests itself as an internal exile. Thus, Molefi Asante (1993:137,141) writes: "Was I conflicted about my identity? Not for one moment did I experience any sense of personal or cultural confusion about my origins, community, and struggle. . . . I was straight up and down an African in my consciousness." In other words, the excluded embraces the imputed identity as a foreigner within, living in the ghetto of expatriates or exiles. Alternatively, the excluded may literally accept the racist cry of "go home." Marcus Garvey (1987:211), among others, called for people of African descent in the United States to return to Africa. Although fueled by racial pride, it is consistent with racist thinking that sought ethnic cleansing. As he ordained: "Insist in a campaign of race purity. . . . It is natural that it is a disgrace to mix your race with other races. . . . It will be a beautiful thing when we have a standard Negro race" (Garvey 1987:204). Mass exodus, however, entails a massive settler-colonization project. The success of Zionism is inextricably intertwined with post-Nazi and post-Holocaust geopolitics. Because there is hardly any land without prior inhabitants and the excluded nonetheless have homes, neighbors, relations, and jobs, the strategy of exit usually requires a situation of extreme exigency.

A more radical collective strategy is to challenge racial hierarchy itself. As I suggested, individual or collective passing, accommodation, and exit do not challenge the status quo. When most members of the discriminated group occupy the same subjugated status, not only is racial hierarchy naturalized, but also few have the capacity to articulate their oppression and to pursue its destruction. The situation is different when some are capable of resisting calumny. Charges of and challenges to racism proliferate precisely when exclusion or domination is in decline—this is the paradox of oppression. It is not during the heyday of slavery or even of Jim Crow that the United States was castigated as racist, but after the civil rights movement and legislation of the 1960s. In other words, racism becomes discredited precisely when its structural force has weakened. The status mismatch between the dominant group and the dominated group generates racial erethism. That is, the relatively privileged members of the minority group develop heightened sensitivity to the slights and injustices of racism. The rise of an empowered minority and the persistence of racism mobilize counter-racist movement and ideology. It is not an accident that Theodor Herzl and Franz Rosenzweig—two leading exponents of Jewish identity in modern Europe—were both assimilated and privileged Europeans or that Zionism should have emerged in a very auspicious time for European Jewry (Vital 1975:223–237; cf. Avineri 1981:5).

The emergence of minority peoplehood transforms a population (defined by racist exclusion) into a people. The crucible of minority peoplehood is forged by racism. Racist exclusion creates the very categories against which counter-racist discourses and movements are mobilized. Because racism imputes peoplehood identity to the excluded, individuals who struggle against racism, like those who combat colonialism, accept the imposed category. Because successful counter-racist struggle requires a fairly widespread support, there is a tendency to form a large agglomeration, which is precisely what racist discourse presumes. Political expediency often underlies pan-racial solidarity. Although Japanese, Koreans, and Chinese in the United States distinguish themselves sharply from one another—it is not so long ago that Japan colonized Korea and China—they fuse as Asian Americans because of anti-Asian racism (cf. Kibria 1998:955) as well as to forge a sizable bloc.

In contrast to the state that was the central organization of modern peoplehood, minority peoplehood relies on religious, economic, or political organizations to forge minority networks and to disseminate a common identity. Counter-racist movements in turn generate intellectual products that promote group solidarity. Hence, history books are written as Asian American history, and university courses are offered as Asian American studies courses. Material benefits and symbolic pride intensify peoplehood identity.

As I noted, African Americans exhibited little common consciousness across the divides of North and South, free and slave, African-born and American-born, as well as languages and cultures into the nineteenth century (Kolchin 1993:19,41). Although slaves shared a common status identity, we should recall that of a half million free blacks in the United States in 1860, half lived in the slave states (Genovese 1974:400). Negro or black identity coalesced in the nineteenth century. Cultural integration occurred along with status integration. The nationalization of black life bridged the gulf between North and South and that between urban and rural. Simultaneously, mass integration occurred, exemplified by Du Bois's discovery of the black "soul" in the Southern folk. The black or the Negro in this conceptualization shared ancestry (out of Africa) and commonality (cultural and status integration).

Nonetheless, black identity was far from being singular or settled. Because the chief organizational basis of black mobilization was the church, black identity carried a strong religious overtone (cf. Rawick 1972:50; Genovese 1974:658). Furthermore, many black leaders actively identified themselves as Americans (Stein 1989:81). Thus the leading secular counter-racist organizations, such as the National Association for the Advancement of Colored People (1909) and the National Urban League (1910), were interracial organizations (Clark 1967:602). The leading ideology of counter-racist mobilization was probably Marxism or socialism, with its explicit goal of integration or assimilation. The leading African American social scientists of the time, ranging from Abram Harris to Ralph Bunche, stressed economics and class, rather than race in and of itself (Holloway 2002:196). The radical sociologist Oliver Cox (1959:572) wrote: "The destruction of Negroes is cultural and biological integration and fusion with the larger American society." The liberal Bunche declared in 1939: "The Negro is an American citizen" (Banks 1996:107). Perhaps the most eloquent expression of black identity, the Harlem Renaissance, is indicative. While Jean Toomer explicitly identified himself as American, others distinguished the elite, or the talented tenth, from the rest (cf. Banks 1996: 80,87). Some even contested African ancestry. Noble Drew Ali proclaimed the "Asiatic" root of African Americans, whereas the Nation of Islam claimed African Americans to be a "lost nation of Islam" (Lincoln 1994: 48,66).

Given class, region, religion, and other sources of differential experience (Myrdal 1962:702; Litwack 1998:377), few foresaw the eruption of black power in the 1960s (cf. McKee 1993:1). In the classic trope of nationalist writings, Clayborne Carson (1981:215) wrote: "The black struggles of the 1960s had awakened dormant traditions of black radicalism and racial separatism by fostering among black people a greater sense of pride, confidence, and racial identity." Although the most important institution of counter-racist mobilization was the black church (Morris 1984:77–80), the black power movement resulted in a virtual cultural revolution. Black pride generated a search for roots that claimed pan-African solidarity and culture. In particular, the civil rights movement mobilized public opinion and disseminated a common identity (cf. Lee 2002:69). Thus, a distinct black culture emerged in the United States. Soul food, for example, arose as a distinct cuisine in the 1960s (Witt 1999:80–83). Although it drew on U.S. Southern and even African traditions of cookery, its specificity was as an expression of a social movement. Ethnic chic—distinct clothing to express a particular identification of peoplehood—gained currency in the United States only after the 1960s (Lurie 1981:92–96). Black pride also led to a search for African origins of African American literature (Gates 1988:40; 1992:xvii).

The exact meaning of black nationalism remained contested, however. The most eloquent spokesperson of black nationalism, Malcolm X, advocated pan-African and universal Muslim ideals (Banks 1996:147–154). By the end of the twentieth century, however, few questioned the centrality of black identity in American life (Dawson 2001:65). Yet racial identity was strongest among the most educated and politically active (Sniderman and Piazza 2002:60,180).

The belated emergence of minority consciousness can also be seen among Native Americans or American Indians. In spite of centuries of European incursion, roughly four-fifths of the present-day continental and contiguous United States was populated by distinct and sovereign American Indian nations at the beginning of the nineteenth century (Cornell 1988:34,45–50). Not surprisingly, there was little in the way of pan–Native American identity: "Many groups identified themselves with names that meant simply 'persons,' 'people,' or 'human beings' " (Cornell 1988:106). Educated professionals first articulated pan–Native American identification by forming the Society of American Indians in 1911 (Cornell 1988:115–118). Yet Native American identity was not widely disseminated even then.

"As late as the 1940s it is difficult to speak of American Indians as forming a self-consciously solidary group" (Cornell 1988:126).

The situation transformed drastically after the 1950s. Although about 350,000 people identified themselves as Native Americans in the 1950 census, the number reached nearly 2 million by the 1990 census (Nagel 1996:5). The reasons for the renewed interest and pride in Native American identity were manifold. As they emigrated into cities from reservations, they faced discrimination qua American Indians (Cornell 1988:132–138). Educated Native Americans led an intellectual and social movement to construct a pan-American Indian identity as they emulated the example of African American civil rights movements. There were also new benefits of Native American identity, ranging from preferential access to educational institutions and governmental subventions (Nagel 1996:122–126). The Lumbee Indians of North Carolina provide an interesting instance. They have "no records of treaties, reservations, an Indian language, or peculiarly 'Indian' customs" (Blu 1980:1). After being classified variously as "free persons of color" and "free Negroes" in the nineteenth century, they established their identity by distinguishing themselves from whites and blacks (Blu 1980:32,46–61). Their success in maintaining their distinctive identity owes in no small part to their ability to claim the larger national classification of Native Americans (Blu 1980:201).

5

The structure of minority peoplehood is homologous to that of majority peoplehood. The European idea redounds in the pioneering visionaries of minority peoplehood. Du Bois (1986c:817) defined race as "a vast family of human beings, generally of common blood and language, always of common history, traditions and impulses, who are both voluntarily and involuntarily striving together for the accomplishment of certain more or less vividly conceived ideals of life." In asserting common descent and contemporary commonality, minority peoplehood perforce presumes its distinctiveness from majority peoplehood. Yet they are often more alike than different. Majority and minority groups often share the same language, religion, and culture. The potentially contradictory claims of belonging and exclusion generate the particularities and paradoxes of minority identity.

Consider Isaiah Berlin's (1980:345) claim for national identity: "the belief in the overriding need to belong to a nation; in the organic relationships of all the elements that constitute a nation; in the value of our own simply because it is ours; and, finally, faced by rival contenders for authority or loyalty, in the supremacy of its claims." Because of the inevitable heterogeneity of any nation, as well as competing ideas of what it means to be authentically and organically a member of a particular peoplehood, there are always grounds for thicker identity formation. Following Berlin's logic, African Americans may plausibly claim the supremacy of their group loyalty against their American identity. This is the sense in which the historian Thomas Holt (2000:13) writes: "Blackness was in many ways 'home'—it connected them to a particular community, to institutions, to a culture and an identity." In this line of thinking, African Americans share the mystic chords of blood and memory, such as African origins and the legacy of slavery and racism (cf. Eyerman 2001:75–88).

The experiential thickness of minority identity belies the historical shallowness of its emergence. There are no transcendental standpoints from which to define minority membership. Because the institutional basis of minority identity, such as a social movement or a religious organization, is weaker than the modern state, minority identity relies more on consciousness-raising. Whereas majority identity exists as an unquestioned norm, minority identity must be consciously and continuously asserted. Thus, Du Bois and Hurston recapitulated the European Romantic project of finding identity in the folk. In turn, their followers learned how to be black. As Henry Louis Gates, Jr. (1997:24) reminisced: "In 1970, I was in college, majoring in history but pursuing extracurricular studies in how to be black."

The reactive and reflexive character of minority identity emphasizes authenticity. Deviants are derided as inauthentic, whether as "Oreos" for blacks (black outside, white inside) or "Bananas" for Asians (yellow exterior, white interior). Yet the claim of authenticity is at best ambiguous and contested. While James Baldwin was hailed as "*the* voice of black America" in the early 1960s, the rise of black nationalism led Eldridge Cleaver to dismiss him as "the most shameful" a few years later (Gates 1997:8,12). In other words, the symbolic stress on authenticity renders the foundation of minority peoplehood precarious. The integrity and indivisibility of minority peoplehood can be challenged by ideological contestation and social diversity. The economist Glenn Loury (1993:7) bemoans the peril of ideological nonconformity: "I was still a 'nigger' to the working-class toughs waiting to punish with their fists my trespass on to their white turf, yet I could not be a 'brother' to the middle-class blacks with whom I shared so much history and circumstance." Heterogeneity provides the bases for thicker identity formation. Whether in terms of history or culture, recent immigrants from Africa or West Indies are distinct from long-term American residents (Waters 1999:91). African American women may very well make a claim for a distinct ontology and identity. As Anna Julia Cooper (1988:30) put it in 1892: "No man can represent the race . . . he can never be regarded as identical with or representative of the whole" (cf. Collins 1991:22; Carby 1998:5). African American feminists may in turn divide along any number of axes, such as class, sexuality, and political identity.

The search for thicker identity has no obvious terminus. The stress on authenticity in the era of individualism holds open voluntary choice as the basis of minority peoplehood. In this sense Jean-Paul Sartre (1948:26) wrote: "Jewish authenticity consists in choosing oneself *as Jew*—that is, in realizing one's Jewish condition." The potential absurdity of voluntaristic identification is inescapable.

Indeed, the only certainty is counter-racist racism. That is, the non-excluded (the racist majority) cannot be part of the excluded (the victimized minority). Although black nationalism may have white origins (Woodward 1974:200) and black identity may be something that is learned, no amount of achievement enables nonblacks to join its ranks. Consider the African American entertainer Harry Belafonte. He divorced a black woman who studied at the Sorbonne and Heidelberg and married a woman of "Russian-Jewish ancestry [who] knew a lot more about African and African-American culture than Belafonte did" and "was involved with the N.A.A.C.P." (Gates 1997:165). Belafonte and his black wife are obviously black; his white wife cannot be. Similarly, Jane Lazarre (1996:xvf) writes: "I discovered that African American literature often described my own deepest emotions, presenting a vision of the world and experience that was profoundly familiar to me, a white, Jewish woman." In spite of having "black" children, she is doomed to her "whiteness." In the world of modern peoplehood—even or especially in its counter-racist articulation—birth is destiny. When Richard Rodriguez (1989:11) writes, "I was a Negro reading James Baldwin," it is taken as a statement of inauthenticity, rather than the power of writing and reading or the universality of the human spirit. The emphasis on authenticity, in other words, reinforces the very racist thinking that it criticizes.

The stress on authenticity also generates pseudo-problems of identity.

In seeking roots, people claim solidarity with others sharing the same ancestry. Auto-essentialism claims pure ancestry and contemporary commonality. As I argued in Chapter 2, however, purity is possible only by pruning unwanted branches. Frederick Douglass, for example, wrote of his white father in 1845 but denied it by 1881. His commitment to proto-black nationalism effaced his white father and his marriage to a white woman in the name of racial purity and pride (Martin 1984:97). Beyond mistaking human beings for plants, the language of roots invites uncomfortable company. The racialized notion of Jewry claims the essential solidarity of the Diaspora (Auerbach 2001:200). Yet divides between Jews residing in Christian or Muslim countries or Ashkenazic and Sephardic Jews are deep. Levantine Jews seem racially distinct by almost any definition from the Ashkenazic norm (Benbassa and Rodrigue 2000:34; cf. Malcolm 1996:1–27). Primo Levi (1988:100) found that in the Lagers: "The Polish, Russian, and Hungarian Jews were astonished that we Italians did not speak [a Jewish language]: we were suspect Jews, not to be trusted, besides being 'Mussolinis' for the French, Greeks, and political prisoners." Few regarded Falashas as Jews until the twentieth century, and many continue to regard them as blacks or Ethiopians (Summerfield 2003:129). Indeed, the question of Jewish identity cannot be resolved within the cognitive matrix of modern peoplehood.

The search for authenticity leads to the quest for roots, but diasporic people are not necessarily connected to their homeland. In fact, African Americans before World War II tended to be indifferent to or claimed superiority toward Africans (Staniland 1991:108). As Countee Cullen (1991:104–105) put it in 1925: "What is Africa to me? . . . Africa? A book one thumbs / Listlessly, till slumber comes." Melville J. Herskovits (1968: 359) found in Harlem in the early twentieth century: "Of the African culture, not a trace," and E. Franklin Frazier's *The Negro Family in the United States* (1939) stressed the American character of black life. Yet the search for African American peoplehood sought distinction from the majority American identity, contrasting the African origins of the former against the European origins of the latter. As Du Bois (1986b:639) declared: "Africa is, of course, my fatherland." The problem, as I stressed in Chapter 2, is that such an assertion is a willful projection. As Du Bois (1986b:639) acknowledges: "Yet neither my father nor my father's father ever saw Africa or knew its meaning or cared overmuch for it." Indeed, his grandfather was "white," which would make his "fatherland" Europe (Du Bois 1986b: 630).

Homeland identification intensified with the rise of the black power movement. The assertion of African roots led St. Clair Drake (1987:xv) to state: "Crucial in the Afro-Americans' coping process has been their identification, over a time span of more than two centuries, with ancient Egypt and Ethiopia as symbols of black initiative and success long before their enslavement on the plantations of the New World" (cf. Feagin and Sikes 1994:356). While their ancestors struggled for inclusion and integration and against the taunt to "go home," the assertion of racial pride manifests itself in the desire to "go home." Yet pan-racial or pan-national claim falters against the inevitable reality of international differences. Eddy Harris (1992: 27) stated: "Africa beats in my blood and shows itself in my hair, my skin, my eyes." African Americans visiting Africa, however, discover the substantive divides of language, religion, and culture that are inimical to facile racial solidarity. As Harris (1992:13) observed after a tour of Africa: "I am not African. If I didn't know it then, I know it now." There is, after all, no quintessential Africa: "Whatever Africans share, we do not have a common traditional culture, common languages, a common religious or conceptual vocabulary . . . we do not even belong to a common race" (Appiah 1992:26).

Beyond the search for roots, the belief in distinct racial ontology denies the category of the mixed race. Until the conceptual dominance of modern peoplehood, intermarriage or mixed marriage often implied cross-status or cross-religious marriages. In addition, many African Americans—as well as European Americans—were already mixed; perhaps three-fourths of African Americans have elements of European descent (Williamson 1980: 125). Yet racist castigations and counter-racist assertions insist passionately on the significance of purity (Reed 1993:271; cf. Holt 2000:10). As I have noted, both Douglass and Du Bois denied their white paternity. Assortative mating comes to denote unions across peoplehood divides. Guardians of identity often condemn such crossings in the name of racial purity. Thus Martin Luther King, Jr., did not marry the white woman he wished to marry (Frady 2002:22). Just as interracial sex often led to death in colonial fiction (Ware 1992:233), interracial sex leads to social death in race pride fiction (cf. Shell 1993:16).

In the world of modern peoplehood, mixed-raced children constitute a group that generates endless worries about acceptance and belonging (cf. Frankenberg 1993:93). They recapitulate the logical development of minority peoplehood, from passing to identity assertion. In the United States, many "mixed race" children identified with one of the parents' races. For example, Frederick August Kittel—with a German father—asserts himself as the black playwright August Wilson (Lahr 2001:55). In the late twentieth century, the mixed-race identity became an identity in its own right (Nobles 2000:138–144).

In the U.S. 2000 Census, seven million Americans identified themselves as "mixed race" (Schmitt 2001:A1). The rise of the mixed-race identities challenges the seemingly settled categories and identities in the United States. Indeed, the exact meanings of race, ethnicity, and nation have shifted dramatically, whether in the form of popular classificatory schemes or scientific definitions. Simultaneously, numerous individuals are re-thinking the messy facts of individual reality against the blunt abstraction of received categories. Distinct racial formations and scenarios challenge the black-white biracial order in the contemporary United States (cf. Hollinger 1995:chaps. 4–6).

6

Why does minority identity become so significant? Precisely when structural racism is waning, the claim of racism and the action of counter-racism proliferate. The paradox of oppression fuses with the search for authenticity to fan the ideological and emotional fervor of minority identity.

Consider in this regard Jean Améry. Born to a Catholic mother and a Jewish father (religious affiliation) in Austria (nation), his childhood "identity was bound to a plain German name [Hans Maier] and to the dialect of my more immediate place of origin." Cultural (pan-German) and regional (linguistic) identities were irrelevant when he was arrested as a German in 1940. Later, he was transported to a Nazi concentration camp as a Jew even though he was not Jewish by the halakhic definition. Furthermore, as he (1990:83) observed, "if being a Jew means sharing a religious creed with other Jews, participating in Jewish cultural and family tradition, cultivating a Jewish national ideal, then I find myself in a hopeless situation." Despite the absence of commonality with other Jews, he nonetheless faced the recalcitrant reality of the Nuremberg Laws and the Nazi domination of Austria. As he (1990:94) wrote: "As a Non-non-non Jew, I am a Jew. . . . In Auschwitz . . . the isolated individual had to relinquish all of German culture, including Dürer and Reger, Gryphius and Trakl, to even the lowest SS man" (Améry 1990:8). The contrast between Améry the intellectual, who had mastered German culture, and "the lowest SS man," who did not have an inkling of Reger or Gryphius, is striking. Améry points to the contradiction between Jewish Germans of immense cultural capital being reduced to the racial other by ordinary Germans of low intellectual standing.

Améry's situation is symptomatic of many individuals who are forced by racist exclusion to explore and confront their identity. The plaintive query of "who am I?" finds a ready description in what Du Bois called "double consciousness," of belonging and not belonging. In a racist universe, a black Harvard Ph.D. is symbolically inferior to an ill-educated white person. Having assimilated far, the remaining distance seems unbridgeable. That is, even as structural racism is lightening, symbolic racism may weigh all the more heavily. Of the Swiss village where he spent some summers, James Baldwin (1998:117) reported: "There is no movie house, no bank, no library, no theater; very few radios, one jeep, one station wagon, and, at the moment, one typewriter, mine, an invention which the woman next door to me here had never seen." In spite of the "backwardness" of the villagers, Baldwin (1998:121) envies the racial unity of the "white people": "These people cannot be, from the point of view of power, strangers anywhere in the world: they have made the modern world, in effect, even if they do not know it. The most illiterate among them is related, in a way that I am not, to Dante, Shakespeare, Michelangelo, Aeschylus, Da Vinci, Rembrandt, and Racine." Only an educated soul tortured by racism can make such an association, at once misrecognizing the status of poor villagers and their ancestry. Who has a spiritual or material claim to be the heir of European civilization? Baldwin, who has read Shakespeare and Dante and owns a typewriter, or poor, ill-educated villagers? Surely the Swiss villager would be dumbfounded to realize her kinship to an "Italian" poet or an "English" playwright.

Symbolic slights accentuate the sense of inauthenticity experienced by those who have assiduously sought to assimilate. The incendiary mixture of pride and humiliation, envy and resentment is corrosive, as expressed trenchantly by L.-G. Damas's poem "Solde" [Balance] (1962:39): "I feel ridiculous / In their shoes / In their tuxedo / . . . I feel ridiculous / . . . Among them a supporter / Among them a murderer / Hands horribly red / From the blood of their ci-vi-li-za-tion." Damas of course had to experience France and to learn French in order to write the poem. But its passion derives from his ire at his exclusion. The poem is a record of achievement and accusation, pride and anger.

The contradictory impulses of structural and symbolic racism can be seen in the impassioned debate in the United States in the 1990s regarding the conditions of African Americans (cf. Hochschild 1995:39–51). Stephen and Abigail Thernstrom (1997:533,pt.2) adduced statistical evidence to demonstrate the progress of African Americans in terms of education, income, and other metrics. As the African American actor Will Smith said: "We've got Bentleys. We can't even relate to not being able to sit in somebody's lunch counter. I'll buy the counter and throw you out" (Cagle 2001: 70; cf. Steele 1990:169). In contrast, David Shipler (1997:17,563) conducted innumerable interviews that revealed racism to be as bad as, if not worse, than ever. Shipler's conclusion is seconded by Cornel West (1993: xv): "The decline and decay in American life *appears,* at the moment, to be irreversible." From the privileged perch of Princeton professorship, he wrote: "Not since the 1920s have so many black folk been disappointed and disillusioned with America. I partake of this black zeitgeist; I share these sentiments" (West 1993:xvii; cf. Bell 1987:3).

One resolution of this debate is to frame it as a paradox of oppression. It is precisely the partially assimilated who most profoundly experience racism (cf. Patterson 1997:54–65). As Ellis Cose (1993:1) writes: "Despite its very evident prosperity, much of America's black middle class is in excruciating pain." Or as Joe Feagin and Melvin Sikes (1994:ix) declare: "Clearly, no amount of hard work and achievement, no amount of money, resources, and success, can protect black people from the persisting ravages of white racism in their everyday lives." They provide one compelling interpretation—the persistence of racism—but there is another. Middle-class African Americans should be more likely to register symbolic slight and to articulate their wrath. Indeed, they are the normative blacks who speak for their people (cf. Dawson 1994:61,196–199).

A similar dynamic can be seen among Asian Americans. The very term is a counter-racist expression against racist essentializing that arose in the 1960s (Wei 1993:118). Many Asian Americans experience educational and professional success, yet they also insist on the eviscerating impact of racism. The sense of symbolic exclusion from American life—"forever foreigners" (Tuan 1998:155–164)—supersedes the structural reality of economic and educational integration. Symbolic racism—dealing with issues in the realm of pride and dignity—is a matter of subjective definition. Apprehension of racism is a reflexive act. As Yi-fu Tuan (1999:92)—the self-described Greek scholar we encountered in the Prelude—warned: "Thanks to a nationwide movement to raise consciousness in regard to the color of one's skin, I am now—white friends, beware!—on guard for every slur or slight."

Racism is recognized belatedly, and in so doing its very meaning shifts. Symbolic slights sting long after structural racism has dissipated. Having broken down the significant barrier of structural racism, the sensitivity to its surviving legacy is heightened. If structural racism had insinuated itself in every nook and cranny of social life, then its destruction nonetheless unleashes the seemingly never-ending task of eradicating its surviving fragments and detritus. Manning Marable (1995:7) claims: "At its essential core, racism is most keenly felt in its smallest manifestations: the white merchant who drops change on the sales counter. . . . These minor actions reflect a structure of power, privilege and violence which most blacks can never forget." In turn his children "complain that their high-school textbooks don't have sufficient information about the activities and events related to African-Americans" (Marable 1995:8). Marable and his children are right to complain about racial insults and injustices, but how significant are the "smallest manifestations" of racism? While the Nazis incinerated Jews, few worried about anti-Semitism. When graffiti grace a Jewish cemetery today, however, a national self-reckoning is mandated. While the KKK openly marched and lynched blacks, few fought publicly to combat racism. When someone utters a racial epithet today, however unintentionally, a full-scale antiracist campaign is waged (cf. Delgado 1995:162–165). While many white Americans received the news of Martin Luther King, Jr.'s, death in 1968 ambivalently, by 1986 his birthday had become a national holiday, and by the early twenty-first century he had become a nationally revered figure on par with the Founding Fathers (cf. Blauner 1989:1–4). While Du Bois or Locke could not have imagined a professorship at a major white university, African-American studies programs proliferate at major "white" universities. Yet the former Harvard Law School professor Derrick Bell (1992:12) declares: "Racial oppression [is a] permanent status in this country. . . . *Black people will never gain full equality in this country.*" It is not professional success that is a barometer of weakening structural racism, but a slight—to be misrecognized by a white person or to fail to hail a cab— that proves the persistence of racism (Jordan 1992:162). Indeed, the very existence of racism, especially against African Americans, comes to be viewed as a source of American exceptionalism, or an American essence (Kovel 1988:177; Quadagno 1994:187; cf. Sniderman and Piazza 1993: 56).

More generally, the world comes to seem awash with racism. Albert

Memmi (2000:131) announces: "*In almost every person there is a tendency toward a racist mode of thinking*" and goes on to announce: "*Racism . . . is ultimately the most widely shared attitude in the world*" (Memmi 2000:132). The philosopher Charles W. Mills (1997:31) proposes the existence of the racial contract, which is "an exploitation contract that creates global European economic domination and national white racial privilege." That is, racism is everywhere (Goldberg 1983:6). Being inside everyone and everywhere, counter-racist intellectuals spearhead the effort to transform populations into peoples. Census categories and other public records dutifully reproduce the contingent world of peoplehood identity (cf. Skerry 2000: 199–202). Even objective and empiricist social scientists perpetuate and reify racist categories. By producing generalizations based on population categories, social scientists lend scientific legitimacy to the primacy of peoples. Well-meaning historians in turn write chronicles of minority peoplehood. While nationalist historians and social scientists initially crystallized the world of modern peoplehood, counter-racist historians and social scientists reify the counter-racist identity of the excluded. In a matter of years, political organization and market research, literary anthology and musicology all presume the categorical reality of minority peoplehood.

Privileged intellectuals, precisely because they have the resource and sensibility, are wont to highlight symbolic racism. The renowned feminist Julia Kristeva (1993:38) insists that in France "foreigners experience more strongly than elsewhere the scorn and rejection that is inflicted upon them by a civilization sure of itself." Needless to say, symbolic pain is difficult to calibrate, but France, after all, prides itself on its republican principles, and Kristeva herself has scaled the summit of French intellectual life, yet her singular conclusion is that: "Nowhere is one *more* a foreigner than in France" (Kristeva 1991:38, 1993:30). "What do you think is common to all the Jews," asked Isaiah Berlin to Avishai Margalit (2001:149): "A sense of social unease. Nowhere do Jews feel entirely at home." Ironically, everyone around Berlin found him "entirely at home" at Oxford (Lilla, Dworkin, and Silvers 2001:188).

Consider in this regard Frantz Fanon's (1967:chap. 5) response to a child's gaze. The perceived slight unleashes a philosophical tour de force. Invoking Hegel and Sartre, Aeschylus and Artaud, Fanon's reflexive response is paradoxically presented as an unmediated experience. "There is nothing more exasperating than to be asked: 'How long have you been in France? You speak French so well' " (Fanon 1967:35). Naïve, though probably innocent, questions or well-intended compliments merely confirm the intransigent racism of French people. After all, the other had painfully acquired the universal civilization of France: "The black schoolboy in the Antilles, who in his lessons is forever talking about 'our ancestors, the Gauls,' identifying himself with the explorer, the bringer of civilization, the white man who carries truth to savages—an all-white truth" (Fanon 1967:142). Years of study, decades of reading cannot fortify the assimilationist project against a mere child's gaze.

The French child in Fanon's allegory of racism cannot represent himself; he must be represented. There is an asymmetry at work in the world of symbolic racism. Take the example of facial recognition. People who do not have extensive contact with an unfamiliar group lack the capacity to recognize intra-group differences (cf. Bruce and Young 1988:112–133). The critic Roger Shattuck (2001:22) writes: "Some years ago when I arrived in Dakar, Senegal, to teach . . . all my students and all my colleagues were black as ebony. For a month they all looked the same. I couldn't recognize people I had met recently two or three times. The usual cues for distinguishing one person from another were drowned in a single all-absorbing color. I felt deeply humiliated and lost confidence in my most basic faculties of perception." Such perceptual difficulties with the unknown are wont to reify the received distinction between Americans and Senegalese or whites and blacks. To Carlo Levi (1963:79), southern peasants "all seemed alike, short, sunburned, with dull, expressionless black eyes like the empty windows of a dark room." Yet surely Levi was not a racist against his fellow Italians with whom he empathized deeply. What may strike Shattuck as innocent undoubtedly struck Senegalese—especially privileged, educated, and proud Senegalese—as profoundly offensive. Imagine Fanon's wrath at Shattuck should Shattuck have mistaken Fanon for a cab driver. Insensitive and offensive though symbolic slights may be, they should not be equated with the social evil of structural racism: systematic segregation and discrimination.

Those who scale the professional heights of a society have both the motivation and the ability to bemoan the limitations of horizontal integration, when vertical hierarchy silently continues to wreak havoc on the poor and the marginalized. The ill educated who spout the occasional racist epithet—the respected scientific opinion of mere decades ago—are reviled as despicable racists. Quite frequently, it justifies unrestrained expressions of class prejudice, which function as a quasi-racist discourse in its own right. That is, there is an asymmetry in stressing the horizontal and ignoring the vertical.

My intention is not to belittle the eviscerating impact of symbolic racism. One does not need to be conversant in the elevated esoterica of European culture to feel the sting of racial epithets by an illiterate, whose only claim to Western civilization may well be her or his European ancestry. Symbolic slights, exclusions, and denigration are the stuff of a society in which dignified life is not possible. Certainly, it would be disingenuous to deny the existence of symbolic racism or belittle efforts to eradicate it.

Nonetheless, think of "rednecks," who have distinct regional and quasi-ethnic origins, such as "Okies" (U.S. Southwest) and "Hillbillies" (Appalachia). As a form of Orientalism, Appalachia is viewed as a distant land with a strange people. More crudely, Appalachians are seen as violent and stupid (Blee and Billings 1999:124). Because Southwesterners constituted a seemingly distinct subculture and were largely poor and ill educated, they faced discrimination that was tantamount to racist exclusion (cf. Gregory 1989: 164–169). And it remains permissible to invoke negative stereotypes with abandon (Shelby 1999:153). The last redoubt of permissible racism in the United States may very well be against poor European Americans, or "white trash" who are deemed "poor, dirty, drunken, criminally minded, and sexually perverse people" (Newitz and Wray 1997:2)—and racist to boot.

Given the proliferation of symbolic slights, the temptation to highlight the evil of racism is rampant, especially among the educated elite. The phenomenological basis of racism finds ready confirmation in the spread of genocide and other instances of putatively racial, ethnic, or national conflict. Yet it is not during the Holocaust that world Jewry rises to combat Nazism, but when its memory is being assaulted after the tragedy. It is not during slavery or Jim Crow that race and racism are important, but when white supremacy begins to crumble that race and racism become national obsessions. It is not during the internment of Japanese Americans that anti-Asian racism became a serious topic, but a generation later that Japanese Americans and other Asian Americans find it to be a linchpin of anti-Japanese or anti-Asian racism in the United States. In the meantime, all of human history is rewritten in the language of modern peoplehood. Races and racisms come to seem ubiquitous and permanent, and therefore invincible: the master explanation of human affairs. Symptomatically, *Romeo and Juliet*—love thwarted by clan conflict—becomes *West Side Story*—love thwarted by ethnic conflict. In the reflexive spiral, all of history comes to be seen as racial and racist. Counter-racist movements and identities generate generic racial pride shared by everyone (cf. Rhea 1997:6). Intellectuals discern autonomous racial dynamics in the form of the racial state or racial identity, racial conflict or racial cooperation, racial language or racial literature (cf. Omi and Winant 1994:56–61; Patterson 1997:4).

Being a positive symbol of distinction, peoplehood identity is extended even to descendants of groups who had struggled so valiantly to be white (Waters 1990:92,97). Although whiteness defined normality—the state of raceless, colorless being—it becomes uninteresting. Like individual identity that valorizes deviance, the claim of modern individuality seeks ethnicity as a form of authenticity and individuality: different and therefore interesting and meaningful. Symbolic ethnicity becomes something that everyone must have, whether in terms of racial pride (black power, red power, yellow power, and so on) or national ancestry (Gutiérrez 1995:183–187). It also fuses with the persistence of traditional racial and ethnic identities (cf. Alba 1990:71). Being costless but with symbolic benefits, the choice of ethnic ancestry becomes yet another expression of individuality. Indeed, even those who resisted peoplehood identity in the past are ensnared by its latter-day advocates. We cannot but remember Jean Toomer or Countee Cullen as black writers (cf. Fields 1990:97).

If the dead are retrospectively granted peoplehood pride, then the living are actively goaded to embrace it. Peoplehood identity is a transnational, global identity and ideology, whether for supranational or subnational groups. Pan-Gypsy or pan-Maya movements emerged recently yet have come to assert a long history of oppression and identity (Fonseca 1995: 293–299; Fischer 2001:84–89). Diasporic groups seek solidarities of their own, constituting supranationalist nationalism or diasporic nationalism (cf. Clifford 1997:276). Counter-racist scholars and activists come to bemoan the belated emergence of racial consciousness elsewhere. Michael Hanchard (1994:6) writes: "the overall inability of Afro-Brazilian activists to mobilize people on the basis of racial identity, [is] due in large part to the general inability of Brazilians to identify patterns of violence and discrimination that are racially specific" (cf. Marx 1998:253). As Hanchard acknowledges, however, "black" consciousness arose principally among college-educated African Americans in the 1970s. Thus, some Brazilians learn their "black" identity upon arriving in the United States: "I say I'm from Brazil. They say, 'No, you are from Africa' " (Fears 2003:29).

More generally, nonracial groups begin to mobilize as distinct peoples.

The discourses of human rights and group dignity inform any number of hitherto excluded and discriminated collectives (cf. Skrentny 2002:354–357). Struggling against the regime of normalcy, the politics of identity assumes the form of modern peoplehood, with its own guardians of identity who define the normative mode of conduct and belief (D'Emilio 1992:246–256; Escoffier 1998:57–62). Physically and mentally disabled people also become distinct peoples (cf. Oliver 1996:152–156). As I argued in Chapter 4, biosociality becomes a potent basis for identity, whether as "deaf people" or "short people." Indeed, the Deaf not only share a language and culture, but they also tend to marry each other and reproduce the community (Davis 1995:78; cf. Lane 1992:191–200).

Struggles over symbolic racism and the politics of identity are important. Although racism—and its allied manifestations, such as tribal conflict, ethnic hatred, racial war—seems to dominate the modern world, it exists much less as a cause but rather as a consequence of power struggles. Counter-racist struggles are often backward looking, combating past evils and present slights. In the meantime, persisting sources of poverty or inequality are passed over in silence. Beyond the welter of racist and counter-racist discourses continues savage inequalities and mass murders. Claiming the ubiquity of racism ultimately renders it impossible to deal with the transhistorical and transcultural phenomenon and obfuscates the challenges of the here and now.

Postlude

Modernity—a topic that generates grandiose and pretentious pronouncements, and hence provokes profound suspicion and skepticism—has been associated among others with the rise of capitalism and industrialization, science and technology, democracy and civil society, urbanism and the public sphere, alienation and meaninglessness, and rationality and secularization. Following an old-fashioned approach, I wish to highlight it as an epistemic shift, or the transition from Christian worldview to secular Enlightenment. Modernity denotes the disenchantment of the world, and, in particular, the decline of religion as a dominant imaginary and institution of Christendom.

What is Enlightenment? *"Enlightenment is man's emergence from his self-incurred immaturity. Immaturity* is the inability to use one's own understanding without the guidance of another. . . . The motto of enlightenment is therefore: *Sapere aude!* Have courage to use your *own* understanding!" (Kant 1991:54). Immanuel Kant's celebrated 1784 essay on the Enlightenment offers a ringing rhetoric for epistemic equality and freedom. From political and religious tutelage, individual maturity marks the autonomy of reason and the rise of the self-reliant and self-reflexive subject. Rather than being in the thrall of throne and altar, the self-legislating subject claims the legitimacy of critical reflection and reason. In particular, Kant (1991:59) highlights *"matters of religion* as the focal point of enlightenment." He states: "As things are at present, we still have a long way to go before men as a whole can be in a position . . . of using their own understanding confidently and well in religious matters, without outside guidance" (Kant 1991: 58). If phylogeny follows ontogeny, then the autonomy of the self amounts to the secularization of society.

Enlightenment superseded Christianity. To be sure, just as Christianity was not a singular, homogenous entity, Enlightenment showed great diversity across place and time (Outram 1995:4–8). The modal contrast between science, secularism, and disenchantment against superstition, religion, and magic is liable to caricature the past and to celebrate the present. As Carl Becker (1932:31) observed: "There is more of Christian philosophy in the writings of the *Philosophes* than has yet been dreamt of in our histories." Consider two thinkers widely celebrated today for their modernity: Vico and Hegel. But Vico thought of "religion as the underlying and unifying force of history" (Mazzotta 1999:254), and Hegel's thought from the 1793 Tübingen essay to the 1821 *Philosophie des Rechts* [The Philosophy of the Right] was steeped in theological and religious problematics (Hegel 1977:5; cf. Harris 1983:557–572). One of the putative fathers of nationalism, Fichte, generated contemporary controversy for his alleged atheism, not his proto-nationalism (La Vopa 2001:chap. 12). Science and religion were far from antagonistic until the late nineteenth century (Chadwick 1975:161–188; Bowler 2001:19–24). Only then did Christianity collapse as a metaphysical backdrop of European thought. Nietzsche's proclamation of God's demise may have been a logical culmination of Kant's declaration of the autonomy of reason, but he was the first to say so loudly and clearly.

By the late nineteenth century, Enlightenment as an epistemic worldview was dominant in western and central Europe. Long-term trends were unmistakable. Instead of intensively reading the Bible, people read widely and of profane matters to boot (cf. Engelsing 1974:339–343; Watt 1957:35–59). Rather than the church and its teachings, the public sphere and public opinion ruled the world of the mind (Habermas 1962:101–127). Society or nation emerged as a meaningful unit of experience and analysis. Not surprisingly, modern social theory—the work of Marx, Durkheim, and Weber—and artistic expressions of modernity—modernism—flowered in the late nineteenth and early twentieth centuries.

The triumph of Enlightenment reason hastened the disenchantment of the world, and promised epistemic individualism and social equality. The rise of the individual as a sovereign subject is a complex process with long antecedents. Even in preliterate, nomadic groups, the physiological separation of persons provided a potent ground for individuation (Lienhardt 1985:153). However, the idea of the individual as an autonomous and self-legislating subject began to be explicitly articulated by Descartes and others in seventeenth-century Europe, and it became widespread in the nineteenth century (Lukes 1973:1).

In addition to abstract, epistemic individualism arose the ideal of egalitarianism. What had been the preserve of the privileged was now open to every individual, regardless of status, who was to exercise her or his will and, moreover, to be recognized as a being with dignity and respect. Many individuals experienced sovereignty not only in the epistemological but also in the political realm by the twentieth century. People gained votes, social citizenship, and moral recognition. The idea of the individual as somebody worthy of respect and recognition, someone who demands attributes of a dignified life, became regnant. Whether working class or women, minorities or minors, everyone gained rights as individuals. Everyone has a descent or lineage worth recording and celebrating.

Modern social theory sought to capture these epochal shifts, whether from *Gemeinschaft* to *Gesellschaft* or from status to contract. In each of these accounts, certitude leads to uncertainty, meaningfulness denudes into meaninglessness, and communalism dissolves into individualism. In one of the founding texts of modern social theory, *De la division du travail social* [The Division of Labor] (1893), Émile Durkheim (1984:83–86) posited the fundamental distinction between tradition and modernity as different types of social solidarity. The source of social solidarity in preindustrial societies presumes the fundamental similarity among members. In contrast, modern solidarity is predicated on division of labor and social differentiation. What holds society together is not the sameness of members, but their difference. Durkheim (1973:56) himself concluded that in a modern, complex society, the individual is the least common denominator and the source of solidarity. Social differentiation, in other words, gives rise to individualism as a source of cohesion.

The socio-political face of modernity that spawned abstract and egalitarian individualism simultaneously pulverized received identities and senses of belonging. Capitalist industrialization and modern state making engulfed the world and transformed it beyond recognition. In that memorable phrase from *The Communist Manifesto* (1844): "all that is solid melts into air" (Marx and Engels 1974:70). Convulsions of modernity—despite recurrent attempts to belittle them—left few stones unturned. Social differentiation, urbanization, modernization, space-time compression, and other processes became undeniable trends by the nineteenth century. Status—that ultimate determinant of one's role in most spheres of premodern social life—declined in significance. Villages and towns were no longer relatively autonomous entities that circumscribed most lives. Consolations of faith and community faded as individuals increasingly faced death alone.

Epistemic and ontological individualism generated the paradigmatic modern individual, staring alone into the abyss of mortality and nothingness. From being a bearer of naturalized identities, individuals found an absent center in the socialized self. The Enlightenment ideal projected the individual as a being with nonidentity, or as an ontological subject sui generis. And the individual faced the Simmelian world of the stranger, at once everywhere and indifferent. Human beings encountered the horror of existence and nothingness without the helping hands of metaphysical salvation or the suffocating intimacy of traditional faith and community.

Modernity seemed alienating and meaningless. As Friedrich Schiller (1967:35) trenchantly and presciently put it in his 1795 treatise: "Everlastingly chained to a single little fragment of the Whole, man himself develops into nothing but a fragment . . . [h]e becomes nothing more than the imprint of his occupation or of his specialized knowledge." How do we gain a sense of self from fragments? Precisely when answers were needed, confessional identities were less convincing in the secular world of wealth and power. As Hegel (1977:340) queried: "If all prejudice and superstition have been banished, the question arises: *What next? What is the truth Enlightenment has propagated in their stead?*" Individualism? Autonomy? Dignity? Sex? Art? Money? Alas, they lacked the majesty and grandeur, consolation and comfort, of old-time religion. Christianity—at least in premodern Europe—valorized the soul, promised redemption, and provided reassurance (Delumeau 1989:14–20). As Marx (1994:57) astutely put it—before pointing out that it was "the *opium* of the people"—"Religion is the sigh of the oppressed creature, the heart of a heartless world and the soul of soulless conditions." Given that oppression did not disappear or the world did not cease to be heartless—indeed, secularization merely accentuated our soulless condition—what was to replace religion?

The consolation of modernity was the possibility of social transformation and redemption, the secular religion of revolutionary ideals and individual metamorphoses. In spite of their persistent appeals, abstract individualism and Enlightenment cosmopolitanism seemed colorless, rootless, and homeless. When individualism was thrust on everyone, traditional identities were in decline. When everyone had to be something or someone, people in fact faced the abstract universal of Enlightenment individualism and the concrete particular of the world they appeared to be losing.

The idea of modern peoplehood served as a floating signifier to denote disparate conceptualizations about its principal predicates and substantive meanings. By definition, however, it provided an identity that was simultaneously different and significant. It was ascribed, primordial, and ineffable. The generative discourse of modern peoplehood provided ready-made narratives of its geography and history, its glorious past and brilliant future. Particularistic elements—everything from biological to religious inheritance—constituted the claim of difference. By grounding it in the most cogent discourses of biology and history, modern peoplehood sealed its dominance. Modern peoplehood restored certainty, meaning, and community. It provided the soul and spirit for modern individuals.

Modern peoplehood creates a fiction of homogeneity, of holistic essences. Among available identities, ones that dominate are those that seem most deep and natural, such as blood and ancestry. Ironically, then, most modern articulations of social identity express mechanical, not organic, solidarity. In discourses of nationalism or racism, the predominant trope is to identify essential characteristics of a group. Far from finding complexity and differentiation, the language of modern peoplehood everywhere expresses simplicity and homogeneity. By friends or foes, essentialism— Durkheim's mechanical solidarity—is the dominant mode of describing people. While social life was fluid and complex, identity became stable and simple. If preliterate, preindustrial life featured fluctuating and overlapping memberships, postliterate, postindustrial life demanded a reified and singular identity. Paradoxically, but perhaps predictably, the age of achievement turned out to be the age of ascription.

Counter-Enlightenment thinkers offered the initial articulation of modern peoplehood. Whether emphasizing horizontal distinction (Herder) or vertical hierarchy (Gobineau), they reacted to the ongoing horizontal and vertical integration of their world. Against Enlightenment universalism and egalitarianism—the world of the modern, autonomous individual— they championed particularism and distinction—the world of the premodern, embedded individual. Whether to defend hierarchical and hereditary privilege or to promote political unification and cultural autonomy, these discourses of difference, in turn, profoundly shaped the discourse of modern peoplehood. Herder's stress on belonging or Hegel's emphasis on reconciliation found numerous successors. Most critically, the contradictions between the theory of abstract universals and the practice of concrete particulars—the very questions of Enlightenment and modernity—were conceptualized and debated principally in the national frame, usually in the national vernacular. In short, the ideology of tradition sustained the myth of homogeneity and continuity. Modern peoplehood became a dominant metaphysic of modernity.

If Kant's 1784 essay on the Enlightenment stands at the beginnings of modernity, replete with emancipatory ideals and promises, then Theodor Adorno and Max Horkheimer's 1944 *Dialectic of Enlightenment* marks its nadir, its dark and dystopian underside. Written during World War II, Adorno and Horkheimer (1979:xiii) proffer a dirge for "the self-destruction of the Enlightenment": "The Enlightenment has always aimed at liberating men from fear and establishing their sovereignty. Yet the fully enlightened earth radiates disaster triumphant" (Adorno and Horkheimer 1979:3). If they express one facet of Enlightenment ideals—the power of critique and the sense of dissatisfaction—they also confess the inability to elude—indeed, to abet—mythology and domination (Adorno and Horkheimer 1979: 27,41).

The dream of universal reason redounds in the nightmare of particularistic irrationality. Reason, rather than unleashing illumination and emancipation, generates deception and domination. Far from achieving self-legislation and self-invention, we witness governmental control and manipulation of society and self. Instead of autonomy and reason, we find the domination of the culture industry and the irrationality of anti-Semitism. Universals are false, manifesting themselves as either colonial or national universals: indeed, the more transcendent in theory, the more practical in politics, wreaking the terror of absolute conviction on the hapless and concrete reality. Disturbingly, one of the fathers of modern social theory, Herbert Spencer (1851:416), had written: "The forces which are working out the great scheme of perfect happiness, taking no account of incidental suffering, exterminate such sections of mankind as stand in their way with the same sternness that they exterminate beasts of prey and herds of useless ruminants. . . . Be he human or be he brute, the hindrance must be got rid of." Certainly, few would wish away Spencer's claim or commitment to reason; fewer would be able to deny a particular conception of modernity that saw its horrific manifestation in the Holocaust. More mundanely, the universalistic pretensions of the social sciences frequently occlude their parochialism (cf. Wallerstein et al. 1996:48–60). Theoretical freedom, equality, and fraternity coincide with practical unfreedom, inequality, and estrangement. That is, reason created its own myth, modern peoplehood and its negative hallucination, racism. The reductio ad absurdum is that we remember Kant as a racist and the Enlightenment as a point in the trajectory toward the Holocaust.

In the early twenty-first century, we encounter the detritus of the developments I have delineated. In the guise of globalization, abstract individualism marches on, generating fundamentalist reactions everywhere. The desire for distinction and the paradox of oppression heighten struggles for state power that find their ne plus ultra in genocide. In the heartless world, then, people seek shards of meaning in the illusory community of modern peoplehood. If grand narratives have lost their hold, then they have merely dispersed and disseminated themselves as personal and particular narratives. Here again, the irrepressible trend toward individualism is undeniable. The efflorescence of subnational peoplehood is intimately related to the desire for thick identities that thin identities—with their systematic disjunction between the whole and the part—cannot bridge. Racial, ethnic, or national pride appears as the maximally possible mode of symbolic solidarity.

Should we bury Enlightenment universalism because of its perverse consequences? The obviousness and inevitability of the aristocratic and religious hierarchy and worldview took centuries of political agitation and intellectual ferment to dismantle. Modern peoplehood, however contingent and constructed, is no less entrenched. Yet the flux of people—moving, intermarrying—and the trend toward individuation are irrepressible. Critical reflection—that hallmark of modernity—continues to shatter all forms of transcendental illusion. Just as Enlightenment reason destroyed throne and altar, it continues to undermine the modern state and modern peoplehood. This is precisely the reason that we come to see modern peoplehood as contingent and constructed, and ultimately implausible and impossible. If the owl of Minerva does indeed fly at dusk, then the demise of modern peoplehood is probably not so far off.

Abstract universals promised by the Enlightenment were empty, as counter-Enlightenment thinkers gleefully pointed out. But claims of modern peoplehood were in fact equally abstract, however concrete and particular they may have intended them to be. George Eliot's (1994:147) statement in 1879 that "I am not bound to feel for a Chinaman as I feel for my fellow-countryman" may seem to be an instance of extreme particularism, but in fact, it is also an example of expansionary consciousness. Mancunians of the past may well have said that "I am not bound to feel for a Liverpudlian as I feel for my fellow Mancunians." The nobility and the peasantry of Manchester or Liverpool did not claim a singular identity. Why is the other necessarily racial, ethnic, or national (cf. Schnapper 1998: 35–39)? Any identity claim is an abstraction. The universe of modern peoplehood forces people to argue endlessly with reified relations and categories. Particular individuality is bypassed in the name of an abstract collectivity. In denying the full repertoire of overlapping belongings and the inevitable flux of populations, the world of modern peoplehood weighs like a nightmare on the minds of the living.

In the name of concrete authenticity, counter-racist thinkers most trenchantly criticized the hollowness of modern peoplehood. Yet authenticity and plenitude promised by antiracist racism (Sartre 2001:118) were no more concrete or meaningful than modern peoplehood. Consider Negritude, one of its most articulate expressions. As Wole Soyinka (1976: 136) writes: "Negritude stayed within a pre-set system of Eurocentric intellectual analysis both of man and society and tried to re-define the African and his society in those externalized terms." As I noted, the process is facilitated by symbolic racism, as the very Western-educated intellectuals take leadership in counter-racist struggles. Soyinka (1976:131) continues: "A totally artificial angst fabricated by a handful of writers *after* Negritude revealed to them the very seductive notion that they had to commence a search for their Africanness. Until then, they were never even aware that it was missing." This is the sense in which Fanon said, "Black soul was but a white artifact," and Sartre (2001:137) saw expressions of Negritude as "a passage and not an outcome, a means and not an ultimate end." All these claims are in fact articulations of alienated categories. The paradox of identity is that there are no essences.

In order to overcome racism, counter-racist racialization is necessary, however illusory its claims of authenticity and liberation may be. Dialectical negation and transformation are part and parcel of the inevitable human struggle in a world of power and inequality. The oppressed at once resist and use the oppressor's language, ideals, and methods. In so doing, counter-racism aspires only to the goals of modern peoplehood. As that memorable passage in *A Dream of John Ball* put it: "how men fight and lose the battle, and the thing that they fought for comes about in spite of their defeat, and when it comes turns out not to be what they meant, and other men have to fight for what they meant under another name" (Morris 1888: 31). Rather than the freedom to choose peoplehood identity, perhaps the time has come for us to seek to be free from it. Refracting ripples of power, modern peoplehood promises neither emancipation nor redemption. Neither, alas, does counter-racist identity hold the key to liberation or salvation.

There is, then, life still in abstract universals, ideals of a well-tempered humanism (Todorov 1993:399). The regulative ideal of the Enlightenment—utopian though it may sound—provides a backdrop against which we can criticize the present and ponder a future, whether to vilify crimes against humanity or to champion nonracist thought. To condemn it as Eurocentric—a genetic fallacy—does disservice to Europe's singular contribution to the human race. The voice of reason, ever fragile and easily mocked, is soft but not silent, a minor but resonant note in the cacophonic world in which we somehow strain to hear and play the chords of knowledge, hope, and love.

References

Aarne, Antti. [1910/1961] 1981. *The Types of the Folktale: A Classification and Bibliography*, 2nd ed., trans. and enlarged Stith Thompson. Helsinki: Academia Scientiarum Fennica.

Abel, Theodore. [1938] 1986. *Why Hitler Came into Power.* Cambridge, Mass.: Harvard University Press.

Abelmann, Nancy, and John Lie. 1995. *Blue Dreams: Korean Americans and the Los Angeles Riots.* Cambridge, Mass.: Harvard University Press.

Abraham, Gary A. 1992. *Max Weber and the Jewish Question: A Study of the Social Outlook of His Sociology.* Urbana: University of Illinois Press.

Ackerman, Jennifer. 2001. *Chance in the House of Fate: A Natural History of Heredity.* Boston: Houghton Mifflin.

Acton, John Emerich Edward Dalberg-Acton, Baron. [1862] 1985. "Nationality." In John Emerich Edward Dalberg-Acton, First Baron Acton, *Selected Writings of Lord Acton,* vol. 1: *Essays in the History of Liberty,* ed. J. Rufus Fears, pp. 409–433. Indianapolis: LibertyClassics.

Adam, Uwe Dietrich. 1972. *Judenpolitik im Dritten Reich.* Düsseldorf: Droste.

Adams, Mark B. 1990. "Towards a Comparative History of Eugenics." In Mark B. Adams, ed., *The Wellborn Science: Eugenics in Germany, France, Brazil, and Russia,* pp. 217–231. New York: Oxford University Press.

Adorno, T. W., Else Frenkel-Brunswik, Daniel J. Levinson, and R. Nevitt Sanford. [1950] 1964. *The Authoritarian Personality,* 2 vols. New York: John Wiley & Sons.

Adorno, Theodor, and Max Horkheimer. [1944/1972] 1979. *Dialectic of Enlightenment,* trans. John Cumming. London: Verso.

African Rights [Rakiya Omaar]. [1994] 1995. *Rwanda: Death, Despair and Defiance,* rev. ed. London: African Rights.

———. 1996. *Rwanda, Killing the Evidence: Murder, Attacks, Arrests and Intimidation of Survivors and Witnesses.* London: African Rights.

Agulhon, Maurice. [1979] 1981. *Marianne into Battle: Republican Imagery and Symbolism in France, 1789–1880,* trans. Janet Lloyd. Cambridge: Cambridge University Press.

———. [1970/1979] 1982. *The Republic in the Village: The People of the Var from the French Revolution to the Second Republic*, trans. Janet Lloyd. Cambridge: Cambridge University Press.

———. [1973] 1983. *The Republican Experiment, 1848–1852*, trans. Janet Lloyd. Cambridge: Cambridge University Press.

Ahmad, Aziz. 1964. *Studies in Islamic Culture in the Indian Environment.* Oxford: Clarendon Press.

Akisada Yoshikazu. 1993. *Kindai to buraku sangyō.* Osaka: Buraku Kaihō Kenkyūsho.

Alba, Richard D. 1990. *Ethnic Identity: The Transformation of White America.* New Haven, Conn.: Yale University Press.

Alinei, Mario. 1984. *Lingua e dialetti: Struttura, storia et geografia.* Bologna: Il Mulino.

Allen, Irving Lewis. 1983. *The Language of Ethnic Conflict: Social Organization and Lexical Culture.* New York: Columbia University Press.

Allen, Theodore W. 1994. *The Invention of the White Race,* vol. 1: *Racial Oppression and Social Control.* London: Verso.

Allen, William Sheridan. [1965] 1984. *The Nazi Seizure of Power: The Experience of a Single German Town 1922–1945,* rev. ed. New York: Franklin Watts.

Alliès, Paul. 1980. *L'invention du territoire.* Grenoble: Presses Universitaires de Grenoble.

Allport, Gordon W. [1954] 1979. *The Nature of Prejudice,* 25th anniversary ed. Reading, Mass.: Addison-Wesley.

Almaguer, Tomás. 1994. *Racial Faultlines: The Historical Origins of White Supremacy in California.* Berkeley: University of California Press.

Almog, Oz. [1997] 2000. *The Sabra: The Creation of the New Jew,* trans. Haim Watzman. Berkeley: University of California Press.

Alperovitz, Gar. 1995. *The Decision to Use the Atomic Bombs and the Architecture of an American Myth.* New York: Alfred A. Knopf.

Alter, Peter. [1985/1989] 1994. *Nationalism,* 2nd ed. London: Edward Arnold.

Alter, Robert. 1988. *The Invention of Hebrew Prose: Modern Fiction and the Language of Realism.* Seattle: University of Washington Press.

Altgeld, Wolfgang. 1999. "German Catholics." In Rainer Liedtke and Stephan Wenderhorst, eds., *The Emancipation of Catholics, Jews and Protestants: Minorities and the Nation State in Nineteenth-Century Europe,* pp. 100–121. Manchester: Manchester University Press.

Altmann, Alexander. 1991. *The Meaning of Jewish Existence: Theological Essays, 1930–1939,* ed. Alfred L. Ovry, trans. Edith Ehrlich and Leonard H. Ehrlich. Hanover, N.H.: Brandeis University Press/University Press of New England.

Aly, Götz. 1994. "Medicine against the Useless." In Götz Aly, Peter Chroust, and Christian Pross, *Cleansing the Fatherland: Nazi Medicine and Racial Hygiene,* trans. Belinda Cooper, pp. 22–98. Baltimore: Johns Hopkins University Press.

————. 1995. *"Endlösung": Völkerverschiebung und der Mord an den europäischen Juden.* Frankfurt am Main: S. Fischer.

Aly, Götz, and Susanne Heim. 1991. *Vordenker der Vernichtung: Auschwitz und die deutschen Pläne für eine neue europäische Ordnung.* Hamburg: Hoffman und Campe.

Ambler, Charles H. 1988. *Kenyan Communities in the Age of Imperialism: The Central Region in the Late Nineteenth Century.* New Haven, Conn.: Yale University Press.

American Kennel Club. [1941] 1985. *The Complete Dog Book,* 17th ed. New York: Howell Book House.

Améry, Jean. [1976/1980] 1990. *At the Mind's Limits: Contemplations by a Survivor on Auschwitz and Its Realities,* trans. Sidney Rosenfeld and Stella P. Rosenfeld. New York: Schocken.

Amino Yoshihiko. 1991. *Nihon no rekishi o yominaosu.* Tokyo: Chikuma Shobō.

Amory, Patrick. 1997. *People and Identity in Ostrogothic Italy, 489–554.* Cambridge: Cambridge University Press.

Ancel, Jacques. 1936. *Géopolitique.* Paris: Librairie Delagrave.

Anderson, Benedict. [1983] 1991. *Imagined Communities: Reflections on the Origin and Spread of Nationalism,* rev. ed. London: Verso.

Anderson, Bonnie S. 2000. *Joyous Greetings: The First International Women's Movement, 1830–1860.* New York: Oxford University Press.

Anderson, M. S. [1982] 1988. *War and Society in Europe of the Old Regime, 1618–1789.* Leicester: Leicester University Press.

Anderson, Nels. 1942. *Desert Saints: The Mormon Frontier in Utah.* Chicago: University of Chicago Press.

Anene, J. C. 1970. *The International Boundaries of Nigeria, 1885–1960: The Framework of an Emergent African Nation.* Harlow, U.K.: Longman.

Antonius, George. 1938. *The Arab Awakening: The Story of the Arab National Movement.* Beirut, Lebanon: Khayats.

Appiah, Kwame Anthony. 1992. *In My Father's House: Africa in the Philosophy of Culture.* New York: Oxford University Press.

———— [K. Anthony Appiah]. 1996. "Race, Culture, Identity: Misunderstood Connections." In K. Anthony Appiah and Amy Gutmann, *Color Conscious: The Political Morality of Race,* pp. 30–105. Princeton, N.J.: Princeton University Press.

Applegate, Celia. 1990. *A Nation of Provincials: The German Idea of Heimat.* Berkeley: University of California Press.

Apter, David E. [1955] 1963. *Ghana in Transition,* rev. ed. New York: Atheneum.

Arad, Gulie Ne'eman. 1997. "Rereading an Unsettling Past: American Jews during the Nazi Era." In Alvin H. Rosenfeld, ed., *Thinking about the Holocaust: After Half a Century,* pp. 182–209. Bloomington: Indiana University Press.

Ardant, Gabriel. 1975. "Financial Policy and Economic Infrastructure of Modern States and Nations." In Charles Tilly, ed., *The Formation of National States in*

Western Europe, pp. 164–242. Princeton, N.J.: Princeton University Press.

Arendt, Hannah. [1951] 1968. *The Origins of Totalitarianism,* new ed. New York: Harcourt Brace Jovanovich.

———. [1954/1968] 1977a. *Between Past and Future: Eight Exercises in Political Thought,* enlarged ed. Harmondsworth, U.K.: Penguin.

———. [1963/1965] 1977b. *Eichmann in Jerusalem: A Report on the Banality of Evil,* rev. ed. Harmondsworth, U.K.: Penguin.

Ariès, Philippe. [1982] 1985. "Thoughts on the History of Homosexuality." In Philippe Ariès and André Béjin, eds., *Western Sexuality: Practice and Precept in Past and Present Times,* trans. Anthony Forster, pp. 62–75. Oxford: Blackwell.

Aristotle. 1984. *The Complete Works of Aristotle,* 2 vols., ed. Jonathan Barnes. Princeton, N.J.: Princeton University Press.

Arlettaz, Gérard, and Silvia Arlettaz. 1996. "La 'question des étrangers' en Suisse 1880–1914." In Daniel Fabre, ed., *L'Europe entre cultures et nations,* pp. 257–268. Paris: Éditions de la maison des sciences de l'homme.

Armitage, David. 2000. *The Ideological Origins of the British Empire.* Cambridge: Cambridge University Press.

Arnold, Matthew. [1867–69] 1993. "Culture and Anarchy: An Essay in Political and Social Criticism." In Matthew Arnold, *Culture and Anarchy and Other Writings,* ed. Stefan Collini, pp. 53–211. Cambridge: Cambridge University Press.

Arranz Márquez, Luis. 1991. *Repartimientos y Encomiendas en la Isla Española (El Repartimiento de Alburquerque de 1514).* Madrid: Ediciones Fundación García Arévalo.

Arrington, Leonard J., and Davis Bitton. [1979] 1992. *The Mormon Experience: A History of the Latter-Day Saints,* 2nd ed. Urbana: University of Illinois Press.

Asante, Molefi Kete. 1993. "Racism, Consciousness, and Afrocentricity." In Gerald Early, ed., *Lure and Loathing: Essays on Race, Identity, and the Ambivalence of Assimilation,* pp. 127–143. New York: Viking Penguin.

Asch, Solomon E. 1955. "Opinions and Social Pressure." *Scientific American* November, pp. 31–35.

Aschheim, Steven E. 1982. *Brothers and Strangers: The East European Jew in Germany and German Jewish Consciousness, 1800–1923.* Madison: University of Wisconsin Press.

Ashworth, John. 1995. *Slavery, Capitalism, and Politics in the Antebellum Republic,* vol. 1: *Commerce and Compromise, 1820–1850.* Cambridge: Cambridge University Press.

Assmann, Jan. 1997. *Moses the Egyptian: The Memory of Egypt in Western Monotheism.* Cambridge, Mass.: Harvard University Press.

Astourian, Stephan H. 1999. "Modern Turkish Identity and the Armenian Genocide: From Prejudice to Racist Nationalism." In Richard G. Hovannisian, ed., *Remembrance and Denial: The Case of the Armenian Genocide,* pp. 23–49. Detroit: Wayne State University Press.

Auerbach, Jerold S. 2001. *Are We One? Jewish Identity in the United States and Israel.* New Brunswick, N.J.: Rutgers University Press.

Augustine, Saint, Bishop of Hippo. [400] 1991. *Confessions,* trans. Henry Chadwick. Oxford: Oxford University Press.

—————. [426] 1998. *The City of God against the Pagans,* trans. R. W. Dyson. Cambridge: Cambridge University Press.

Avineri, Shlomo. 1981. *The Making of Modern Zionism: The Intellectual Origins of the Jewish State.* New York: Basic Books.

—————. 1985. *Moses Hess: Prophet of Communism and Zionism.* New York: New York University Press.

Axtell, James. 1992. *Beyond 1492: Encounters in Colonial North America.* New York: Oxford University Press.

Ayass, Wolfgang. 1988. "Vagrants and Beggars in Hitler's Reich." In Richard J. Evans, ed., *The German Underworld: Deviants and Outcasts in German History,* pp. 210–237. London: Routledge.

Bachman, John. 1850. *The Doctrine of the Unity of the Human Race Examined on the Principles of Science.* Charleston, S.C.: C. Canning.

Bacon, Roger [Rogeri Baconis]. 1953. *Moralis Philosophia,* ed. Eugenio Massa. Turici, Italy: Thesaurus Mundi.

Bade, Klaus J., ed. 1992. *Deutsche im Ausland—Fremde in Deutschland: Migration in Geschichte und Gegenwart.* München: C. H. Beck.

Badian, E. [1965] 1968. *Roman Imperialism and the Late Republic,* 2nd ed. Ithaca, N.Y.: Cornell University Press.

Badie, Bertrand. 1992. *L'état importé: l'occidentalisation de l'ordre politique.* Paris: Fayard.

Baker, John R. 1974. *Race.* New York: Oxford University Press.

Baker, Leonard. [1978] 1980. *Days of Sorrow and Pain: Leo Baeck and the Berlin Jews.* New York: Oxford University Press.

Bakos, Adrianna. 1997. *Images of Kingship in Early Modern France: Louis XI in Political Thought, 1560–1789.* London: Routledge.

Baldry, H. C. 1965. *The Unity of Mankind in Greek Thought.* Cambridge: Cambridge University Press.

Baldwin, James. [1953] 1998. "Stranger in the Village." In James Baldwin, *Collected Essays,* ed. Toni Morrison, pp. 117–129. New York: Library of America.

Baldwin, Kate A. 2002. *Beyond the Color Line and the Iron Curtain: Reading Encounters between Black and Red, 1922–1963.* Durham, N.C.: Duke University Press.

Baldwin, Peter. 1999. *Contagion and the State in Europe, 1830–1930.* Cambridge: Cambridge University Press.

Bales, Kevin. 1999. *Disposable People: New Slavery in the Global Economy.* Berkeley: University of California Press.

Balfour, Ian. 2002. *The Rhetoric of Romantic Prophecy.* Stanford, Calif.: Stanford University Press.

Balibar, Etienne, and Immanuel Wallerstein. [1988] 1991. *Race, Nation, Class: Ambiguous Identities,* trans. Chris Turner. London: Verso.

Balibar, Renée, and Dominique Laporte. 1974. *Le français national: politique et pratiques de la langue nationale sous la Révolution française.* Paris: Hachette.

Balsdon, J. P. V. D. 1979. *Romans and Aliens.* Chapel Hill: University of North Carolina Press.

Banac, Ivo. 1984. *The National Question in Yugoslavia: Origins, History, Politics.* Ithaca, N.Y.: Cornell University Press.

Banaji, Mahzarin R., and R. Bhaskar. 2000. "Implicit Stereotypes and Memory: The Bounded Rationality of Social Beliefs." In Daniel L. Schacter and Elaine Scarry, eds., *Memory, Brain, and Belief,* pp. 139–175. Cambridge, Mass.: Harvard University Press.

Bankier, David. 1992. *The Germans and the Final Solution: Public Opinion under Nazism.* Oxford: Blackwell.

Banks, Marcus. 1992. *Organizing Jainism in India and England.* Oxford: Clarendon Press.

Banks, William M. 1996. *Black Intellectuals: Race and Responsibility in American Life.* New York: W. W. Norton.

Banton, Michael. 1996. *International Action against Racial Discrimination.* Oxford: Clarendon Press.

———. [1987] 1998. *Racial Theories,* 2nd ed. Cambridge: Cambridge University Press.

———. 2002. *The International Politics of Race.* Cambridge: Polity.

Barclay, John. 1996. *Jews in the Mediterranean Diaspora: From Alexander to Trajan (323 BCE–117 CE).* Edinburgh: T&T Clark.

Bardakjian, Kevork B. 1985. *Hitler and the Armenian Genocide.* Cambridge, Mass.: Zoryan Institute.

Barkai, Avraham. [1987] 1989. *From Boycott to Annihilation: The Economic Struggle of German Jews, 1933–1943,* trans. William Templer. Hanover, N.H.: University Press of New England.

———. [1977] 1990. *Nazi Economics: Ideology, Theory, and Policy,* trans. Ruth Hadass-Vashitz. New Haven, Conn.: Yale University Press.

Barkan, Elazar. 1992. *The Retreat of Scientific Racism: Changing Concepts of Race in Britain and the United States between the World Wars.* Cambridge: Cambridge University Press.

Barnett, Michael N. 1996. "The Politics of Indifference at the United Nations and Genocide in Rwanda and Bosnia." In Thomas Cushman and and Stjepan G. Meštrović, eds., *This Time We Knew: Western Responses to Genocide in Bosnia,* pp. 128–162. New York: New York University Press.

Barraclough, Geoffrey. [1946] 1963. *The Origins of Modern Germany.* New York: G. P. Putnam's Sons.

Barth, Fredrik. 1969. "Introduction." In Fredrik Barth, ed., *Ethnic Groups and*

Boundaries: The Social Organization of Cultural Difference, pp. 7–38. Boston: Little, Brown.

Barthes, Roland. [1957] 1972. *Mythologies,* trans. Annette Lavers. New York: Hill & Wang.

Bartlett, John R. 1985. *Jews in the Hellenistic World: Josephus, Aristeas, the Sibylline Oracles, and Eupolemus.* Cambridge: Cambridge University Press.

Bartlett, Robert. 1993. *The Making of Europe: Conquest, Colonization and Cultural Change 950–1350.* Princeton, N.J.: Princeton University Press.

Bartov, Omer. 1991. *Hitler's Army: Soldiers, Nazis, and War in the Third Reich.* New York: Oxford University Press.

———. 1996. *Murder in Our Midst: The Holocaust, Industrial Killing, and Representation.* New York: Oxford University Press.

———. 2000. *Mirrors of Destruction: War, Genocide, and Modern Identity.* Oxford: Oxford University Press.

Barzun, Jacques. 1937. *Race: A Study in Modern Superstition.* New York: Harcourt, Brace.

Baudet, Henri. [1959/1965] 1988. *Paradise on Earth: Some Thoughts on European Images of Non-European Man,* trans. Elizabeth Wentholt. Middletown, Conn.: Wesleyan University Press.

Bauer, Otto. [1907/1924] 1975. "Die Nationalitätenfrage und die Sozialdemokratie." In Otto Bauer, *Werkausgabe,* vol. 1, pp. 49–622. Vienna: Europaverlag.

Bauer, Yehuda. 1994. *Jews for Sale? Nazi-Jewish Negotiations, 1933–1945.* New Haven, Conn.: Yale University Press.

———. 2001. *Rethinking the Holocaust.* New Haven, Conn.: Yale University Press.

Bauman, Zygmunt. 1989. *Modernity and the Holocaust.* Ithaca, N.Y.: Cornell University Press.

Bayly, Susan. 1999. *The New Cambridge History of India,* vol. 4, pt. 3: *Caste, Society and Politics in India from the Eighteenth Century to the Modern Age.* Cambridge: Cambridge University Press.

Beaglehole, J. C. 1974. *The Life of Captain James Cook.* Stanford, Calif.: Stanford University Press.

Beaton, Roderick. 1988. "Romanticism in Greece." In Roy Porter and Mikuláš Teich, eds., *Romanticism in National Context,* pp. 92–108. Cambridge: Cambridge University Press.

Beaune, Colette. 1985. *Naissance de la nation France.* Paris: Gallimard.

Becker, Carl L. 1932. *The Heavenly City of the Eighteenth Century Philosophers.* New Haven, Conn.: Yale University Press.

Becker, Jasper. 1996. *Hungry Ghosts: China's Secret Famine.* London: John Murray.

Becker, Jean Jacques. 1977. *1914, comment les Français sont entrés dans la guerre: contribution à l'étude de l'opinion publique printemps-été 1914.* Paris: Presses de la Fondation nationale des sciences politiques.

Becker, Jean Jacques, Jay M. Winter, Gerd Krumeich, Annette Becker, and Stéphane Audoin-Rouzeau. 1994. *Guerre et cultures, 1914–1918.* Paris: Armand Colin.

Becker, Marjorie. 1995. *Setting the Virgin on Fire: Lázaro Cárdenas, Michoacán Peasants, and the Redemption of the Mexican Revolution.* Berkeley: University of California Press.

Behrens, C. B. A. 1985. *Society, Government, and the Enlightenment: The Experiences of Eighteenth-Century France and Prussia.* New York: Harper & Row.

Beinin, Joel. 1998. *The Dispersion of Egyptian Jewry: Culture, Politics, and the Formation of a Modern Diaspora.* Berkeley: University of California Press.

Beiser, Frederick C. 1992. *Enlightenment, Revolution, and Romanticism: The Genesis of Modern German Political Thought, 1790–1800.* Cambridge, Mass.: Harvard University Press.

Bell, Daniel. [1975] 1980. "The End of American Exceptionalism." In Daniel Bell, *The Winding Passage: Essays and Sociological Journeys 1960–1980*, pp. 245–271. Cambridge, Mass.: Abt Books.

Bell, Derrick A. 1987. *And We Are Not Saved: The Elusive Quest for Racial Justice.* New York: Basic Books.

———. 1992. *Faces at the Bottom of the Well: The Permanence of Racism.* New York: Basic Books.

Bell, Quentin. [1947] 1976. *On Human Finery,* 2nd ed. New York: Schocken.

Benbassa, Esther. [1997] 1999. *The Jews of France: A History from Antiquity to the Present,* trans. M. B. DeBevoise. Princeton, N.J.: Princeton University Press.

Benbassa, Esther, and Aron Rodrigue. [1993/1995] 2000. *Sephardi Jewry: A History of the Judeo-Spanish Community, 14th–20th Centuries.* Berkeley: University of California Press.

Bendix, Reinhard. 1978. *Kings or People: Power and the Mandate to Rule.* Berkeley: University of California Press.

Benner, Erica. 1995. *Really Existing Nationalisms: A Post-Communist View from Marx and Engels.* Oxford: Clarendon Press.

Ben-Rafael, Eliezer. 1994. *Language, Identity, and Social Division: The Case of Israel.* Oxford: Clarendon Press.

Benveniste, Emile. [1969] 1973. *Indo-European Language and Society,* trans. Elizabeth Palmer. Coral Gables, Fla.: University of Miami Press.

Benz, Wolfgang. 1987. "Die Abwehr der Vergangenheit: Ein Problem nur für Historiker und Moralisten?" In Dan Diner, ed., *Ist der Nationalsozialismus Geschichte? Zu Historisierung und Historikerstreit*, pp. 17–33. Frankfurt am Main: Fischer.

———. 1990. *Herrschaft und Gesellschaft im nationalsozialistischen Staat.* Frankfurt am Main: Fischer.

———. 1995. *Der Holocaust.* München: C. H. Beck.

Berenbaum, Michael. 1990. *After Tragedy and Triumph: Essays in Modern Jewish Thought and the American Experience.* Cambridge: Cambridge University Press.

Berlin, Brent. 1992. *Ethnobiological Classification: Principles of Categorization of Plants and Animals in Traditional Societies*. Princeton, N.J.: Princeton University Press.

Berlin, Ira. 1998. *Many Thousands Gone: The First Two Centuries of Slavery in North America*. Cambridge, Mass.: Harvard University Press.

Berlin, Isaiah. 1976. *Vico and Herder: Two Studies in the History of Ideas*. London: Hogarth Press.

———. [1979] 1980. *Against the Current: Essays in the History of Ideas*, ed. Henry Hardy. New York: Viking.

Berman, Bruce, and John Lonsdale. 1992. *Unhappy Valley: Conflict in Kenya and Africa*. London: James Currey.

Bernasconi, Robert. 2001. "Who Invented the Concept of Race? Kant's Role in the Enlightenment Construction of Race." In Robert Bernasconi, ed., *Race*, pp. 11–36. Oxford: Blackwell.

Bessel, Richard. 1984. *Political Violence and the Rise of Nazism: The Storm Troopers in Eastern Germany, 1925–1934*. New Haven, Conn.: Yale University Press.

Best, Geoffrey. 1982. *War and Society in Revolutionary Europe, 1770–1870*. New York: St. Martin's Press.

Béteille, André. 1965. *Caste, Class, and Power: Changing Patterns of Stratification in a Tanjore Village*. Berkeley: University of California Press.

———. 1996. "Caste in Contemporary India." In C. J. Fuller, ed., *Caste Today*, pp. 150–179. Delhi: Oxford University Press.

Betzig, Laura. 2002. "British Polygyny." In Malcolm Smith, ed., *Human Biology and History*, pp. 30–97. London: Taylor & Francis.

Bible. 1991. *The New Oxford Annotated Bible: New Revised Standard Version*, eds. Bruce M. Metzger and Roland E. Murphy. New York: Oxford University Press.

Biddis, Michael D. 1970. *Father of Racist Ideology: The Social and Political Thought of Count Gobineau*. New York: Weybright and Talley.

Biesold, Horst. [1988] 1999. *Crying Hands: Eugenics and Deaf People in Nazi Germany*, trans. William Sayers. Washington, D.C.: Gallaudet University Press.

Bindman, David. 2002. *Ape to Apollo: Aesthetics and the Idea of Race in the 18th Century*. Ithaca, N.Y.: Cornell University Press.

Binyon, T. J. 2002. *Pushkin: A Biography*. New York: Alfred A. Knopf.

Birdsell, Joseph B. 1993. *Microevolutionary Patterns in Aboriginal Australia: A Gradient Analysis of Clines*. New York: Oxford University Press.

Birnbaum, Pierre. 1993. *"La France aux Français": histoire des haines nationalistes*. Paris: Seuil.

———. [1995] 2000. *Jewish Destinies: Citizenship, State, and Community in Modern France*. New York: Hill & Wang.

Blackbourn, David. 1987. *Populists and Patricians: Essays in Modern German History*. London: Allen & Unwin.

————. [1997] 1998. *The Long Nineteenth Century: A History of Germany, 1780–1918.* New York: Oxford University Press.

Blackbourn, David, and Geoff Eley. 1984. *The Peculiarities of German History: Bourgeois Society and Politics in Nineteenth-Century Germany.* Oxford: Oxford University Press.

Blalock, Hubert M., Jr. 1982. *Race and Ethnic Relations.* Englewood Cliffs, N.J.: Prentice-Hall.

Blanning, T. C. W. 1983. *The French Revolution in Germany: Occupation and Resistance in the Rhineland, 1792–1802.* Oxford: Clarendon Press.

Blauner, Bob. 1989. *Black Lives, White Lives: Three Decades of Race Relations in America.* Berkeley: University of California Press.

Bledsoe, Albert Taylor. 1860. "Liberty and Slavery: Or, Slavery in the Light of Moral and Political Philosophy." In E. N. Elliott, ed., *Cotton Is King, and Pro-Slavery Arguments,* pp. 269–458. Augusta, Ga.: Pritchard, Abbott & Loomis.

Blee, Kathleen M., and Dwight B. Billings. 1999. "Where 'Bloodshed Is a Pastime': Mountain Feuds and Appalachian Stereotyping." In Dwight B. Billings, Gurney Norman, and Katherine Ledford, eds., *Confronting Appalachian Stereotypes: Back Talk from an American Region,* pp. 119–137. Louisville: University Press of Kentucky.

Bleicken, Jochen. 1985. *Die athenische Demokratie.* Paderborn, Germany: Ferdinand Schöningh.

Bloch, Marc. 1961. *Feudal Society,* trans. L. A. Manyon. Chicago: University of Chicago Press.

————. [1933] 1963. "Liberté et servitude personnelles au moyen âge, particularièment en France: contribution à une etude des classes." In *Mélanges historiques,* vol. 1, pp. 286–355. Paris: S.E.V.P.E.N.

————. [1931] 1966. *French Rural History: An Essay on Its Basic Characteristics,* trans. Janet Sondheimer. Berkeley: University of California Press.

————. [1954] 1970. "Les aliments de l'ancienne France." In Jean-Jacques Hémardinquer, ed., *Pour une histoire de l'alimentation,* pp. 231–235. Paris: Armand Colin.

Blu, Karen I. 1980. *The Lumbee Problem: The Making of an American Indian People.* Cambridge: Cambridge University Press.

Bluhm, William T. 1973. *Building an Austrian Nation: The Political Integration of a Western State.* New Haven, Conn.: Yale University Press.

Blum, Jerome. 1961. *Lord and Peasant in Russia: From the Ninth to the Nineteenth Century.* Princeton, N.J.: Princeton University Press.

————. 1978. *The End of the Old Order in Rural Europe.* Princeton, N.J.: Princeton University Press.

Blumenbach, Johann Friedrich. [1775/1865] 1973a. "On the Natural Variety of Mankind, ed. 1775." In Johann Friedrich Blumenbach, *The Anthropological*

Treatises of Johann Friedrich Blumenbach, ed. and trans. Thomas Bendyshe, pp. 69–143. Boston: Milford House.

———. [1795/1865] 1973b. "On the Natural Variety of Mankind, ed. 1795." In Johann Friedrich Blumenbach, *The Anthropological Treatises of Johann Friedrich Blumenbach,* ed. and trans. Thomas Bendyshe, pp. 145–276. Boston: Milford House.

———. [1806/1865] 1973c. "Contributions to Natural History, Part the First." In Johann Friedrich Blumenbach, *The Anthropological Treatises of Johann Friedrich Blumenbach,* ed. and trans. Thomas Bendyshe, pp. 277–324. Boston: Milford House.

Boas, Franz. 1912. *Changes in Body Form of the Descendants of Immigrants.* New York: Columbia University Press.

———. [1945] 1969. *Race and Democratic Society.* New York: Biblo and Tannen.

Boas, George. [1948] 1966. *Essays on Primitivism and Related Ideas in the Middle Ages.* New York: Octagon.

Boateng, E. A. 1978. *A Political Geography of Africa.* Cambridge: Cambridge University Press.

Bober, Phyllis Pray. 1999. *Art, Culture, and Cuisine: Ancient and Medieval Gastronomy.* Chicago: University of Chicago Press.

Bock, Gisela. 1984. "Racism and Sexism in Nazi Germany: Motherland, Compulsory Sterilization and the State." In Renate Bridenthal, Atina Grossmann, and Marion Kaplan, eds., *When Biology Became Destiny: Women in Weimar and Nazi Germany,* pp. 271–296. New York: Monthly Review Press.

———. 1986. *Zwangssterilisation im Nationalsozialismus: Studien zur Rassenpolitik und Frauenpolitik.* Opladen, Germany: Westdeutscher Verlag.

Bodin, Jean. [1567/1606] 1962. *The Six Bookes of a Commonweale,* ed. Kenneth Douglas McRae, trans. Richard Knolles. Cambridge, Mass.: Harvard University Press.

Bohannan, Paul, and Philip Curtin. [1964] 1971. *Africa and Africans,* rev. ed. Garden City, N.Y.: Natural History Press.

Bolingbroke, Henry St. John, Viscount. [1749] 1965. *The Idea of a Patriot King,* ed. Sidney W. Jackman. Indianapolis: Bobbs-Merrill.

Boltanski, Luc. [1993] 1999. *Distant Suffering: Morality, Media and Politics,* trans. Graham Burchell. Cambridge: Cambridge University Press.

Bonacich, Edna. 1973. "A Theory of Ethnic Antagonism: The Split Labor Market." *American Sociological Review* 37:547–559.

Bond, Brian. 1983. *War and Society in Europe 1870–1970.* Leicester: Leicester University Press.

Book of Mormon. 1986. *Book of Mormon,* trans. Joseph Smith, Jr. Salt Lake City, Utah: Church of Jesus Christ of Latter-Day Saints.

Boon, James A. 1973. "Further Operations of Culture in Anthropology: A Synthesis of and for Debate." In Louis Schneider and Charles Bonjean, eds., *The Idea of Culture in the Social Sciences*, pp. 1–32. Cambridge: Cambridge University Press.

———. 1977. *The Anthropological Romance of Bali, 1597–1972: Dynamic Perspectives in Marriage and Caste, Politics and Religion.* Cambridge: Cambridge University Press.

Borges, Jorge Luis. 1995. "Borges and I," trans. Alastair Reid. In Daniel Halpern, ed., *Who's Writing This? Notations on the Authorial I with Self-Portraits*, pp. 3–5. New York: Ecco.

Borst, Arno. 1957. *Der Turmbau von Babel: Geschichte der Meinungen über Ursprung und Vielfalt der Sprachen und Völker, band 1: Fundamente und Aufbau.* Stuttgart: Anton Hiersemann.

———. 1992. *Medieval Worlds: Barbarians, Heretics and Artists*, trans. Eric Hansen. Chicago: University of Chicago Press.

Borstelmann, Thomas. 2001. *The Cold War and the Color Line: American Race Relations in the Global Arena.* Cambridge, Mass.: Harvard University Press.

Bossy, John. 1982. "Catholicity and Nationality in the Northern Counter-Reformation." In Stuart Mews, ed., *Religion and National Identity*, pp. 285–296. Oxford: Blackwell.

Bourne, Randolph S. [1916] 1964. "Trans-National America." In Randolph S. Bourne, *War and the Intellectuals: Collected Essays, 1915–1919*, ed. Carl Resek, pp. 107–123. New York: Harper & Row.

Bowersock, G. W. 1988. "Palestine: Ancient History and Modern Politics." In Edward Said and Christopher Hitchens, eds., *Blaming the Victims: Spurious Scholarship and the Palestinian Questions*, pp. 181–191. London: Verso.

Bowker, Geoffrey C., and Susan Leigh Star. 1999. *Sorting Things Out: Classification and Its Consequences.* Cambridge, Mass.: MIT Press.

Bowler, Peter J. 1986. *Theories of Human Evolution: A Century of Debate, 1844–1944.* Baltimore: Johns Hopkins University Press.

———. 2001. *Reconciling Science and Religion: The Debate in Early-Twentieth-Century Britain.* Chicago: University of Chicago Press.

Boyajian, Dickran H. 1972. *Armenia: The Case for a Forgotten Genocide.* Westwood, N.J.: Educational Book Crafters.

Boyarin, Daniel. 1994. *A Radical Jew: Paul and the Politics of Identity.* Berkeley: University of California Press.

Brace, C. Loring. 1964. "A Nonracial Approach towards the Understanding of Human Diversity." In Ashley Montagu, ed., *The Concept of Race*, pp. 103–152. New York: Free Press.

Bradley, Keith. 1994. *Slavery and Society at Rome.* Cambridge: Cambridge University Press.

Bradley, R. N. 1926. *Racial Origins of English Character.* London: George Allen & Unwin.

Braeckman, Colette. 1994. *Rwanda: histoire d'un génocide.* Paris: Fayard.

———. 1996. *Terreur africaine: Burundi, Rwanda, Zaïre, les racines de la violence.* Paris: Fayard.

Brandenberger, David. 2002. *National Boshevism: Stalinist Mass Culture and the Formation of Modern Russian National Identity, 1931–1956.* Cambridge, Mass.: Harvard University Press.

Brandon, William. 1986. *New Worlds for Old: Reports from the New World and Their Effect on the Development of Social Thought in Europe, 1500–1800.* Athens: Ohio University Press.

Braun, Rudolf. 1975. "Taxation, Sociopolitical Structure, and State-Building: Great Britain and Brandenburg-Prussia." In Charles Tilly, ed., *The Formation of National States in Western Europe,* pp. 243–327. Princeton, N.J.: Princeton University Press.

———. [1960/1979] 1990. *Industrialisation and Everyday Life,* trans. Sarah Hanbury Tenison. Cambridge: Cambridge University Press.

Brecht, Martin. [1987] 1993. *Martin Luther,* vol. 3: *The Preservation of the Church, 1532–1546,* trans. James L. Schaaf. Minneapolis: Fortress Press.

Breisach, Ernst. [1983] 1994. *Historiography: Ancient, Medieval, and Modern,* 2nd ed. Chicago: University of Chicago Press.

Breitman, Richard. 1991. *The Architect of Genocide: Himmler and the Final Solution.* New York: Alfred A. Knopf.

Breitman, Richard, and Alan M. Kraut. 1987. *American Refugee Policy and European Jewry, 1933–1945.* Bloomington: Indiana University Press.

Brenner, Michael. [1995] 1997. *After the Holocaust: Rebuilding Jewish Lives in Postwar Germany,* trans. Barbara Harshav. Princeton, N.J.: Princeton University Press.

Breuilly, John. [1982] 1994. *Nationalism and the State,* 2nd ed. Chicago: University of Chicago Press.

Bridenthal, Renate, and Claudia Koontz. "Beyond *Kinder, Küche, Kirche:* Weimar Women in Politics and Work." In Renate Bridenthal, Atina Grossmann, and Marion Kaplan, eds., *When Biology Became Destiny: Women in Weimar and Nazi Germany,* pp. 33–65. New York: Monthly Review Press.

Briggs, Asa. [1960] 1985. "The Language of 'Class' in Early Nineteenth-Century England." In Asa Briggs, *The Collected Essays of Asa Briggs,* vol. 1: *Words, Numbers, Places, People,* pp. 3–33. Urbana: University of Illinois Press.

Briggs, Jean L. 1970. *Never in Anger: Portrait of an Eskimo Family.* Cambridge, Mass.: Harvard University Press.

Briggs, Robin. 1996. *Witches & Neighbors: The Social and Cultural Context of European Witchcraft.* New York: Viking.

Brillat-Savarin, Jean Anthelme. [1825]. 1995. *The Physiology of Taste or Meditations on Transcendental Gastronomy,* trans. M. F. K. Fisher. Washington, D.C.: Counterpoint.

Bringa, Tone. 1995. *Being Muslim the Bosnian Way: Identity and Community in a Central Bosnian Village.* Princeton, N.J.: Princeton University Press.

Broca, Paul. 1864. *On the Phenomena of Hybridity in the Genus Homo,* ed. C. Carter Blake. London: Longman, Green, Longman, and Roberts.

Brogan, Patrick. [1989] 1998. *World Conflicts,* 3rd ed. London: Bloomsbury.

Bromley, Yu. 1978. *Ethnography and Ethnic Processes,* ed. V. Paritsky. Moscow: USSR Academy of Sciences.

Brooker, Paul. 1991. *The Faces of Fraternalism: Nazi Germany, Fascist Italy, and Imperial Japan.* Oxford: Clarendon Press.

Broszat, Martin. [1965] 1968. "The Concentration Camps 1933–45," trans. Marian Jackson. In Helmut Krausnick, Hans Buchheim, Martin Broszat, and Hans-Adolf Jacobsen, *Anatomy of the SS State,* pp. 397–504. New York: Walker.

———. [1969] 1981. *The Hitler State: The Foundation and Development of the Internal Structure of the Third Reich,* trans. John W. Hiden. London: Longman.

Brown, Howard G. 1995. *War, Revolution, and the Bureaucratic State: Politics and Army Administration in France, 1791–1799.* Oxford: Clarendon Press.

Brown, Judith M. [1985] 1994. *Modern India: The Origins of an Asian Democracy,* 2nd ed. Oxford: Oxford University Press.

Browning, Christopher R. 1985. *Fateful Months: Essays on the Emergence of the Final Solution.* New York: Holmes & Meier.

———. 1992a. *The Path to Genocide: Essays on Launching the Final Solution.* Cambridge: Cambridge University Press.

———. 1992b. *Ordinary Men: Reserve Police Battalion 101 and the Final Solution in Poland.* New York: HarperCollins.

———. 2000. *Nazi Policy, Jewish Workers, German Killers.* Cambridge: Cambridge University Press.

Brubaker, Rogers. 1992. *Citizenship and Nationhood in France and Germany.* Cambridge, Mass.: Harvard University Press.

———. 1996. *Nationalism Reframed: Nationhood and the National Question in the New Europe.* Cambridge: Cambridge University Press.

Bruce, Vicki, and Andy Young. 1998. *In the Eye of the Beholder: The Science of Face Perception.* Oxford: Oxford University Press.

Bruford, W. H. 1935. *Germany in the Eighteenth Century: The Social Background of the Literary Revival.* Cambridge: Cambridge University Press.

———. 1962. *Culture and Society in Classical Weimar, 1775–1806.* Cambridge: Cambridge University Press.

Brun, Auguste. 1927. *La langue française en Provence de Louis XIV au Félibrige.* Marseille: Institut Historique de Provence.

Brunot, Ferdinand. 1891. *La doctrine de Malherbe d'après son commentaire sur Desportes.* Paris: G. Masson.

————. 1905–72. *Histoire de la langue française: des origins à 1900,* 13 vols. Paris: Armand Colin.

Brunt, P. A. 1990. *Roman Imperial Themes.* Oxford: Clarendon Press.

————. 1993. *Studies in Greek History and Thought.* Oxford: Clarendon Press.

Buchanan, Allen. 1991. *Secession: The Morality of Political Divorce from Fort Sumter to Lithuania and Quebec.* Boulder, Colo.: Westview Press.

Bullock, Alan. 1964. *Hitler: A Study in Tyranny,* rev. ed. New York: Harper & Row.

Bultmann, Rudolf. 1957. *The Presence of Eternity.* New York: Harper & Brothers.

Burg, Steven L., and Paul S. Shoup. 1999. *The War in Bosnia-Herzegovina: Ethnic Conflict and International Intervention.* Armonk, N.Y.: M. E. Sharpe.

Burke, Edmund. [1757/1958] 1968. *A Philosophical Enquiry into the Origin of Our Ideas of the Sublime and Beautiful,* ed. James T. Boulton, 2nd ed. Notre Dame, Ind.: University of Notre Dame Press.

Burke, Kenneth. [1941] 1973. *The Philosophy of Literary Form,* 3rd ed. Berkeley: University of California Press.

Burke, Peter. 1990. *The French Historical Revolution: The Annales School, 1929–89.* Stanford, Calif.: Stanford University Press.

Burleigh, Michael. 1988. *Germany Turns Eastwards: A Study of Ostforschung in the Third Reich.* Cambridge: Cambridge University Press.

————. 1994. *Death and Deliverance: "Euthanasia" in Germany 1900–1945.* Cambridge: Cambridge University Press.

————. 1997. *Ethics and Extermination: Reflections on Nazi Genocide.* Cambridge: Cambridge University Press.

————. 2000. *The Third Reich: A New History.* New York: Hill & Wang.

Burleigh, Michael, and Wolfgang Wippermann. 1991. *The Racial State: Germany 1933–1945.* Cambridge: Cambridge University Press.

Burrow, J. W. 1966. *Evolution and Society: A Study in Victorian Social Theory.* Cambridge: Cambridge University Press.

————. 2000. *The Crisis of Reason: European Thought, 1848–1914.* New Haven, Conn.: Yale University Press.

Bury, J. B. [1932] 1955. *The Idea of Progress: An Inquiry into Its Origin and Growth.* New York: Dover.

Bushman, Richard L. 1984. *Joseph Smith and the Beginnings of Mormonism.* Urbana: University of Illinois Press.

Butler, E. M. [1935] 1958. *The Tyranny of Greece over Germany: A Study of the Influence Exercised by Greek Art and Poetry over the Great German Writers of the 18th, 19th and 20th Centuries.* Boston: Beacon Press.

Cabral, Amilcar. [1975] 1979. *Unity and Struggle: Speeches and Writings of Amilcar Cabral,* trans. Michael Wolfers. New York: Monthly Review Press.

Cagle, Jess. 2001. "Lord of the Ring." *Time* December 24, pp. 69–75.

Calhoun, Craig. 1997. *Nationalism*. Minneapolis: University of Minnesota Press.

Calvet, Louis-Jean. 1974. *Linguistique et colonialisme: petit traité de glottophagie*. Paris: Payot.

———. [1987] 1998. *Language Wars and Linguistic Politics*, trans. Michel Petheram. Oxford: Oxford University Press.

Calvino, Italo. [1956] 1980. *Italian Folktales Selected and Retold by Italo Calvino*, trans. George Martin. New York: Pantheon.

Cameron, Euan. 1991. *The European Reformation*. Oxford: Clarendon Press.

Cannadine, David. 1990. *The Decline and Fall of the British Aristocracy*. New Haven, Conn.: Yale University Press.

———. 1995. "British History as a 'New Subject': Politics, Perspectives and Prospects." In Alexander Grant and Keith J. Stringer, eds., *Uniting the Kingdom? The Making of British History*, pp. 12–28. London: Routledge.

———. 1999. *The Rise and Fall of Class in Britain*. New York: Columbia University Press.

———. 2001. *Ornamentalism: How the British Saw Their Empire*. Harmondsworth, U.K.: Allen Lane.

Caplan, Jay. 1999. *In the King's Wake: Post-Absolutist Culture in France*. Chicago: University of Chicago Press.

Carby, Hazel V. 1998. *Race Men*. Cambridge, Mass.: Harvard University Press.

Cardoza, Anthony L. 1997. *Aristocrats in Bourgeois Italy: The Piedmontese Nobility, 1861–1930*. Cambridge: Cambridge University Press.

Carlyle, Thomas. [1830] n.d. "On History." In Thomas Carlyle, *Works*, vol. 16, pp. 149–162. Chicago: Belford, Clarke.

Caron, Jean-Claude. 1995. *La nation, l'état et la démocratie en France de 1789 à 1914*. Paris: Armand Colin.

Carr, Edward Hallett. [1930] 1946. *The Twenty Years' Crisis 1919–1939: An Introduction to the Study of International Relations*, 2nd ed. London: Macmillan.

Carrasco, Davíd. 1982. *Quetzalcoatl and the Irony of Empire: Myths and Prophecies in the Aztec Tradition*. Chicago: University of Chicago Press.

Carson, Clayborne. 1981. *In Struggle: SNCC and the Black Awakening of the 1960s*. Cambridge, Mass.: Harvard University Press.

Carsten, F. L. [1967] 1980. *The Rise of Fascism*, 2nd ed. Berkeley: University of California Press.

Cartledge, Paul. 1993. *The Greeks: A Portrait of Self and Others*. Oxford: Oxford University Press.

———. 2001. *Spartan Reflections*. Berkeley: University of California Press.

Cartwright, S. A. 1860. "Slavery in the Light of Ethnology." In E. N. Elliott, ed., *Cotton Is King, and Pro-Slavery Arguments*, pp. 659–728. Augusta, Ga.: Pritchard, Abbott & Loomis.

Casanova, Pascale. 1999. *La république mondiale des lettres*. Paris: Seuil.

Cavalli-Sforza, L. Luca, Paolo Menozzi, and Alberto Piazza. 1994. *The History and Geography of Human Genes.* Princeton, N.J.: Princeton University Press.

Certeau, Michel de, Dominique Julia, and Jacques Revel. 1975. *Une politique de la langue: la Révolution française et les patois: L'enquête de Grégoire.* Paris: Gallimard.

Chabod, Federico. [1961] 1991. *Storia dell'idea d'Europa,* ed. Ernesto Sestan and Armando Saitta. Bari: Laterza.

Chadwick, H. Munro. [1945] 1973. *The Nationalities of Europe and the Growth of National Ideologies.* New York: Cooper Square.

Chadwick, Owen. 1975. *The Secularization of the European Mind in the Nineteenth Century.* Cambridge: Cambridge University Press.

———. 1981. "The Italian Enlightenment." In Roy Porter and Mikuláš Teich, eds., *The Enlightenment in National Context,* pp. 90–105. Cambridge: Cambridge University Press.

Chakravarti, Uma. 1987. *The Social Dimensions of Early Buddhism.* Delhi: Oxford University Press.

Chaliand, Gérard. [1992] 1994. *The Kurdish Tragedy,* trans. Philip Black. London: Zed.

Chalk, Frank, and Kurt Jonassohn. 1990. *The History and Sociology of Genocide: Analyses and Case Studies.* New Haven, Conn.: Yale University Press.

Chamberlain, Houston Stewart. [1899/1910] 1968. *Foundations of the Nineteenth Century,* vol. 1, trans. John Lees. New York: Howard Fertig.

Chandler, David P. 1991. *The Tragedy of Cambodian History: Politics, War, and Revolution since 1945.* New Haven, Conn.: Yale University Press.

———. 1999. *Brother Number One: A Political Biography of Pol Pot,* rev. ed. Boulder, Colo.: Westview Press.

Chang, Iris. 1997. *The Rape of Nanking: The Forgotten Holocaust of World War II.* New York: Basic Books.

Chang, Joseph T. 1999. "Recent Common Ancestors of All Present-Day Individuals." *Advances in Applied Probability* 31:1002–1026.

Charle, Christophe. 2001. *La crise des sociétés imperiales: Allemagne, France, Grande-Bretagne 1900–1940: Essai d'histoire sociale comparée.* Paris: Seuil.

Chatterjee, Partha. [1986] 1993. *Nationalist Thought and the Colonial World: A Derivative Discourse.* Minneapolis: University of Minnesota Press.

Chaumont, Jean-Michel. 1997. *La concurrence des victimes: genocide, identité, reconnaissance.* Paris: La Découverte.

Chaunu, Pierre. 1969. *Conquête et exploitation des nouveaux mondes.* Paris: Presses Universitaires de France.

———. 1981. *Histoire et décadence.* Paris: Perrin.

Chaussinand-Nogaret, Guy. [1976] 1985. *The French Nobility in the Eighteenth Century: From Feudalism to Enlightenment,* trans. William Doyle. Cambridge: Cambridge University Press.

Chazan, Robert. 1987. *European Jewry and the First Crusade*. Berkeley: University of California Press.

———. 1989. *Daggers of Faith: Thirteenth-Century Christian Missionizing and Jewish Response*. Berkeley: University of California Press.

Cheng, Robert L. [1979] 1994. "Language Unification in Taiwan: Present and Future." In Murray A. Rubinstein, ed., *The Other Taiwan: 1945 to the Present*, pp. 357–391. Armonk, N.Y.: M. E. Sharpe.

Chevalier, François. [1952] 1963. *Land and Society in Colonial Mexico: The Great Hacienda*, ed. Lesley Byrd Simpson, trans. Alvin Eustis. Berkeley: University of California Press.

Chevalier, Louis. [1958/1973] 1981. *Laboring Classes and Dangerous Classes in Paris during the First Half of the Nineteenth Century*, trans. Frank Jellinek. Princeton, N.J.: Princeton University Press.

Chrétien, Jean-Pierre. 1997. *Le défi de l'ethnisme: Rwanda et Burundi: 1990–1996*. Paris: Karthala.

Chrétien, Jean-Pierre, Jean-François Dupaquier, Narcel Kabanda, and Joseph Ngarmbe. 1995. *Rwanda: les médias du génocide*. Paris: Karthala.

Clark, Christopher. 1999. "German Jews." In Rainer Liedtke and Stephan Wenderhorst, eds., *The Emancipation of Catholics, Jews and Protestants: Minorities and the Nation State in Nineteenth-Century Europe*, pp. 122–147. Manchester: Manchester University Press.

Clark, Kenneth B. [1965–66] 1967. "The Civil Rights Movement: Momentum and Organization." In Talcott Parsons and Kenneth B. Clark, eds., *The Negro American*, pp. 595–625. Boston: Beacon Press.

Clark, Samuel. 1995. *State and Status: The Rise of the State and Aristocratic Power in Western Europe*. Montreal: McGill-Queen's University Press.

Clarke, Colin. 2000. *Class, Ethnicity, and Community in Southern Mexico: Oaxaca's Peasantries*. Oxford: Oxford University Press.

Clausewitz, Carl von. 1992. *Historical and Political Writings*, ed. and trans. Peter Paret and Daniel Moran. Princeton, N.J.: Princeton University Press.

Claussen, Detlev. 1987. *Grenzen der Aufklärung: Zur gesellschaftlichen Geschichte des modernen Antisemitismus*. Frankfurt am Main: Fischer.

Clawson, Mary Ann. 1989. *Constructing Brotherhood: Class, Gender, and Fraternalism*. Princeton, N.J.: Princeton University Press.

Clendinnen, Inga. 1987. *Ambivalent Conquests: Maya and Spaniard in Yucatan, 1517–1570*. Cambridge: Cambridge University Press.

———. 1999. *Reading the Holocaust*. Cambridge: Cambridge University Press.

Clifford, James. 1997. *Routes: Travel and Translation in the Late Twentieth Century*. Cambridge, Mass.: Harvard University Press.

Clogg, Richard. 1992. *A Concise History of Greece*. Cambridge: Cambridge University Press.

Coakley, J. F. 1992. *The Church of the East and the Church of England: A History of the Archbishop of Canterbury's Assyrian Mission.* Oxford: Clarendon Press.

Cohen, Abner. 1969. *Custom and Politics in Urban Africa: A Study of Hausa Migrants in Yoruba Towns.* Berkeley: University of California Press.

———. 1974. "Introduction: The Lesson of Ethnicity." In Abner Cohen, ed., *Urban Ethnicity,* pp. ix–xxiv. London: Tavistock.

Cohen, Amnon. 1984. *Jewish Life under Islam: Jerusalem in the Sixteenth Century.* Cambridge, Mass.: Harvard University Press.

Cohen, Edward E. 2000. *The Athenian Nation.* Princeton, N.J.: Princeton University Press.

Cohen, Shaye J. D. 1987. *From the Maccabees to the Mishnah.* Philadelphia: Westminster Press.

———. 1992. "The Place of the Rabbi in Jewish Society of the Second Century." In Lee I. Levine, ed., *The Galilee in Late Antiquity,* pp. 157–173. New York: Jewish Theological Seminary of America.

———. 1999. *The Beginnings of Jewishness: Boundaries, Varieties, Uncertainties.* Berkeley: University of California Press.

Cohen, Stanley. 2001. *States of Denial: Knowing about Atrocities and Suffering.* Cambridge: Polity.

Cohen, William B. 1980. *The French Encounter with Africans: White Response to Blacks, 1530–1880.* Bloomington: Indiana University Press.

Cohn, Norman. 1967. *Warrant for Genocide: The Myth of the Jewish World-Conspiracy and the Protocols of the Elders of Zion.* New York: Harper & Row.

Cole, Tim. 1999. *Images of the Holocaust: The Myth of the "Shoah Business."* London: Duckworth.

Colley, Linda. 1992. *Britons: Forging the Nation 1707–1837.* New Haven, Conn.: Yale University Press.

———. 2002. *Captives: Britain, Empire and the World, 1600–1850.* London: Jonathan Cape.

Collins, Patricia Hill. 1991. *Black Feminist Thought: Knowledge, Consciousness, and the Politics of Empowerment.* London: Routledge.

Colls, Robert. 2002. *Identity of England.* Oxford: Oxford University Press.

Colson, Elizabeth. 1967. "Contemporary Tribes and the Development of Nationalism." In June Helm, ed., *Essays on the Problem of Tribe,* pp. 201–206. Seattle: University of Washington Press.

Comrie, Bernard. 1981. *The Languages of the Soviet Union.* Cambridge: Cambridge University Press.

Connell, R. W. 1995. *Masculinities.* Cambridge: Polity.

Connerton, Paul. 1989. *How Societies Remember.* Cambridge: Cambridge University Press.

Connor, W. Robert. 1994. "The Problem of Athenian Civic Identity." In Alan L.

Boegehold and Adele C. Scafuro, eds., *Athenian Identity and Civic Ideology*, pp. 34–44. Baltimore: Johns Hopkins University Press.

Connor, Walker. 1994. *Ethnonationalism: The Quest for Understanding*. Princeton, N.J.: Princeton University Press.

Conquest, Robert. 1990. *The Great Terror: A Reassessment*. New York: Oxford University Press.

———. 2000. *Reflections on a Ravaged Century*. New York: W. W. Norton.

Constable, Giles. 1995. *Three Studies in Medieval Religious and Social Thought*. Cambridge: Cambridge University Press.

Constantine, Stephen. 1999. "Migrants and Settlers." In Judith M. Brown and Wm. Roger Louis, eds., *The Oxford History of the British Empire*, vol. 4: *The Twentieth Century*, pp. 162–187. Oxford: Oxford University Press.

Conze, Werner. 1984. "Rasse." In Otto Brunner, Werner Conze, and Reinhardt Koselleck, eds., *Geschichtliche Grundbegriffe: Historisches Lexikon zur politisch-sozialen Sprache in Deutschland, band 5: Pro-Soz*, pp. 135–178. Stuttgart: Klett-Cotta.

Cook, Noble David. 1981. *Demographic Collapse in Indian Peru, 1520–1620*. Cambridge: Cambridge University Press.

———. 1998. *Born to Die: Disease and New World Conquest, 1492–1650*. Cambridge: Cambridge University Press.

Cook, Sherburne F., and Woodrow Borah. 1971. *Essays in Population History: Mexico and the Caribbean*, vol. 1. Berkeley: University of California Press.

———. 1979. *Essays in Population History: Mexico and California*, vol. 3. Berkeley: University of California Press.

Coon, Carleton S. 1963. *The Origin of Races*. New York: Alfred A. Knopf.

———. 1965. *The Living Races of Man*. New York: Alfred A. Knopf.

Cooper, Anna Julia. [1892] 1988. *A Voice from the South*. New York: Oxford University Press.

Cooper, Frederick, and Randall Packard. 1997. "Introduction." In Frederick Cooper and Randall M. Packard, eds., *International Development and the Social Sciences: Essays on the History and Politics of Knowledge*, pp. 1–41. Berkeley: University of California Press.

Cooper, Robert L. 1989. *Language Planning and Social Change*. Cambridge: Cambridge University Press.

Cope, R. Douglas. 1994. *The Limits of Racial Domination: Plebeian Society in Colonial Mexico City, 1660–1720*. Madison: University of Wisconsin Press.

Coquery-Vidrovitch, Catherine. [1985] 1988. *Africa: Endurance and Change South of the Sahara*, trans. David Maisel. Berkeley: University of California Press.

Corbin, Alain. 1998. *Le monde retrouvé de Louis-François Pinagot: sur les traces d'un inconnu 1798–1876*. Paris: Flammarion.

Cornell, John B. 1967. "Individual Mobility and Group Membership: The Case of the Burakumin." In R. P. Dore, ed., *Aspects of Social Change in Modern Japan*, pp. 337–372. Princeton, N.J.: Princeton University Press.

Cornell, Stephen. 1988. *The Return of the Native: American Indian Political Resurgence*. New York: Oxford University Press.

Cortés, Hernán. [1519–26/1971] 1986. *Letters from Mexico*, ed. and trans. Anthony Pagden. New Haven, Conn.: Yale University Press.

Cose, Ellis. 1993. *The Rage of a Privileged Class*. New York: HarperCollins.

Coser, Lewis A. 1972. "The Alien as a Servant of Power: Court Jews and Christian Renegades." *American Sociological Review* 37:574–581.

Cox, Oliver C. [1948] 1959. *Caste, Class, and Race: A Study in Social Dynamics*. New York: Monthly Review Press.

Craig, Gordon A. 1978. *Germany 1866–1945*. Oxford: Oxford University Press.

Crone, Patricia 1986. "The Tribe and the State." In John A. Hall, ed., *States in History*, pp. 48–77. Oxford: Blackwell.

Crookshank, F. G. 1924. *The Mongol in Our Midst: A Study of Man and His Three Faces*, 3rd ed. London: Kegan, Paul, Treuch, and Trubner.

Crosby, Alfred W. 1986. *Ecological Imperialism: The Biological Expansion of Europe, 900–1900*. Cambridge: Cambridge University Press.

———. 1994. *Germs, Seeds, and Animals: Studies in Ecological History*. Armonk, N.Y.: M. E. Sharpe.

Crossley, Pamela Kyle. 1999. *A Translucent Mirror: History and Identity in Qing Imperial Ideology*. Berkeley: University of California Press.

Cruse, Harold. 1967. *The Crisis of the Negro Intellectual*. New York: William Morrow.

Crystal, David. 2000. *Language Death*. Cambridge: Cambridge University Press.

Cullen, Countee. [1925] 1991. "Heritage." In Countee Cullen, *My Soul's High Song: The Collected Writings of Countee Cullen, Voice of the Harlem Renaissance*, ed. Gerald Early, pp. 104–108. New York: Doubleday.

Curtin, Philip D. 1964. *The Image of Africa: British Ideas and Action, 1780–1850*, 2 vols. in 1. Madison: University of Wisconsin Press.

Curtius, Ernst Robert. [1948] 1953. *European Literature and the Latin Middle Ages*, trans. Willard R. Trask. Princeton, N.J.: Princeton University Press.

Cushman, Thomas, and Stjepan G. Meštrović. 1996. "Introduction." In Thomas Cushman and Stjepan G. Meštrović, eds., *This Time We Knew: Western Responses to Genocide in Bosnia*, pp. 1–38. New York: New York University Press.

Cyprian. [251] 1840. "On the Unity of the Church." In Cyprian, *The Treatises of Cyprian, Bishop of Carthage, and Martyr*, ed. E. B. Pusey, John Keble, and J. H. Newman, trans. Charles Thornton, pp. 131–152. Oxford: John Henry Parker.

Dadrian, Vahakn N. 1999. *Warrant for Genocide: Key Elements of Turko-Armenian Conflict.* New Brunswick, N.J.: Transaction.

Dahlberg, Gunnar. 1942. *Race, Reason, and Rubbish: A Primer of Race Biology.* New York: Columbia University Press.

Dahrendorf, Ralf. [1965] 1967. *Society and Democracy in Germany.* New York: W. W. Norton.

Dain, Bruce. 2002. *A Hideous Monster of the Mind: American Race Theory in the Early Republic.* Cambridge, Mass.: Harvard University Press.

Dalby, Andrew. 1998. *Dictionary of Languages.* New York: Columbia University Press.

Damas, L.-G. 1962. *Pigments.* Paris: Présence Africaine.

Dandamaev, Muhammad A. 1992. *Iranians in Achaemenid Babylonia.* Costa Mesa, Calif.: Mazda.

Dann, Otto. 1988. "Introduction." In Otto Dann and John Dinwiddy, eds., *Nationalism in the Age of the French Revolution,* pp. 1–11. London: Hambledon Press.

Dante. [1305?] 1996. *De vulgari eloquentia,* ed. and trans. Steven Botterill. Cambridge: Cambridge University Press.

Darnton, Robert. 1984. *The Great Cat Massacre and Other Episodes in French Cultural History.* New York: Basic Books.

Darwin, Charles. [1871] 1981. *The Descent of Man, and Selection in Relation to Sex.* Princeton, N.J.: Princeton University Press.

——. [1859] 1993. *The Origin of Species.* New York: Random House.

Davenport, Charles B. 1911. *Heredity in Relation to Eugenics.* New York: Henry Holt.

Davies, Sarah. [1997] 2000. " 'Us against Them': Social Identity in Soviet Russia, 1934–41." In Sheila Fitzpatrick, ed., *Stalinism: New Directions,* pp. 47–70. London: Routledge.

Davis, David Brion. 1975. *The Problem of Slavery in the Age of Revolution 1770–1823.* Ithaca, N.Y.: Cornell University Press.

——. 1984. *Slavery and Human Progress.* New York: Oxford University Press.

Davis, Fred. 1992. *Fashion, Culture, and Identity.* Chicago: University of Chicago Press.

Davis, Lennard J. 1995. *Enforcing Normalcy: Disability, Deafness, and the Body.* London: Routledge.

Davis, Natalie Zemon. 1975. *Society and Culture in Early Modern France.* Stanford, Calif.: Stanford University Press.

Dawson, Michael C. 1994. *Behind the Mule: Race and Class in African-American Politics.* Princeton, N.J.: Princeton University Press.

——. 2001. *Black Visions: The Roots of Contemporary African-American Political Ideologies.* Chicago: University of Chicago Press.

De Lange, Nicholas. 1986. *Judaism*. Oxford: Oxford University Press.

De Mauro, Tullio. [1963] 1972. *Storia linguistica dell'Italia unita*, 3rd ed. Bari: Editori Laterza.

De Waal, Alexander. 1989. *Famine That Kills: Darfur, Sudan, 1984–1985*. Oxford: Clarendon Press.

Deák, István. 1990. *Beyond Nationalism: A Social and Political History of the Habsburg Officer Corps, 1848–1918*. New York: Oxford University Press.

Deane, Seamus. 1997. *Strange Country: Modernity and Nationhood in Irish Writing since 1790*. Oxford: Clarendon Press.

Dégh, Linda. [1962] 1969. *Folktales and Society: Story-Telling in a Hungarian Peasant Community*, trans. Emily M. Schossberger. Bloomington: Indiana University Press.

Degler, Carl N. 1971. *Neither Black nor White: Slavery and Race Relations in Brazil and the United States*. New York: Macmillan.

Dehio, Ludwig. 1959. *Germany and World Politics in the Twentieth Century*, trans. Dieter Pevsner. New York: W. W. Norton.

Delacampagne, Christian. 1983. *L'invention de racisme: antiquité et Moyen Age*. Paris: Seuil.

———. 1998. *De l'indifférence: essai sur la banalisation du mal*. Paris: Odile Jacob.

Delbo, Charlotte. 1995. *Auschwitz and After*, trans. Rosette C. Lamont. New Haven, Conn.: Yale University Press.

Delft, Louis van. 1993. *Littérature et anthropologie: Nature humaine et caractère à l'âge classique*. Paris: Presses Universitaires de France.

Delgado, Richard. [1982] 1995. "Words That Wound: A Tort Action for Racial Insults, Epithets, and Name-Calling." In Richard Delgado, ed., *Critical Race Theory: The Cutting Edge*, pp. 159–168. Philadelphia: Temple University Press.

Déloye, Yves. 1997. "Commémoration et imaginaire national en France (1896–1996)." In Pierre Birnbaum, ed., *Sociologie des nationalismes*, pp. 55–84. Paris: Presses Universitaires de France.

Delumeau, Jean. 1989. *Rassurer et protéger: le sentiment de sécurité dans l'Occident d'autrefois*. Paris: Fayard.

———. [1971] 1992. *Le Catholicisme entre Luther et Voltaire*, 4th ed. Paris: Presses Universitaires de France.

D'Emilio, John. 1992. *Making Trouble: Essays on Gay History, Politics, and the University*. New York: Routledge.

d'Entrèves, Alexander Passerin. 1967. *The Notion of the State: An Introduction to Political Theory*. Oxford: Clarendon Press.

Derr, Mark. 1997. *Dog's Best Friend: Annals of the Dog-Human Relationship*. New York: Henry Holt.

Destexhe, Alain. [1994] 1995. *Rwanda and Genocide in the Twentieth Century*, trans. Alison Marschner. New York: New York University Press.

Deutsch, Helen, and Felicity Nussbaum. 2000. "Introduction." In Helen Deutsch and Felicity Nussbaum, eds., *"Defects": Engendering the Modern Body*, pp. 1–28. Ann Arbor: University of Michigan Press.

Deutsch, Karl W. [1953] 1966. *Nationalism and Social Communication: An Inquiry into the Foundations of Nationality,* 2nd ed. Cambridge, Mass.: MIT Press.

Deutscher, Isaac. [1968] 1972. *The Non-Jewish Jew and Other Essays,* ed. Tamara Deutscher. Boston: Alyson.

Devoto, Giacomo. [1974] 1978. *The Languages of Italy,* trans. V. Louise Katainen. Chicago: University of Chicago Press.

Dewald, Jonathan. 1996. *The European Nobility, 1400–1800.* Cambridge: Cambridge University Press.

Díaz del Castillo, Bernal. 1956. *The Discovery and Conquest of Mexico 1517–1521,* ed. Genaro García, trans. A. P. Maudslay. New York: Farrar, Straus & Giroux.

Dickens, Charles. [1850] 1948. *The Personal History of David Copperfield.* Oxford: Oxford University Press.

Diderot, Denis, and Jean Le Rond d'Alembert, eds. [1747–73] n.d. *Encyclopédie, ou Dictionnaire raisonné des sciences, des arts et des métiers,* compact ed., 5 vols. Elmsford, N.Y.: Pergamon Press.

Dippel, John V. H. 1996. *Bound upon a Wheel of Fire: Why So Many German Jews Made the Tragic Decision to Remain in Nazi Germany.* New York: Basic Books.

Dippie, Brian W. 1982. *The Vanishing American: White Attitudes and U.S. Indian Policy.* Middletown, Conn.: Wesleyan University Press.

Dirks, Nicholas B. 2001. *Castes of Mind: Colonialism and the Making of Modern India.* Princeton, N.J.: Princeton University Press.

Dittmer, Lowell. 1974. *Liu Shao-Ch'i and the Chinese Cultural Revolution: The Politics of Mass Criticism.* Berkeley: University of California Press.

———. 1987. *China's Continuous Revolution: The Post-Liberation Epoch 1949–1981.* Berkeley: University of California Press.

Dixon, Roland B. 1923. *The Racial History of Man.* New York: Charles Scribner's Sons.

Długoborski, Wacław. 1993. "On the History of the Gypsy Camp at Auschwitz-Birkenau." In State Museum of Auschwitz-Birkenau, ed., *Memorial Book: The Gypsies at Auschwitz-Birkenau,* vol. 1, pp. 1–5. München: K. G. Saur.

Dobzhansky, Theodosius. 1962. *Mankind Evolving: The Evolution of the Human Species.* New Haven, Conn.: Yale University Press.

———. [1937] 1982. *Genetics and the Origins of Species.* New York: Columbia University Press.

Doder, Dusko, and Louise Branson. 1999. *Milosevic: Portrait of a Tyrant.* New York: Free Press.

Dollard, John. [1937] 1957. *Caste and Class in a Southern Town,* 3rd ed. New York: Anchor.

Douglas, Mary. 1966. *Purity and Danger: An Analysis of the Concepts of Pollution and Taboo.* London: RKP.

———. 1970. *Natural Symbols: Explorations in Cosmology.* New York: Pantheon.

Dower, John W. 1986. *War without Mercy: Race and Power in the Pacific War.* New York: Pantheon.

Doyle, Michael W. 1986. *Empires.* Ithaca, N.Y.: Cornell University Press.

Drake, Christine. 1989. *National Integration in Indonesia: Patterns and Policies.* Honolulu: University of Hawaii Press.

Drake, St. Claire. 1987. *Black Folk Here and There: An Essay in History and Anthropology,* vol. 1. Los Angeles: Center for Afro-American Studies, University of California.

Drèze, Jean, and Amartya Sen. 1989. *Hunger and Public Action.* Oxford: Clarendon Press.

Du Bois, W. E. B. [1903] 1986a. "The Souls of Black Folk." In W. E. B. Du Bois, *Writings,* ed. Nathan Huggins, pp. 357–547. New York: Library of America.

———. [1940] 1986b. "Dusk of Dawn: An Essay Toward an Autobiography of a Race Concept." In W. E. B. Du Bois, *Writings,* ed. Nathan Huggins, pp. 549–802. New York: Library of America.

———. [1897] 1986c. "The Conservation of Races." In W. E. B. Du Bois, *Writings,* ed. Nathan Huggins, pp. 815–826. New York: Library of America.

Duby, Georges. [1978] 1980a. *The Three Orders: Feudal Society Imagined,* trans. Arthur Goldhammer. Chicago: University of Chicago Press.

———. [1977] 1980b. *The Chivalrous Society,* trans. Cynthia Postan. Berkeley: University of California Press.

Dudziak, Mary L. 2000. *Cold War Civil Rights: Race and the Image of American Democracy.* Princeton, N.J.: Princeton University Press.

Dundes, Alan. 1989. *Folklore Matters.* Knoxville: University of Tennessee Press.

Dunn, James. 1995. "The Timor Affair in International Perspective." In Peter Carey and G. Carter Bentley, eds., *East Timor at the Crossroads: The Forging of a Nation,* pp. 59–72. Honolulu: University of Hawai'i Press.

———. [1983] 1996. *Timor: A People Betrayed,* new ed. Sydney, Australia: ABC Books.

Dunn, John. [1979] 1993. *Western Political Theory in the Face of the Future,* 2nd ed. Cambridge: Cambridge University Press.

Dunn, John, and A. F. Robertson. 1973. *Dependence and Opportunity: Political Change in Ahafo.* Cambridge: Cambridge University Press.

Durkheim, Emile. [1898] 1973. "Individualism and the Intellectuals," trans. Mark Traugott. In Emile Durkheim, *Emile Durkheim on Morality and Society,* ed. and trans. Robert N. Bellah, pp. 43–60. Chicago: University of Chicago Press.

———. [1893] 1984. *The Division of Labor in Society,* trans. W. D. Halls. New York: Free Press.

————. [1912] 1995. *The Elementary Forms of Religious Life,* trans. Karen E. Fields. New York: Free Press.

Dyer, Richard. 1997. *White.* London: Routledge.

Eberhard, Wolfram. [1952] 1965. *Conquerors and Rulers: Social Forces in Medieval China.* Leiden: E. J. Brill.

Economist. 1995–96. "Short Guys Finish Last." *The Economist* December 23–January 5, pp. 19–22.

Eggert, Karl. 1986. "Mahafaly as Misnomer." In Conrad Phillip Kottak, Jean-Aimé Rakotoarisoa, Aidan Southall, and Pierre Vérin, eds., *Madagascar: Society and History,* pp. 321–335. Durham, N.C.: Carolina Academic Press.

Ehmann, Annegret. 1998. "From Colonial Racism to Nazi Population Policy: The Role of the So-called Mischlinge." In Michael Berenbaum and Abraham J. Peck, eds., *The Holocaust and History: The Known, the Unknown, the Disputed, and the Reexamined,* pp. 115–133. Bloomington: Indiana University Press.

Ehrenberg, Victor. [1960] 1969. *The Greek State,* 2nd ed. London: Methuen.

Eicher, Joanne B. 1995. "Introduction: Dress as Expression of Ethnic Identity." In Joanne B. Eicher, ed., *Dress and Ethnicity: Change across Space and Time,* pp. 1–5. Oxford: Berg.

Eisen, Arnold M. 1998. *Rethinking Modern Judaism: Ritual, Commandment, Community.* Chicago: University of Chicago Press.

Eley, Geoff. 1980. *Reshaping the German Right: Radical Nationalism and Political Change after Bismarck.* New Haven, Conn.: Yale University Press.

Elias, Norbert, and John L. Scotson. [1965] 1994. *The Established and the Outsiders.* London: Sage.

Eliot, George. [1879] 1994. *Impressions of Theophrastus Such,* ed. Nancy Henry. Iowa City: University of Iowa Press.

Eliot, T. S. [1948] 1968. "Notes towards the Definition of Culture." In T. S. Eliot, *Christianity and Culture,* pp. 79–202. New York: Harcourt Brace Jovanovich.

Elkins, Stanley M. [1959] 1976. *Slavery: A Problem in American Institutional and Intellectual Life,* 3rd ed. Chicago: University of Chicago Press.

Ellen, Roy. 1993. *The Cultural Relations of Classification: An Analysis of Nuaulu Animal Categories from Central Seram.* Cambridge: Cambridge University Press.

Elliott, J. H. 1970. *The Old World and the New 1492–1650.* Cambridge: Cambridge University Press.

Elliott, Mark C. 2001. *The Manchu Way: The Eight Banners and Ethnic Identity in Late Imperial China.* Stanford, Calif.: Stanford University Press.

Ellis, Harold A. 1988. *Boulainvilliers and the French Monarchy: Aristocratic Politics in Early Eighteenth-Century France.* Ithaca, N.Y.: Cornell University Press.

Ellis, John M. 1983. *One Fairy Story Too Many: The Brothers Grimm and Their Tales.* Chicago: University of Chicago Press.

Ellison, Ralph. [1970] 1995. "What America Would Be Like without Blacks." In Ralph Ellison, *The Collected Essays of Ralph Ellison,* ed. John F. Callahan, pp. 577–584. New York: Modern Library.

Elshtain, Jean Bethke. 1987. *Women and War.* New York: Basic Books.

Elton, Hugh. 1996. *Frontiers of the Roman Empire.* Bloomington: Indiana University Press.

Engelmann, Bernt. [1982–83] 1986. *In Hitler's Germany: Daily Life in the Third Reich,* trans. Krishna Winston. New York: Pantheon.

Engelsing, Rolf. 1974. *Der Bürger als Leser: Lesergeschichte in Deutschland 1500–1800.* Stuttgart: J. B. Meltzerlsche Verlagsbuchhandlung.

Enloe, Cynthia. [1989] 1990. *Bananas, Beaches & Bases: Making Feminist Sense of International Politics.* Berkeley: University of California Press.

Ens, Adolf. 1994. *Subjects or Citizens? The Mennonite Experience in Canada, 1870–1925.* Ottawa: University of Ottawa Press.

Epstein, A. L. 1958. *Politics in an Urban African Community.* Manchester: Manchester University Press.

Epstein, Isidore. 1959. *Judaism: A Historical Presentation.* Harmondsworth, U.K.: Penguin.

Epstein, Klaus. 1966. *The Genesis of German Conservatism.* Princeton, N.J.: Princeton University Press.

Ereshefsky, Marc, ed. 1992. *The Units of Evolution: Essays on the Nature of Species.* Cambridge, Mass.: MIT Press.

Erikson, Erik H. 1958. *Luther: A Study in Psychoanalysis and History.* New York: W. W. Norton.

———. [1950] 1985. *Childhood and Society,* 35th anniversary ed. New York: W. W. Norton.

Escoffier, Jeff. 1998. *American Homo: Community and Perversity.* Berkeley: University of California Press.

Esman, Milton J. 1994. *Ethnic Politics.* Ithaca, N.Y.: Cornell University Press.

Evans, Eric. 1995. "Englishness and Britishness: National Identities, c.1790–c.1870." In Alexander Grant and Keith J. Stringer, eds., *Uniting the Kingdom? The Making of British History,* pp. 223–243. London: Routledge.

Evans-Pritchard, E. E. 1940. "The Nuer of the Southern Sudan." In M. Fortes and E. E. Evans-Pritchard, ed., *African Political Systems,* pp. 272–296. London: Oxford University Press.

Ewen, C. L'Estrange. [1938] 1945. *The British Race—Germanic or Celtic?.* Paignton, U.K.: C. L. Ewen.

Eyerman, Ron. 2001. *Cultural Trauma: Slavery and the Formation of African American Identity.* Cambridge: Cambridge University Press.

Ezekiel, Raphael S. 1995. *The Racist Mind: Portraits of American Neo-Nazis and Klansmen.* New York: Viking Penguin.

Fabian, Johannes. 1983. *Time and the Other: How Anthropology Makes Its Object.* New York: Columbia University Press.

Fairbank, John K. 1968. "A Preliminary Framework." In John King Fairbank, ed., *The Chinese World Order: Traditional China's Foreign Relations,* pp. 1–19. Cambridge, Mass.: Harvard University Press.

———. 1992. *China: A New History.* Cambridge, Mass.: Harvard University Press.

Fanon, Frantz. [1959] 1965. *A Dying Colonialism,* trans. Haakon Chevalier. New York: Grove Press.

———. [1963] 1965b. *The Wretched of the Earth.* New York: Grove Press.

———. [1952] 1967. *Black Skin, White Masks,* trans. Charles Lam Markmann. New York: Grove Press.

Fauré, Christine. [1985] 1991. *Democracy without Women: Feminism and the Rise of Individualism in France,* trans. Claudia Gorbman and John Berks. Bloomington: Indiana University Press.

Faust, Drew Gilpin. 1981. "Introduction: The Proslavery Argument in History." In Drew Gilpin Faust, ed., *The Ideology of Slavery: Proslavery Thought in the Antebellum South, 1830–1860,* pp. 1–20. Baton Rouge: Louisiana State University Press.

Favre, Pierre. 1989. *Naissances de la science politique en France, 1870–1914.* Paris: Fayard.

Feagin, Joe R., and Melvin P. Sikes. 1994. *Living with Racism: The Black Middle-Class Experience.* Boston: Beacon Press.

Fears, Darryl. 2003. "Racial Label Surprises Latino Immigrants." *Manchester Guardian Weekly* January 9–15, p. 29.

Febvre, Lucien. 1942. *Le Problème de l'incroyance au XVIe siècle: la religion de Rabelais.* Paris: Albin Michel.

———. 1973. *A New Kind of History: From the Writings of Febvre,* ed. Peter Burke, trans. K. Folca. New York: Harper & Row.

Fehrenbacher, Don E. 2001. *The Slaveholding Republic: An Account of the United States Government's Relations to Slavery,* ed. Ward M. McAfee. New York: Oxford University Press.

Feierman, Steven. 1990. *Peasant Intellectuals: Anthropology and History in Tanzania.* Madison: University of Wisconsin Press.

Feldman, Louis H. 1993. *Jew and Gentile in the Ancient World: Attitudes and Interactions from Alexander to Justinian.* Princeton, N.J.: Princeton University Press.

Fest, Joachim C. [1963] 1970. *The Face of the Third Reich: Portraits of the Nazi Leadership,* trans. Michael Bullock. New York: Pantheon.

Fichte, Johann Gottlieb. [1808] 1997. "Reden an die deutsche Nation." In Johann Gottlieb Fichte, *Schriften zur angewandten Philosophie,* ed. Peter Lothar Oesterreich, pp. 539–788. Frankfurt am Main: Deutscher Klassiker Verlag.

Field, Martha A., and Valeria A. Sanchez. 1999. *Equal Treatment for People with Mental Retardation: Having and Raising Children.* Cambridge, Mass.: Harvard University Press.

Fields, Barbara Jeanne. 1990. "Slavery, Race and Ideology in the United States of America." *New Left Review* 181:95–118.

Fine, Gary Alan, and Patricia A. Turner. 2001. *Whispers on the Color Line: Rumor and Race in America.* Berkeley: University of California Press.

Finer, Samuel E. 1975. "State- and Nation-Building in Europe: The Role of the Military." In Charles Tilly, ed., *The Formation of National States in Western Europe,* pp. 84–163. Princeton, N.J.: Princeton University Press.

Finkelstein, Norman G. 1995. *Image and Reality of the Israel-Palestine Conflict.* London: Verso.

———. 1998. "Daniel Jonah Goldhagen's 'Crazy' Thesis: A Critique of *Hitler's Willing Executioners.*" In Norman G. Finkelstein and Ruth Bettina Birn, *A Nation on Trial: The Goldhagen Thesis and Historical Truth,* pp. 1–100. New York: Metropolitan.

Finley, M. I. 1980. *Ancient Slavery and Modern Ideology.* New York: Viking.

———. [1970] 1981. *Early Greece: The Bronze and Archaic Ages,* rev. ed. London: Chatto & Windus.

———. 1983. *Politics in the Ancient World.* Cambridge: Cambridge University Press.

Firth, Raymond. [1936] 1963. *We, the Tikopia: A Sociological Study of Kinship in Primitive Polynesia,* 2nd ed. Boston: Beacon Press.

———. 1973. *Symbols: Public and Private.* Ithaca, N.Y.: Cornell University Press.

Fisch, Jörg. 1992. "Zivilisation, Kultur." In Otto Brunner, Werner Conze, and Reinhardt Koselleck, eds., *Geschichtliche Grundbegriffe: Historisches Lexikon zur politisch-sozialen Sprache in Deutschland, band 7: Verw—Z,* pp. 679–774. Stuttgart: Klett-Cotta.

Fischer, Edward F. 2001. *Cultural Logics and Global Economies: Maya Identity in Thought and Practice.* Austin: University of Texas Press.

Fischer, Fritz. [1965] 1974. *World Power or Decline: The Controversy over Germany's Aims in the First World War,* trans. Lancelot L. Farrar, Robert Kimber, and Rita Kimber. New York: W. W. Norton.

Fischer, Wolfram, and Peter Lundgreen. 1975. "The Recruitment and Training of Administrative and Technical Personnel." In Charles Tilly, ed., *The Formation of National States in Western Europe,* pp. 456–561. Princeton, N.J.: Princeton University Press.

Fishman, Joshua A. 1972. *Language and Nationalism: Two Integrative Essays.* Rowley, Mass.: Newbury House.

Fitzgerald, F. Scott. [1934] 1982. *Tender Is the Night.* New York: Limited Editions Club.

Fitzgerald, John. 1996. *Awakening China: Politics, Culture, and Class in the Nationalist Revolution.* Stanford, Calif.: Stanford University Press.

Fitzhugh, George. [1850] 1965. *Sociology for the South or the Failure of Free Society.* New York: Burton Franklin.

———. [1857] 1960. *Cannibals All! Or, Slaves without Masters,* ed. C. Vann Woodward. Cambridge, Mass.: Harvard University Press.

Fitzpatrick, David. 1994. *Oceans of Consolation: Personal Accounts of Irish Migration to Australia.* Ithaca, N.Y.: Cornell University Press.

Fitzpatrick, Sheila. 1999. *Everyday Stalinism: Ordinary Life in Extraordinary Times: Soviet Russia in the 1930s.* New York: Oxford University Press.

———. [1993] 2000. "Ascribing Class: The Construction of Social Identity in Soviet Russia." In Sheila Fitzpatrick, ed., *Stalinism: New Directions,* pp. 20–46. London: Routledge.

Flandrin, Jean-Louis. 1984. "Internationalisme, nationalisme et régionalisme dans la cuisine des XIVe et XVe siècles: Le témoignage des livres et cuisine." In Centre d'Études Médiévales de Nice, ed., *Manger et boire au Moyen Age,* vol. 2: *cuisine, manières de table, régimes alimentaire,* pp. 75–91. Paris: Belles Lettres.

Flapan, Simha. 1987. *The Birth of Israel: Myths and Realities.* New York: Pantheon.

Flaubert, Gustave. [1857] 1993. *Madame Bovary,* trans. Francis Steegmuller. New York: Alfred A. Knopf.

Flood, Gavin. 1996. *An Introduction to Hinduism.* Cambridge: Cambridge University Press.

Floud, Roderick, Kenneth Wachter, and Annabel Gregory. 1990. *Height, Health and History: Nutritional Status in the United Kingdom, 1750–1980.* Cambridge: Cambridge University Press.

Foley, Neil. 1997. *The White Scourge: Mexicans, Blacks, and Poor Whites in Texas Cotton Culture.* Berkeley: University of California Press.

Foner, Eric. 1970. *Free Soil, Free Labor, Free Men: The Ideology of the Republican Party before the Civil War.* New York: Oxford University Press.

———. 1988. *Reconstruction 1863–1877: America's Unfinished Revolution.* New York: Harper & Row.

Foner, Nancy. 2000. *From Ellis Island to JFK: New York's Two Great Waves of Immigration.* New Haven, Conn.: Yale University Press.

Fonseca, Isabel. 1995. *Bury Me Standing: The Gypsies and Their Journey.* New York: Alfred A. Knopf.

Forbes, H. D. 1997. *Ethnic Conflict: Commerce, Culture, and the Contact Hypothesis.* New Haven, Conn.: Yale University Press.

Forman, Michael. 1998. *Nationalism and the International Labor Movement: The Idea of the Nation in Socialist and Anarchist Theory.* University Park: Pennsylvania State University Press.

Forrest, Alan. 1989. *Conscripts and Deserters: The Army and French Society during the Revolution and Empire.* New York: Oxford University Press.

———. 1996. *The Revolution in Provincial France: Aquitaine, 1790–1799.* Oxford: Clarendon Press.

Forster, Jürgen. [1996] 1998. "Operation Barbarossa in Historical Perspective." In Militärgeschichtliches Forschungsamt, ed., *Germany and the Second World War,* vol. 4: *The Attack on the Soviet Union,* trans. Dean S. McMurry, Ewald Osers, and Louise Willmot, pp. 1245–1255. Oxford: Clarendon Press.

Forster, Peter G. 1982. *The Esperanto Movement.* The Hague: Mouton.

Fortes, M., and E. E. Evans-Pritchard. 1940. "Introduction." In M. Fortes and E. E. Evans-Pritchard, ed., *African Political Systems,* pp. 1–23. London: Oxford University Press.

Fortes, Meyer. [1959] 1983. *Oedipus and Job in West African Religion.* Cambridge: Cambridge University Press.

Foster, George M. [1967] 1988. *Tzintzuntzan: Mexican Peasants in a Changing World.* Prospect Heights, Ill.: Waveland Press.

Foucher, Michel. 1988. *Fronts et frontières: un tour du monde géopolitique.* Paris: Fayard.

Fowden, Garth. 1993. *Empire to Commonwealth: Consequences of Monotheism in Late Antiquity.* Princeton, N.J.: Princeton University Press.

Frady, Marshall. 2002. *Martin Luther King, Jr.* New York: Viking.

Frankenberg, Ruth. 1993. *White Women, Race Matters: The Social Construction of Whiteness.* Minneapolis: University of Minnesota Press.

Franklin, Benjamin. [1751] 1987. "Observations Concerning the Increase of Mankind, Peopling of Countries, etc." In Benjamin Franklin, *Writings,* ed. J. A. Leo Lemay, pp. 367–374. New York: Library of America.

Fredrickson, George M. 1981. *White Supremacy: A Comparative Study in American and South African History.* New York: Oxford University Press.

———. [1971] 1987. *The Black Image in the White Mind: The Debate on Afro-American Character and Destiny, 1817–1914.* Middletown, Conn.: Wesleyan University Press.

———. 1988. *The Arrogance of Race: Historical Perspectives on Slavery, Racism, and Social Inequality.* Middletown, Conn.: Wesleyan University Press.

———. 1995. *Black Liberation: A Comparative History of Black Ideologies in the United States and South Africa.* New York: Oxford University Press.

———. 2002. *Racism: A Short History.* Princeton, N.J.: Princeton University Press.

Freedman, Paul. 1999. *Images of the Medieval Peasant.* Stanford, Calif.: Stanford University Press.

Freeman, Kathleen. 1948. *Ancilla to the Pre-Socratic Philosophers.* Cambridge, Mass.: Harvard University Press.

French, Howard W. 2001. "The Japanese, It Seems, Are Outgrowing Japan." *New York Times,* February 1, p. A4.

Freud, Sigmund. [1930/1948] 1999. "Vorrede." In Sigmund Freud, *Gesammelte Werke,* vol. 14: *Werke aus den Jahren 1925–1931,* p. 569. Frankfurt am Main: Fischer.

Fried, Morton H. 1967. "On the Concepts of 'Tribe' and 'Tribal Society.' " In June Helm, ed., *Essays on the Problem of Tribe,* pp. 3–20. Seattle: University of Washington Press.

———. 1975. *The Notion of Tribe.* Menlo Park, Calif.: Cummings.

Friedlander, Henry. 1995. *The Origins of Nazi Genocide: From Euthanasia to the Final Solution.* Chapel Hill: University of North Carolina Press.

Friedländer, Saul. [1982] 1984: *Reflections on Nazism: An Essay on Kitsch and Death,* trans. Thomas Weyr. New York: Harper & Row.

Friedlaender, Jonathan Scott. 1975. *Patterns of Human Variation: The Demography, Genetics, and Phenetics of Bougainville Islanders.* Cambridge, Mass.: Harvard University Press.

Friedman, John Block. 1981. *The Monstrous Races in Medieval Art and Thought.* Cambridge, Mass.: Harvard University Press.

Fritzsche, Peter. 1998. *Germans into Nazis.* Cambridge, Mass.: Harvard University Press.

Fulbrook, Mary. 1991. *The Fontana History of Germany 1918–1990: The Divided Nation.* London: Fontana.

———. 1999. *German National Identity after the Holocaust.* Cambridge: Polity.

Fumaroli, Marc. 1980. *L'age de l'eloquence: rhétorique et "res literaria" de la Renaissance au seuil de l'époque classique.* Genève: Droz.

Funkenstein, Amos. 1993. *Perceptions of Jewish History.* Berkeley: University of California Press.

Furet, François. [1988] 1992. *Revolutionary France, 1770–1880,* trans. Antonia Nevill. Oxford: Blackwell.

Futuyma, Douglas J. [1986] 1998. *Evolutionary Biology,* 3rd ed. Sunderland, Mass.: Sinauer Associates.

Gabaccia, Donna R. 1998. *We Are What We Eat: Ethnic Food and the Making of Americans.* Cambridge, Mass.: Harvard University Press.

Gadamer, H. G. 1942. *Volk und Geschichte im Denken Herders.* Frankfurt am Main: Vittorio Klostermann.

Gadd, C. J. 1971. "Babylonia c. 2120–1800 B.C." In I. E. S. Edwards, C. J. Gadd, and N. G. L. Hammond, eds., *Cambridge Ancient History,* vol. 1, pt. 2, 3rd ed., pp. 595–643. Cambridge: Cambridge University Press.

———. 1973. "Hammurabi and the End of His Dynasty." In I. E. S. Edwards, C. J. Gadd, N. G. L. Hammond, and E. Sollberger, eds., *Cambridge Ancient History,* vol. 2, pt. 1, 3rd ed., pp. 176–227. Cambridge: Cambridge University Press.

Gager, John. 1983. *The Origins of Anti-Semitism: Attitude toward Judaism in Pagan and Christian Antiquity.* New York: Oxford University Press.

Gagliardo, John G. 1980. *Reich and Nation: The Holy Roman Empire as Idea and Reality, 1763–1806.* Bloomington: Indiana University Press.

Galenson, David. 1981. *White Servitude in Colonial America: An Economic Analysis.* Cambridge: Cambridge University Press.

Galler, Roberta. 1984. "The Myth of the Perfect Body." In Carole S. Vance, ed., *Pleasure and Danger: Exploring Female Sexuality,* pp. 165–172. Boston: Routledge & Kegan Paul.

Gallie, W. B. 1991. *Understanding War.* London: Routledge.

Galton, Francis. [1869] 1892. *Hereditary Genius: An Inquiry into Its Laws and Consequences,* 2nd ed. London: Macmillan.

———. 1909. *Essays in Eugenics.* London: Eugenics Education Society.

Garlan, Yvon. [1982] 1988. *Slavery in Ancient Greece,* rev. ed., trans. Janet Lloyd. Ithaca, N.Y.: Cornell University Press.

Garn, Stanley M. [1961] 1971. *Human Races,* 3rd ed. Springfield, Ill.: Charles C. Thomas.

Garnsey, Peter. 1970. *Social Status and Legal Privilege in the Roman Empire.* Oxford: Clarendon Press.

———. 1996. *Ideas of Slavery from Aristotle to Augustine.* Cambridge: Cambridge University Press.

———. 1998. *Cities, Peasants and Food in Classical Antiquity: Essays in Social and Economic History,* ed. Walter Scheidel. Cambridge: Cambridge University Press.

———. 1999. *Food and Society in Classical Antiquity.* Cambridge: Cambridge University Press.

Garvey, Marcus. 1987. *Marcus Garvey: Life and Lessons: A Centennial Companion to the Marcus Garvey and Universal Negro Improvement Association Papers,* ed. Robert A. Hill. Berkeley: University of California Press.

Gates, Henry Louis, Jr. 1988. *The Signifying Monkey: A Theory of Afro-American Literary Criticism.* New York: Oxford University Press.

———. 1992. *Loose Canons: Notes on the Culture Wars.* New York: Oxford University Press.

———. 1997. *Thirteen Ways of Looking at a Black Man.* New York: Random House.

Gates, R. Ruggles. 1949. *Pedigrees of Negro Families.* Philadelphia: Blakiston.

Gauchet, Marcel. 1995. *La révolution des pouvoirs: la souveraineté, le peuple et la représentation 1789–1799.* Paris: Gallimard.

Gaulle, Charles de. [1970–71] 1971. *Memoirs of Hope: Renewal and Endeavor,* trans. Terence Kilmartin. New York: Simon & Schuster.

Gaunt, David. 2001. "Kinship: Thin Red Lines or Thick Blue Blood." In David I. Kertzer and Marzio Barbagli, eds., *The History of the European Family,* vol. 1:

Family Life in Early Modern Times, 1500–1789, pp. 257–287. New Haven, Conn.: Yale University Press.

Gay, Peter. 1998. *My German Question: Growing Up in Nazi Berlin.* New Haven, Conn.: Yale University Press.

Geary, Patrick J. 2002. *The Myth of Nations: The Medieval Origins of Europe.* Princeton, N.J.: Princeton University Press.

Geertz, Clifford. 1960. *The Religion of Java.* New York: Free Press of Glencoe.

———. 1963. "The Integrative Revolution: Primordial Sentiments and Civil Politics in the New States." In Clifford Geertz, ed., *Old Societies and New States: The Quest for Modernity in Asia and Africa,* pp. 105–157. New York: Free Press.

Gehring, Albert. 1908. *Racial Contrasts: Distinguishing Traits of the Graeco-Latins and Teutons.* New York: G. P. Putnam's Sons.

Geiss, Immanuel. 1988. *Geschichte des Rassismus.* Frankfurt am Main: Suhrkamp.

Gelder, Geert Jan van. 2000. *God's Banquet: Food in Classical Arabic Literature.* New York: Columbia University Press.

Gellately, Robert. 1990. *The Gestapo and German Society: Enforcing Racial Policy 1933–1945.* Oxford: Clarendon Press.

———. 2001. *Backing Hitler: Consent and Coercion in Nazi Germany.* Oxford: Oxford University Press.

Gellner, Ernest. 1983. *Nations and Nationalism.* Ithaca, N.Y.: Cornell University Press.

———. 1997. *Nationalism.* New York: New York University Press.

Gelman, Susan A. 2003. *The Essential Child: Origins of Essentialism in Everyday Thought.* Oxford: Oxford University Press.

Genovese, Eugene D. 1974. *Roll, Jordan, Roll: The World the Slaves Made.* New York: Pantheon.

———. 1994. *The Southern Tradition: The Achievement and Limitations of an American Conservatism.* Cambridge, Mass.: Harvard University Press.

Gentile, Giovanni. [1946] 1960. *Genesis and Structure of Society,* trans. H. S. Harris. Urbana: University of Illinois Press.

Geras, Norman. 1998. *The Contract of Mutual Indifference: Political Philosophy after the Holocaust.* London: Verso.

Gerbi, Antonello. 1955. *La disputa del Nuovo Mondo: storia di una polemica, 1750–1900.* Milano: Riccardo Ricciardi.

Geremek, Bronislaw. [1987] 1990. "The Marginal Man." In Jacques Le Goff, ed., *Medieval Callings,* trans. Lydia G. Cochrane, pp. 347–373. Chicago: University of Chicago Press.

———. [1991] 1996. *The Common Roots of Europe,* trans. Jan Aleksandrowicz, J. K. Fedorowicz, Rosemary Hunt, Agnieszka Kolakowska, and Shayne Mitchell. Cambridge: Polity.

Gergen, Kenneth J. 1991. *The Saturated Self: Dilemmas of Identity in Contemporary Life.* New York: Basic Books.

Gernet, Jacques. [1959] 1970. *Daily Life in China on the Eve of the Mongol Invasion, 1250–1276,* trans. H. M. Wright. Stanford, Calif.: Stanford University Press.

Gernet, Louis. [1968] 1981. *The Anthropology of Ancient Greece,* trans. John Hamilton, S.J., and Blaise Nagy. Baltimore: Johns Hopkins University Press.

Gerstle, Gary. 2001. *American Crucible: Race and Nation in the Twentieth Century.* Princeton, N.J.: Princeton University Press.

Getty, J. Arch, and Oleg V. Naumov. 1999. *The Road to Terror: Stalin and the Self-Destruction of the Bolsheviks, 1932–1939.* New Haven, Conn.: Yale University Press.

Geyer, Michael, and John W. Boyer, eds. [1992] 1994. *Resistance against the Third Reich, 1933–1990.* Chicago: University of Chicago Press.

Giddens, Anthony. 1991. *Modernity and Self-Identity: Self and Society in the Late Modern Age.* Stanford, Calif.: Stanford University Press.

Giesen, Bernhard. 1993. *Die Intellektuellen und die Nation: Eine deutsche Achsenzeit.* Frankfurt am Main: Suhrkamp.

Gil, Moshe. [1983] 1992. *A History of Palestine, 634–1099,* trans. Ethel Broido. Cambridge: Cambridge University Press.

Gilbert, Felix. 1988. *A European Past: Memoirs, 1905–1945.* New York: W. W. Norton.

———. 1990. *History: Politics or Culture? Reflections on Ranke and Burckhardt.* Princeton, N.J.: Princeton University Press.

Gildea, Robert. 1987. *Barricades and Borders: Europe, 1800–1914.* Oxford: Oxford University Press.

Gilman, Sander L. 1986. *Jewish Self-Hatred: Anti-Semitism and the Hidden Language of the Jews.* Baltimore: Johns Hopkins University Press.

———. 1991. *The Jew's Body.* New York: Routledge.

Gilroy, Paul. [1987] 1991. *"There Ain't No Black in the Union Jack": The Cultural Politics of Race and Nation.* Chicago: University of Chicago Press.

———. 2000. *Against Race: Imagining Political Culture beyond the Color Line.* Cambridge, Mass.: Harvard University Press.

Ginsburg, Faye D., and Rayna Rapp. 1995. "Introduction: Conceiving the New World Order." In Faye D. Ginsburg and Rayna Rapp, eds., *Conceiving the New World Order: The Global Politics of Reproduction,* pp. 1–17. Berkeley: University of California Press.

Ginzburg, Carlo. [1976/1980] 1982. *The Cheese and the Worms: The Cosmos of a Sixteenth-Century Miller,* trans. John Tedeschi and Anne Tedeschi. Harmondsworth, U.K.: Penguin.

Girardet, Raoul, ed. 1966. *Le nationalisme française 1871–1914.* Paris: Armand Colin.

Gittings, John. 1993. "The Indonesian Massacres, 1965–1966: Image and Reality." In Mark Levene and Penny Roberts, eds., *The Massacre in History,* pp. 247–262. New York: Berghahn Books.

Gjerset, Knut. 1924. *History of Iceland.* New York: Macmillan.

Glacken, Clarence J. 1967. *Traces on the Rhodian Shore: Nature and Culture in Western Thought from Ancient Times to the End of the Eighteenth Century.* Berkeley: University of California Press.

Glazer, Nathan. [1957/1972] 1989. *American Judaism,* 2nd ed., rev. Chicago: University of Chicago Press.

Glazer, Nathan, and Daniel P. Moynihan. [1963] 1970. *Beyond the Melting Pot: The Negroes, Puerto Ricans, Jews, Italians, and Irish of New York City,* 2nd ed. Cambridge, Mass.: MIT Press.

———. 1975. "Introduction." In Nathan Glazer and Daniel P. Moynihan, eds., *Ethnicity: Theory and Experience,* pp. 1–26. Cambridge, Mass.: Harvard University Press.

Gluckman, Max. 1940. "The Kingdom of the Zulu of South Africa." In M. Fortes and E. E. Evans-Pritchard, ed., *African Political Systems,* pp. 25–55. London: Oxford University Press.

Gobineau, Arthur de. [1853] 1966. *The Inequality of the Human Races,* trans. Adrian Collins. Torrance, Calif.: Noontide Press.

Godechot, Jacques. [1956] 1983. *La grande nation: l'expansion révolutionnaire de la France dans le monde de 1789 à 1799,* 2nd ed. Paris: Aubier Montaigne.

———. 1988. "The New Concept of the Nation and Its Diffusion in Europe." In Otto Dann and John Dinwiddy, eds., *Nationalism in the Age of the French Revolution,* pp. 13–26. London: Hambledon Press.

Goebbels, Joseph. [1940] 1979. *My Part in Germany's Fight,* trans. Kurt Fiedler. New York: Howard Fertig.

Goering, Hermann. 1934. *Germany Reborn.* London: Elkin Mathews & Marrot.

Goethe, Johann Wolfgang von. 1986. *Essays on Art and Literature,* ed. John Gearey, trans. Ellen von Nardroff and Ernest H. von Nardroff. New York: Suhrkamp.

Goffman, Erving. 1959. *The Presentation of Self in Everyday Life.* Garden City, N.Y.: Doubleday Anchor.

———. [1963] 1974. *Stigma: Notes on the Management of Spoiled Identity.* New York: Jason Aronson.

Goitein, S. D. 1999. *A Mediterranean Society,* an abridgment in 1 vol., rev. and ed. Jacob Lassner. Berkeley: University of California Press.

Goldberg, David Theo. 1993. *Racist Culture: Philosophy and the Politics of Meaning.* Oxford: Blackwell.

Goldhill, Simon. 2002. *Who Needs Greek? Contests in the Cultural History of Hellenism.* Cambridge: Cambridge University Press.

Goldsby, Richard. [1971] 1977. *Race and Races,* 2nd ed. New York: Macmillan.

Goldthorpe, John H., David Lockwood, Frank Bechhofer, and Jennifer Platt. 1968. *The Affluent Worker,* vol. 2: *Political Attitudes and Behaviour.* Cambridge: Cambridge University Press.

Goldziher, Ignaz. [1889–90] 1966. *Muslim Studies,* vol. 1, ed. S. M. Stern, trans. C. R. Barber and S. M. Stern. London: George Allen & Unwin.

Gomme, A. W. 1933. *The Population of Athens in the Fifth and Fourth Centuries B.C.* Oxford: Oxford University Press.

Goodman, David G., and Masanori Miyazawa. 1995. *Jews in the Japanese Mind: The History and Uses of a Cultural Stereotype.* New York: Free Press.

Goodman, Martin. 1983. *State and Society in Roman Galilee, A.D. 132–212.* Totowa, N.J.: Rowman and Allanheld.

———. 1987. *The Ruling Class of Judaea: The Origins of the Jewish Revolt against Rome: A.D. 66–70.* Cambridge: Cambridge University Press.

———. 1994. *Mission and Conversion: Proselytizing in the Religious History of the Roman Empire.* Oxford: Clarendon Press.

———. 1998. "Jews, Greeks, and Romans." In Martin Goodman, ed., *Jews in a Graeco-Roman World,* pp. 3–14. Oxford: Clarendon Press.

Goody, Jack. 1982. *Cooking, Cuisine and Class: A Study in Comparative Sociology.* Cambridge: Cambridge University Press.

———. 1998. *Food and Love: A Cultural History of East and West.* London: Verso.

Gordon, Sarah. 1984. *Hitler, Germans and the "Jewish Question."* Princeton, N.J.: Princeton University Press.

Gossett, Thomas F. [1963] 1997. *Race: The History of an Idea in America,* new ed. New York: Oxford University Press.

Gottwald, Norman K. 1979. *The Tribes of Yahweh: A Sociology of the Religion of Liberated Israel, 1250–1050 B.C.E.* Maryknoll, N.Y.: Orbis Books.

Goubert, Pierre. [1982] 1986. *The French Peasantry in the Seventeenth Century,* trans. Ian Patterson. Cambridge: Cambridge University Press.

Gould, Stephen Jay. [1981] 1996. *The Mismeasure of Man,* rev. ed. New York: W. W. Norton.

———. 1999. *Rocks of Ages: Science and Religion in the Fullness of Life.* New York: Ballantine.

Gourevitch, Philip. 1998. *We Wish to Inform You That Tomorrow We Will Be Killed with Our Families: Stories from Rwanda.* New York: Farrar, Straus & Giroux.

———. 2003. "The Optimist." *New Yorker* March 3, pp. 50–73.

Gourgouris, Stathis. 1996. *Dream Nation: Enlightenment, Colonization and the Institution of Modern Greece.* Stanford, Calif.: Stanford University Press.

Graetz, H. 1891. *History of the Jews,* vol. 1: *From the Earliest Period to the Death of Simon the Maccabee (135 B.C.E.),* trans. Bella Löwy. Philadelphia: Jewish Publication Society of America.

Graml, Hermann. [1988] 1992. *Anti-semitism in the Third Reich,* trans. Tim Kirk. Oxford: Blackwell.

Grant, Madison. 1916. *The Passing of the Great Race or the Racial Basis of European History.* New York: Charles Scribner's Sons.

Grau, Günter, ed. 1993. *Homosexualität in der NS-Zeit: Dokumente einer Diskriminierung und Verfolgung.* Frankfurt am Main: Fischer.

Gray, J. Glenn. [1959] 1970. *The Warriors: Reflections on Men in Battle,* 2nd ed. New York: Harper & Row.

Green, Abigail. 2001. *Fatherlands: State-Building and Nationhood in Nineteenth-Century Germany.* Cambridge: Cambridge University Press.

Greenfeld, Liah. 1992. *Nationalism: Five Roads to Modernity.* Cambridge, Mass.: Harvard University Press.

Gregory, James N. 1989. *American Exodus: The Dust Bowl Migration and Okie Culture in California.* New York: Oxford University Press.

Greisch, Jean. 2002. *Le buisson ardent et les lumières de la raison: l'invention de la philosophie de la religion, tome 1: héritages et héritiers du XIXᵉ siècle.* Paris: Cerf.

Grenville, John A. S. 1998. "Neglected Holocaust Victims: The Mischlinge, the Jüdischversippte, and the Gypsies." In Michael Berenbaum and Abraham J. Peck, eds., *The Holocaust and History: The Known, the Unknown, the Disputed, and the Reexamined,* pp. 315–326. Bloomington: Indiana University Press.

Griffin, Roger. 1991. *The Nature of Fascism.* London: Pinter.

Grillo, R. D. 1989. *Dominant Languages: Language and Hierarchy in Britain and France.* Cambridge: Cambridge University Press.

Grimm, Jacob, and Wilhelm Grimm. [1812–15] 1997. *Kinder- und Hausmärchen,* ed. Heinz Rölleke. Stuttgart: Philipp Reclam jun.

Grossmann, Atina. 1995. *Reforming Sex: The German Movement for Birth Control and Abortion Reform, 1920–1950.* New York: Oxford University Press.

Gruen, Erich S. 1998. *Heritage and Hellenism: The Reinvention of Jewish Tradition.* Berkeley: University of California Press.

Gruzinski, Serge. 1988. *La colonisation de l'imaginaire: sociétés indigènes et occidentalisation dans le Mexique espagnol XVIᵉ–XVIIIᵉ siècle.* Paris: Gallimard.

Gschnitzer, Fritz. 1981. *Griechische Sozialgeschichte: Von der mykenischen bis zum Ausgang der klassischen Zeit.* Wiesbaden, Germany: Steiner.

Guérin, Daniel. 1994. *The Brown Plague: Travels in Late Weimar and Early Nazi Germany,* trans. Robert Schwartzwald. Durham, N.C.: Duke University Press.

Gulick, Edward Vose. [1955] 1967. *Europe's Classical Balance of Power.* New York: W. W. Norton.

Gumplowicz, Ludwig. [1883] 1928. *Der Rassenkampf.* Innsbruck: Universitäts-Verlag Wagner.

Gunn, Geoffrey C. 1994. *A Critical View of Western Journalism and Scholarship on East Timor.* Manila, Philippines: Journal of Contemporary Asia Publishers.

Guterl, Matthew Pratt. 2001. *The Color of Race in America, 1900–1940.* Cambridge, Mass.: Harvard University Press.

Gutiérrez, David G. 1995. *Walls and Mirrors: Mexican Americans, Mexican Immigrants, and the Politics of Ethnicity.* Berkeley: University of California Press.

Gutiérrez, Ramón A. 1991. *When Jesus Came, the Corn Mothers Went Away: Marriage, Sexuality, and Power in New Mexico, 1500–1846.* Stanford, Calif.: Stanford University Press.

Guyot, Gary W. 1998. "Attachment in Mammals." In Gary Greenberg and Maury M. Haraway, eds., *Comparative Psychology: A Handbook,* pp. 509–516. New York: Garland.

Habermas, Jürgen. 1962. *Strukturwandel der Öffentlichkeit.* Darmstadt, Germany: Hermann Luchterhand.

Hadas, Moses. [1959] 1972. *Hellenistic Culture: Fusion and Diffusion.* New York: W. W. Norton.

Haddon, A. C. 1925. *The Races of Man and Their Distribution.* New York: Macmillan.

Hagen, William W. 1980. *Germans, Poles, and Jews: The Nationality Conflict in the Prussian East, 1772–1914.* Chicago: University of Chicago Press.

Haldane, J. B. S. [1932] 1990. *The Causes of Evolution.* Princeton, N.J.: Princeton University Press.

Hall, Edith. 1989. *Inventing the Barbarian: Greek Self-Definition through Tragedy.* Oxford: Clarendon Press.

Hall, Jonathan M. 1997. *Ethnic Identity in Greek Antiquity.* Cambridge: Cambridge University Press.

———. 2002. *Hellenicity: Between Ethnicity and Culture.* Chicago: University of Chicago Press.

Hall, Stuart. 1990. "Cultural Identity and Diaspora." In Jonathan Rutherford, ed., *Identity: Community, Culture, Difference,* pp. 222–237. London: Lawrence & Wishart.

———. 1996. "The Formation of a Diasporic Intellectual: An Interview with Stuart Hall by Kuan-Hsing Chen." In David Morley and Kuan-Hsing Chen, eds., *Stuart Hall: Critical Dialogues in Cultural Studies,* pp. 484–503. London: Routledge.

Haller, Mark H. 1963. *Eugenics: Hereditarian Attitudes in American Thought.* New Brunswick, N.J.: Rutgers University Press.

Hamann, Brigitte. 1999. *Hitler's Vienna: A Dictator's Apprenticeship,* trans. Thomas Thornton. New York: Oxford University Press.

Hamerow, Theodore S. 1958. *Restoration, Revolution, Reaction: Economics and Politics in Germany, 1815–1871.* Princeton, N.J.: Princeton University Press.

———. 1969–72. *The Social Foundations of German Unification 1858–1871,* 2 vols. Princeton, N.J.: Princeton University Press.

———. 1997. *On the Road to the Wolf's Lair: German Resistance to Hitler.* Cambridge, Mass.: Harvard University Press.

Hammond, N. G. L. 1989. *The Macedonian State: Origins, Institutions, and History.* Oxford: Clarendon Press.

Hance, William A. [1964] 1975. *The Geography of Modern Africa,* 2nd ed. New York: Columbia University Press.

Hanchard, Michael George. 1994. *Orpheus and Power: The Movimento Negro of Rio de Janeiro and São Paulo, Brazil, 1945–1988.* Princeton, N.J.: Princeton University Press.

Hanke, Lewis. [1959] 1970. *Aristotle and the American Indians: A Study in Race Prejudice in the Modern World.* Bloomington: Indiana University Press.

———. 1974. *All Mankind Is One: A Study of the Disputation between Bartolomé de Las Casas and Juan Ginés de Sepúlveda in 1550 on the Intellectual and Religious Captivity of the American Indians.* DeKalb: Northern Illinois University Press.

Hankins, Frank H. 1926. *The Racial Basis of Civilization: A Critique of the Nordic Doctrine.* New York: Alfred A. Knopf.

Hannaford, Ivan. 1996. *Race: The History of an Idea in the West.* Washington, D.C.: Woodrow Wilson Center Press.

Hannerz, Ulf. 1974. "Ethnicity and Opportunity in Urban America." In Abner Cohen, ed., *Urban Ethnicity,* pp. 37–76. London: Tavistock.

Hansen, Klaus J. 1981. *Mormonism and the American Experience.* Chicago: University of Chicago Press.

Hansen, Thomas Blom. 1999. *The Saffron Wave: Democracy and Hindu Nationalism in Modern India.* Princeton, N.J.: Princeton University Press.

Hanson, Paul D. 1978. *Dynamic Transcendence.* Philadelphia: Fortress Press.

Hardach, Karl. [1976] 1980. *The Political Economy of Germany in the Twentieth Century.* Berkeley: University of California Press.

Hardacre, Helen. 1989. *Shintō and the State, 1868–1988.* Princeton, N.J.: Princeton University Press.

Harding, Harry. [1993] 1997. "The Chinese State in Crisis, 1966–9." In Roderick MacFarquhar, ed., *The Politics of China: The Eras of Mao and Deng,* 2nd ed., pp. 148–247. Cambridge: Cambridge University Press.

Harff, Barbara. 1992. "Recognizing Genocides and Politicides." In Helen Fein, ed., *Genocide Watch,* pp. 27–41. New Haven, Conn.: Yale University Press.

Hargreaves, John D. [1988] 1996. *Decolonization in Africa,* 2nd ed. London: Longman.

Harrington, James. [1656] 1992. "The Commonwealth of Oceana." In James Harrington, *The Commonwealth of Oceana and a System of Politics,* ed. J. G. A. Pocock, pp. 1–266. Cambridge: Cambridge University Press.

Harris, Eddy L. 1992. *Native Stranger: A Black American's Journey into the Heart of Africa.* New York: Simon & Schuster.

Harris, H. S. 1983. *Hegel's Development: Night Thoughts (Jena 1801–1806).* Oxford: Clarendon Press.

Harris, Leonard. 2001. " 'Outing' Alain Locke: Empowering the Silenced." In Mark Blasius, *Sexual Identities, Queer Politics,* pp. 321–342. Princeton, N.J.: Princeton University Press.

Harrison, G. Ainsworth. 1995. *The Human Biology of the English Village.* Oxford: Oxford University Press.

Harrison, Peter. 1990. *"Religion" and the Religions in the English Enlightenment.* Cambridge: Cambridge University Press.

Harshav, Benjamin. 1993. *Language in Time of Revolution.* Berkeley: University of California Press.

Hart, John Mason. 1987. *Revolutionary Mexico: The Coming and Process of the Mexican Revolution.* Berkeley: University of California Press.

Hartog, François. [1980] 1988. *The Mirror of Herodotus: The Representation of the Other in the Writing of History,* trans. Janet Lloyd. Berkeley: University of California Press.

Hartz, Louis. 1955. *The Liberal Tradition in America: An Interpretation of American Political Thought since the Revolution.* New York: Harcourt, Brace.

Harvey, Graham. 1996. *The True Israel: Uses of the Names Jew, Hebrew and Israel in Ancient Jewish and Early Christian Literature.* Leiden: E. J. Brill.

Haslam, Jonathan. 2002. *No Virtue Like Necessity: Realist Thought in International Relations since Machiavelli.* New Haven, Conn.: Yale University Press.

Hastrup, Kirsten. 1985. *Culture and History in Medieval Iceland: An Anthropological Analysis of Structure and Change.* Oxford: Clarendon Press.

———. 1990a. *Island of Anthropology: Studies in Past and Present Iceland.* Odense: Odense University Press.

———. 1990b. *Nature and Policy in Iceland 1400–1800: An Anthropological Analysis of History and Mentality.* Oxford: Clarendon Press.

———. 1998. *A Place Apart: An Anthropological Study of the Icelandic World.* Oxford: Clarendon Press.

Haugen, Einar. 1966. *Language Conflict and Language Planning: The Case of Modern Norwegian.* Cambridge, Mass.: Harvard University Press.

Haupt, Georges. [1965] 1972. *Socialism and the Great War: The Collapse of the Second International.* Oxford: Clarendon Press.

Hayes, Carlton J. H. 1931. *The Historical Evolution of Modern Nationalism.* New York: Richard R. Smith.

Hazareesingh, Sudhir. 1994. *Political Traditions in Modern France.* Oxford: Oxford University Press.

———. 1998. *From Subject to Citizen: The Second Empire and the Emergence of Modern French Democracy.* Princeton, N.J.: Princeton University Press.

Hechter, Michael. 1975. *Internal Colonialism: The Celtic Fringe in British National Development, 1536–1966.* Berkeley: University of California Press.

———. 2000. *Containing Nationalism.* Oxford: Oxford University Press.

Heers, Jacques. 1995. *Libérer Jérusalem: la première croisade (1095–1107)*. Paris: Perrin.

Hegel, G. W. F. [1807] 1977. *Phenomenology of Spirit*, trans. A. V. Miller. Oxford: Clarendon Press.

———. [1820] 1991. *Elements of the Philosophy of Right*, ed. Allen W. Wood, trans. H. B. Nisbet. Cambridge: Cambridge University Press.

Heidegger, Martin. [1927] 1962. *Being and Time*, trans. John Macquarrie and Edward Robinson. New York: Harper & Row.

Hengel, Martin. [1976] 1980. *Jews, Greeks and Barbarians: Aspects of the Hellenization of Judaism in the pre-Christian Period*, trans. John Bowden. Philadelphia: Fortress Press.

———. 1989. *The "Hellenization" of Judaea in the First Century after Christ*, trans. John Bowden. London: SCM Press.

Herbert, Ulrich. [1986] 1990. *A History of Foreign Labor in Germany, 1880–1980: Seasonal Workers/Forced Laborers/Guest Workers*, trans. William Templer. Ann Arbor: University of Michigan Press.

———. 1998. "Vernichtungspolitik: Neue Antworten und Fragen zur Geschichte des 'Holocaust.' " In Ulrich Herbert, ed., *Nationalsozialistische Vernichtungspolitik 1939–1945: Neue Forschungen und Kontroversen*, pp. 9–66. Frankfurt am Main: Fischer.

———. 2001. *Geschichte der Ausländerpolitik in Deutschland: Saisonarbeiter, Zwangsarbeiter, Gastarbeiter, Flüchtlinge*. München: C. H. Beck.

Herder, Johann Gottfried. [1793–97] 1991. *Werke, bard 7: Briefe zu Beförderung der Humanität*, ed. Hans Dietrich Irmscher. Frankfurt am Main: Deutscher Klassiker Verlag.

Herodotus. 1987. *The History*, trans. David Grene. Chicago: University of Chicago Press.

Herskovits, Melville J. 1930. *The Anthropometry of the American Negro*. New York: Columbia University Press.

———. [1925] 1968. "The Negro's Americanism." In Alain Locke, ed., *The New Negro: An Interpretation*, pp. 353–360. New York: Arno Press.

Hertz, Friedrich. [1928] 1970. *Race and Civilization*, trans. A. S. Levetus and W. Entz. n.p.: KTAV.

Hertzberg, Arthur, ed. [1959] 1969. *The Zionist Idea: A Historical Analysis and Reader*. New York: Atheneum.

Herzl, Theodor. [1896] 1946. *The Jewish State: An Attempt at a Modern Solution of the Jewish Question*, trans. Jacob M. Alkow. New York: American Jewish Emergency Council.

Hewitson, Mark. 2000. *National Identity and Political Thought in Germany: Wilhelmine Depictions of the French Third Republic, 1890–1914*. Oxford: Clarendon Press.

Higham, John. [1955] 1974. *Strangers in the Land: Patterns of American Nativism 1860–1925.* New York: Atheneum.

Higonnet, Patrice. 1994. "The Harmonization of the Spheres: Goodness and Dysfunctions in the Provincial Clubs." In Keith Michael Baker, ed., *The French Revolution and the Creation of Modern Culture,* vol. 4: *The Terror,* pp. 117–137. Oxford: Pergamon Press.

Hilberg, Raul. 1985. *The Destruction of the European Jews,* rev. ed., 3 vols. New York: Holmes & Meier.

———. [1985] 1989. "The Statistic." In François Furet, ed., *Unanswered Questions: Nazi Germany and the Genocide of the Jews,* pp. 155–171. New York: Schocken.

Hill, Polly. 1986. *Development Economics on Trial: The Anthropological Case for a Prosecution.* Cambridge: Cambridge University Press.

Himmelfarb, Gertrude. 1983. *The Idea of Poverty: England in the Early Industrial Age.* New York: Alfred A. Knopf.

Hinsley, F. H. 1963. *Power and the Pursuit of Peace: Theory and Practice in the History of Relations between States.* Cambridge: Cambridge University Press.

———. [1966] 1986. *Sovereignty,* 2nd ed. Cambridge: Cambridge University Press.

Hintze, Otto. [1906] 1975. "Military Organization and the Organization of the State." In Otto Hintze, ed., *The Historical Essays of Otto Hintze,* ed. Felix Gilbert, pp. 178–215. New York: Oxford University Press.

Hirschfeld, Lawrence A. 1996. *Race in the Making: Cognition, Culture, and the Child's Construction of Human Kinds.* Cambridge, Mass.: MIT Press.

Hitchins, Keith. 1969. *The Rumanian National Movement in Transylvania, 1780–1849.* Cambridge, Mass.: Harvard University Press.

Hitler, Adolf. [1925] 1943. *Mein Kampf,* trans. Ralph Manheim. Boston: Houghton Mifflin.

Hitti, Philip K. [1937] 1970. *History of the Arabs: From the Earliest Times to the Present,* 10th ed. New York: St. Martin's Press.

Hobbes, Thomas. [1651] 1996. *Leviathan,* rev. student ed., ed. Richard Tuck. Cambridge: Cambridge University Press.

———. [1647] 1998. *On the Citizen,* ed. and trans. Richard Tuck and Michael Silverthorne. Cambridge: Cambridge University Press.

Hoberman, John. 1997. *Darwin's Athletes: How Sport Has Damaged Black America and Preserved the Myth of Race.* Boston: Houghton Mifflin.

Hobsbawm, E. J. [Eric]. 1983a. "Introduction: Inventing Traditions." In Eric Hobsbawm and Terence Ranger, eds., *The Invention of Tradition,* pp. 1–14. Cambridge: Cambridge University Press.

———. 1983b. "Mass-Producing Traditions: Europe, 1870–1914." In Eric Hobsbawm and Terence Ranger, eds., *The Invention of Tradition,* pp. 263–307. Cambridge: Cambridge University Press.

――――. [1990] 1992. *Nations and Nationalism since 1780: Programme, Myth, Reality*, 2nd ed. Cambridge: Cambridge University Press.

――――. 2002. "War and Peace in the 20th Century." *London Review of Books* February 21, pp. 16–18.

Hochschild, Jennifer L. 1995. *Facing Up to the American Dream: Race, Class, and the Soul of the Nation*. Princeton, N.J.: Princeton University Press.

Hodgen, Margaret T. 1964. *Early Anthropology in the Sixteenth and Seventeenth Centuries*. Philadelphia: University of Pennsylvania Press.

Hodgkin, Thomas. [1956] 1957. *Nationalism in Colonial Africa*. New York: New York University Press.

Hodgson, Marshall G. S. 1974. *The Venture of Islam*, 3 vols. Chicago: University of Chicago Press.

Hödl, Klaus. 1997. *Die Pathologisierung des jüdischen Körpers: Antisemitismus, Geschlecht und Medizin im Fin de Siècle*. Wien: Picus.

Hoerder, Dirk. 2002. *Cultures in Contact: World Migrations in the Second Millennium*. Durham, N.C.: Duke University Press.

Hoess, Rudolf. [1951] 1959. *Commandant of Auschwitz: The Autobiography of Rudolf Hoess*, trans. Constantine FitzGibbon. Cleveland: World Publishing.

Hoffman, Stanley. 1974. *Decline or Renewal? France since the 1930s*. New York: Viking.

Hoffmann, Peter. [1969] 1996. *The History of the German Resistance, 1933–1945*, 3rd ed., trans. Richard Barry. Montreal: McGill-Queen's University Press.

Hofstadter, Richard. [1965] 1996. *The Paranoid Style in American Politics and Other Essays*. Cambridge, Mass.: Harvard University Press.

Hogben, Lancelot. 1932. *Genetic Principles in Medicine and Social Science*. New York: Alfred A. Knopf.

――――. 1939. *Dangerous Thoughts*. London: George Allen & Unwin.

Hoggart, Richard. [1957] 1958. *The Uses of Literacy: Aspects of Working-Class Life with Special Reference to Publications and Entertainments*. Harmondsworth, U.K.: Penguin.

Hohmann, Joachim. 1981. *Geschichte der Zigeunerverfolgung in Deutschland*. Frankfurt am Main: Campus.

Holcomb, Bonnie K., and Sisai Ibssa. 1990. *The Invention of Ethiopia*. Trenton, N.J.: Red Sea Press.

Hollinger, David A. 1995. *Postethnic America: Beyond Multiculturalism*. New York: Basic Books.

Holloway, Jonathan Scott. 2002. *Confronting the Veil: Abram Harris Jr., E. Franklin Frazier, and Ralph Bunche, 1919–1941*. Chapel Hill: University of North Carolina Press.

Holmes, Samuel J. 1921. *The Trend of the Race: A Study of Present Tendencies in the Biological Development of Civilized Mankind*. New York: Harcourt, Brace.

Holt, Thomas C. 2000. *The Problem of Race in the 21st Century*. Cambridge, Mass.: Harvard University Press.

Homze, Edward L. 1967. *Foreign Labor in Nazi Germany*. Princeton, N.J.: Princeton University Press.

Honda Katsuichi. 1993. *The Impoverished Spirit in Contemporary Japan*, ed. John Lie, trans. Eri Fujieda, Masayuki Hamazaki, and John Lie. New York: Monthly Review Press.

Hong, Young-Sun. 1998. *Welfare, Modernity, and the Weimar State, 1919–1933*. Princeton, N.J.: Princeton University Press.

Honig, Bonnie. 2001. *Democracy and the Foreigner*. Princeton, N.J.: Princeton University Press.

Honig, Emily. 1992. *Creating Chinese Ethnicity: Subei People in Shanghai, 1850–1980*. New Haven, Conn.: Yale University Press.

Hopkins, John Henry. 1864. *Scriptural, Ecclesiastical, and Historical View of Slavery, from the Days of the Patriarch Abraham, to the Nineteenth Century*. New York: W. I. Pooley.

Hopkins, Keith. 1978. *Conquerors and Slaves*. Cambridge: Cambridge University Press.

Horowitz, Donald L. 1985. *Ethnic Groups in Conflict*. Berkeley: University of California Press.

———. 2001. *The Deadly Ethnic Riot*. Berkeley: University of California Press.

Horowitz, Irving Louis. 1976. *Genocide: State Power and Mass Murder*. New Brunswick, N.J.: Transaction.

Horrocks, Geoffrey C. 1997. *Greek: A History of the Language and Its Speakers*. London: Longman.

Horsley, Richard A. 1995. *Galilee: History, Politics, People*. Valley Forge, Penn.: Trinity Press International.

———. 1996. *Archaeology, History, and Society in Galilee: The Social Context of Jesus and the Rabbis*. Valley Forge, Penn.: Trinity Press International.

Horsman, Reginald. 1981. *Race and Manifest Destiny: The Origins of American Racial Anglo-Saxonism*. Cambridge, Mass.: Harvard University Press.

Hosking, Geoffrey. 1985. *The First Socialist Society: A History of the Soviet Union from Within*. Cambridge, Mass.: Harvard University Press.

———. 1998. "Can Russia Become a Nation-State?" *Nations and Nationalism* 4: 449–462.

Houghton, Philip. 1996. *People of the Great Ocean: Aspects of Human Biology of the Early Pacific*. Cambridge: Cambridge University Press.

Hourani, Albert. [1962] 1983. *Arabic Thought in the Liberal Age 1798–1939*. Cambridge: Cambridge University Press.

Hovannisian, Richard G. 1986. "The Historical Dimensions of the Armenian Question, 1878–1923." In Richard G. Hovannisian, ed., *The Armenian Genocide in Perspective*, pp. 19–41. New Brunswick, N.J.: Transaction.

———. 1992. "Intervention and Shades of Altruism during the Armenian Genocide." In Richard G. Hovannisian, ed., *The Armenian Genocide: History, Politics, Ethics,* pp. 173–207. New York: St. Martin's Press.

———. 1999. "Introduction: The Armenian Genocide: Remembrance and Denial." In Richard G. Hovannisian, ed., *Remembrance and Denial: The Case of the Armenian Genocide,* pp. 13–21. Detroit: Wayne State University Press.

Howard, Michael. 1978. *War and the Liberal Conscience.* New Brunswick, N.J.: Rutgers University Press.

———. 1983. *The Causes of Wars and Other Essays.* Cambridge, Mass.: Harvard University Press.

———. 2000. *The Invention of Peace: Reflections on War and International Order.* New Haven, Conn.: Yale University Press.

Howe, Irving. [1976] 1994. *World of Our Fathers: The Journey of the East European Jews to America and the Life They Found and Made.* New York: Galahad.

Hroch, Miroslav. 1985. *Social Preconditions of National Revival in Europe: A Comparative Analysis of the Social Composition of Patriotic Groups among the Smaller European Nations,* trans. Ben Fowkes. Cambridge: Cambridge University Press.

Hsieh, Shih-Chung. 1994. "From *Shanbao* to *Yuanzhumin:* Taiwan Aborigines in Transition." In Murray A. Rubinstein, ed., *The Other Taiwan: 1945 to the Present,* pp. 404–419. Armonk, N.Y.: M. E. Sharpe.

Hughes, Henry. 1854. *Treatise on Sociology, Theoretical and Practical.* Philadelphia: Lippincott, Grambo.

Hughes, Michael. 1988. *Nationalism and Society: Germany 1800–1945.* London: Edward Arnold.

Human Rights Watch [Alison Des Forges]. 1999. *"Leave None to Tell the Story":
Genocide in Rwanda.* New York: Human Rights Watch.

Human Rights Watch/Africa. 1994. *Civilian Devastation: Abuses by All Parties in the War in Southern Sudan.* New York: Human Rights Watch.

———. 1996. *Behind the Red Line: Political Repression in Sudan.* New York: Human Rights Watch.

Human Rigths Watch/Asia. 1997. *Indonesia/East Timor: Deteriorating Human Rights in East Timor.* New York: Human Rights Watch.

Hume, David. [1777/1888] 1978. *A Treatise on Human Nature,* 2nd ed., ed. L. A. Selby-Bigge. Oxford: Clarendon Press.

———. [1777/1985] 1987. *Essays, Moral, Political, and Literary,* rev. ed., ed. Eugene F. Miller. Indianapolis: LibertyClassics.

Hunczak, Taras. 1990. "The Ukrainian Losses during World War II." In Michael Berenbaum, ed., *A Mosaic of Victims: Non-Jews Persecuted and Murdered by the Nazis,* pp. 116–127. New York: New York University Press.

Hunt, Lynn. 1984. *Politics, Culture, and Class in the French Revolution.* Berkeley: University of California Press.

Hutchinson, George. 1995. *The Harlem Renaissance in Black and White.* Cambridge, Mass.: Harvard University Press.

Hutchinson, Sharon E. 1996. *Nuer Dilemmas: Coping with Money, War, and the State.* Berkeley: University of California Press.

Huxley, Julian S., and A. C. Haddon. 1935. *We Europeans: A Survey of "Racial" Problems.* London: Jonathan Cape.

Hymes, Dell. 1967. "Linguistic Problems in Defining the Concept of 'Tribe.' " In June Helm, ed., *Essays on the Problem of Tribe,* pp. 23–48. Seattle: University of Washington Press.

Ignatieff, Michael. 1993. *Blood and Belonging: Journeys into the New Nationalism.* New York: Farrar, Straus & Giroux.

Ignatiev, Noel. 1995. *How the Irish Became White.* New York: Routledge.

Iliffe, John. 1979. *A Modern History of Tanganyika.* Cambridge: Cambridge University Press.

———. 1995. *Africans: The History of a Continent.* Cambridge: Cambridge University Press.

Im Hof, Ulrich, and François de Capitani. 1983. *Die helvetische Gesellschaft: Spätaufklärung und Vorrevolution in der Schweiz,* 2 vols. Franenfeld: Huber.

Inden, Ronald. 1990. *Imagining India.* Oxford: Blackwell.

Iriye, Akira. 2002. *Global Community: The Role of International Organizations in the Making of the Contemporary World.* Berkeley: University of California Press.

Irschick, Eugene F. 1994. *Dialogue and History: Constructing South India, 1795–1895.* Berkeley: University of California Press.

Isaacs, Harold R. 1975. "Basic Group Identity: The Idols of the Tribe." In Nathan Glazer and Daniel P. Moynihan, eds., *Ethnicity: Theory and Experience,* pp. 29–52. Cambridge, Mass.: Harvard University Press.

Isherwood, Christopher. 1976. *Christopher and His Kind, 1929–1939.* New York: Farrar, Straus & Giroux.

Jäckel, Eberhard. 1981. *Hitler's World View: A Blueprint for Power,* trans. Herbert Arnold. Cambridge, Mass.: Harvard University Press.

———. 1984. *Hitler in History.* Hanover, N.H.: University Press of New England.

Jackson, Karl D. 1989a. "Introduction: The Khmer Rouge in Context." In Karl D. Jackson, ed., *Cambodia 1975–1978: Rendezvous with Death,* pp. 3–11. Princeton, N.J.: Princeton University Press.

———. 1989b. "The Ideology of Total Revolution." In Karl D. Jackson, ed., *Cambodia 1975–1978: Rendezvous with Death,* pp. 37–78. Princeton, N.J.: Princeton University Press.

Jacobsen, Hans-Adolf. [1965] 1968. "The *Kommissarbefehl* and Mass Executions of Soviet Russian Prisoners of War," trans. Dorothy Long. In Helmut Krausnick, Hans Buchheim, Martin Broszat, and Hans-Adolf Jacobsen, *Anatomy of the SS State,* pp. 505–535. New York: Walker.

Jacobsen, Thorkild. 1976. *The Treasures of Darkness: A History of Mesopotamian Religion*. New Haven, Conn.: Yale University Press.

Jacobson, Matthew Frye. 1998. *Whiteness of a Different Color: European Immigrants and the Alchemy of Race*. Cambridge, Mass.: Harvard University Press.

Jaeger, Werner. 1939. *Paideia: The Ideals of Greek Culture*, vol. 1, trans. Gilbert Highet. Oxford: Blackwell.

Jaffrelot, Christophe. [1993] 1996. *The Hindu Nationalist Movement in India*. New York: Columbia University Press.

Jaher, Frederic Cople. 1994. *A Scapegoat in the New Wilderness: The Origins and Rise of Anti-Semitism in America*. Cambridge, Mass.: Harvard University Press.

James, Allison. 1996. "Cooking the Books: Global or Local Identities in Contemporary British Food Cultures?" In David Howes, ed., *Cross-Cultural Consumption: Global Markets, Local Realities*, pp. 77–92. London: Routledge.

James, Harold. 1986. *The German Slump: Politics and Economics 1924–1936*. Oxford: Clarendon Press.

———. 1989. *A German Identity 1770–1990*. London: Routledge.

James, Wendy. 1988. *The Listening Ebony: Moral Knowledge, Religion, and Power among the Uduk of Sudan*. Oxford: Clarendon Press.

Janowitz, Morris. 1975. *Military Conflict: Essays in the Institutional Analysis of Peace*. Beverly Hills, Calif.: Sage.

Janton, Pierre. 1973. *L'espéranto*. Paris: Presses Universitaires de France.

Jaspars, Jos, and Miles Hewstone. 1990. "Social Categorization, Collective Beliefs, and Causal Attribution." In Colin Fraser and George Gaskell, eds., *The Social Psychological Study of Widespread Beliefs*, pp. 121–141. Oxford: Clarendon Press.

Jaspers, Karl. 1946. *Die Schuldfrage: Ein Beitrag zur deutschen Frage*. Zürich: Artemis.

———. 1949. *Vom Ursprung und Ziel der Geschichte*. Zürich: Artemis.

Jaurès, Jean. [1902] 1931. "Le Prolétariat, la patrie et la paix." In Jean Jaurès, ed., *Oeuvres de Jean Jaurès*, vol. 1, ed. Max Bonnafous, pp. 275–326. Paris: Rieder.

Jayawardena, Kumari. 1986. *Feminism and Nationalism in the Third World*. London: Zed.

Jeismann, Michael. 1992. *Das Vaterland der Feinde: Studien zum nationalen Feindbegriff und Selbstverständnis in Deutschland und Frankreich 1792–1918*. Stuttgart: Klett-Cotta.

Jelavich, Barbara. 1987. *Modern Austria: Empire and Republic, 1815–1986*. Cambridge: Cambridge University Press.

Jellonnek, Burkhard. 1990. *Homosexuelle unter dem Hakenkreuz: Die Verfolgung von Homosexuellen im Dritten Reich*. Paderborn, Germany: Ferdinand Schöningh.

Jenkins, Richard. 1998. "Culture, Classification and (In)competence." In Richard Jenkins, ed., *Questions of Competence: Culture, Classification and Intellectual Disability*, pp. 1–24. Cambridge: Cambridge University Press.

Jennings, Francis. [1975] 1976. *The Invasion of America: Indians, Colonialism, and the Cant of Conquest.* New York: W. W. Norton.

Johnson, Charles S. 1939. "Race Relations and Social Change." In Edgar T. Thompson, ed., *Race Relations and the Race Problem: A Definition and an Analysis,* pp. 271–303. Durham, N.C.: Duke University Press.

Johnson, Douglas H. 1994. *Nuer Prophets: A History of Prophecy from the Upper Nile in the Nineteenth and Twentieth Centuries.* Oxford: Clarendon Press.

Johnson, Walter. 1974. *The Roman Economy: Studies in Ancient Economic and Administrative History,* ed. P. A. Brunt. Oxford: Blackwell.

———. 1999. *Soul by Soul: Life inside the Antebellum Slave Market.* Cambridge, Mass.: Harvard University Press.

Jones, Howard Mumford. [1948] 1965. *The Theory of American Literature.* Ithaca, N.Y.: Cornell University Press.

Jones, P. M. 1988. *The Peasantry in the French Revolution.* Cambridge: Cambridge University Press.

———. 1995. *Reform and Revolution in France: The Politics of Transition, 1774–1791.* Cambridge: Cambridge University Press.

Jordan, June. 1992. *Technical Difficulties: African-American Notes on the State of the Union.* New York: Pantheon.

Jordan, Winthrop D. 1968. *White over Black: American Attitudes toward the Negro, 1550–1812.* Chapel Hill: University of North Carolina Press.

Jouvenel, Bertrand de. 1957. *Sovereignty: An Inquiry into the Political Good,* trans. J. F. Huntington. Chicago: University of Chicago Press.

Judah, Tim. 1997. *The Serbs: History, Myth and the Destruction of Yugoslavia.* New Haven, Conn.: Yale University Press.

———. 2000. *Kosovo: War and Revenge.* New Haven, Conn.: Yale University Press.

Judt, Tony. 1996. *A Grand Illusion? An Essay on Europe.* New York: Hill & Wang.

Jung, Courtney. 2000. *Then I Was Black: South African Political Identities in Transition.* New Haven, Conn.: Yale University Press.

Jünger, Ernst. [1921] 1929. *The Storm of Steel: From the Diary of a German Storm-Troop Officer on the Western Front,* trans. Basil Creighton. London: Chatto & Windus.

Kafka, Franz. [1937/1990] 1994. *Tagebücher band 2: 1912–1914.* Frankfurt am Main: Fischer.

Kahan, Arcadius. 1967. "Nineteenth-Century European Experience with Policies of Economic Nationalism." In Harry G. Johnson, ed., *Economic Nationalism in Old and New States,* pp. 17–30. Chicago: University of Chicago Press.

Kahler, Miles. 1984. *Decolonization in Britain and France: The Domestic Consequences of International Relations.* Princeton, N.J.: Princeton University Press.

Kallen, Horace M. 1924. *Culture and Democracy in the United States: Studies in the Group Psychology of the American Peoples.* New York: Boni and Liveright.

Kāmil, ʿAbd-al-ʿAzīz ʿAbd-al-Qādir. 1970. *Islam and the Race Question.* Paris: UNESCO.

Kant, Immanuel. [1798–1800] 1965. "Anthropologie in pragmatischer Hinsicht." In Immanuel Kant, *Werke,* ed. Wilhelm Weischedel, vol. 10, pp. 395–690. Wiesbaden, Germany: Insel.

——. [1784/1970] 1991. "An Answer to the Question: 'What is Enlightenment?' " In Immanuel Kant, *Political Writings,* 2nd ed., ed. Hans Reiss, trans. H. B. Nisbet, pp. 54–60. Cambridge: Cambridge University Press.

Kaplan, Marion A. 2001. "When the Ordinary Became Extraordinary: German Jews Reacting to Nazi Persecution, 1933–1939." In Robert Gellately and Nathan Stoltzfus, eds., *Social Outsiders in Nazi Germany,* pp. 66–98. Princeton, N.J.: Princeton University Press.

Karsh, Efraim, and Inari Karsh. 1999. *Empires of the Sand: The Struggle for Mastery in the Middle East, 1789–1923.* Cambridge, Mass.: Harvard University Press.

Karakasidou, Anastasia N. 1997. *Fields of Wheat, Hills of Blood: Passages to Nationhood in Greek Macedonia, 1870–1990.* Chicago: University of Chicago Press.

Kashner, Sam. 1999. "The Color of Love." *Vanity Fair* April, pp. 378–409.

Kästli, Tobias. 1998. *Die Schweiz—Eine Republik in Europa: Geschichte des Nationalstaats seit 1798.* Zürich: Neue Zürcher Zeitung.

Kater, Michael H. 1983. *The Nazi Party: A Social Profile of Members and Leaders, 1919–1945.* Cambridge, Mass.: Harvard University Press.

Katz, Steven T. 1994. *The Holocaust in Historical Context,* vol. 1: *The Holocaust and Mass Death before the Modern Age.* New York: Oxford University Press.

Kauders, Anthony. 1996. *German Politics and the Jews: Düsseldorf and Nuremberg 1910–1933.* Oxford: Clarendon Press.

Kautsky, Karl. [1908]. 1925. *Foundations of Christianity: A Study in Christian Origins.* New York: International Publishers.

——. [1914/1921] 1926. *Are the Jews a Race?* New York: International Publishers.

——. [1892] 1971. *The Class Struggle,* trans. William E. Bohn. New York: W. W. Norton.

Keats, John. 1990. *John Keats,* ed. Elizabeth Cook. Oxford: Oxford University Press.

Kee, Howard Clark. 1995. *Who Are the People of God? Early Christian Models of Community.* New Haven, Conn.: Yale University Press.

Keen, David. 1994. *The Benefits of Famine: A Political Economy of Famine and Relief in Southwestern Sudan, 1983–1989.* Princeton, N.J.: Princeton University Press.

Keen, Ian. 1994. *Knowledge and Secrecy in an Aboriginal Religion.* Oxford: Clarendon Press.

Keil, Frank C. 1989. *Concepts, Kinds, and Cognitive Development.* Cambridge, Mass.: MIT Press.

Kelley, Donald R. 1984. *Historians and the Law in Postrevolutionary France.* Princeton, N.J.: Princeton University Press.

Kellner, Menachem. 1991. *Maimonides on Judaism and the Jewish People.* Albany: State University of New York Press.

Kenyatta, Jomo. 1953. *Facing Mount Kenya: The Tribal Life of the Gikuyu.* London: Secker & Warburg.

Keohane, Nannerl O. 1980. *Philosophy and the State in France: The Renaissance to the Enlightenment.* Princeton, N.J.: Princeton University Press.

Kershaw, Ian. 1983. *Popular Opinion and Political Dissent in the Third Reich: Bavaria 1933–1945.* Oxford: Clarendon Press.

———. 1987. *The "Hitler Myth": Image and Reality in the Third Reich.* Oxford: Clarendon Press.

———. [1998] 1999. *Hitler: 1889–1936: Hubris.* New York: W. W. Norton.

———. 2000. *Hitler: 1936–1945: Nemesis.* New York: W. W. Norton.

Kerswill, Paul. 1994. *Dialects Converging: Rural Speech in Urban Norway.* Oxford: Clarendon Press.

Kete, Kathleen. 1994. *The Beast in the Boudoir: Petkeeping in Nineteenth-Century Paris.* Berkeley: University of California Press.

Kevles, Daniel J. 1985. *In the Name of Eugenics: Genetics and the Uses of Human Heredity.* New York: Alfred A. Knopf.

Keynes, John Maynard. [1919] 1971. *The Collected Writings of John Maynard Keynes,* vol. 2: *The Economic Consequences of Peace.* London: Macmillan.

Khalidi, Rashid. 1997. *Palestinian Identity: The Construction of Modern National Consciousness.* New York: Columbia University Press.

Khazanov, Anatoly M. [1983] 1994. *Nomads and the Outside World,* 2nd ed., trans. Julia Crookenden. Madison: University of Wisconsin Press.

———. 1995. *After the USSR: Ethnicity, Nationalism, and Politics in the Commonwealth of Independent States.* Madison: University of Wisconsin Press.

Kibria, Nazli. 1998. "The Contested Meanings of 'Asian American': Racial Dilemmas in the Contemporary US." *Ethnic and Racial Studies* 21:939–958.

Kiernan, Ben. 1996. *The Pol Pot Regime: Race, Power, and Genocide in Cambodia under the Khmer Rouge, 1975–79.* New Haven. Conn.: Yale University Press.

Kiernan, V. G. [1957] 1965. "Foreign Mercenaries and Absolute Monarchy." In Trevor Aston, ed., *Crisis in Europe, 1560–1660,* pp. 117–140. London: RKP.

———. [1969] 1986. *The Lords of Human Kind: Black Man, Yellow Man, and White Man in an Age of Empire.* New York: Columbia University Press.

Kimelman, Reuven. 1981. "*Birkat Ha-Minim* and the Lack of Evidence for an Anti-Christian Jewish Prayer in Late Antiquity." In E. P. Sanders, ed., *Jewish and Christian Self-Definition,* vol. 2:*Aspects of Judaism in the Greco-Roman Period,* pp. 226–244. Philadelphia: Fortress Press.

Kinder, Donald R., and Lynn M. Sanders. 1996. *Divided by Color: Racial Politics and Democratic Ideals.* Chicago: University of Chicago Press.

King, James C. [1971] 1981. *The Biology of Race,* rev. ed. Berkeley: University of California Press.

King, Jeremy. 2002. *Budweisers into Czechs and Germans: A Local History of Bohemian Politics, 1848–1948.* Princeton, N.J.: Princeton University Press.

King, Victor T. 1993. *The Peoples of Borneo.* Oxford: Blackwell.

Kissinger, Henry A. 1958. *A World Restored: Metternich, Castlereagh and the Problems of Peace, 1812–1822.* Boston: Houghton Mifflin.

Kitcher, Philip.1985. *Vaulting Ambition: Sociobiology and the Quest for Human Nature.* Cambridge, Mass.: MIT Press.

Kittredge, George Lyman. [1929] 1972. *Witchcraft in Old and New England.* New York: Atheneum.

Klingenstein, Grete. 1997. "The Meaning of 'Austria' and 'Austrian' in the Eighteenth Century," trans. Sabina Krause and Grete Klingenstein. In Robert Oresko, G. C. Gibbs, and H. M. Scott, eds., *Royal and Republican Sovereignty in Early Modern Europe,* pp. 423–478. Cambridge: Cambridge University Press.

Knox, Robert. 1850. *The Races of Men: A Fragment.* Philadelphia: Lea & Blanchard.

Knudsen, Jonathan B. 1986. *Justus Möser and the German Enlightenment.* Cambridge: Cambridge University Press.

Kobayashi Shigeru. 1979. *Buraku "kaihōrei" no kenkyū.* Osaka: Buraku Kaihō Shuppansha.

Koerner, Lisbet. 1999. *Linnaeus: Nature and Nation.* Cambridge, Mass.: Harvard University Press.

Kogon, Eugen. [1950] 1958. *The Theory and Practice of Hell: The German Concentration Camps and the System Behind Them,* trans. Heinz Norden. New York: Berkley.

Kohn, Hans. 1944. *The Idea of Nationalism: A Study in Its Origins and Background.* New York: Macmillan.

———. [1953] 1960. *Pan-Slavism: Its History and Ideology,* 2nd ed. New York: Vintage.

Kolchin, Peter. 1993. *American Slavery, 1619–1877.* New York: Hill & Wang.

König, René [1971] 1973. *A La Mode: On the Social Psychology of Fashion,* trans. F. Bradley. New York: Seabury Press.

Konvitz, Milton R. 1946. *The Alien and the Asiatic in American Law.* Ithaca, N.Y.: Cornell University Press.

Koonz, Claudia. 1987. *Mothers in the Fatherland: Women, the Family, and Nazi Politics.* New York: St. Martin's Press.

Korinman, Michel. 1999. *Deutschland über alles: le pangermanisme 1890–1945.* Paris: Fayard.

Koshar, Rudy. 1986. *Social Life, Local Politics, and Nazism: Marburg, 1880–1935.* Chapel Hill: University of North Carolina Press.

Kossmann, E. H. 1978. *The Low Countries, 1780–1940.* Oxford: Clarendon Press.

Kotkin, Stephen. 1995. *Magnetic Mountain: Stalinism as a Civilization.* Berkeley: University of California Press.

Kovel, Joel. [1970/1984] 1988. *White Racism: A Psychohistory.* London: Free Association Books.

Kramer, Lloyd. 1998. *Nationalism: Political Cultures in Europe and America, 1775–1865.* New York: Twayne.

Krasner, Stephen D. 1999. *Sovereignty: Organized Hypocrisy.* Princeton, N.J.: Princeton University Press.

Krausnick, Helmut. [1965] 1968. "The Persecution of the Jews," trans. Dorothy Long. In Helmut Krausnick, Hans Buchheim, Martin Broszat, and Hans-Adolf Jacobsen, *Anatomy of the SS State,* pp. 1–124. New York: Walker.

———. 1981. "Die Einsatzgruppen vom Anschluß Österreichs bis zum Feldzug gegen die Sowjetunion: Entwicklung und Verhältnis zur Wehrmacht." In Helmut Krausnick and Hans-Heinrich Wilhelm, eds., *Die Truppe des Weltanschauungskrieges: Die Ensatzgruppen der Sicherheitspolizei und des SD 1938–1942,* pp. 11–278. Stuttgart: Deutsche Verlags-Anstalt.

Kreissig, Heinz. 1970. *Die sozialen Zusammenhänge des judäischen Krieges.* Berlin: Akademie Verlag.

Kripke, Saul A. 1980. *Naming and Necessity.* Cambridge, Mass.: Harvard University Press.

Kristeva, Julia. 1991. *Strangers to Ourselves,* trans. Leon S. Roudiez. New York: Columbia University Press.

———. [1990] 1993. *Nations without Nationalism,* trans. Leon S. Roudiez. New York: Columbia University Press.

Kroll, Frank-Lothar. 1998. *Utopie als Ideologie: Geschichtsdenken und politisches Handeln im Dritten Reich.* Paderborn, Germany: Ferdinand Schöningh.

Krüger, Peter. 1993. "Auf der Suche nach Deutschland—ein historischer Streifzug ins Ungewisse." In Peter Krüger, ed., *Deutschland, deutscher Staat, deutsche Nation: Historische Erkundungen eines Spannungsverhältnisses,* pp. 41–70. Marburg, Germany: Hitzeroth.

Kuehn, Manfred. 2001. *Kant: A Biography.* Cambridge: Cambridge University Press.

Kühl, Stefan. 1994. *The Nazi Connection: Eugenics, American Racism, and German National Socialism.* New York: Oxford University Press.

Kumar, Radha. 1997. *Divide and Fall? Bosnia in the Annals of Partition.* London: Verso.

Kuper, Adam. 1988. *The Invention of Primitive Society: Transformations of an Illusion.* London: Routledge.

———. 1999. *Culture: The Anthropologists' Account.* Cambridge, Mass.: Harvard University Press.

Kuper, Leo. 1981. *Genocide: Its Political Use in the Twentieth Century.* New Haven, Conn.: Yale University Press.

Kutter, Markus. 1995. *Die Schweizer und die Deutschen.* Zürich: Ammann.

Kvistad, Gregg. 1998. "Segmented Politics: Xenophobia, Citizenship, and Political

Loyalty in Germany." In Norbert Finzsch and Dietmar Schirmer, eds., *Identity and Intolerance: Nationalism, Racism, and Xenophobia in Germany and the United States,* pp. 43–69. Cambridge: Cambridge University Press.

Kwiet, Konrad. 1988. "Nach dem Pogrom stufen der Ausgrenzung." In Wolfgang Benz, ed., *Die Juden in Deutschland 1933–1945: Leben unter nationalsozialistischer Herrschaft,* pp. 545–659. München: C. H. Beck.

La Vopa, Anthony J. 2001. *Fichte: The Self and the Calling of Philosophy, 1762–1799.* Cambridge: Cambridge University Press.

Lach, Donald F. 1965. *Asia in the Making of Europe,* vol. 1: *The Century of Discovery,* 2 parts. Chicago: University of Chicago Press.

———. 1977. *Asia in the Making of Europe,* vol. 2: *A Century of Wonder, Book 3: The Scholarly Disciplines.* Chicago: University of Chicago Press.

Lacy, Terry G. 1998. *Ring of Seasons: Iceland—Its Culture and History.* Ann Arbor: University of Michigan Press.

Lafaye, Jacques. [1974] 1976. *Quetzalcóatl and Guadalupe: The Formation of Mexican National Consciousness 1531–1813,* trans. Benjamin Keen. Chicago: University of Chicago Press.

Lahr, John. 2001. "Been Here and Gone." *New Yorker* April 16, pp. 50–65.

Laitin, David. 1992. *Language Repertoires and State Construction in Africa.* Cambridge: Cambridge University Press.

Lamont, Michèle. 2000. *The Dignity of Working Men: Morality and the Boundaries of Race, Class, and Immigration.* Cambridge, Mass.: Harvard University Press.

Lampe, John R. [1996] 2000. *Yugoslavia as History: Twice There Was a Country,* 2nd ed. Cambridge: Cambridge University Press.

Lamphear, John. 1992. *The Scattering Time: Turkana Responses to Colonial Rule.* Oxford: Clarendon Press.

Landau, Jacob M. 1993. *The Arab Minority in Israel 1967–1991: Political Aspects.* Oxford: Clarendon Press.

Lane, Barbara Miller, and Leila J. Rupp. 1978. "Introduction." In Barbara Miller Lane and Leila J. Rupp, eds., *Nazi Ideology before 1933: A Documentation,* pp. ix–xxviii. Austin: University of Texas Press.

Lane, Harlan. 1992. *The Mask of Benevolence: Disabling the Deaf Community.* New York: Alfred A. Knopf.

Langer, William L. 1965. *Gas and Flame in World War I.* New York: Alfred A. Knopf.

Langford, Paul. 1991. *Public Life and the Propertied Englishman, 1689–1798.* Oxford: Clarendon Press.

———. 2000. *Englishness Identified: Manners and Character, 1650–1850.* Oxford: Oxford University Press.

Langmuir, Gavin I. 1990. *History, Religion, and Antisemitism.* Berkeley: University of California Press.

Laqueur, Walter. [1980] 1982. *The Terrible Secret: Suppression of the Truth about Hitler's "Final Solution."* Harmondsworth, U.K.: Penguin.

Large, David Clay, ed. 1991. *Contending with Hitler: Varieties of German Resistance in the Third Reich.* Cambridge: Cambridge University Press.

Larkin, Maurice. [1988] 1997. *France since the Popular Front: Government and People, 1936–1986,* 2nd ed. Oxford: Clarendon Press.

Larsen, Clark Spencer. 1997. *Bioarchaeology: Interpreting Behavior from the Human Skeleton.* Cambridge: Cambridge University Press.

Larsen, J. A. O. 1968. *Greek Federal States: Their Institutions and History.* Oxford: Clarendon Press.

Las Casas, Bartolomé de. [1552] 1974. *The Devastation of the Indies: A Brief Account,* trans. Herma Briffault. New York: Seabury Press.

Lasker, G. W. 1969. "Human Biological Adaptability: The Ecological Approach in Physical Anthropology." *Science* 166:1480–1486.

———. 1985. *Surnames and Genetic Structure.* Cambridge: Cambridge University Press.

Laurence, Ray. 1998. "Territory, Ethnonyms and Geography: The Construction of Identity in Roman Italy." In Ray Laurence and Joanne Berry, eds., *Cultural Identity in the Roman Empire,* pp. 95–110. London: Routledge.

Laurens, Henry. 1999. *La question de Palestine,* vol. 1: *1799–1922: l'invention de la terre sainte.* Paris: Fayard.

Lautmann, Ruediger. 1990. "Gay Prisoners in Concentration Camps as Compared with Jehovah's Witnesses and Political Prisoners." In Michael Berenbaum, ed., *A Mosaic of Victims: Non-Jews Persecuted and Murdered by the Nazis,* pp. 200–206. New York: New York University Press.

Lavisse, Ernest. 1918. *France=Humanité: lettres à une normalienne.* Paris: I. Rirachovski.

Lawrence, D. H. [1923] 1971. *Studies in Classical American Literature.* Harmondsworth, U.K.: Penguin.

Lazarre, Jane. 1996. *Beyond the Whiteness of Whiteness: Memoir of a White Mother of Black Sons.* Durham, N.C.: Duke University Press.

Le Bras, Hervé. 2000. *Naissance de la mortalité: l'origine politique de la statistique et de la démographie.* Paris: Gallimard.

Le Goff, Jacques. 1980. *Time, Work, and Culture in the Middle Ages,* trans. Arthur Goldhammer. Chicago: University of Chicago Press.

———. [1964] 1988. *Medieval Civilization 400–1500,* trans. Julia Barrow. Oxford: Blackwell.

Le Roy Ladurie, Emmanuel. [1975/1978] 1979. *Montaillou: The Promised Land of Error,* trans. Barbara Bray. New York: Vintage.

———. [1978] 1981. *The Mind and Method of the Historian,* trans. Siân Reynolds and Ben Reynolds. Chicago: University of Chicago Press.

————. [1980/1982] 1984. *Love, Death and Money in the Pays d'Oc,* trans. Alan Sheridan. Harmondsworth, U.K.: Penguin.

————. [1977] 1987. *The French Peasantry 1450–1660,* trans. Alan Sheridan. Berkeley: University of California Press.

Leach, E. R. [1954] 1965. *Political Systems of Highland Burma: A Study of Kachin Social Structure.* Boston: Beacon Press.

Lebovics, Herman. 1992. *True France: The Wars over Cultural Identity, 1900–1945.* Ithaca, N.Y.: Cornell University Press.

Lebow, Richard Ned. 1976. *White Britain and Black Ireland: The Influence of Stereotypes on Colonial Policy.* Philadelphia: Institute for the Study of Human Issues.

Lee, Richard Borsay. 1979. *The !Kung San: Men, Women, and Work in a Foraging Society.* Cambridge: Cambridge University Press.

Lee, Taeku. 2002. *Mobilizing Public Opinion: Black Insurgency and Racial Attitudes in the Civil Rights Era.* Chicago: University of Chicago Press.

Leed, Eric J. 1979. *No Man's Land: Combat and Identity in World War I.* Cambridge: Cambridge University Press.

Lefebvre, Georges. [1932] 1973. *The Great Fear of 1789: Rural Panic in Revolutionary France,* trans. Joan White. New York: Pantheon.

Leibowitz, Yeshayahu. 1992. *Judaism, Human Values, and the Jewish State,* ed. Eliezer Goldman, trans. Eliezer Goldman et al. Cambridge, Mass.: Harvard University Press.

Lemkin, Raphael. [1944] 1973. *Axis Rule in Occupied Europe: Laws of Occupation, Analysis of Government, Proposals for Redress.* New York: Howard Fertig.

Lemon, Alaina. 2000. *Between Two Fires: Gypsy Performance and Romani Memory from Pushkin to Postsocialism.* Durham, N.C.: Duke University Press.

Lenin, V. I. [1916] 1964. "Speech Delivered at an International Meeting in Berne, February 8, 1916." In V. I. Lenin, *Collected Works,* vol. 22: *December 1915–July 1916,* ed. George Hanna, trans. Yuri Sdobnikov, pp. 123–126. Moscow: Progress Publishers.

Leone, Mark P. 1979. *Roots of Modern Mormonism.* Cambridge, Mass.: Harvard University Press.

Lepsius, M. Rainer. 1966. *Extremer Nationalismus: Strukturbedingungen vor der nationalsozialistischen Machtergreifung.* Stuttgart: W. Kohlhammer.

Letwin, Shirley Robin. 1982. *The Gentleman in Trollope: Individuality and Moral Conduct.* Cambridge, Mass.: Harvard University Press.

Levi, Carlo. [1945/1947] 1963. *Christ Stopped at Eboli: The Story of a Year,* trans. Frances Frenaye. New York: Farrar, Straus & Giroux.

Levi, Primo. [1986] 1988. *The Drowned and the Saved,* trans. Raymond Rosenthal. New York: Summit Books.

Levillain, Philippe. 1992. "1871–1898: les droites en République." In Jean-François

Sirinelli, ed., *Histoire des droites en France,* vol. 1, pp. 147–212. Paris: Gallimard.

Levin, Michael. 1997. *Why Race Matters: Race Differences and What They Mean.* Westport, Conn.: Praeger.

Levinas, Emmanuel. [1963] 1990. *Difficult Freedom: Essays on Judaism,* trans. Seán Hand. London: Athlone Press.

Levine, Hillel. 1996. *In Search of Sugihara: The Elusive Japanese Diplomat Who Risked His Life to Rescue 10,000 Jews from the Holocaust.* New York: Free Press.

Levine, Lee I. 1998. *Judaism and Hellenism in Antiquity: Conflict or Confluence?* Seattle: University of Washington Press.

Levine, Philippa. 1986. *The Amateur and the Professional: Antiquarians, Historians and Archaeologists in Victorian England, 1838–1886.* Cambridge: Cambridge University Press.

Levins, Richard, and Richard Lewontin. 1985. *The Dialectical Biologist.* Cambridge, Mass.: Harvard University Press.

Lévi-Strauss, Claude. [1962] 1963. *Totemism,* trans. Rodney Needham. Boston: Beacon Press.

Lévy, Bernard-Henri. 1981. *L'idéologie française.* Paris: Grasset.

Lewis, Bernard. [1950] 1967. *The Arabs in History,* rev. ed. New York: Harper & Row.

——. 1982. *The Muslim Discovery of Europe.* New York: W. W. Norton.

——. 1984. *The Jews of Islam.* Princeton, N.J.: Princeton University Press.

——. 1988. *The Political Language of Islam.* Chicago: University of Chicago Press.

——. 1990. *Race and Slavery in the Middle East: An Historical Enquiry.* New York: Oxford University Press.

——. 1995. *Cultures in Conflict: Christians, Muslims, and Jews in the Age of Discovery.* New York: Oxford University Press.

——. 1998. *The Multiple Identities of the Middle East.* New York: Schocken.

Lewis, Julian Herman. 1942. *The Biology of the Negro.* Chicago: University of Chicago Press.

Lewis, Martin, and Kären E. Wigen. 1997. *The Myth of Continents: A Critique of Metageography.* Berkeley: University of California Press.

Lewis, W. Arthur. 1985. *Racial Conflict and Economic Development.* Cambridge, Mass.: Harvard University Press.

Lewontin, R. C. 1974. *The Genetic Basis of Evolutionary Change.* New York: Columbia University Press.

——. 2000. *The Triple Helix: Gene, Organism, and Environment.* Cambridge, Mass.: Harvard University Press.

Lewy, Guenter. 2000. *The Nazi Persecution of the Gypsies.* New York: Oxford University Press.

Liber, George O. 1998. "Imagining Ukraine: Regional Differences and the Emergence of an Integrated State Identity, 1926–1944." *Nations and Nationalism* 4: 187–206.

Lidtke, Vernon L. 1985. *The Alternative Culture: Socialist Labor in Imperial Germany.* New York: Oxford University Press.

Lie, John. 1998. *Han Unbound: The Political Economy of South Korea.* Stanford, Calif.: Stanford University Press.

———. 2001. *Multiethnic Japan.* Cambridge, Mass.: Harvard University Press.

Lieberson, Stanley. 1980. *A Piece of the Pie: Blacks and White Immigrants since 1880.* Berkeley: University of California Press.

Liebman, Charles S., and Eliezer Don-Yehiya. 1983. *Civil Religion in Israel: Traditional Judaism and Political Culture in the Jewish State.* Berkeley: University of California Press.

Lienhardt, Godfrey. 1985. "Self: Public, Private. Some African Representation." In Michael Carrithers, Steven Collins, and Steven Lukes, eds., *The Category of the Person: Anthropology, Philosophy, History,* pp. 141–155. Cambridge: Cambridge University Press.

Lifton, Robert Jay. 1986. *The Nazi Doctors: Medical Killing and the Psychology of Genocide.* New York: Basic Books.

Lilla, Mark, Ronald Dworkin, and Robert B. Silvers, eds. 2001. *The Legacy of Isaiah Berlin.* New York: New York Review Books.

Lin, Yueh-hua. 1961. *The Lolo of Liang Shan,* ed. Wu-Chi Liu, trans. Ju-Shu Pan. New Haven, Conn.: HRAF Press.

Lincoln, Bruce. 1999. *Theorizing Myth: Narrative, Ideology, and Scholarship.* Chicago: University of Chicago Press.

Lincoln, C. Eric. [1961] 1994. *The Black Muslims in America,* 3rd ed. Grand Rapids, Mich.: William B. Eerdmans.

Lindee, M. Susan. 1994. *Suffering Made Real: American Science and the Survivors at Hiroshima.* Chicago: University of Chicago Press.

Lipovetsky, Gilles. [1987] 1994. *The Empire of Fashion: Dressing Modern Democracy,* trans. Catherine Porter. Princeton, N.J.: Princeton University Press.

Liss, Peggy K. 1975. *Mexico under Spain, 1521–1556: Society and the Origins of Nationality.* Chicago: University of Chicago Press.

Littlefield, Daniel C. 1981. *Rice and Slaves: Ethnicity and the Slave Trade in Colonial South Carolina.* Baton Rouge: Louisiana State University Press.

Litwack, Leon F. 1961. *North of Slavery: The Negro in the Free States 1790–1860.* Chicago: University of Chicago Press.

———. 1998. *Trouble in Mind: Black Southerners in the Age of Jim Crow.* New York: Alfred A. Knopf.

Liu, Lydia H. 1995. *Translingual Practice: Literature, National Culture, and Translated Modernity: China, 1900–1937.* Stanford, Calif.: Stanford University Press.

Livingstone, Frank B. 1962. "On the Non-Existence of Human Races." *Current Anthropology* 3:279–281.

Lloyd, G. E. R. 1966. *Polarity and Analogy: Two Types of Argumentation in Early Greek Thought.* Cambridge: Cambridge University Press.

Locke, Alain. [1925] 1968. "The New Negro." In Alain Locke, ed., *The New Negro: An Interpretation,* pp. 3–16. New York: Arno Press.

———. [1942] 1989. "Who and What Is 'Negro'?" In Leonard Harris, ed., *The Philosophy of Alain Locke: Harlem Renaissance and Beyond,* pp. 207–228. Philadelphia: Temple University Press.

Locke, John. [1689] 1975. *An Essay Concerning Human Understanding,* ed. Peter H. Nidditch. Oxford: Clarendon Press.

Lockhart, James. 1991. *Nahuas and Spaniards: Postconquest Central Mexican History and Philology.* Stanford, Calif.: Stanford University Press.

———. 1992. *The Nahuas after the Conquest: A Social and Cultural History of the Indians of Central Mexico, Sixteenth through Eighteenth Centuries.* Stanford, Calif.: Stanford University Press.

———. [1968] 1994. *Spanish Peru, 1532–1560: A Social History.* Madison: University of Wisconsin Press.

Longerich, Peter. 1998. *Politik der Vernichtung: Eine Gesamtdarstellung der nationalsozialistischen Judenverfolgung.* München: Piper.

Longerich, Peter, ed. 1990. *"Was Ist des Deutschen Vaterland?": Dokumente zur Frage der deutschen Einheit 1800 bis 1900.* München: Piper.

Lonsdale, John. 1985. "The European Scramble and Conquest in African History." In Roland Oliver and G. N. Sanderson, eds., *The Cambridge History of Africa,* vol. 6: *From 1870 to 1905,* pp. 680–766. Cambridge: Cambridge University Press.

Loury, Glenn C. 1993. "Free at Last? A Personal Perspective on Race and Identity in America." In Gerald Early, ed., *Lure and Loathing: Essays on Race, Identity, and the Ambivalence of Assimilation,* pp. 1–12. New York: Viking Penguin.

———. 2002. *The Anatomy of Racial Inequality.* Cambridge, Mass.: Harvard University Press.

Lowenthal, David. 1996. *The Heritage Crusade and the Spoils of History.* New York: Free Press.

Lowie, Robert H. 1954. *Toward Understanding Germany.* Chicago: University of Chicago Press.

Luckham, Robin. 1971. *The Nigerian Military: A Sociological Analysis of Authority and Revolt 1960–1967.* Cambridge: Cambridge University Press.

———. 1979. "Militarism: Force, Class and International Conflict." In Mary Kaldor and Asbjørn Eide, eds., *The World Military Order: The Impact of Military Technology on the Third World,* pp. 232–256. London: Macmillan.

Ludmerer, Kenneth M. 1972. *Genetics and American Society: A Historical Appraisal.* Baltimore: Johns Hopkins University Press.

Ludwig, Emil. 1931. *Geschenke des Lebens: Ein Rückblick.* Berlin: Ernst Rowohlt.

Lukács, Georg. [1962] 1980. *The Destruction of Reason,* trans. Peter Palmer. London: Merlin Press.

Lukas, Richard C. 1990. "The Polish Experience during the Holocaust." In Michael Berenbaum, ed., *A Mosaic of Victims: Non-Jews Persecuted and Murdered by the Nazis,* pp. 88–95. New York: New York University Press.

Lukes, Steven. 1973. *Individualism.* Oxford: Blackwell.

Lumans, Valdis O. 1993. *Himmler's Auxiliaries: The Volksdeutsche Mittelstelle and the German National Minorities of Europe, 1933–1945.* Chapel Hill: University of North Carolina Press.

Lundgren, Svante. 1992. *Moses Hess on Religion, Judaism and the Bible.* Åbo: Åbo Akademis Förlag.

Lurie, Alison. 1981. *The Language of Clothes.* New York: Random House.

MacBeth, Helen. 1997. "What Is an Ethnic Group? A Biological Perspective." In Angus Clarke and Evelyn Parsons, eds., *Culture, Kinship and Genes: Towards Cross-Cultural Genetics,* pp. 54–66. Houndsmills, U.K.: Macmillan.

MacDougall, Hugh A. 1982. *Racial Myth in English History: Trojans, Teutons, and Anglo-Saxons.* Montreal: Harvest House.

Macfarlane, Alan. 1970. *Witchcraft in Tudor and Stuart England: A Regional and Comparative Study.* London: Routledge and Kegan Paul.

MacFarquhar, Roderick. 1997. *The Origins of the Cultural Revolution,* vol. 3: *The Coming of the Cataclysm 1961–1966.* Oxford: Oxford University Press.

Machiavelli, Niccolò. 1970. *The Discourses,* ed. Bernard Crick, trans. Leslie J. Walker, rev. Brian Richardson. Harmondsworth, U.K.: Penguin.

Mack Smith, Denis. 1994. *Mazzini.* New Haven, Conn.: Yale University Press.

MacKenzie, John M. 1999. "The Popular Culture of Empire in Britain." In Judith M. Brown and Wm. Roger Louis, eds., *The Oxford History of the British Empire,* vol. 4: *The Twentieth Century,* pp. 212–231. Oxford: Oxford University Press.

MacMullen, Ramsay. 2000. *Romanization in the Time of Augustus.* New Haven, Conn.: Yale University Press.

MacNamara, Nottidge Charles. 1900. *Origin and Character of the British People.* London: Smith, Elder.

Maguire, G. Andrew. 1969. *Toward "Uhuru" in Tanzania: The Politics of Participation.* Cambridge: Cambridge University Press.

Mahler, Sarah J. 1995. *American Dreaming: Immigrant Life on the Margins.* Princeton, N.J.: Princeton University Press.

Maiden, Martin. 1995. *A Linguistic History of Italian.* London: Longman.

Maier, Charles S. 1988. *The Unmasterable Past: History, Holocaust, and German National Identity*. Cambridge, Mass.: Harvard University Press.

Maistre, Joseph de. [1965] 1971. *The Works of Joseph de Maistre*, ed. and trans. Jack Lively. New York: Schocken.

———. [1797/1974] 1994. *Considerations on France*, ed. and trans. Richard A. Lebrun. Cambridge: Cambridge University Press.

Malcolm, José V. 1996. *The African Origins of Modern Judaism: From Hebrews to Jews*. Trenton, N.J.: African World Press.

Malcolm, Noel. 1994. *Bosnia: A Short History*. New York: New York University Press.

———. 1998. *Kosovo: A Short History*. New York: New York University Press.

Maleville, Georges de. 1988. *La Tragédie Arménienne de 1915*. Paris: Lanore.

Malkin, Irad. 1998. *The Returns of Odysseus: Colonization and Ethnicity*. Berkeley: University of California Press.

Malkki, Liisa H. 1995. *Purity and Exile: Violence, Memory, and National Cosmology among Hutu Refugees in Tanzania*. Chicago: University of Chicago Press.

Mallon, Florencia E. 1995. *Peasant and Nation: The Making of Postcolonial Mexico and Peru*. Berkeley: University of California Press.

Mamdani, Mahmood. 1996. *Citizen and Subject: Contemporary Africa and the Legacy of Late Colonialism*. Princeton, N.J.: Princeton University Press.

———. 2001. *When Victims Become Killers: Colonialism, Nativism, and the Genocide in Rwanda*. Princeton, N.J.: Princeton University Press.

Mandelbaum, David G. 1970. *Society in India*, 2 vols. Berkeley: University of California Press.

Mandelstam, Nadezhda. 1970. *Hope against Hope: A Memoir*, trans. Max Hayward. New York: Atheneum.

Mandler, Peter. 2000. " 'Race' and 'Nation' in Mid-Victorian Thought." In Stefan Collini, Richard Whatmore, and Brian Young, eds., *History, Religion, and Culture: British Intellectual History 1750–1950*, pp. 224–244. Cambridge: Cambridge University Press.

Mann, Michael. 1993. *The Sources of Social Power*, vol. 2: *The Rise of Classes and Nation-States, 1760–1914*. Cambridge: Cambridge University Press.

Manning, Frederic. [1929] 1979. *The Middle Parts of Fortune*. New York: Plume.

Manville, Philip Brook. 1990. *The Origins of Citizenship in Ancient Athens*. Princeton, N.J.: Princeton University Press.

Marable, Manning. 1995. *Beyond Black & White: Transforming African-American Politics*. London: Verso.

Marcuse, Harold. 2001. *Legacies of Dachau: On Uses and Abuses of a Concentration Camp, 1933–2001*. Cambridge: Cambridge University Press.

Margalit, Avishai. 1998. *Views in Review: Politics and Culture in the State of the Jews*. New York: Farrar, Straus & Giroux.

————. 2001. "The Crooked Timber of Nationalism." In Mark Lilla, Ronald Dworkin, and Robert B. Silvers, ed., *The Legacy of Isaiah Berlin*, pp. 147–159. New York: New York Review Books.

Markman, Ellen M. 1989. *Categorization and Naming in Children: Problems of Induction*. Cambridge, Mass.: MIT Press.

Markus, R. A. 1980. "The Problem of Self-Definition: From Sect to Church." In E. P. Sanders, ed., *Jewish and Christian Self-Definition*, vol. 1: *The Shaping of Christianity in the Second and Third Centuries*, pp. 1–15. Philadelphia: Fortress Press.

Markusen, Eric, and David Kopf. 1995. *The Holocaust and Strategic Bombing: Genocide and Total War in the Twentieth Century*. Boulder, Colo.: Westview Press.

Marquand, David. 1996. "The Twilight of the British State? Henry Dubb versus Sceptred Awe." In S. J. D. Green and R. C. Whiting, eds., *The Boundaries of the State in Modern Britain*, pp. 57–69. Cambridge: Cambridge University Press.

Marrus, Michael R. 1971. *The Politics of Assimilation: The French Jewish Community at the Time of the Dreyfus Affair*. Oxford: Clarendon Press.

————. 1985. *The Unwanted: European Refugees in the Twentieth Century*. New York: Oxford University Press.

————. 1987. *The Holocaust in History*. Hanover, N.H.: University Press of New England.

Marshall, P. J. 1995. "A Nation Defined by Empire, 1755–1776." In Alexander Grant and Keith J. Stringer, eds., *Uniting the Kingdom? The Making of British History*, pp. 208–222. London: Routledge.

Marshall, Peter. 1992. *Demanding the Impossible: A History of Anarchism*. London: HarperCollins.

Marshall, T. H. 1964. *Class, Citizenship, and Social Development: Essays*. Garden City, N.Y.: Doubleday.

Martin, Douglas. 2001. "Charles Johnson, 76, Proponent of Flat Earth." *New York Times* March 25, p. 31.

Martin, Waldo E., Jr. 1984. *The Mind of Frederick Douglass*. Chapel Hill: University of North Carolina Press.

Marwick, Arthur. [1965] 1970. *The Deluge: British Society and the First World War*. New York: W. W. Norton.

Marx, Anthony W. 1998. *Making Race and Nation: A Comparison of South Africa, the United States, and Brazil*. Cambridge: Cambridge University Press.

Marx, Jörg. 1997. *Völkermord in Rwanda: Zur Genealogie einer unheilvollen Kulturwirkung: Eine diskurshistorische Untersuchung*. Hamburg: LIT Verlag.

Marx, Karl. [1844] 1994. "A Contribution to the Critique of Hegel's Philosophy of Right: Introduction." In Karl Marx, *Early Political Writings*, ed. and trans. Joseph J. O'Malley, pp. 57–70. Cambridge: Cambridge University Press.

Marx, Karl, and Frederick Engels. [1844/1973] 1974. "Manifesto of the Communist

Party." In Karl Marx, *Political Writings*, vol. 1: *The Revolutions of 1848*, pp. 62–98. New York: Vintage.

Mascie-Taylor, C. G. N., and Barry Bogin, eds. 1995. *Human Variability and Plasticity.* Cambridge: Cambridge University Press.

Mason, Timothy W. [1977] 1993. *Social Policy in the Third Reich: The Working Class and the "National Community,"* trans. John Broadwin. Providence, R.I.: Berg.

——— [Tim]. 1995. *Nazism, Fascism and the Working Class,* ed. Jane Caplan. Cambridge: Cambridge University Press.

Maurras, Charles. 1937. *Mes idées politiques,* ed. Pierre Chardon. Paris: Fayard.

Mauss, Armand L. 1994. *The Angel and the Beehive: The Mormon Struggle with Assimilation.* Urbana: University of Illinois Press.

Mayer, Arno J. 1981. *The Persistence of the Old Regime: Europe to the Great War.* New York: Pantheon.

———. 1988. *Why Did the Heavens Not Darken? The "Final Solution" in History.* New York: Pantheon.

Mayr, Ernst. [1951] 1976. "Taxonomic Categories in Fossil Hominids." In Ernst Mayr, *Evolution and the Diversity of Life: Selected Essays,* pp. 530–545. Cambridge, Mass.: Harvard University Press.

———. [1942] 1982. *Systematics and the Origin of Species: From the Viewpoint of a Zoologist.* New York: Columbia University Press.

———. 1991. *One Long Argument: Charles Darwin and the Genesis of Modern Evolutionary Thought.* Cambridge, Mass.: Harvard University Press.

———. 1997. *This Is Biology: The Science of the Living World.* Cambridge, Mass.: Harvard University Press.

Mazower, Mark. 2001. "The G-Word." *London Review of Books* February 8, pp. 19–21.

Mazrui, Ali A., and Michael Tidy. 1984. *Nationalism and New States in Africa from about 1935 to the Present.* London: Heinemann.

Mazumdar, Pauline M. H. 1995. *Species and Specificity: An Interpretation of the History of Immunology.* Cambridge: Cambridge University Press.

Mazzini, Joseph [Giuseppe]. 1907. *The Duties of Man and Other Essays.* London: J. M. Dent & Sons.

Mazzotta, Giuseppe. 1999. *The New Map of the World: The Poetic Philosophy of Giambattista Vico.* Princeton, N.J.: Princeton University Press.

McClain, Charles J. 1994. *In Search of Equality: The Chinese Struggle against Discrimination in Nineteenth-Century America.* Berkeley: University of California Press.

McCullum, Hugh. 1995. *The Angels Have Left Us: The Rwanda Tragedy and the Churches.* Geneva: World Council of Churches.

McDonald, Maryon. 1989. *"We Are Not French!": Language, Culture and Identity in Brittany.* London: Routledge.

McGarty, Craig, Vincent Y. Yzerbyt, and Russell Spears. 2002. "Social, Cultural and Cognitive Factors in Stereotype Formation." In Craig McGarty, Vincent Y. Yzerbyt, and Russell Spears, eds., *Stereotypes as Explanations: The Formation of Meaningful Beliefs about Social Groups,* pp. 1–15. Cambridge: Cambridge University Press.

McGrane, Bernard. 1989. *Beyond Anthropology: Society and the Other.* New York: Columbia University Press.

McGreevy, John T. 1996. *Parish Boundaries: The Catholic Encounter with Race in the Twentieth-Century Urban North.* Chicago: University of Chicago Press.

McKee, James B. 1993. *Sociology and the Race Problem: The Failure of a Perspective.* Urbana: University of Illinois Press.

McKibbin, Ross. 1998. *Classes and Cultures: England 1918–1951.* Oxford: Oxford University Press.

McLeod, W. H. 1989. *Who Is a Sikh? The Problem of Sikh Identity.* Oxford: Oxford University Press.

McNeill, William H. 1976. *Plagues and Peoples.* Garden City, N.Y.: Anchor/Doubleday.

———. 1986. *Polyethnicity and National Unity in World History.* Toronto: University of Toronto Press.

Mearsheimer, John J. 2001. *The Tragedy of Great Power Politics.* New York: W. W. Norton.

Medawar, P. B., and J. S. Medawar. 1983. *Aristotle to Zoos: A Philosophical Dictionary of Biology.* Cambridge, Mass.: Harvard University Press.

Medvedev, Roy. [1972] 1989. *Let History Judge: The Origins and Consequences of Stalinism,* rev. and exp. ed., ed. and trans. George Shriver. New York: Columbia University Press.

Meier, Christian. [1980] 1990. *The Greek Discovery of Politics,* trans. David McLintock. Cambridge, Mass.: Harvard University Press.

Meillet, A. 1918. *Les langues dans l'Europe nouvelle.* Paris: Payot.

Meinecke, Friedrich. [1946/1950] 1963. *The German Catastrophe: Reflections and Recollections,* trans. Sidney B. Fay. Boston: Beacon Press.

———. [1907/1963] 1970. *Cosmopolitanism and the National State,* trans. Robert B. Kimber. Princeton, N.J.: Princeton University Press.

———. [1959] 1972. *Historism: The Rise of a New Historical Outlook,* trans. J. E. Anderson. London: Routledge & Kegan Paul.

———. [1906/1957] 1977. *The Age of German Liberation, 1795–1815,* ed. Peter Paret, trans. Peter Paret and Helmuth Fischer. Berkeley: University of California Press.

Melson, Robert F. 1992. *Revolution and Genocide: On the Origins of the Armenian Genocide and the Holocaust.* Chicago: University of Chicago Press.

Memmi, Albert. [1994] 2000. *Racism,* trans. Steve Martinot. Minneapolis: University of Minnesota Press.

Mendel, Douglas. 1970. *The Politics of Formosan Nationalism.* Cambridge, Mass.: Harvard University Press.

Mengaldo, Pier Vincenzo. 1994. *Storia della lingua italiana: Novecento.* Bologna: Il Mulino.

Mennell, Stephen. 1985. *All Manners of Food: Eating and Taste in England and France from the Middle Ages to the Present.* Oxford: Blackwell.

Merk, Frederick. [1963] 1966. *Manifest Destiny and Mission in American History: A Reinterpretation.* New York: Vintage.

Mertus, Julie A. 1999. *Kosovo: How Myths and Truths Started a War.* Berkeley: University of California Press.

Metcalf, Barbara Daly, ed. 1996. *Making Muslim Space in North America and Europe.* Berkeley: University of California Press.

Metcalf, Thomas R. 1994. *Ideologies of the Raj.* Cambridge: Cambridge University Press.

Meyer, Michael A. 1990. *Jewish Identity in the Modern World.* Seattle: University of Washington Press.

Michelet, Jules. 1973. *The People,* trans. John P. McKay. Urbana: University of Illinois Press.

Mies, Maria. 1986. *Patriarchy and Accumulation on a World Scale: Women in the International Division of Labour.* London: Zed.

Migliorini, Bruno 1990. *La lingua italiana nel Novecento,* ed. Massimo L. Fanfani. Firenze: Casa Editrice Le Lettere.

Migliorini, Bruno, and T. Gwynfor Griffith. [1960] 1984. *The Italian Language,* rev. ed. London: Faber and Faber.

Miles, Robert. 1989. *Racism.* London: Routledge.

———. 1993. *Racism after "Race Relations".* London: Routledge.

Milgram, Stanley. 1974. *Obedience to Authority: An Experimental View.* New York: Harper & Row.

Mill, John Stuart. [1861] 1977. "Considerations on Representative Government." In John Stuart Mill, *Collected Works,* vol. 19: *Essays on Politics and Society,* pt.2, ed. J. M. Robson, pp. 371–613. Toronto: University of Toronto Press.

Miller, David. 1995. *On Nationality.* Oxford: Clarendon Press.

Miller, Donald E., and Lorna Touryan Miller. 1993. *Survivors: An Oral History of the Armenian Genocide.* Berkeley: University of California Press.

Miller, George. 1956. "The Magical Number Seven Plus or Minus Two: Some Limits on Our Capacity for Processing Information." *Psychological Review* 63:581–597.

Miller, Karl. 1985. *Doubles: Studies in Literary History.* Oxford: Oxford University Press.

Miller, Perry. [1953] 1961. *The New England Mind: From Colony to Province.* Boston: Beacon Press.

Miller, William Lee. 1996. *Arguing about Slavery: The Great Battle in the United States Congress.* New York: Alfred A. Knopf.

Mills, Charles W. 1997. *The Racial Contract.* Ithaca, N.Y.: Cornell University Press.

Milner, Murray, Jr. 1994. *Status and Sacredness: A General Theory of Status Relations and an Analysis of Indian Culture.* New York: Oxford University Press.

Milton, Sybil H. 2001. " 'Gypsies' as Social Outsiders in Nazi Germany." In Robert Gellately and Nathan Stoltzfus, eds., *Social Outsiders in Nazi Germany,* pp. 212–232. Princeton, N.J.: Princeton University Press.

Mintz, Sidney. [1974] 1984. *Caribbean Transformations.* Baltimore: Johns Hopkins University Press.

Mitchell, J. Clyde. [1956] 1968. *The Kalela Dance: Aspects of Social Relationships among Urban Africans in Northern Rhodesia.* Manchester: Manchester University Press.

Mitchell, Robert W. 1994. "Multiplicities of Self." In Sue Taylor Parker, Robert W. Mitchell, and Maria L. Boccia, eds., *Self-Awareness in Animals and Humans: Developmental Perspectives,* pp. 81–107. Cambridge: Cambridge University Press.

Mitchell, Stephen. 1993. *Anatolia: Land, Men, and Gods in Asia Minor,* vol. 2: *The Rise of the Church.* Oxford: Clarendon Press.

Moerman, Michael. 1967. "Being Lue: Uses and Abuses of Ethnic Identification." In June Helm, ed., *Essays on the Problem of Tribe,* pp. 153–169. Seattle: University of Washington Press.

Moir, J. Reid. 1927. *The Antiquity of Man in East Anglia.* Cambridge: Cambridge University Press.

Momigliano, Arnaldo. 1975. *Alien Wisdom: The Limits of Hellenization.* Cambridge: Cambridge University Press.

Mommsen, Hans. 1991. *From Weimar to Auschwitz,* trans. Philip O'Connor. Princeton, N.J.: Princeton University Press.

———. 1997. "Cumulative Radicalisation and Progressive Self-Destruction as Structural Determinants of the Nazi Dictatorship." In Ian Kershaw and Moshe Lewin, eds., *Stalinism and Nazism: Dictatorships in Comparison,* pp. 75–87. Cambridge: Cambridge University Press.

———. 1998. "The Civil Service and the Implementation of the Holocaust: From Passive to Active Complicity." In Michael Berenbaum and Abraham J. Peck, eds., *The Holocaust and History: The Known, the Unknown, the Disputed, and the Reexamined,* pp. 219–227. Bloomington: Indiana University Press.

Mommsen, Wolfgang J. 1990. "The Varieties of the Nation State in Modern History: Liberal, Imperialist, Fascist and Contemporary Notions of Nation and Nationality." In Michael Mann, ed., *The Rise and Decline of the Nation State,* pp. 210–226. Oxford: Blackwell.

Montagu, M. F. Ashley. 1965. *The Idea of Race.* Lincoln: University of Nebraska Press.

Montaigne, Michel de. 1991. *The Complete Essays,* trans. M. A. Screech. London: Allen Lane.

Montanari, Massimo. 1994. *The Culture of Food,* trans. Carl Ipsen. Oxford: Blackwell.

Moore, R. I. [1977] 1997. *The Origins of European Dissent.* Toronto: University of Toronto Press.

———. 2000. *The First European Revolution, c. 970–1215.* Oxford: Blackwell.

Moran, Rachel F. 2001. *Interracial Intimacy: The Regulation of Race and Romance.* Chicago: University of Chicago Press.

Moretti, Franco. [1997] 1998. *Atlas of the European Novel, 1800–1900.* London: Verso.

Morgan, Edmund S. 1975. *American Slavery, American Freedom: The Ordeal of Colonial Virginia.* New York: W. W. Norton.

Morgan, Philip D. 1998. *Slave Counterpoint: Black Culture in the Eighteenth-Century Chesapeake and Lowcountry.* Chapel Hill: University of North Carolina Press.

Morgenthau, Hans J. 1946. *Scientific Man vs. Power Politics.* Chicago: University of Chicago Press.

Morin, Edgar. 2001. *La methode,* vol. 5: *l'humanité de l'humanité, pt.1: l'identité humaine.* Paris: Seuil.

Morris, Aldon D. 1984. *The Origins of the Civil Rights Movement: Black Communities Organizing for Change.* New York: Free Press.

Morris, Benny. 1993. *Israel's Border Wars 1949–1956: Arab Infiltration, Israeli Retaliation, and the Countdown to the Suez War.* Oxford: Clarendon Press.

———. 1999. *Righteous Victims: A History of the Zionist-Arab Conflict, 1881–1999.* New York: Alfred A. Knopf.

Morris, Christopher W. 1998. *An Essay on the Modern State.* Cambridge: Cambridge University Press.

Morris, William. 1888. "A Dream of John Ball." In William Morris, *A Dream of John Ball and A King's Lesson.* London: Reeves & Turner.

Mortimer, Rex. 1978. *Indonesian Communism under Sukarno: Ideology and Politics, 1959–1965.* Ithaca, N.Y.: Cornell University Press.

Moskoff, William. 1990. *The Bread of Affliction: The Food Supply in the USSR during World War II.* Cambridge: Cambridge University Press.

Mosse, George L. [1964] 1981. *The Crisis of German Ideology: Intellectual Origins of the Third Reich.* New York: Schocken.

———. 1985. *German Jews beyond Judaism.* Bloomington: Indiana University Press.

Mote, F. W. 1999. *Imperial China 900–1800.* Cambridge, Mass.: Harvard University Press.

Mournier, Roland. [1967] 1970. *Peasant Uprisings in Seventeenth-Century France, Russia, and China,* trans. Brian Pearce. New York: Harper & Row.

———. [1969] 1973. *Social Hierarchies 1450 to the Present,* ed. Margaret Clarke, trans. Peter Evans. New York: Schocken.

Mourant, A. E., Ada C. Kopec, and Kazimiera Domaniewska-Sobczak. 1978. *The Genetics of the Jews.* Oxford: Clarendon Press.

Muchembled, Robert. [1978] 1985. *Popular Culture and Elite Culture in France 1400–1750,* trans. Lydia Cochrane. Baton Rouge: Louisiana State University Press.

———. 1990. *Société, cultures et mentalités dans la France moderne XVIᵉ–XVIIIᵉ siècle.* Paris: Armand Colin.

Mulford, Elisha. [1887] 1971. *The Nation: The Foundations of Civil Order and Political Life in the United States.* New York: Kelley.

Müller, Horst. 1989. *Fürstenstaat oder Bürgernation: Deutschland 1763–1815.* Berlin: Siedler.

Müller, Jan-Werner. 2000. *Another Country: German Intellectuals, Unification and National Identity.* New Haven, Conn.: Yale University Press.

Müller-Hill, Benno. 1988. *Murderous Science: Elimination by Scientific Selection of Jews, Gypsies, and Others in Germany, 1933–1945.* Oxford: Oxford University Press.

———. 1998. "Human Genetics and the Mass Murder of Jews, Gypsies, and Others." In Michael Berenbaum and Abraham J. Peck, eds., *The Holocaust and History: The Known, the Unknown, the Disputed, and the Reexamined,* pp. 103–114. Bloomington: Indiana University Press.

Mungeam, G. H. 1966. *British Rule in Kenya, 1895–1912: The Establishment of Administration in the East Africa Protectorate.* Oxford: Clarendon Press.

Murphy, Robert F. 1987. *The Body Silent.* New York: Henry Holt.

Murphy-Lawless, Jo. 1998. *Reading Birth and Death: A History of Obstetric Thinking.* Bloomington: Indiana University Press.

Myrdal, Gunnar. [1944] 1962. *An American Dilemma: The Negro Problem and Modern Democracy,* 20th anniversary ed. New York: Harper & Row.

Nagahara Keiji. 1990. "The Medieval Peasant," trans. Suzanne Gay. In Kozo Yamamura, ed., *The Cambridge History of Japan,* vol. 3: *Medieval Japan,* pp. 301–343. Cambridge: Cambridge University Press.

Nagel, Joane. 1996. *American Indian Ethnic Renewal: Red Power and the Resurgence of Identity and Culture.* New York: Oxford University Press.

Naimark, Norman M. 2001. *Fires of Hatred: Ethnic Cleansing in Twentieth-Century Europe.* Cambridge, Mass.: Harvard University Press.

Nairn, Tom. [1977] 1981. *The Break-Up of Britain,* new ed. London: Verso.

Nakamura Hajime. 1985. *Genshi butten o yomu.* Tokyo: Iwanami Shoten.

Nash, Gary B. 1999. "The Hidden History of Mestizo America." In Martha Hodes, ed., *Sex, Love, Race: Crossing Boundaries in North American History,* pp. 10–32. New York: New York University Press.

Natsume Sōseki. [1912] 1986. "Gendai Nihon no kaika." In Sōseki Natsume, *Sōseki bunmeironshū*, ed. Yukio Miyoshi, pp. 7–38. Tokyo: Iwanami Shoten.

Neary, Ian. 1989. *Political Protest and Social Control in Pre-War Japan: The Origins of Buraku Liberation.* Atlantic Highlands, N.J.: Humanities Press International.

Nebrija, Antonio de. [1492] 1946. *Gramática castellana,* ed. Pascual Galindo Romeo and Luis Ortiz Muñoz. Madrid: Edición de la Junta del Centenario.

Neiman, Susan. 1994. "In Defense of Ambiguity." In Sander L. Gilman and Karen Remmler, eds., *Reemerging Jewish Culture in Germany: Life and Literature since 1989,* pp. 253–265. New York: New York University Press.

Neisser, Arden. 1983. *The Other Side of Silence: Sign Language and the Deaf Community in America.* New York: Alfred A. Knopf.

Neumann, Franz. [1942/1944] 1966. *Behemoth: The Structure and Practice of National Socialism, 1933–1944.* New York: Harper & Row.

Neumann, Iver B. 1999. *Uses of the Other: "The East" in European Identity Formation.* Minneapolis: University of Minnesota Press.

Neusner, Jacob. 1983. *Midrash in Context: Exegesis in Formative Judaism.* Philadelphia: Fortress Press.

———. 1987. *Judaism and Christianity in the Age of Constantine: History, Messiah, Israel, and the Initial Confrontation.* Chicago: University of Chicago Press.

Newbury, Catharine. 1988. *The Cohesion of Oppression: Clientship and Ethnicity in Rwanda 1860–1960.* New York: Columbia University Press.

Newitz, Annalee, and Matt Wray. 1997. "Introduction." In Matt Wray and Annalee Newitz, eds., *White Trash: Race and Class in America,* pp. 1–12. New York: Routledge.

Newman, Gerald. 1987. *The Rise of English Nationalism: A Cultural History, 1740–1830.* New York: St. Martin's Press.

Newman, John Henry, Cardinal. [1870] 1947. *An Essay in Aid of a Grammar of Assent,* new ed., ed. Charles Frederick Harrold. New York: Longmans, Green.

Niebuhr, H. Richard. [1929] 1957. *The Social Sources of Denominationalism.* New York: World Publishing.

Niebuhr, Reinhold. 1941–43. *The Nature and Destiny of Man: A Christian Interpretation,* 2 vols. New York: Charles Scribner's Sons.

Nietzsche, Friedrich. [1882/1887] 2001. *The Gay Science,* ed. Bernard Williams, trans. Josefine Nauckhoff and Adrian Del Caro. Cambridge: Cambridge University Press.

———. [1886] 1999. *Beyond Good and Evil: Prelude to the Philosophy of the Future,* trans. Marion Faber. Oxford: Oxford University Press.

Niezen, Ronald. 2003. *The Origins of Indigenism: Human Rights and the Politics of Identity.* Berkeley: University of California Press.

Nippel, Wilfried. 1990. *Griechen, Barbaren und "Wilde": Alte Geschichte und Sozialanthropologie.* Frankfurt am Main: Fischer.

Nirenberg, David. 1996. *Communities of Violence: Persecution of Minorities in the Middle Ages.* Princeton, N.J.: Princeton University Press.

Nisbet, Robert. 1980. *History of the Idea of Progress.* New York: Basic Books.

Nisbett, Richard, and Lee Ross. 1980. *Human Inference: Strategies and Shortcomings of Social Judgment.* Englewood Cliffs, N.J.: Prentice-Hall.

Nissen, Hans J. [1983] 1988. *The Early History of the Ancient Near East, 9000–2000 B.C.,* trans. Elizabeth Lutzeier, with Kenneth J. Northcott. Chicago: University of Chicago Press.

Nkrumah, Kwame. [1979] 1997. *Speeches of Kwame Nkrumah,* vol. 1, ed. Samuel Oberg. Accra, Ghana: Afram.

Noakes, Jeremy, ed. 1998. *Nazism 1919–1945,* vol. 4: *The German Home Front in World War II: A Documentary Reader.* Exeter, U.K.: University of Exeter Press.

Noakes, Jeremy, and Geoffrey Pridham, eds. 1984. *Nazism 1919–1945,* vol. 2: *State, Economy and Society, 1933–39: A Documentary Reader.* Exeter, U.K.: University of Exeter.

——. 1988. *Nazism 1919–1945,* vol. 3: *Foreign Policy, War and Racial Extermination: A Documentary Reader.* Exeter, U.K.: University of Exeter.

Nobles, Melissa. 2000. *Shades of Citizenship: Race and the Census in Modern Politics.* Stanford, Calif.: Stanford University Press.

Noethlichs, Karl Leo. 1996. *Das Judentum und der römische Staat: Minderheitenpolitik im antiken Rom.* Darmstadt, Germany: Wissenschaftlicher Buchgesellschaft.

Noiriel, Gérard. 1988. *Le creuset français: histoire de l'immigration XIXᵉ–XXᵉ siècle.* Paris: Seuil.

——. 1992. *Population, immigration et identité nationale en France XIXᵉ–XXᵉ siècle.* Paris: Hachette.

Nott, Josiah C. 1844. *Two Lectures on the Natural History of the Caucasian and Negro Races.* Mobile, Ala.: Dade and Thompson.

Novak, David. 1995. *The Election of Israel: The Idea of the Chosen People.* Cambridge: Cambridge University Press.

Novick, Peter. 1999. *The Holocaust in American Life.* Boston: Houghton Mifflin.

Nowak, Kurt. 1978. *"Euthanasie" und Sterilisierung im "Dritten Reich": Die Konfrontation der evangelischen und katholischen Kirche mit dem "Gesetz zur Verhütung erbkranken Nachwuchses" und der "Euthanasie" Aktion.* Göttingen: Vandenhoeck & Ruprecht.

Nugent, David. 1997. *Modernity at the Edge of Empire: State, Individual, and Nation in the Northern Peruvian Andes, 1885–1935.* Stanford, Calif.: Stanford University Press.

Nyerere, Julius K. 1966. *Freedom and Unity—Uhuru na Umoja: A Selection from Writings and Speeches, 1952–1965.* London: Oxford University Press.

Ó Gráda, Cormac. 1994. *Ireland: A New Economic History 1780–1939.* Oxford: Clarendon Press.

———. [1989] 1995. *The Great Irish Famine.* Cambridge: Cambridge University Press.

———. 1999. *Black '47 and Beyond: The Great Irish Famine in History, Economy, and Memory.* Princeton, N.J.: Princeton University Press.

Oakes, James. 1990. *Slavery and Freedom: An Interpretation of the Old South.* New York: Alfred A. Knopf.

Ober, Josiah. 1989. *Mass and Elite in Democratic Athens: Rhetoric, Ideology, and the Power of the People.* Princeton, N.J.: Princeton University Press.

O'Dea, Thomas F. 1957. *The Mormons.* Chicago: University of Chicago Press.

Odlum, E. 1916. *God's Covenant Man: British—Israel.* London: Robert Banks & Son.

Offen, Karen. 2000. *European Feminisms, 1700–1950: A Political History.* Stanford, Calif.: Stanford University Press.

Ogden, C. K., and Mary Sargant Florence. [1915] 1987. "Militarism versus Feminism: An Enquiry and a Policy Demonstrating That Militarism Involves the Subjection of Women." In Catherine Marshall, C. K. Ogden, and Mary Sargant Florence, *Militarism versus Feminism: Writings on Women and War,* ed. Margaret Kamester and Jo Vellacott, pp. 53–140. London: Virago Press.

Ohnuki-Tierney, Emiko. 1993. *Rice as Self: Japanese Identities through Time.* Princeton, N.J.: Princeton University Press.

Oldfield, Adrian. 1990. *Citizenship and Community: Civic Republicanism and the Modern World.* London: Routledge.

Olender, Maurice. 1992. *The Language of Paradise: Race, Religion, and Philology in the Nineteenth Century,* trans. Arthur Goldhammer. Cambridge, Mass.: Harvard University Press.

Oliver, Douglas L. [1955] 1967. *A Solomon Island Society: Kinship and Leadership among the Siuai of Bougainville.* Boston: Beacon Press.

Oliver, Michael. 1990. *The Politics of Disablement: A Sociological Approach.* New York: St. Martin's Press.

———. 1996. *Understanding Disability: From Theory to Practice.* New York: St. Martin's Press.

Omi, Michael, and Howard Winant. [1986] 1994. *Racial Formation in the United States: From the 1960s to the 1990s,* 2nd ed. New York: Routledge.

O'Neill, J. C. 1995. *Who Did Jesus Think He Was?* Leiden: E. J. Brill.

Ooms, Herman. 1996. *Tokugawa Village Practice: Class, Status, Power, Law.* Berkeley: University of California Press.

Oppenheim, A. Leo. [1964] 1977. *Ancient Mesopotamia: Portrait of a Dead Civilization,* rev. ed. Chicago: University of Chicago Press.

Ornan, Uzzi. 1985. "Hebrew Is Not a Jewish Language." In Joshua A. Fishman, ed., *Readings in the Sociology of Jewish Languages,* pp. 22–24. Leiden: E. J. Brill.

Orozco y Berra, Manuel. [1880] 1960. *Historia antigua y de la conquista de Mexico,* vol. 4. Mexico City: Porrúa.

Orwell, George. [1937] 1986. *The Complete Works of George Orwell,* vol. 5: *The Road to Wigan Pier,* ed. Peter Davison. London: Secker & Warburg.

Osborne, M. J. 1981–83. *Naturalization in Athens,* 4 vols. Brussels: AWLSK.

Osiander, Andreas. 1994. *The States System of Europe, 1640–1990: Peacemaking and the Conditions of International Stability.* Oxford; Clarendon Press.

Outram, Dorinda. 1995. *The Enlightenment.* Cambridge: Cambridge University Press.

Padley, G. A. 1988. *Grammatical Theory in Western Europe, 1500–1700: Trends in Vernacular Grammar II.* Cambridge: Cambridge University Press.

Pagden, Anthony. [1982] 1986. *The Fall of Natural Man: The American Indian and the Origins of Comparative Ethnology,* 2nd ed. Cambridge: Cambridge University Press.

———. 1990. *Spanish Imperialism and the Political Imagination: Studies in European and Spanish-American Social and Political Theory 1513–1830.* New Haven, Conn.: Yale University Press.

———. 1993. *European Encounters with the New World.* New Haven, Conn.: Yale University Press.

———. 2001. *Peoples and Empires: A Short History of European Migration, Exploration, and Conquest, from Greece to the Present.* New York: Modern Library.

Paine, Thomas. [1776] 1995. "Common Sense." In Thomas Paine, *Collected Writings,* ed. Eric Foner, pp. 5–59. New York: Library of America.

Palmer, R. R. [1941] 1969. *Twelve Who Ruled: The Year of the Terror in the French Revolution.* Princeton, N.J.: Princeton University Press.

Pálsson, Gísli. 1989. "Language and Society: The Ethnolinguistics of Icelanders." In E. Paul Durrenberger and Gísli Pálsson, eds., *The Anthropology of Iceland,* pp. 121–139. Iowa City: University of Iowa Press.

Pandey, Gyanendra. 1993. "The Civilized and the Barbarian: The 'New' Politics of Late Twentieth Century India and the World." In Gyanendra Pandey, ed., *Hindus and Others: The Question of Identity in India Today,* pp. 1–23. New Dehli: Viking.

Pannenberg, Wolfhart. [1977] 1983. *The Church,* trans. Keith Crim. Philadelphia: Westminster Press.

Paret, Peter. 1992. *Understanding War: Essays on Clausewitz and the History of Military Power.* Princeton, N.J.: Princeton University Press.

Parfit, Derek. 1984. *Reasons and Persons.* Oxford: Clarendon Press.

Parker, Geoffrey. 1988. *The Military Revolution: Military Innovation and the Rise of the West, 1500–1800.* Cambridge: Cambridge University Press.

———. 1998. *Geopolitics: Past, Present and Future.* London: Pinter.

Parker, Robert. 1996. *Athenian Religion: A History.* Oxford: Clarendon Press.

Parry, J. H. [1963] 1981. *The Age of Reconnaisance: Discovery, Exploration and Settlement 1450–1650.* Berkeley: University of California Press.

Parsons, Talcott. [1948] 1986. "Social Science: A Basic National Resource." In Samuel Z. Klausner and Victor M. Lidz, eds., *The Nationalization of the Social Sciences,* pp. 41–112. Philadelphia: University of Pennsylvania Press.

Pateman, Carole. 1988. *The Sexual Contract.* Stanford, Calif.: Stanford University Press.

Patterson, Orlando. 1975. "Context and Choice in Ethnic Allegiance: A Theoretical Framework and Caribbean Case Study." In Nathan Glazer and Daniel P. Moynihan, eds., *Ethnicity: Theory and Experience,* pp. 305–349. Cambridge, Mass.: Harvard University Press.

———. 1982. *Slavery and Social Death: A Comparative Study.* Cambridge, Mass.: Harvard University Press.

———. 1997. *The Ordeal of Integration: Progress and Resentment in America's "Racial" Crisis.* Washington, D.C.: Civitas.

Paul, Kathleen. 1997. *Whitewashing Britain: Race and Citizenship in the Postwar Era.* Ithaca, N.Y.: Cornell University Press.

Pawełczyńska, Anna. [1973] 1979. *Values and Violence in Auschwitz: A Sociological Analysis,* trans. Catherine S. Leach. Berkeley: University of California Press.

Paxton, Robert O. [1972] 1982. *Vichy France: Old Guard and New Order, 1940–1944.* New York: Columbia University Press.

Payne, Stanley G. 1995. *A History of Fascism, 1914–1945.* Madison: University of Wisconsin Press.

Pearson, Karl. [1892] 1937. *Grammar of Science,* Everyman ed. London: J. M. Dent.

Pélassy, Dominique. 1983. *Le signe nazi: l'univers symbolique d'une dictature.* Paris: Fayard.

Perrot, Philippe. [1981] 1994. *Fashioning the Bourgeoisie: A History of Clothing in the Nineteenth Century,* trans. Richard Bienvenu. Princeton, N.J.: Princeton University Press.

Peters, Edward, ed. [1971] 1998. *The First Crusade: The Chronicle of Fulcher of Chartres and Other Source Materials,* 2nd ed. Philadelphia: University of Pennsylvania Press.

Petersen, Roger D. 2002. *Understanding Ethnic Violence: Fear, Hatred, and Resentment in Twentieth-Century Eastern Europe.* Cambridge: Cambridge University Press.

Peterson, T. Sarah. 1994. *Acquired Taste: The French Origins of Modern Cooking.* Ithaca, N.Y.: Cornell University Press.

Peukert, Detlev J. K. [1982] 1987. *Inside Nazi Germany: Conformity, Opposition and Racism in Everyday Life,* trans. Richard Deveson. London: B. T. Batsford.

Peyre, Henri. 1933. *La royauté et les langues provinciales.* Paris: Les Presses Modernes.

Pflanze, Otto. 1990. *Bismarck and the Development of Germany,* 3 vols. Princeton, N.J.: Princeton University Press.

Phillipson, Robert. 1992. *Linguistic Imperialism.* Oxford: Oxford University Press.

Pick, Daniel. 1989. *Faces of Degeneration: A European Disorder, c. 1848–c. 1918.* Cambridge: Cambridge University Press.

Pinchuk, Ben-Cion. 1990. *Shtetl Jews under Soviet Rule: Eastern Poland on the Eve of the Holocaust.* Oxford: Blackwell.

Pine, Lisa. 1997. *Nazi Family Policy, 1933–1945.* Oxford: Berg.

Pinkney, David H. 1986. *Decisive Years in France, 1840–1847.* Princeton, N.J.: Princeton University Press.

Pipes, Richard. 1974. *Russia under the Old Regime.* New York: Scribner.

Pitkin, Hanna Fenichel. 1967. *The Concept of Representation.* Berkeley: University of California Press.

Plamenatz, John. 1960. *On Alien Rule and Self-Government.* London: Longmans, Green.

Planhol, Xavier de. 1988. *Géographie historique de la France.* Paris: Fayard.

Plant, Richard. 1986. *The Pink Triangle: The Nazi War against Homosexuals.* New York: Henry Holt.

Plischke, Hans. 1937. *Johann Friedrich Blumenbachs Einfluß auf die Entdeckungs- reisenden seiner Zeit.* Göttingen: Vandenhoeck & Ruprecht.

Plum, Günter. 1988. "Deutsche Juden oder Juden in Deutschland." In Wolfgang Benz, ed., *Die Juden in Deutschland 1933–1945: Leben unter nationalsozialistischer Herrschaft,* pp. 35–74. München: C. H. Beck.

Pocock, J. G. A. 1975. *The Machiavellian Moment: Florentine Political Thought and the Atlantic Republican Tradition.* Princeton, N.J.: Princeton University Press.

Poggi, Gianfranco. 1978. *The Development of the Modern State: A Sociological Intro- duction.* Stanford, Calif.: Stanford University Press.

Poliakov, Leon. 1955–77. *Histoire de l'antisémitisme,* 4 vols. Paris: Calmann-Lévy.

———. [1951/1954] 1979. *Harvest of Hate: The Nazi Program for the Destruction of the Jews of Europe,* rev. and exp. ed. New York: Holocaust Library.

Pollock, Susan. 1999. *Ancient Mesopotamia: The Eden That Never Was.* Cambridge: Cambridge University Press.

Pomeroy, Sarah B. 1997. *Families in Classical and Hellenistic Greece: Representations and Realities.* Oxford: Clarendon Press.

Pomian, Krzysztof. 1996. "Nation et patrimoine." In Daniel Fabre, ed., *L'Europe entre cultures et nations,* pp. 85–97. Paris: Éditions de la maison des sciences de l'homme.

Pommerin, Reiner. 1979. *Sterilisierung der Rheinlandbastarde: Das Schicksal einer farbigen deutschen Minderheit 1918–1937.* Düsseldorf: Droste.

Ponchaud, François. 1989. "Social Change in the Vortex of Revolution." In Karl D. Jackson, ed., *Cambodia 1975–1978: Rendezvous with Death,* pp. 151–177. Princeton, N.J.: Princeton University Press.

Porat, Dina. [1986] 1990. *The Blue and the Yellow Stars of David: The Zionist Leadership in Palestine and the Holocaust 1939–1945,* trans. David Ben-Nahum. Cambridge, Mass.: Harvard University Press.

Porath, Yehoshua. 1986. *In Search of Arab Unity.* London: Frank Cass.

Porter, Roy. 1982. *English Society in the Eighteenth Century.* Harmondsworth, U.K.: Penguin.

Post, Gaines. 1964. *Studies in Medieval Legal Thought: Public Law and the State, 1100–1322.* Princeton, N.J.: Princeton University Press.

Pound, Ezra. [1926] 1990. *Personae: The Shorter Poems,* rev. ed., ed. Lea Baechler and A. Walton Litz. New York: New Directions.

Power, Samantha. 2002. *"A Problem from Hell": America and the Age of Genocide.* New York: Basic Books.

Prawer, Joshua. 1988. *The History of the Jews in the Latin Kingdom of Jerusalem.* Oxford: Clarendon Press.

Prescott, J. R. V. 1987. *Political Frontiers and Boundaries.* London: Allen & Unwin.

Pressly, Thomas J. [1954] 1965. *Americans Interpret Their Civil War.* New York: Free Press.

Proctor, Robert. 1988. *Racial Hygiene: Medicine under the Nazis.* Cambridge, Mass.: Harvard University Press.

Prunier, Gérard. 1995. *The Rwanda Crisis: History of a Genocide.* New York: Columbia University Press.

Pulzer, Peter. [1964] 1988. *The Rise of Political Anti-Semitism in Germany and Austria,* rev. ed. Cambridge, Mass.: Harvard University Press.

———. 1998. "Between Hope and Fear: Jews and the Weimar Republic." In Wolfgang Benz, Arnold Paucker, and Peter Pulzer, eds., *Jüdisches Leben in der Weimarer Republik,* pp. 271–279. Tübingen: Mohr Siebeck.

Quadagno, Jill S. 1994. *The Color of Welfare: How Racism Undermined the War on Poverty.* New York: Oxford University Press.

Quigley, Declan. 1993. *The Interpretation of Caste.* Oxford: Clarendon Press.

Quinn, Kenneth M. 1989. "The Pattern and Scope of Violence." In Karl D. Jackson, ed., *Cambodia 1975–1978: Rendezvous with Death,* pp. 179–208. Princeton, N.J.: Princeton University Press.

Qur'an [1984] 1988. *Al-Qur'an: A Contemporary Translation,* rev. ed., trans. Ahmed Ali. Princeton, N.J.: Princeton University Press.

Rabinovitz, Dan. 1997. *Overlooking Nazareth: The Ethnography of Exclusion in Galilee.* Cambridge: Cambridge University Press.

Radcliffe-Brown, A. R. 1950. "Introduction." In A. R. Radcliffe-Brown and Daryll Forde, eds., *African Systems of Kinship and Marriage,* pp. 1–85. London: Oxford University Press.

———. [1922] 1964. *The Andaman Islanders.* New York: Free Press.

Radin, Paul. 1934. *The Racial Myth.* New York: McGraw-Hill.

Rae, Heather. 2002. *State Identities and the Homogenization of Peoples.* Cambridge: Cambridge University Press.

Rahman, Fazlur. 1982. *Islam and Modernity: Transformation of an Intellectual Tradition.* Chicago: University of Chicago Press.

Rahner, Karl. [1976] 1978. *Foundations of Christian Faith: An Introduction to the Idea of Christianity,* trans. William V. Dych. New York: Crossroad.

Rampersad, Arnold. [1976] 1990. *The Art and Imagination of W. E. B. Du Bois.* New York: Schocken.

Ramsey, S. Robert. 1987. *The Languages of China.* Princeton, N.J.: Princeton University Press.

Randal, Jonathan C. 1997. *After Such Knowledge, What Forgiveness? My Encounters with Kurdistan.* New York: Farrar, Straus & Giroux.

Ranger, Terence. 1983. "The Invention of Tradition in Colonial Africa." In Eric Hobsbawm and Terence Ranger, eds., *The Invention of Tradition,* pp. 211–262. Cambridge: Cambridge University Press.

———. 1989. "Missionaries, Migrants and the Manyika: The Invention of Ethnicity in Zimbabwe." In Leroy Vail, ed., *The Creation of Tribalism in Southern Africa,* pp. 118–150. London: James Currey.

Rankin, David. 1995. *Tertullian and the Church.* Cambridge: Cambridge University Press.

Rapaport, Lynn. 1997. *Jews in Germany after the Holocaust: Memory, Identity and Jewish-German Relations.* Cambridge: Cambridge University Press.

Ratzel, Friedrich. [1897] 1923. *Politische Geographie,* 3rd ed. München: R. Oldenbourg.

Rawick, George P. 1972. *The American Slave: A Composite Autobiography,* vol. 1: *From Sundown to Sunup: The Making of the Black Community.* Westport, Conn.: Greenwood.

Rawson, Claude. 2001. *God, Gulliver, and Genocide: Barbarism and the European Imagination, 1492–1945.* Oxford: Oxford University Press.

Rayside, David. 2001. "The Structuring of Sexual Minority Activity Opportunities in the Political Mainstream: Britain, Canada, and the United States." In Mark Blasius, ed., *Sexual Identities, Queer Politics,* pp. 23–55. Princeton, N.J.: Princeton University Press.

Redford, Donald B. 1992. *Egypt, Canaan, and Israel in Ancient Times.* Princeton, N.J.: Princeton University Press.

Reed, Ishmael. 1989. "America's 'Black Only' Ethnicity." In Werner Sollors, ed., *The Invention of Ethnicity,* pp. 226–229. New York: Oxford University Press.

———. 1993. *Airing Dirty Laundry.* Reading, Mass.: Addison-Wesley.

Reed, Nelson. 1964. *The Caste War of Yucatan.* Stanford, Calif.: Stanford University Press.

Reid, Anthony. 1994. "Early Southeast Asian Categorizations of Europeans." In Stuart B. Schwartz, ed., *Implicit Understandings: Observing, Reporting, and Reflecting on the Encounters between Europeans and Other Peoples in the Early Modern Era*, pp. 268–294. Cambridge: Cambridge University Press.

Reid, James J. 1992. "Total War, the Annihilation Ethic, and the Armenian Genocide, 1870–1918." In Richard G. Hovannisian, ed., *The Armenian Genocide: History, Politics, Ethics*, pp. 21–52. New York: St. Martin's Press.

Reid, Thomas. [1785] 1846. "Essays on the Intellectual Powers of Man." In Thomas Reid, *The Works of Thomas Reid*, ed. William Hamilton, pp. 213–508. Edinburgh: Maclachlan, Stewart.

Remarque, Erich Maria. [1928] 1958. *All Quiet on the Western Front*. Greenwich, Conn.: Fawcett Crest.

Renan, Ernest. [1882] 1990. "What Is a Nation?" trans. Martin Thom. In Homi K. Bhabha, ed., *Nation and Narration*, pp. 8–22. London: Routledge.

Repp, Kevin. 2000. *Reformers, Critics, and the Paths of German Modernity: Anti-Politics and the Search for Alternatives, 1890–1914*. Cambridge, Mass.: Harvard University Press.

Revel, Jean-François. [1979] 1982. *Culture and Cuisine: A Journey through the History of Food*, trans. Helen R. Lane. Garden City, N.Y.: Doubleday.

Rex, John. [1970] 1983. *Race Relations in Sociological Theory*, 2nd ed. London: RKP.

Reynolds, Susan. 1984. *Kingdoms and Communities in Western Europe, 900–1300*. Oxford: Clarendon Press.

Rhea, Joseph Tilden. 1997. *Race Pride and the American Identity*. Cambridge, Mass.: Harvard University Press.

Riasanovsky, Nicholas V. 1992. *The Emergence of Romanticism*. New York: Oxford University Press.

Rich, Paul B. [1986] 1990. *Race and Empire in British Politics*, 2nd ed. Cambridge: Cambridge University Press.

Richards, John F. 1993. *The Mughal Empire*. Cambridge: Cambridge University Press.

Ricklefs, M. C. [1981] 1993. *A History of Modern Indonesia since c. 1300*, 2nd ed. Stanford, Calif.: Stanford University Press.

Rieder, Jonathan 1985. *Canarsie: The Jews and Italians of Brooklyn against Liberalism*. Cambridge, Mass.: Harvard University Press.

Rieff, David. 1995. *Slaughterhouse: Bosnia and the Failure of the West*. New York: Simon & Schuster.

Rigg, Bryan Mark. 2002. *Hitler's Jewish Soldiers: The Untold Story of Nazi Racial Laws and Men of Jewish Descent in the German Military*. Lawrence: University Press of Kansas.

Riley-Smith, Jonathan. 1977. *What Were the Crusades?* Totowa, N.J.: Rowman & Littlefield.

————. 1997. *The First Crusaders, 1095–1131.* Cambridge: Cambridge University Press.

Rinderle, Walter, and Bernard Norling. 1993. *The Nazi Impact on a German Village.* Lexington: University of Kentucky Press.

Ripley, William Z. 1923. *The Races of Europe: A Sociological Study.* New York: Appleton.

Ritter, Joachim. [1969] 1982. *Hegel and the French Revolution: Essays on the Philosophy of Right,* trans. Richard Dien Winfield. Cambridge, Mass.: MIT Press.

Ritvo, Harriet. 1987. *The Animal Estate: The English and Other Creatures in the Victorian Age.* Cambridge, Mass.: Harvard University Press.

————. 1997. *The Platypus and the Mermaid and Other Figments of the Classifying Imagination.* Cambridge, Mass.: Harvard University Press.

Rivière, Peter. 1984. *Individual and Society in Guiana: A Comparative Study of Amerindian Social Organization.* Cambridge: Cambridge University Press.

Roach, Mary Ellen, and Joanne Bubolz Eicher, eds. 1965. *Dress, Adornment, and the Social Order.* New York: John Wiley & Sons.

Robb, Peter. 1995. "South Asia and the Concept of Race." In Peter Robb, ed., *The Concept of Race in South Asia,* pp. 1–76. Delhi: Oxford University Press.

Roberts, D. F. 1995. "The Pervasiveness of Plasticity." In C. G. N. Mascie-Taylor, and Barry Bogin, eds., *Human Variability and Plasticity,* pp. 1–17. Cambridge: Cambridge University Press.

Robins, Ashley H. 1991. *Biological Perspectives on Human Pigmentation.* Cambridge: Cambridge University Press.

Robinson, Geoffrey. 1995. *The Dark Side of Paradise: Political Violence in Bali.* Ithaca, N.Y.: Cornell University Press.

Roche, Daniel. [1989] 1996. *The Culture of Clothing: Dress and Fashion in the Ancien Regime,* trans. Jean Birrell. Cambridge: Cambridge University Press.

Rochebrune, Renaud de, and Jean-Claude Hazera. 1995. *Les patrons sous l'Occupation.* Paris: Odile Jacob.

Rodriguez, Richard. 1989. "An American Writer." In Werner Sollors, ed., *The Invention of Ethnicity,* pp. 3–13. New York: Oxford University Press.

Roediger, David R. 1991. *The Wages of Whiteness: Race and the Making of the American Working Class.* London: Verso.

Roger, Jacques. [1963] 1997. *The Life Sciences in Eighteenth-Century French Thought,* ed. Keith R. Benson, trans. Robert Ellrich. Stanford, Calif.: Stanford University Press.

Rogers, Spencer L. 1990. *The Colors of Mankind: The Range and Role of Human Pigmentation.* Springfield, Ill.: Charles C. Thomas.

Romaine, Suzanne. 1992. *Language, Education, and Development: Urban and Rural Tok Pisin in Papua New Guinea.* Oxford: Clarendon Press.

Romein, Jan. [1967] 1978. *The Watershed of Two Eras: Europe in 1900,* trans. Arnold Pomerans. Middletown, Conn.: Wesleyan University Press.

Rosdolsky, Roman. 1979. *Zur nationalen Frage: Friedrich Engels und das Problem der "geschichtslosen" Völker.* Berlin: Olle & Wolter.

Rose, Anne C. 2001. *Beloved Strangers: Interfaith Families in Nineteenth-Century America.* Cambridge, Mass.: Harvard University Press.

Rose, Romani. 1993. "Preface." In State Museum of Auschwitz-Birkenau, ed., *Memorial Book: The Gypsies at Auschwitz-Birkenau,* vol. 1, pp. xiii–xviii. München: K. G. Saur.

Rose, Steven. 1997. *Lifelines: Biology beyond Determinism.* Oxford: Oxford University Press.

Rosenberg, Alfred. 1970. *Selected Writings,* ed. Robert Pois. London: Jonathan Cape.

Rosenberg, Hans. [1958] 1966. *Bureaucracy, Aristocracy and Autocracy: The Prussian Experience 1660–1815.* Boston: Beacon Press.

Rosenberg, Justin. 1994. *The Empire of Civil Society: A Critique of the Realist Theory of International Relations.* London: Verso.

Rosenthal, Michael. 1986. *The Character Factory: Baden-Powell's Boy Scouts and the Imperatives of Empire.* New York: Pantheon.

Rosenzweig, Franz. [1919/1971] 1972. *The Star of Redemption,* trans. William W. Hallo. Boston: Beacon Press.

Ross, Fred A. 1857. *Slavery Ordained by God.* Philadelphia: J. B. Lippincott.

Ross, Lee, and Nisbett, Richard E. 1991. *The Person and the Situation: Perspectives of Social Psychology.* Boston: McGraw-Hill.

Ross, Ronald J. 1976. *Beleaguered Tower: The Dilemma of Political Catholicism in Wilhelmine Germany.* Notre Dame, Ind.: University of Notre Dame Press.

———. 1998. *The Failure of Bismarck's Kulturkampf: Catholicism and State Power in Imperial Germany, 1871–1887.* Washington, D.C.: Catholic University of America Press.

Roth, Joseph. [1927/1976] 2001. *The Wandering Jews: The Classic Portrait of a Vanished People,* trans. Michael Hofmann. New York: W. W. Norton.

Rouhana, Nadim N. 1997. *Palestinian Citizens in an Ethnic Jewish State: Identities in Conflict.* New Haven, Conn.: Yale University Press.

Rousseau, Jean-Jacques. [1752] 1994. "On the Social Contract, or Principles of Political Right." In Jean-Jacques Rousseau, *Social Contract, Discourse on the Virtue Most Necessary for a Hero, Political Fragments, and Geneva Manuscript,* ed. Roger D. Masters and Christopher Kelly, trans. Judith R. Bush, Roger D. Masters, and Chrisopher Kelly, pp. 127–224. Hanover, N.H.: University Press of New England.

———. [1782–98] 1995. "Confessions." In Jean-Jacques Rousseau, *The Confessions and Correspondence, Including the Letters to Malesherbes,* ed. Christopher

Kelly, Roger D. Masters, and Peter G. Stillman, trans. Christopher Kelly, pp. 1–550. Hanover, N.H.: University Press of New England.

Rousseau, Jérôme. 1990. *Central Borneo: Ethnic Identity and Social Life in a Stratified Community.* Oxford: Clarendon Press.

Roy, Olivier. [1992] 1994. *The Failure of Political Islam,* trans. Carol Volk. Cambridge, Mass.: Harvard University Press.

Rubin, Barry. 1999. *The Transformation of Palestinian Politics: From Revolution to State-Building.* Cambridge, Mass.: Harvard University Press.

Rubin, Gayle. 1984. "Thinking Sex: Notes for a Radical Theory of the Politics of Sexuality." In Carole S. Vance, ed., *Pleasure and Danger: Exploring Female Sexuality,* pp. 267–319. Boston: Routledge & Kegan Paul.

Rubinstein, Murray A. 1999. "Postscript and Conclusion." In Murray A. Rubinstein, ed., *Taiwan: A New History,* pp. 481–500. Armonk, N.Y.: M. E. Sharpe.

Rudé, George. 1959. *The Crowd in the French Revolution.* London: Oxford University Press.

Rummel, R. J. 1990. *Soviet Genocide and Mass Murder since 1917.* New Brunswick, N.J.: Transaction.

Rupp, Leila J. 1978. *Mobilizing Women for War: German and American Propaganda, 1939–1945.* Princeton, N.J.: Princeton University Press.

Rürup, Reinhard. 1975. *Emanzipation und Antisemitismus.* Göttingen: Vandenhoeck & Ruprecht.

———. 1991. "Jüdische Geschichte in Deutschland: Von der Emanzipation bis zur nationalsozialistischen Gewaltherrschaft." In Dirk Blasius and Dan Diner, eds., *Zerbrochene Geschichte: Leben und Selbstverständnis der Juden in Deutschland,* pp. 79–101. Frankfurt am Main: Fischer.

Rushton, J. Philippe. 1995. *Race, Evolution, and Behavior: A Life History Perspective.* New Brunswick, N.J.: Transaction.

Russell, Jeffrey B. 1980. *A History of Witchcraft: Sorcerers, Heretics and Pagans.* London: Thames & Hudson.

Rygiel, Kim. 1998. "Stabilizing Borders: The Geopolitics of National Identity Construction in Turkey." In Gearóid Ó Tuathail and Simon Dalby, eds., *Rethinking Geopolitics,* pp. 106–130. London: Routledge.

Sack, Robert David. 1986. *Human Territoriality: Its Theory and History.* Cambridge: Cambridge University Press.

Safrian, Hans. 1993. *Die Eichmann-Männer.* Wien: Europaverlag.

Sahagún, Bernardino de. 1990. *Historia general de las cosas de Nueva España,* 2 vols., ed. Juan Carlos Temprano. Madrid: Historia 16.

Sahlins, Marshall. 1995. *How "Natives" Think: About Captain Cook, for Example.* Chicago: University of Chicago Press.

Sahlins, Peter. 1989. *Boundaries: The Making of France and Spain in the Pyrenees.* Berkeley: University of California Press.

Said, Edward. [1978] 1979. *Orientalism.* New York: Vintage.

———. 1994. *The Politics of Dispossession: The Struggle for Palestinian Self-Determination, 1969–1994.* New York: Pantheon.

Saldarini, Anthony J. 1988. *Pharisees, Scribes and Sadducees in Palestinian Society.* Edinburgh: T&T Clark.

Samir, Samir Khalil. 1998. "The Christian Communities, Active Members of Arab Society throughout History." In Andrea Pacini, ed., *Christian Communities in the Arab Middle East: The Challenge of the Future*, pp. 67–91. Oxford: Clarendon Press.

Sanders, E. P. 1985. *Jesus and Judaism.* Philadelphia: Fortress Press.

Sanderson, G. N. 1985. "The European Partition of Africa: Origins and Dynamics." In Roland Oliver and G. N. Sanderson, eds., *The Cambridge History of Africa*, vol. 6: *From 1870 to 1905*, pp. 96–158. Cambridge: Cambridge University Press.

Sandkühler, Thomas. 1996. *"Endlösung" in Galizien: Der Judenmord in Ostpolen und die Rettungsinitiativen von Berthold Beitz 1941–1944.* Bonn: Dietz.

Sartre, Jean-Paul. [1946] 1948. *Anti-Semite and Jew,* trans. George J. Becker. New York: Schocken.

———. [1971] 1981. *The Family Idiot: Gustave Flaubert 1821–1857*, vol. 1, trans. Carol Cosman. Chicago: University of Chicago Press.

———. [1946] 2001. "The Black Orpheus," trans. John MacCombie. In Robert Bernasconi, ed., *Race*, pp. 115–142. Oxford: Blackwell.

Saussure, Ferdinand de. 1980. *Cours de linguistique générale*, ed. Tullio De Mauro. Paris: Payot.

Sayigh, Yezid. 1997. *Armed Struggle and the Search for State: The Palestinian National Movement 1949–1993.* Oxford: Clarendon Press.

Schaepdrijver, Sophie de. 1999. "Occupation, Propaganda and the Idea of Belgium." In Aviel Roshwald and Richard Stites, eds., *European Culture in the Great War: The Arts, Entertainment, and Propaganda, 1914–1918*, pp. 267–294. Cambridge: Cambridge University Press.

Schäfer, Peter. 1983. *Geschichte der Juden in der Antike: Die Juden Palästinas von Alexander dem Großen bis zur arabischen Eroberung.* Stuttgart: Katholisches Bibelwerk.

Scheffler, Wolfgang. 1989. "The Forgotten Part of the 'Final Solution': The Liquidation of the Ghettos," trans. Nina Morris-Farber. In Michael R. Marrus, ed., *The Nazi Holocaust: Historical Articles on the Destruction of European Jews, 3: The 'Final Solution': The Implementation of Mass Murder*, vol. 2, pp. 809–829. Westport, Conn.: Meckler.

Scheler, Max. [1914] 1982. "Der Genius des Krieges und der deutsche Krieg." In Max Scheler, *Gesammelte Werke*, vol. 4: *Politisch-pädagogische Schriften*, ed. Manfred S. Frings, pp. 7–250. Bern: Francke.

Schiffman, Lawrence H. 1985. *Who Was a Jew? Rabbinic and Halakhic Perspectives on the Jewish-Christian Schism.* Hoboken, N.J.: KTAV.

Schiller, Friedrich. [1759] 1967. *On the Aesthetic Education of Man, in a Series of Letters,* ed. and trans. Elizabeth M. Wilkinson and L. A. Willoughby. Oxford: Clarendon Press.

Schivelbusch, Wolfgang. [1977/1979] 1986. *The Railway Journey: The Industrialization of Time and Space in the 19th Century.* Berkeley: University of California Press.

Schleunes, Karl A. [1970] 1990. *The Twisted Road to Auschwitz: Nazi Policy toward German Jews, 1933–1939,* Illini Book ed. Urbana: University of Illinois Press.

Schmitt, Carl. 1976. *The Concept of the Political,* trans. George Schwab. New Brunswick, N.J.: Rutgers University Press.

———. 1985. *Political Theology: Four Chapters on the Concept of Sovereignty,* trans. George Schwab. Cambridge, Mass.: MIT Press.

Schmitt, Eric. 2001. "For 7 Million People in Census, One Race Category Isn't Enough." *New York Times* March 13, pp. A1, A14.

Schnapper, Dominique. 1991. *France de l'integration: sociologie de la nation en 1990.* Paris: Gallimard.

———. 1998. *La relation à l'autre: au coeur de la pensée sociologique.* Paris: Gallimard.

Schoenbaum, David. 1966. *Hitler's Social Revolution: Class and Status in Nazi Germany 1933–1939.* Garden City, N.Y.: Doubleday.

Scholem, Gershom. [1957] 1973. *Sabbatai Sevi: The Mystical Messiah 1626–1676,* trans. R.J. Zwi Werblowski. Princeton, N.J.: Princeton University Press.

Schorske, Carl E. 1994. "Introduction." In Nicolas Bouvier, Gordon A. Craig, and Lionel Gossman, eds., *Geneva, Zurich, Basel: History, Culture, and National Identity,* pp. 1–15. Princeton, N.J.: Princeton University Press.

———. 1995. "History and the Study of Culture." In Ralph Cohen and Michael S. Roth, eds., *History and . . . Histories within the Human Sciences,* pp. 382–395. Charlottesville: University Press of Virginia.

Schroeder, Paul W. 1994. *The Transformation of European Politics, 1763–1848.* Oxford: Clarendon Press.

Schulze, Hagen. [1985] 1991. *The Course of German Nationalism: From Frederick the Great to Bismarck, 1763–1867,* trans. Sarah Hanbury-Tenison. Cambridge: Cambridge University Press.

———. [1994] 1996. *States, Nations and Nationalism: From the Middle Ages to the Present,* trans. William E. Yuill. Oxford: Blackwell.

———. [1996] 1998. *Germany: A New History,* trans. Deborah Lucas Schneider. Cambridge, Mass.: Harvard University Press.

Schumann, Willy. 1991. *Being Present: Growing Up in Hitler's Germany.* Kent, Ohio: Kent State University Press.

Schumpeter, Joseph A. [1918/1954] 1991. "The Crisis of the Tax State." In Joseph A. Schumpeter, *The Economics and Sociology of Capitalism,* ed. Richard Swedberg, pp. 99–140. Princeton, N.J.: Princeton University Press.

Schwarz, Adam. 1994. *A Nation in Waiting: Indonesia in the 1990s.* Boulder, Colo.: Westview.

Scott, H. M., and Christopher Storrs. 1995. "Introduction: The Consolidation of Noble Power in Europe, c. 1600–1800." In H. M. Scott, ed., *The European Nobilities in the Seventeenth and Eighteenth Centuries,* vol. 1: *Western Europe,* pp. 1–52. London: Longman.

Scott, John Paul, and John L. Fuller. 1965. *Genetics and the Social Behavior of the Dog.* Chicago: University of Chicago Press.

Scott, Rebecca J. 2000. "Fault Lines, Color Lines, and Party Lines." In Frederick Cooper, Thomas C. Holt, and Rebecca J. Scott, *Beyond Slavery: Explorations of Race, Labor, and Citizenship in Postemancipation Societies,* pp. 61–106. Chapel Hill: University of North Carolina Press.

Seabrook, John. 2001. "The Tree of Man." *New Yorker* March 26, pp. 58–71.

Seal, Anil. 1973. "Imperialism and Nationalism in India." In John Gallagher, Gordon Johnson, and Anil Seal, eds., *Locality, Province and Nation: Essays on Indian Politics, 1870 to 1940,* pp. 1–27. Cambridge: Cambridge University Press.

Seale, Clive. 1998. *Constructing Death: The Sociology of Dying and Bereavement.* Cambridge: Cambridge University Press.

Searle, G. R. 1981. "Eugenics and Class." In Charles Webster, ed., *Biology, Medicine and Society, 1840–1940,* pp. 217–242. Cambridge: Cambridge University Press.

Seed, Patricia. 1988. *To Love, Honor, and Obey in Colonial Mexico: Conflicts over Marriage Choice, 1574–1821.* Stanford, Calif.: Stanford University Press.

———. 1995. *Ceremonies of Possession in Europe's Conquest of the New World 1492–1640.* Cambridge: Cambridge University Press.

———. 2001. *American Pentimento: The Invention of Indians and the Pursuit of Riches.* Minneapolis: University of Minnesota Press.

Segal, Alan F. 1986. *Rebecca's Children: Judaism and Christianity in the Roman World.* Cambridge, Mass.: Harvard University Press.

———. 1990. *Paul the Convert: The Apostolate and Apostasy of Saul the Pharisee.* New Haven, Conn.: Yale University Press.

Segalen, Martine. 1986. *Historical Anthropology of the Family,* trans. J. C. Whitehouse and Sarah Matthews. Cambridge: Cambridge University Press.

Segev, Tom. [1986] 1998. *1949: The First Israelis,* ed. Arlen Neal Weinstein. New York: Free Press.

———. [1999] 2000. *One Palestine, Complete: Jews and Arabs under the British Mandate,* trans. Haim Watzman. New York: Metropolitan.

Selden, Mark. 1989. "Introduction: The United States, Japan, and the Atomic

Bomb." In Kyoko Selden and Mark Selden, eds., *The Atomic Bomb: Voices from Hiroshima and Nagasaki,* pp. xi-xxxvi. Armonk, N.Y.: M. E. Sharpe.

Senghor, Léopold. [1977] 2001. "Negritude and Modernity or Negritude as a Humanism for the Twentieth Century," trans. Valentine Moulard. In Robert Bernasconi, ed., *Race,* pp. 143–165. Oxford: Blackwell.

Sereny, Gitta. 1974. *Into That Darkness: From Mercy Killing to Mass Murder.* New York: McGraw-Hill.

Service, Robert. 2000. *Lenin: A Biography.* Cambridge, Mass.: Harvard University Press.

Seton-Watson, Hugh. 1977. *Nations and States.* Boulder, Colo.: Westview Press.

Sewell, William H., Jr. 1980. *Work and Revolution in France: The Language of Labor from the Old Regime to 1848.* Cambridge: Cambridge University Press.

———. 1985. *Structure and Mobility: The Men and Women of Marseille, 1820–1870.* Cambridge: Cambridge University Press.

———. 1994. *A Rhetoric of Bourgeois Revolution: The Abbé Sieyes and What Is the Third Estate?* Durham, N.C.: Duke University Press.

Shanin, Teodor. 1990. *Defining Peasants: Essays Concerning Rural Societies, Expolary Economies, and Learning from Them in the Contemporary World.* Oxford: Blackwell.

Shapira, Anita. [1980] 1984. *Berl: The Biography of a Socialist Zionist: Berl Katznelson 1887–1944,* trans. Haya Galai. Cambridge: Cambridge University Press.

———. 1997. "The Holocaust and World War II as Elements of the Yishuv Psyche until 1948." In Alvin H. Rosenfeld, ed., *Thinking about the Holocaust: After Half a Century,* pp. 61–82. Bloomington: Indiana University Press.

Sharpless, John. 1997. "Population Science, Private Foundations, and Development Aid: The Transformation of Demographic Knowledge in the United States, 1945–1965." In Frederick Cooper and Randall M. Packard, eds., *International Development and the Social Sciences: Essays on the History and Politics of Knowledge,* pp. 176–200. Berkeley: University of California Press.

Shattuck, Roger. 2001. "Farce & Philosophy." *New York Review of Books* February 22, pp. 22–25.

Shaw, Martin. 1988. *Dialectics of War: An Essay in the Social Theory of Total War and Peace.* London: Pluto Press.

———. 1991. *Post-Military Society: Militarism, Demilitarization and War at the End of the Twentieth Century.* Philadelphia: Temple University Press.

———. 1996. *Civil Society and Media in Global Crises: Representing Distant Violence.* London: Pinter.

———. 2000. *Theory of the Global State: Globality as an Unfinished Revolution.* Cambridge: Cambridge University Press.

Sheehan, James J. 1978. *German Liberalism in the Nineteenth Century.* Chicago: University of Chicago Press.

————. 1989. *German History, 1770–1866.* Oxford: Clarendon Press.

————. 1992. "State and Nationality in the Napoleonic Period." In John Breuilly, ed., *The State of Germany: The National Idea in the Making, Unmaking and Remaking of a Modern Nation-State,* pp. 47–59. London: Longman.

Shelby, Anne. 1999. "The 'R' Word: What's So Funny (and Not So Funny) about Redneck Jokes." In Dwight B. Billings, Gurney Norman, and Katherine Ledford, eds., *Confronting Appalachian Stereotypes: Back Talk from an American Region,* pp. 153–160. Louisville: University Press of Kentucky.

Shell, Marc. 1993. *Children of the Earth: Literature, Politics and Nationhood.* New York: Oxford University Press.

Shelley, Percy Bysshe. [1821] 1974. "Hellas: A Lyrical Drama." In Percy Bysshe Shelley, *The Poetical Works of Shelley,* ed. Newell F. Ford, pp. 317–339. Boston: Houghton Mifflin.

Shennan, J. H. 1974. *The Origins of the Modern European State 1450–1725.* London: Hutchinson.

Shepherd, John Robert. 1993. *Statecraft and Political Economy on the Taiwan Frontier, 1600–1800.* Stanford, Calif.: Stanford University Press.

Sherwin, Martin J. [1975] 1977. *A World Destroyed: The Atomic Bomb and the Grand Alliance.* New York: Vintage.

Sherwin-White, A. N. 1939. *The Roman Citizenship.* Oxford: Clarendon Press.

————. 1967. *Racial Prejudice in Imperial Rome.* Cambridge: Cambridge University Press.

Shi Gang. 1993. *Shokuminchi shihai to Nihongo.* Tokyo: Sangensha.

Shils, Edward. 1963. "On the Comparative Study of the New States." In Clifford Geertz, ed., *Old Societies and New States: The Quest for Modernity in Asia and Africa,* pp. 1–26. New York: Free Press.

Shipler, David K. 1997. *A Country of Strangers: Blacks and Whites in America.* New York: Alfred A. Knopf.

Shipps, Jan. 1985. *Mormonism: The Story of a New Religious Tradition.* Urbana: University of Illinois Press.

————. 1994. "Making Saints: In the Early Days and the Latter Days." In Marie Cornwall, Tim B. Heaton, and Lawrence A. Young, eds., *Contemporary Mormonism: Social Science Perspectives,* pp. 64–83. Urbana: University of Illinois Press.

Shklar, Judith N. 1991. *American Citizenship: The Quest for Inclusion.* Cambridge, Mass.: Harvard University Press.

Shore, Cris. [1993] 1997. "Ethnicity as Revolutionary Strategy: Communist Identity Construction in Italy." In Sharon MacDonald, ed., *Inside European Identities: Ethnography in Western Europe,* pp. 27–53. Oxford: Berg.

Shue, Vivienne. 1988. *The Reach of the State: Sketches of the Chinese Body Politic.* Stanford, Calif.: Stanford University Press.

Siberry, Elizabeth. 1985. *Criticism of Crusading 1095–1274*. Oxford: Clarendon Press.

Siegel, James T. 1997. *Fetish, Recognition, Revolution*. Princeton, N.J.: Princeton University Press.

Sieyès, Emmanuel Joseph. [1791] 1963. *What Is the Third Estate?* ed. S. E. Finer, trans. M. Blondel. New York: Frederick A. Praeger.

Simpson, George Gaylord. [1961] 1990. *Principles of Animal Taxonomy*. New York: Columbia University Press.

Singer, Mark. 2001. "Home Is Here." *New Yorker*, October 15, pp. 62–70.

Singh, K. S., V. Bhalla, and V. Kaul. 1994. *The Biological Variation in Indian Populations*. Delhi: Oxford University Press.

Skerry, Peter. 2000. *Counting on the Census? Race, Group Identity, and the Evasion of Politics*. Washington, D.C.: Brookings Institution Press.

Skran, Claudena M. 1995. *Refugees in Inter-War Europe: The Emergence of a Regime*. Oxford: Clarendon Press.

Skrentny, John D. 2002. *The Minority Rights Revolution*. Cambridge, Mass.: Harvard University Press.

Sliwinski, Marek. 1995. *Le génocide Khmer Rouge: une analyse démographique*. Paris: L'Harmattan.

Smith, Anna Marie. 1994. *New Right Discourse on Race & Sexuality: Britain 1968–1990*. Cambridge: Cambridge University Press.

Smith, Anthony D. 1981. *The Ethnic Revival*. Cambridge: Cambridge University Press.

———. 1986. *The Ethnic Origins of Nations*. Oxford: Blackwell.

———. 1991. *National Identity*. Reno: University of Nevada Press.

———. 1995. *Nations and Nationalism in a Global Era*. Cambridge: Polity.

Smith, David Norman. 1998. "The Psychocultural Roots of Genocide: Legitimacy and Crisis in Rwanda." *American Psychologist* 53:743–753.

Smith, Edward E., and Douglas L. Medin. 1981. *Categories and Concepts*. Cambridge, Mass.: Harvard University Press.

Smith, Helmut Walser. 1995. *German Nationalism and Religious Conflict: Culture, Ideology, Politics, 1870–1914*. Princeton, N.J.: Princeton University Press.

———. 1998. "The Talk of Genocide, the Rhetoric of Miscegenation: Notes on Debates in the German Reichstag Concerning Southwest Africa, 1904–14." In Sara Friedrichsmeyer, Sara Lennox, and Susanne Zantop, eds., *The Imperialist Imagination: German Colonialism and Its Legacy*, pp. 107–123. Ann Arbor: University of Michigan Press.

Smith, Jonathan Z. 1990. *Drudgery Divine: On the Comparison of Early Christianities and the Religions of Late Antiquity*. Chicago: University of Chicago Press.

Smith, M. G. 1965. *The Plural Society in the British West Indies*. Berkeley: University of California Press.

Smith, Malcolm T. 1993. "Genetic Adaptation." In G. A. Harrison, ed., *Human Adaptation,* pp. 1–54. Oxford: Oxford University Press.

Smith, Michael G. 1998. *Language and Power in the Creation of the USSR, 1917–1953.* Berlin: Mouton de Gruyter.

Smith, Rogers M. 1997. *Civic Ideals: Conflicting Visions of Citizenship in U.S. History.* New Haven, Conn.: Yale University Press.

Smith, Steve. 1989. "The Fall and Rise of the State in International Politics." In Graeme Duncan, ed., *Democracy and the Capitalist State,* pp. 33–55. Cambridge: Cambridge University Press.

Smith, Wilfred Cantwell. 1957. *Islam in Modern History.* Princeton, N.J.: Princeton University Press.

———. 1977. *Belief and History.* Charlottesville: University of Virginia Press.

———. 1979. *Faith and Belief.* Princeton, N.J.: Princeton University Press.

———. 1981. *Towards a World Theology: Faith and the Comparative History of Religion.* Philadelphia: Westminster Press.

Snell, Daniel C. 1997. *Life in the Ancient Near East, 3100–332 B.C.E.* New Haven, Conn.: Yale University Press.

Snell, K. D. M. 1985. *Annals of the Labouring Poor: Social Change and Agrarian England, 1660–1900.* Cambridge: Cambridge University Press.

Sniderman, Paul M., and Thomas Piazza. 1993. *The Scar of Race.* Cambridge, Mass.: Harvard University Press.

———. 2002. *Black Pride and Black Prejudice.* Princeton, N.J.: Princeton University Press.

Snodgrass, Anthony. 1980. *Archaic Greece: The Age of Experiment.* Berkeley: University of California Press.

Snowden, Frank M., Jr. 1983. *Before Color Prejudice: The Ancient View of Blacks.* Cambridge, Mass.: Harvard University Press.

Snyder, Jack. 2000. *From Voting to Violence: Democratization and Nationalist Conflict.* New York: W. W. Norton.

Snyder, Louis L. 1939. *Race: A History of Modern Ethnic Theories.* New York: Longmans, Green.

Soekarno [Sukarno]. [1954] 1968. *The Meaning of Nationalism.* Westport, Conn.: Greenwood.

———. 1975. *Indonesia Accuses!: Soekarno's Defence Oration in the Political Trial of 1930,* ed. and trans. Roger K. Paget. Kuala Lumpur: Oxford University Press.

Sofsky, Wolfgang. [1993] 1997. *The Order of Terror: The Concentration Camp,* trans. William Templer. Princeton, N.J.: Princeton University Press.

Sollors, Werner. 1986. *Beyond Ethnicity: Consent and Descent in American Culture.* New York: Oxford University Press.

———. 1989. "Introduction: The Invention of Ethnicity." In Werner Sollors, ed., *The Invention of Ethnicity,* pp. ix–xx. New York: Oxford University Press.

————. 1997. *Neither Black nor White yet Both: Thematic Explorations of Interracial Literature.* New York: Oxford University Press.

Solomon, Barbara Miller. 1956. *Ancestors and Immigrants, a Changing New England Tradition.* Cambridge, Mass.: Harvard University Press.

Solomos, John. 1988. *Black Youth, Racism and the State: The Politics of Ideology and Policy.* Cambridge: Cambridge University Press.

Sommer, Doris. 1991. *Foundational Fictions: The National Romances of Latin America.* Berkeley: University of California Press.

Sorkin, David. 1987. *The Transformation of German Jewry, 1780–1840.* New York: Oxford University Press.

Soyinka, Wole. 1976. *Myth, Literature and the African World.* Cambridge: Cambridge University Press.

Soysal, Yasemin Nuhoglu. 1994. *Limits of Citizenship: Migrants and Postnational Membership in Europe.* Chicago: University of Chicago Press.

Spalding, Karen. 1984. *Huarochiri: An Andean Society under Inca and Spanish Rule.* Stanford, Calif.: Stanford University Press.

Speier, Hans. [1977] 1986. *German White-Collar Workers and the Rise of Hitler.* New Haven, Conn.: Yale University Press.

Spence, Jonathan D. 1996. *God's Chinese Son: The Taiping Heavenly Kingdom of Hong Xiuquan.* New York: W. W. Norton.

Spencer, Herbert. 1851. *Social Statics: Or, the Conditions Essential to Human Happiness Specified, and the First of Them Developed.* London: John Chapman.

Speranza, Gino. 1925. *Race or Nation: A Conflict of Divided Loyalties.* Indianapolis: Bobbs-Merrill.

Sperber, Jonathan. 1994. *The European Revolutions, 1848–1851.* Cambridge: Cambridge University Press.

Spinoza, Benedict de. 1951. "A Theologico-Political Treatise." In Benedict de Spinoza, *The Chief Works of Benedict de Spinoza,* vol. 1, trans. R. H. M. Elwes, pp. 1–278. New York: Dover.

Spolsky, Bernard, and Robert L. Cooper. 1991. *The Languages of Jerusalem.* Oxford: Clarendon Press.

Spruyt, Hendrik. 1994. *The Sovereign State and Its Competitors.* Princeton, N.J.: Princeton University Press.

Srinivas, M. N. 1952. *Religion and Society among the Coorgs of South India.* Oxford: Clarendon Press.

————. 1966. *Social Change in Modern India.* Berkeley: University of California Press.

————. 1987. *The Dominant Caste and Other Essays.* Delhi: Oxford University Press.

St. Clair, William. 1972. *That Greece Might Still Be Free: The Philhellenes in the War of Independence.* London: Oxford University Press.

Stampp, Kenneth M. 1956. *The Peculiar Institution: Slavery in the Ante-Bellum South.* New York: Alfred A. Knopf.

Staniland, Martin. 1991. *American Intellectuals and African Nationalists, 1955–1970.* New Haven, Conn.: Yale University Press.

Stannard, David E. 1989. *Before the Horror: The Population of Hawai'i on the Eve of Western Contact.* Honolulu: Social Science Research Institute, University of Hawaii.

———. 1992. *American Holocaust: Columbus and the Conquest of the New World.* New York: Oxford University Press.

Stanton, William. 1960. *The Leopard's Spots: Scientific Attitudes toward Race in America, 1815–59.* Chicago: University of Chicago Press.

Starr, Douglas. 1998. *Blood: An Epic History of Medicine and Commerce.* New York: Alfred A. Knopf.

Steakley, James D. 1975. *The Homosexual Emancipation Movement in Germany.* New York: Arno Press.

Steele, Shelby. 1990. *The Content of Our Character: A New Vision of Race in America.* New York: St. Martin's Press.

Stein, Judith. 1989. "Defining the Race 1890–1930." In Werner Sollors, ed., *The Invention of Ethnicity,* pp. 77–104. New York: Oxford University Press.

Stein, Stanley J., and Barbara H. Stein. 1970. *The Colonial Heritage of Latin America: Essays on Economic Dependence in Perspective.* New York: Oxford University Press.

Steinberg, Jonathan. 1987. "The Historian and the *Questione della Lingua.*" In Peter Burke and Roy Porter, eds., *The Social History of Language,* pp. 198–209. Cambridge: Cambridge University Press.

———. [1976] 1996. *Why Switzerland?* 2nd ed. Cambridge: Cambridge University Press.

Steinberg, Stephen. [1981] 1989. *The Ethnic Myth: Race, Ethnicity, and Class in America,* updated ed. Boston: Beacon Press.

Steinert, Marlis G. 1970. *Hitlers Krieg und die Deutschen: Stimmung und Haltung der deutschen Bevölkerung im Zweiten Weltkrieg.* Düsseldorf: Econ.

Steinmetz, George. 1997. "German Exceptionalism and the Origins of Nazism: The Career of a Concept." In Ian Kershaw and Moshe Lewin, eds., *Stalinism and Nazism: Dictatorships in Comparison,* pp. 251–284. Cambridge: Cambridge University Press.

Stepan, Nancy. 1982. *The Idea of Race in Science: Great Britain 1800–1960.* London: Macmillan.

———. 1991. *The Hour of Eugenics: Race, Gender, and Nation in Latin America.* Ithaca, N.Y.: Cornell University Press.

Stern, Fritz. 1961. *The Politics of Cultural Despair: A Study in the Rise of the Germanic Ideology.* Berkeley: University of California Press.

———. 1972. *The Failure of Illiberalism: Essays on the Political Culture of Modern Germany.* New York: Alfred A. Knopf.

———. 1987. *Dreams and Delusions: The Drama of German History.* New York: Alfred A. Knopf.

Stern, J. P. 1975. *Hitler: The Führer and the People.* Berkeley: University of California Press.

Stern, Sacha. 1994. *Jewish Identity in Early Rabbinic Writings.* Leiden: E. J. Brill.

Stern, Steve J. 1982. *Peru's Indian Peoples and the Challenge of Spanish Conquest: Huamanga to 1640.* Madison: University of Wisconsin Press.

Sternhell, Zeev. [1996] 1998. *The Founding Myths of Israel: Nationalism, Socialism, and the Making of the Jewish State,* trans. David Maisel. Princeton, N.J.: Princeton University Press.

Stevens, Jacqueline. 1999. *Reproducing the State.* Princeton, N.J.: Princeton University Press.

Stewart, J. I. M. 1963. *Eight Modern Writers.* Oxford: Clarendon Press.

Stewart, Michael. 1997. *The Time of the Gypsies.* Boulder, Colo.: Westview Press.

Stier, Haya, and Marta Tienda. 2001. *The Color of Opportunity: Pathways to Family, Welfare, and Work.* Chicago: University of Chicago Press.

Stiker, Henri-Jacques. 1982. *Corps infirmes et sociétés.* Paris: Aubier Montaigne.

Stockton, David. 1990. *The Classical Athenian Democracy.* Oxford: Oxford University Press.

Stoczkowski, Wiktor. 1994. *Anthropologie naïve, anthropologie savante.* Paris: CNRS.

Stoltzfus, Nathan. 1996. *Resistance of the Heart: Intermarriage and the Rosenstrasse Protest in Nazi Germany.* New York: W. W. Norton.

Stone, John. 1985. *Racial Conflict in Contemporary Society.* Cambridge, Mass.: Harvard University Press.

Stouff, Louis. 1970. *Ravitaillement et alimentation en Provence aux XIVᵉ et XVᵉ siècles.* Paris: Mouton.

Strasburger, Hermann. 1976. *Zum antiken Gesellschaftsideal.* Heidelberg: Carl Winter.

Strawson, P. F. 1959. *Individuals: An Essay in Descriptive Metaphysics.* London: Methuen.

Strayer, Joseph R. 1970. *On the Medieval Origins of the Modern State.* Princeton, N.J.: Princeton University Press.

Streit, Christian. [1978] 1991. *Keine Kameraden: Die Wehrmacht und die sowjetischen Kriegsgefangenen 1941–1945.* Bonn: J. H. W. Dietz Nachf.

Stümke, Hans-Georg. 1996. "From the 'People's Consciousness of Right and Wrong' to 'the Hearty Instincts of the Nation': The Persecution of Homosexuals in Nazi Germany." In Michael Burleigh, ed., *Confronting the Nazi Past: New Debates on Modern German History,* pp. 154–166. New York: St. Martin's Press.

Summerfield, Daniel P. 2003. *From Falashas to Ethiopian Jews: The External Influences for Change, c. 1860–1960.* London: RoutledgeCurzon.

Suny, Ronald Grigor. 1993. *Looking toward Ararat: Armenia in Modern History.* Bloomington: Indiana University Press.

———. 1998. *The Soviet Experiment: Russia, the USSR, and the Successor States.* New York: Oxford University Press.

Suny, Ronald Grigor, and Michael Kennedy. 1999. "Toward a Theory of National Intellectual Practice." In Ronald Grigor Suny and Michael Kennedy, eds., *Intellectuals and the Articulation of the Nation,* pp. 383–417. Ann Arbor: University of Michigan Press.

Suttanipāta. 1932. *Buddha's Teachings, Being the Sutta-Nipāta or Discourse-Collection,* ed. Lord Chalmers. Cambridge, Mass.: Harvard University Press.

Sutton, Francis X. 1965. "Education and the Making of Modern Nations." In James S. Coleman, ed., *Education and Political Development,* pp. 51–74. Princeton, N.J.: Princeton University Press.

Swain, Simon. 1996. *Hellenism and Empire: Language, Classicism, and Power in the Greek World, AD 50–250.* Oxford: Clarendon Press.

Sykes, Stephen. 1984. *The Identity of Christianity: Theologians and the Essence of Christianity from Schleiermacher to Barth.* Philadelphia: Fortress Press.

Syme, Ronald. 1958. *Colonial Élites: Rome, Spain and the Americas.* London: Oxford University Press.

Tajfel, Henri. 1981. *Human Groups and Social Categories: Studies in Social Psychology.* Cambridge: Cambridge University Press.

Takakusu, Junjirō. [1947] 1956. *The Essentials of Buddhist Philosophy,* 3rd ed, ed. Wing-Tsit Chan and Charles A. Moore. Delhi: Motilal Banarsidass.

Tal, Uriel. [1969] 1975. *Christians and Jews in Germany: Religion, Politics, and Ideology in the Second Reich, 1870–1914,* trans. Noah Jonathan Jacobs. Ithaca, N.Y.: Cornell University Press.

Talmon, J. L. 1960. *Political Messianism: The Romantic Phase.* London: Secker & Warburg.

———. 1970. *Israel among the Nations.* London: Weidenfeld & Nicholson.

Tarrow, Sidney. 1994. *Power in Movement: Social Movements, Collective Action and Politics.* Cambridge: Cambridge University Press.

Tatar, Maria. 1987. *The Hard Facts of the Grimms' Fairy Tales.* Princeton, N.J.: Princeton University Press.

Taylor, A. J. P. 1954. *The Struggle for Mastery in Europe, 1848–1918.* Oxford: Clarendon Press.

———. 1965. *English History, 1914–1945.* Oxford: Clarendon Press.

Taylor, Charles. 1989. *Sources of the Self: The Making of the Modern Identity.* Cambridge, Mass.: Harvard University Press.

Taylor, John G. 1991. *Indonesia's Forgotten War: The Hidden History of East Timor.* London: Zed.

————. 1995. "The Emergence of a Nationalist Movement in East Timor." In Peter Carey and G. Carter Bentley, eds., *East Timor at the Crossroads: The Forging of a Nation*, pp. 21–41. Honolulu: University of Hawaii Press.

Taylor, William B. 1979. *Drinking, Homicide, and Rebellion in Colonial Mexican Villages*. Stanford, Calif.: Stanford University Press.

te Brake, Wayne. 1998. *Shaping History: Ordinary People in European Politics, 1500–1700*. Berkeley: University of California Press.

Tec, Nechama. 1986. *When Light Pierced the Darkness: Christian Rescue of Jews in Nazi-Occupied Poland*. New York: Oxford University Press.

Teggart, Frederick J. [1941] 1977. *Theory and Processes of History*. Berkeley: University of California Press.

Ternon, Yves. 1995. *L'état criminel: Les génocides au XXᵉ siècle*. Paris: Seuil.

————. 2002. *L'Empire ottoman: Le déclin, la chute, l'effacement*. Paris: Michel de Maule.

Thernstrom, Stephan, and Abigail Thernstrom. 1997. *America in Black and White: One Nation, Indivisible*. New York: Simon & Schuster.

Thomas, Keith. [1971] 1997. *Religion and the Decline of Magic: Studies in Popular Beliefs in Sixteenth and Seventeenth Century England*. New York: Oxford University Press.

Thomas, Nicholas. 1990. *Marquesan Societies: Inequality and Political Transformation in Eastern Polynesia*. Oxford: Clarendon Press.

Thomas, William I., and Florian Znaniecki. 1918–20. *The Polish Peasant in Europe and America: A Monograph of an Immigrant Group*, 5 vols. Chicago: University of Chicago Press.

Thompson, Charis. 2001. "Strategic Naturalizing: Kinship in an Infertility Clinic." In Sarah Franklin and Susan McKinnon, eds., *Relative Values: Reconfiguring Kinship Studies*, pp. 175–202. Durham, N.C.: Duke University Press.

Thompson, Elizabeth. 2000. *Colonial Citizens: Republican Rights, Paternal Privilege, and Gender in French Syria and Lebanon*. New York: Columbia University Press.

Thompson, Leonard. 1985. *The Political Mythology of Apartheid*. New Haven, Conn.: Yale University Press.

Thompson, Lloyd A. 1989. *Romans and Blacks*. London: Routledge.

Thorowgood, Thomas. 1660. *Jews in America*. London: Henry Brome.

Thurner, Erika. [1983] 1998. *National Socialism and Gypsies in Austria*, ed. and trans. Gilya Gerda Schmidt. Tuscaloosa: University of Alabama Press.

Thurston, Robert W. 1996. *Life and Terror in Stalin's Russia, 1934–1941*. New Haven, Conn.: Yale University Press.

Tibi, Bassam. [1971] 1990. *Arab Nationalism: A Critical Enquiry*, 2nd ed., ed. and trans. Marion Farouk-Sluglett and Peter Sluglett. New York: St. Martin's Press.

Tignor, Robert L. 1976. *The Colonial Transformation of Kenya: The Kamba, Kikuyu, and Maasai from 1900 to 1939*. Princeton, N.J.: Princeton University Press.

Tilly, Charles. 1990. *Coercion, Capital, and European States, AD 990–1990.* Oxford: Blackwell.

———. 1998. *Durable Inequality.* Berkeley: University of California Press.

Tilly, Charles, Louise Tilly, and Richard Tilly. 1975. *The Rebellious Century 1830–1930.* Cambridge, Mass.: Harvard University Press.

Tocqueville, Alexis de. [1856] 1955. *The Old Régime and the French Revolution,* trans. Stuart Gilbert. Garden City, N.Y.: Doubleday.

Todorov, Tzvetan. [1982] 1984. *The Conquest of America: The Question of the Other.* New York: Harper & Row.

———. [1989] 1993. *On Human Diversity: Nationalism, Racism, and Exoticism in French Thought,* trans. Catherine Porter. Cambridge, Mass.: Harvard University Press.

Toews, John. 1980. *Hegelianism.* Cambridge: Cambridge University Press.

Tolstoy, Leo. [1900] 1935. "Patriotism and Government." In Leo Tolstoy, *The Works of Leo Tolstoy,* vol. 20, pp. 545–574. London: Oxford University Press.

———. [1884] 1983. *Confession,* trans. David Patterson. New York: W. W. Norton.

Tomasson, Richard F. 1980. *Iceland: The First New Society.* Minneapolis: University of Minnesota Press.

Tombs, Robert. 1996. *France 1814–1914.* London: Longman.

———. 1999. *The Paris Commune 1871.* London: Longman.

Törnquist, Olle. 1984. *Dilemmas of Third World Communism: The Destruction of the PKI in Indonesia.* London: Zed.

Torpey, John. 2000. *The Invention of the Passport: Surveillance, Citizenship and the State.* Cambridge: Cambridge University Press.

Totten, Samuel, William S. Parsons, and Israel W. Charny, eds. 1995. *Genocide in the Twentieth Century: Critical Essays and Eyewitness Accounts.* New York: Garland.

Totten, Samuel, William S. Parsons, and Robert K. Hitchcock. 2002. "Confronting Genocide and Ethnocide of Indigenous Peoples: An Interdisciplinary Approach to Definition, Intervention, Prevention, and Advocacy." In Alexander Laban Hinton, ed., *Annihilating Difference: The Anthropology of Genocide,* pp. 54–91. Berkeley: University of California Press.

Trautmann, Thomas R. 1987. *Lewis Henry Morgan and the Invention of Kinship.* Berkeley: University of California Press.

Trevor-Roper, Hugh. 1983. "The Invention of Tradition: The Highland Tradition of Scotland." In Eric Hobsbawm and Terence Ranger, eds., *The Invention of Tradition,* pp. 15–41. Cambridge: Cambridge University Press.

Trigger, Bruce G. 1989. *A History of Archaeological Thought.* Cambridge: Cambridge University Press.

Tsing, Anna Lowenhaupt. 1993. *In the Realm of the Diamond Queen: Marginality in an Out-of-the-Way Place.* Princeton, N.J.: Princeton University Press.

Tsuboi Hirofumi. 1979. *Imo to Nihonjin.* Tokyo: Miraisha.

Tu Weiming. [1996] 1998. "Cultural Identity and the Politics of Recognition in Contemporary Taiwan." In David Shambaugh, ed., *Contemporary Taiwan*, pp. 71–96. Oxford: Clarendon Press.

Tuan, Mia. 1998. *Forever Foreigners or Honorary Whites? The Asian Ethnic Experience Today.* New Brunswick, N.J.: Rutgers University Press.

Tuan, Yi-fu. 1999. *Who Am I? An Autobiography of Emotion, Mind, and Spirit.* Madison: University of Wisconsin Press.

Tucker, Robert C. 1990. *Stalin in Power: The Revolution from Above, 1928–1941.* New York: W. W. Norton.

Tucker, William H. 1994. *The Science and Politics of Racial Research.* Urbana: University of Illinois Press.

Turner, Frederick Jackson. [1893] 1963. *The Significance of the Frontier in American History,* ed. Harold P. Simonson. New York: Frederick Ungar.

Turner, Henry Ashby, Jr. 1985. *German Big Business and the Rise of Hitler.* New York: Oxford University Press.

Turner, V. W. 1968. *The Drums of Affliction: A Study of Religious Processes among the Ndembu of Zambia.* Oxford: Clarendon Press.

Tushnet, Mark V. 1981. *The American Law of Slavery, 1810–1860: Considerations of Humanity and Interest.* Princeton, N.J.: Princeton University Press.

Tyerman, Christopher. 1998. *The Invention of the Crusade.* Toronto: University of Toronto Press.

Tylor, Edward Burnett. [1871] 1970. *The Origins of Culture (Primitive Culture).* Gloucester, Mass.: Peter Smith.

Updike, John. 1960. *Rabbit, Run.* New York: Alfred A. Knopf.

Usher, Jonathan. 1996. "Origins and Duecento." In Peter Brand and Lino Pertile, eds., *Cambridge History of Italian Literature,* pp. 1–36. Cambridge: Cambridge University Press.

Vagts, Alfred. [1937/1959] 1967. *A History of Militarism: Civilian and Military,* rev. ed. New York: Free Press.

Vail, Leroy. 1989. "Introduction: Ethnicity in Southern African History." In Leroy Vail, ed., *The Creation of Tribalism in Southern Africa,* pp. 1–19. London: James Currey.

Vaillant, Janet G. 1990. *Black, French, and African: A Life of Léopold Sédar Senghor.* Cambridge, Mass.: Harvard University Press.

Van Creveld, Martin. 1991. *The Transformation of War.* New York: Free Press.

Van de Mieroop, Marc. 1997. *The Ancient Mesopotamian City.* Oxford: Clarendon Press.

Van Deburg, William. L. 1992. *New Day in Babylon: The Black Power Movement and American Culture, 1965–1975.* Chicago: University of Chicago Press.

Van den Berghe, Pierre L. [1967] 1978. *Race and Racism: A Comparative Perspective,* 2nd ed. New York: John Wiley & Sons.

Vansina, Jan. 1978. *The Children of Woot: A History of the Kuba People.* Madison: University of Wisconsin Press.

———. [1961] 1985. *Oral Tradition as History.* Madison: University of Wisconsin Press.

Vaughan, Alden T. [1965] 1995. *The New England Frontier: Puritans and Indians 1620–1675,* 3rd ed. Norman: University of Oklahoma Press.

Veer, Peter van der. 1994. *Religious Nationalism: Hindus and Muslims in India.* Berkeley: University of California Press.

Verhey, Jeffrey. 2000. *The Spirit of 1914: Militarism, Myth, and Mobilization in Germany.* Cambridge: Cambridge University Press.

Vernant, Jean-Pierre. [1962] 1982. *The Origins of Greek Thought.* Ithaca, N.Y.: Cornell University Press.

Vick, Brian E. 2002. *Defining Germany: The 1848 Frankfurt Parliamentarians and National Identity.* Cambridge, Mass.: Harvard University Press.

Vickers, Adrian. [1989] 1990. *Bali: A Paradise Created.* Hong Kong: Periplus.

Vidal-Naquet, Pierre. [1981] 1986. *The Black Hunter: Forms of Thought and Forms of Society in the Greek World,* trans. Andrew Szegedy-Maszak. Baltimore: Johns Hopkins University Press.

———. 1987. *Les assassins de la mémoire: "un Eichmann de papier" et autres essais sur le révisionnisme.* Paris: Découverte.

Vierhaus, Rudolf. 1988. *Germany in the Age of Absolutism,* trans. Jonathan B. Knudsen. Cambridge: Cambridge University Press.

Vital, David. 1975. *The Origins of Zionism.* Oxford: Clarendon Press.

———. 1999. *A People Apart: The Jews in Europe 1789–1939.* Oxford: Oxford University Press.

Voegelin, Eric. [1937] 1997. *The Collected Works of Eric Voegelin,* vol. 2: *Race and State.* Baton Rouge: Louisiana State University Press.

Volkov, Shulamit. [1985] 1989. "The Written Matter and the Spoken Word: On the Gap between Pre-1914 and Nazi Anti-Semitism." In François Furet, ed., *Unanswered Questions: Nazi Germany and the Genocide of the Jews,* pp. 33–53. New York: Schocken.

Von Grunebaum, Gustave E. [1946] 1953. *Medieval Islam: A Study in Cultural Orientation,* 2nd ed. Chicago: University of Chicago Press.

Von Klemperer, Klemens. 1992. *German Resistance against Hitler: The Search for Allies Abroad, 1938–1945.* Oxford: Clarendon Press.

Waal, Frans de. 1982. *Chimpanzee Politics: Power & Sex among Apes.* New York: Harper & Row.

Wachman, Alan M. 1994. *Taiwan: National Identity and Democratization.* Armonk, N.Y.: M. E. Sharpe.

Waddell, L. A. 1925. *The Phoenician Origin of Britons, Scots, and Anglo-Saxons.* London: Williams and Northgate.

Walbank, Frank W. 1985. *Selected Papers: Studies in Greek and Roman History and Historiography.* Cambridge: Cambridge University Press.

———— [F. W. Walbank]. [1981] 1992. *The Hellenistic World,* rev. ed. Cambridge, Mass.: Harvard University Press.

Walicki, Andrzej. 1989. *The Enlightenment and the Birth of Modern Nationhood: Polish Political Thought from Noble Republicanism to Tadeusz Kosciuszko,* trans. Emma Harris. Notre Dame, Ind.: University of Notre Dame Press.

Walker, Mack. 1971. *German Home Towns: Community, State, and General Estate, 1648–1817.* Ithaca, N.Y.: Cornell University Press.

Wallerstein, Immanuel. 1974–89. *The Modern World System,* 3 vols. New York and San Diego: Academic Press.

————. 1991. *Geopolitics and Geoculture: Essays on the Changing World-System.* Cambridge: Cambridge University Press.

Wallerstein, Immanuel, et al. 1996. *Open the Social Sciences: Report of the Gulbenkian Commission on the Restructuring of the Social Sciences.* Stanford, Calif.: Stanford University Press.

Walter, Henriette. 1982. *Enquête phonologique et variétés régionales du français.* Paris: Presses Universitaires de France.

————. 1988. *Le Français dans tous les sens.* Paris: Robert Laffont.

Waltz, Kenneth N. 1959. *Man, the State and War: A Theoretical Analysis.* New York: Columbia University Press.

Ward, W. R. 1999. *Christianity under the Ancien Régime, 1648–1789.* Cambridge: Cambridge University Press.

Ware, Vron. 1992. *Beyond the Pale: White Women, Racism and History.* London: Verso.

Warren, Kay B. 1998. *Indigenous Movements and Their Critics: Pan-Maya Activism in Guatemala.* Princeton, N.J.: Princeton University Press.

Washburn, S. L. 1963. "The Study of Race." *American Anthropologist* 65:521–531.

Wasserstein, Bernard. 1979. *Britain and the Jews of Europe 1939–1945.* London: Institute of Jewish Affairs.

Waters, Mary C. 1990. *Ethnic Options: Choosing Identity in America.* Berkeley: University of California Press.

————. 1999. *Black Identities: West Indian Immigrant Dreams and American Realities.* Cambridge, Mass.: Harvard University Press.

Watkins, Susan Cott. 1991. *From Provinces into Nations: Demographic Integration in Western Europe, 1870–1960.* Princeton, N.J.: Princeton University Press.

Watt, Ian. 1957. *The Rise of the Novel: Studies in Defoe, Richardson and Fielding.* London: Chatto & Windus.

Webber, Carolyn, and Aaron Wildavsky. 1986. *A History of Taxation and Expenditure in the Western World.* New York: Simon & Schuster.

Weber, Eugen. 1976. *Peasants into Frenchmen: The Modernization of Rural France, 1870–1914.* Stanford, Calif.: Stanford University Press.

Weeks, Jeffrey. 1981. *Sex, Politics and Society: The Regulation of Sexuality since 1800.* London: Longman.

Wehler, Hans-Ulrich. [1969] 1985. *Bismarck und der Imperialismus,* 2nd ed. Frankfurt am Main: Suhrkamp.

Wei, William. 1993. *The Asian American Movement.* Philadelphia: Temple University Press.

Weinberg, Gerhard L. 2003. "The Politics of War and Peace in the 1920s and 1930s." In Roger Chickering and Stig Förster, eds., *The Shadows of Total War: Europe, East Asia, and the United States, 1919–1939,* pp. 23–34. Cambridge: Cambridge University Press.

Weindling, Paul. 1989. *Health, Race and German Politics between National Unification and Nazism, 1870–1945.* Cambridge: Cambridge University Press.

Weiss, John. 1996. *Ideology of Death: Why the Holocaust Happened in Germany.* Chicago: Ivan R. Dee.

Welch, Holmes. [1957] 1965. *Taoism: The Parting of the Way,* rev. ed. Boston: Beacon Press.

Weller, Georges. [1983] 1993. "The Two Poison Gasses." In Eugen Kogon, Hermann Langbein, and Adalbert Rückerl, eds., *Nazi Mass Murder: A Documentary History of the Use of Poison Gas,* trans. Mary Scott and Caroline Lloyd-Morris, pp. 205–209. New Haven, Conn.: Yale University Press.

Wells, Allen, and Gilbert M. Joseph. 1996. *Summer of Discontent, Seasons of Upheaval: Elite Politics and Rural Insurgency in Yucatán, 1876–1915.* Stanford, Calif.: Stanford University Press.

Wells, Peter S. 1999. *The Barbarians Speak: How the Conquered Peoples Shaped Roman Europe.* Princeton, N.J.: Princeton University Press.

Werth, Nicolas. [1997] 1999. "A State against Its People: Violence, Repression, and Terror in the Soviet Union." In Stéphane Courtois, Nicolas Werth, Jean-Louis Panné, Andrzej Paczkowski, Karel Bartošek, and Jean-Louis Margolin, *The Black Book of Communism: Crimes, Terror, Repression,* trans. Jonathan Murphy and Mark Kramer, pp. 33–268. Cambridge, Mass.: Harvard University Press.

Wertsch, James V. 2002. *Voices of Collective Remembering.* Cambridge: Cambridge University Press.

West, Cornel. 1982. *Prophecy Deliverance! An Afro-American Revolutionary Christianity.* Philadelphia: Westminster Press.

———. 1993. *Keeping Faith: Philosophy and Race in America.* New York: Routledge.

West, M. L. 1997. *The East Face of Helicon: West Asiatic Elements in Greek Poetry and Myth.* Oxford: Clarendon Press.

Westwood, J. N. [1978] 1987. *Endurance and Endeavour: Russian History, 1812–1986,* 3rd ed. Oxford: Oxford University Press.

Wette, Wolfram. 1990. "Ideology, Propaganda, and Internal Politics as Preconditions of the War Policy of the Third Reich." In Militärgeschichtliches Forschungsamt, ed., *Germany and the Second World War,* vol. 1: *The Build-Up of German Aggression,* trans. P. S. Falla, Dean S. McMurry, and Ewald Osers, pp. 9–155. Oxford: Clarendon Press.

Wheeler, Roxann. 2000. *The Complexion of Race: Categories of Difference in Eighteenth-Century British Culture.* Philadelphia: University of Pennsylvania Press.

Whethan, William Cecil Dampier, and Catherine Durning Whethan. 1909. *The Family and the Nation: A Study in Natural Inheritance and Social Responsibility.* London: Longmans, Green.

White, Hayden V. 1978. *Tropics of Discourse: Essays in Cultural Criticism.* Baltimore: Johns Hopkins University Press.

White, Owen. 1999. *Children of the French Empire: Miscegenation and Colonial Society in French West Africa 1895–1960.* Oxford: Clarendon Press.

White, Walter. [1925] 1968. "The Paradox of Color." In Alain Locke, ed., *The New Negro: An Interpretation,* pp. 361–368. New York: Arno Press.

Whitehead, David. 1977. *The Ideology of the Athenian Metic.* Cambridge: Cambridge Philological Society.

———. 1986. *The Demes of Attica, 508/7–ca. 250 B.C.: A Political and Social Study.* Princeton, N.J.: Princeton University Press.

Whitelam, Keith W. 1996. *The Invention of Ancient Israel: The Silencing of Palestinian History.* London: Routledge.

Whitelock, Dorothy. [1952] 1954. *The Beginnings of English Society.* Harmondsworth, U.K.: Penguin.

Whiteside, Andrew G. 1975. *The Socialism of Fools: Georg Ritter von Schönerer and Austrian Pan-Germanism.* Berkeley: University of California Press.

Whittaker, Elvi W. 1986. *The Mainland Haole: The White Experience in Hawaii.* New York: Columbia University Press.

Whorf, Benjamin Lee. 1956. *Language, Thought, and Reality: Selected Writings of Benjamin Lee Whorf,* ed. John B. Carroll. Cambridge, Mass.: MIT Press.

Whyte, Susan Reynolds. 1995. "Disability between Discourse and Experience." In Benedict Ingstad and Susan Reynolds Whyte, eds., *Disability and Culture,* pp. 267–291. Berkeley: University of California Press.

Wiggins, David. 1980. *Sameness and Substance.* Cambridge, Mass.: Harvard University Press.

Wilde, Oscar. [1894/1969] 1982. "Phrases and Philosophies for the Use of the Young." In Oscar Wilde, *The Artist as Critic: Critical Writings of Oscar Wilde,* ed. Richard Ellman, pp. 433–434. Chicago: University of Chicago Press.

Wildenthal, Lora. 1997. "Race, Gender, and Citizenship in the German Colonial Empire." In Frederick Cooper and Ann Laura Stoler, eds., *Tensions of Empire:*

Colonial Cultures in a Bourgeois World, pp. 263–283. Berkeley: University of California Press.

———. 2001. *German Women for Empire, 1884–1945.* Durham, N.C.: Duke University Press.

Wilder, Harris Hawthorne. 1926. *The Pedigree of the Human Race.* New York: Henry Holt.

Wilken, Robert L. 1984. *The Christians as the Romans Saw Them.* New Haven, Conn.: Yale University Press.

Williams, Eric. [1944] 1966. *Capitalism and Slavery.* New York: Capricorn.

Williams, Gwyn A. 1985. *When Was Wales? A History of the Welsh.* London: Black Raven Press.

Williams, Raymond. [1976] 1983. *Keywords: A Vocabulary of Culture and Society,* rev. ed. New York: Oxford University Press.

Williams, Richard. 1990. *Hierarchical Structures and Social Value: The Creation of Black and Irish Identities in the United States.* Cambridge: Cambridge University Press.

Williamson, Joel. 1980. *New People: Miscegenation and Mulattoes in the United States.* New York: Free Press.

———. 1984. *The Crucible of Race: Black-White Relations in the American South since Emancipation.* New York: Oxford University Press.

Willis, Justin. 1993. *Mombasa, the Swahili, and the Making of the Mijikenda.* Oxford: Clarendon Press.

Wilson, Monica. 1977. *For Men and Elders: Change in the Relations of Generations and of Men and Women among the Nyakyusa-Ngonde People 1875–1971.* London: International African Institute.

Wilson, Robert A., ed. 1999. *Species: New Interdisciplinary Essays.* Cambridge, Mass.: MIT Press.

Wilson, William Julius. [1979] 1980. *The Declining Significance of Race,* 2nd ed. Chicago: University of Chicago Press.

———. 1996. *When Work Disappears: The World of the New Urban Poor.* New York: Alfred A. Knopf.

Winant, Howard. 2001. *The World Is a Ghetto: Race and Democracy since World War II.* New York: Basic Books.

Winichakul, Thongchai. 1994. *Siam Mapped: A History of the Geo-Body of a Nation.* Honolulu: University of Hawaii Press.

Winnicott, D. W. 1971. *Playing and Reality.* New York: Basic Books.

Winter, Jay. 1995. *Sites of Memory, Sites of Mourning: The Great War in European Cultural History.* Cambridge: Cambridge University Press.

———. 1996. "British National Identity and the First World War." In S. J. D. Green and R. C. Whiting, eds., *The Boundaries of the State in Modern Britain,* pp. 261–277. Cambridge: Cambridge University Press.

Wistrich, Robert S. [1982] 1995. *Who's Who in Nazi Germany.* London: Routledge.

Witt, Doris. 1999. *Black Hunger: Food and the Politics of U.S. Identity.* New York: Oxford University Press.

Wittgenstein, Ludwig. 1958. *Philosophical Investigations,* 3rd ed., trans. G. E. M. Anscombe. New York: Macmillan.

———. [1922] 2001. *Tractatus Logico-Philosophicus,* trans. D. F. Pears and B. F. McGuiness. London: Routledge.

Wohl, Robert. 1979. *The Generation of 1914.* Cambridge, Mass.: Harvard University Press.

Wolf, Eric R. 2001. *Pathways of Power: Building an Anthropology of the Modern World.* Berkeley: University of California Press.

Wollstonecraft, Mary [1792] 1975. *Vindication of the Rights of Woman,* ed. Miriam Brody Kramnick. Harmondsworth, U.K.: Penguin.

Woods, Frederick Adams. 1906. *Mental and Moral Heredity in Royalty: A Statistical Study in History and Psychology.* New York: Henry Holt.

Woodward, C. Vann. [1955] 1974. *The Strange Career of Jim Crow,* 3rd rev. ed. New York: Oxford University Press.

Woodward, Susan. 1995a. *Socialist Unemployment: The Political Economy of Yugoslavia 1945–1990.* Princeton, N.J.: Princeton University Press.

———. 1995b. *Balkan Tragedy: Chaos and Dissolution after the Cold War.* Washington, D.C.: Brookings Institution.

Woolf, Greg. 1998. *Becoming Roman: The Origins of Provincial Civilization in Gaul.* Cambridge: Cambridge University Press.

Woolf, Stuart. 1991. *Napoleon's Integration of Europe.* London: Routledge.

Wright, Arthur F. 1959. *Buddhism in Chinese History.* Stanford, Calif.: Stanford University Press.

Wright, Lawrence. 2002. "Lives of the Saints." *New Yorker* January 21, pp. 40–57.

Wright, Quincy. [1942] 1964. *A Study of War,* abridged ed., ed. Louise Leonard Wright. Chicago: University of Chicago Press.

Wyatt, David K. 1984. *Thailand: A Short History.* New Haven, Conn.: Yale University Press.

Wyatt-Brown, Bertram. 1982. *Southern Honor: Ethics and Behavior in the Old South.* New York: Oxford University Press.

———. 2001. *The Shaping of Southern Culture: Honor, Grace, and War, 1760s–1890s.* Chapel Hill: University of North Carolina Press.

Wyman, David S. 1984. *The Abandonment of the Jews: America and the Holocaust, 1941–1945.* New York: Pantheon.

X, Malcolm, with Alex Haley. [1965] 1973. *The Autobiography of Malcolm X.* New York: Ballantine.

Yack, Bernard. 1993. *The Problems of a Political Animal: Community, Justice, and Conflict in Aristotelian Political Thought.* Berkeley: University of California Press.

Yahil, Leni. [1987] 1990. *The Holocaust: The Fate of European Jewry, 1932–1945*, trans. Ina Friedman and Haya Galai. New York: Oxford University Press.

Yanagita Kunio. [1952] 1978. *Kaijō no michi*. Tokyo: Iwanami Shoten.

Yoshimoto Takaaki. [1976] 1981. *Saigo no Shinran*, new ed. Tokyo: Shunjūsh.

Yoshimura Tsutomu. 1986. *Buraku sabetsu to rōdō mondai*. Tokyo: Akashi Shoten.

Young, Arthur. [1772] 1970. *Political Essays Concerning the Present State of the British Empire*. New York: Research Reprints.

Young, Crawford. 1994. *The African Colonial State in Comparative Perspective*. New Haven, Conn.: Yale University Press.

Young, James E. 1993. *The Texture of Memory: Holocaust Memorials and Meaning*. New Haven, Conn.: Yale University Press.

Young, Robert J. C. 2001. *Postcolonialism: An Historical Introduction*. Oxford: Blackwell.

Younge, Gary. 1999. *No Place Like Home: A Black Briton's Journey through the American South*. London: Picador.

Zack, Naomi. 1993. *Race and Mixed Race*. Philadelphia: Temple University Press.

——. 2002. *Philosophy of Science and Race*. New York: Routledge.

Zagorin, Perez. 1982. *Rebels & Rulers 1500–1660*, 2 vols. Cambridge: Cambridge University Press.

Zamir, Shamoon. 1995. *Dark Voices: W. E. B. Du Bois and American Thought, 1888–1903*. Chicago: University of Chicago Press.

Zeldin, Theodore. 1958. *The Political System of Napoleon III*. London: Macmillan.

Zertal, Idith. [1996] 1998. *From Catastrophe to Power: Holocaust Survivors and the Emergence of Israel*. Berkeley: University of California Press.

Zheng, Yongnian. 1999. *Discovering Chinese Nationalism in China: Modernization, Identity, and International Relations*. Cambridge: Cambridge University Press.

Ziegler, Herbert F. 1989. *Nazi Germany's New Aristocracy: The SS Leadership, 1925–1939*. Princeton, N.J.: Princeton University Press.

Zimmer, Oliver. 1998. "In Search of Natural Identity: Alpine Landscape and the Reconstruction of the Swiss Nation." *Comparative Studies in Society and History* 40:637–665.

Zimmermann, Michael. 1996. *Rassenutopie und Genozid: Die nationalsozialistische "Lösung der Zigeunerfrage."* Hamburg: Hans Christians Verlag.

Zimmermann, Moshe. 1986. *Wilhelm Marr: The Patriarch of Anti-Semitism*. New York: Oxford University Press.

Zink, Michel. [1996] 1998. *The Enchantment of the Middle Ages*, trans. Jane Marie Todd. Baltimore: Johns Hopkins University Press.

Zola, Irving Kenneth. 1982. *Missing Pieces: A Chronicle of Living with a Disability*. Philadelphia: Temple University Press.

Zürcher, Erik J. 1993. *Turkey: A Modern History*. London: I. B. Tauris.

Zweig, Stefan. [1943] 1987. *The World of Yesterday: An Autobiography*. London: Cassell.

Index

Acton, Lord, 124, 154
Adorno, Theodor, 270
Africa, 10, 52, 59, 82, 174, 188, 206, 254–55;
  anticolonialism and colonialism in, 135–39,
  212; pan-Africanism, 148, 155, 232–33,
  250; pre-colonial, 134–37; 179; slaves of,
  85, 88, 151; tribal societies of, 137–38. *See
  also under specific country names*; African
  Americans; Race; Tribal organization
African Americans, 33, 169, 171, 183, 232–
  33, 240, 244–59, 263; and black pride,
  250; racial identity and racial purity of, 62–
  66, 249–51; and racial science, 88–89; and
  slavery, 85–89; women's identity, 334. *See
  also* Black Power Movement; Racism;
  Slavery; United States
Akif, Mehmet, 236
American Indians, 83, 85, 232, 250–51
Améry, Jean, 256–57
Anarchists, 168
Annan, Kofi, 169
Anthropology, 91, 96, 236; philosophical, 22,
  120, 137; physical, 67; premodern, 75, 83
Anticolonialism, 134, 137–38; in Africa 181–
  85. *See also* Colonialism
Anti-Semitism, 196; rise of, 30–32; in
  Germany, 182–83, 185, 193–99, 240. *See
  also* Hitler; Holocaust; Nazi Germany
Apartheid, 183, 190
Appalachia, 262
Arabs, 11, 14, 24, 28, 38–41, 59, 69, 148,
  186, 246, 271
Archaeology, 122, 159
Aristocracy, 92–93, 104, 108, 112, 116, 119,
  130, 138, 154, 271. *See also* Nobility
Aristotle, 14, 43–45, 82, 125, 237–41;
  Politics, 184
Armenia, 206–8

Arndt, Ernst Moritz, 151
Arnold, Matthew, 34, 181
Asante, Molefi, 247–48
Asian Americans, 248–49
Augustine, Saint, 2, 11, 22
Australia, 17, 26, 52, 62, 70, 166
Austria, 48, 113, 154, 160, 173
Autobiography, 4, 29, 232

Bacon, Francis, 75
Bacon, Roger, 234–35
Baeck, Leo, 32, 194
Baldwin, James, 252–53, 257–58
Bali, 139
Barbarians, 2, 15, 29, 37, 43–44, 49–50, 74–
  78, 82–83, 87, 91, 150, 181, 184, 186,
  191, 238
Barnel, Abbé, 130
Barrès, Maurice, 135, 162
Barthes, Roland, 162
Bebel, August, 185
Beckett, Samuel, 7
Behn, Aphra, 86
Belafonte, Harry, 253–54
Belgium, 106, 134, 160–61
Bell, Derrick, 259–60
Ben-Gurion, David, 28
Berlin, Ira, 89
Berlin, Isaiah, 123, 149, 251, 260
Bernier, François, 89
Bible, 71, 86–87, 121, 266
Biography, 2, 4–6
Biopolitics (biopower), 91, 94, 164–68, 174;
  in Nazi Germany, 198–201, 211
Bismarck, Otto von, 151
Black Power Movement, 250, 255
Blake, William, 67
Blalock, Hubert, 73

377